TEACHING STUDIES OF

SOCIETY
AND
ENVIRONMENT

THIRD EDITION

TEACHING STUDIES OF

SOCIETY
AND
ENVIRONMENT

THIRD EDITION

COLIN MARSH

Prentice
Hall

Copyright © Pearson Education Australia Pty Limited 2001
First published 1994
Second edition published 1998
Third edition published 2001

Pearson Education Australia
Unit 4, Level 2
14 Aquatic Drive
Frenchs Forest NSW 2086

Senior Acquisitions Editor: Cath Godfrey
Project Editor: Sarah Welling
Copy edited by Jennifer Coombs
Proofread by Jane Tyrrell
Index by Garry Cousins
Cover designed by Ramsay Macfarlane Design, Surry Hills, NSW
Typeset by: Midland Typesetters, Maryborough, Victoria

Printed in Malaysia, KVP

4 5 04 03 02

National Library of Australia
Cataloguing-in-Publication data

Marsh, Colin J.
Teaching studies of society and environment.

3rd ed.
Bibliography.
Includes index.

ISBN 1 74009 317 8

1. Social sciences—Study and teaching—Australia.
2. Curriculum planning—Australia. 3. Environmental
education—Australia.

300.71094

An imprint of Pearson Education Australia

Contents

Preface

Studies of society and environment is an exciting and challenging learning area. This title is being used in most states although in New South Wales the title 'Human Society and its Environment' is used. Studies of society and environment encompasses a learning area which was previously titled as 'Social Education', 'Social Science', 'Social Studies', 'Liberal Arts', 'Environmental Studies'.

Studies of society and environment involves the study of people as social beings, as they interact with one another, with the natural and social environment, and in various places through time. A primary purpose is 'to introduce young people to a world of ideas and experiences which will enhance their self knowledge and assist them to participate in their world' (Queensland School Curriculum Council, 1999: 1). Studies of society and environment 'provides a framework for the development of students' knowledge and understanding of Australian society, within the Asia-Pacific region and as a part of the wider global community' (Board of Studies, Victoria, 2000: 417).

This learning area is based on a number of important value orientations relating to the principles of democratic process, social justice and ecologically sustainable development. Further, the learning area is characterised by an inquiry-based method of learning whereby students are encouraged to ask questions and to actively search for answers through investigating, communicating and participating (Board of Studies, New South Wales, 1998a).

This third edition includes a number of major changes to chapters although the existing sequence is maintained. There have been exciting new developments in civics education and the use of the Internet and the World Wide Web has increased exponentially. These and other recent developments are incorporated in the new chapters.

Chapter 1 examines some curriculum theory approaches and practical issues for the field of studies of society and environment. Chapter 2 describes how teaching units can be developed and includes a number of individual and small-group strategies and examples. This is directly linked to Chapter 3 which examines a variety of resources which can be used by teachers and students.

In Chapter 4 a number of teacher-centred and student-centred modes of instruction are presented, including a detailed analysis of cooperative learning. This chapter provides an overview for subsequent chapters which focus upon specific teaching techniques. The teaching of concepts and skills is presented in Chapters 5 and 6. In each of these chapters, a detailed theoretical analysis, together with numerous practical examples, forms the basis for discussion.

Various points of view relating to the study of controversial issues and values are examined in Chapter 7, together with some practical guidelines and examples for use in classrooms.

In Chapter 8 the focus is upon the conceptual strands of studies of society and environment, how they evolved, justification of them in terms of the literature and an analysis of the modifications that have been undertaken by states and territories. This is followed by 'Assessing, Recording and Reporting Student Learning' (Chapter 9) which not only examines purposes and modes of assessment, but provides techniques for assessing students' achievement of outcomes, strands and levels through the use of portfolios and assessment tasks.

Chapter 10, 'Inquiry Approaches and Student Projects', has special application in studies of society and environment and it has been extended in this edition to include cooperative learning techniques. Chapter 11 provides a detailed analysis of simulation games, how they can be designed and developed, and some guidelines for the important element of debriefing.

Some of the challenging possibilities for using computers within the studies of society and environment field are explored in Chapter 12, especially the use of online databases such as the Internet and World Wide Web.

In Chapter 13 the case for including Aboriginal and Torres Strait Islander studies is made very convincingly, and various teaching techniques and resources are described.

'Civics and Citizenship Education', Chapter 14, focuses upon linking schoolwide citizenship to the community and the processes of decision making and citizenship. Details of the Discovering Democracy project are also included.

Chapter 15, 'Multicultural Studies', examines the need for a global perspective, and provides practical examples of how this orientation can be included in classroom teaching. Some of the blatant and the more subtle discriminatory practices against males and females that occur in Australasian society are discussed in the final chapter 'Gender and Schooling' (Chapter 16).

The practical examples, ideas and concepts incorporated by the authors in their respective chapters have been derived from various sources and from many different states of Australia and New Zealand, and so it is difficult, therefore, to acknowledge individual sources. The slides on Kakadu were made available by Dal Anderson. Special thanks are due to Peta Edwards for her expert organisational and word-processing skills.

Colin Marsh
September 2000

Contributors

Associate Professor Bernard Cox, Kenmore, Queensland, **Chapters 5–7**

Professor Kerry Kennedy, University of Canberra, **Chapters 1 and 14**

Professor Colin Marsh, AIUS/Curtin University, **Chapters 2–4, 8–11, 15**

Dr John Pearson, Monash University, **Chapter 12**

Ms Kaye Price, Gordon, ACT, **Chapter 13**

Ms Janet Smith, University of Canberra, **Chapter 16**

1 Theoretical Frameworks for Understanding Studies of Society and Environment

Introduction

On a daily basis, teaching is essentially a practical activity—planning, interacting with students, assessing student progress and evaluating how things might be done better next time. Yet these practical activities also take place in a larger context that influences them. Part of this context is the broad social, political and economic directions of the time and another part is the theoretical ideas that influence the way we see the world around us.

The purpose of this chapter is to consider these contexts—social, political, economic and theoretical—and how they enhance or constrain our understanding of studies of society and the environment. Individuals will have different responses to these contexts so that it is not expected that everyone will agree on their significance or the role they might play in helping to make decisions about teaching. Nevertheless, it is important to understand that our ideas about teaching are influenced by factors outside of ourselves and to take account of these when we come to plan for teaching studies of society and the environment.

A good example of how these larger contexts influence us can be seen when we examine the role recent Australian governments have played in relation to education. Coinciding with Australia's economic problems since the mid-1980s, governments have taken a significant interest in education as an instrument for creating a future in which the productive capacity of the nation will be enhanced. The emphasis on education about Asia, numeracy and literacy skills and the development of a scientifically and technologically literate population must all be seen as part of a broader plan for economic growth and development.

Such a view of education might be seen as instrumental since it shifts the emphasis from the personal and social dimensions of education to education's role in the economic life of the nation. In one sense, however, education seems to have gained a new status as part of a broader policy agenda being pursued by politicians. It is important, therefore, for teachers to be aware that this new interest in education is located in a broader theoretical context. All educational statements, whether made by politicians or professional educators, articulate a set of values and a philosophical framework that have the potential to drive not only policy but also practice.

In this chapter educational theories that influence our thinking about studies of society and the environment will be examined as will issues of social, political and economic significance. By the end of the chapter it is hoped that readers will be able to evaluate the broad contexts that influence studies of society and the environment and will be in a good position to assess the implications for curriculum design and classroom teaching.

■ The Adelaide Declaration on National Goals for Schooling in the Twenty-First Century

The political nature and significance of *The Adelaide Declaration on National Goals for Schooling in the Twenty-First Century* will be discussed in more detail elsewhere. The important point to note for the present purpose is that the statement on national goals highlighted a number of issues related to the study of society and environment. The following have been extracted from the *Goals*:

when students leave school they should:

1.3 have the capacity to exercise judgement and responsibility in matters of morality, ethics and social justice, and the capacity to make sense of their world, to think about how things got to be the way they are, to make rational and informed decisions about their own lives and to accept responsibility for their actions

1.4 be active and informed citizens with an understanding and appreciation of Australia's system of government and civic life

. . .

1.7 have an understanding of, and concern for, stewardship of the natural environment, and the knowledge and skills to contribute to ecologically sustainable development.

An important point to note about these statements is that they provide considerable support at a political level for the inclusion of studies about society and environment in the school curriculum. Yet as educational statements, they raise a number of questions about the **nature of studies of society and environment**, questions that educators need to address:

- There is no specific reference to specific social science disciplines in the *Goals*. What role should traditional disciplines such as history and geography play in studies of society and environment? What is the role of other social science disciplines such as political science, anthropology, sociology and economics? Should the concept of 'sustainable development' be considered through geography or through a broader range of disciplines? Is Australia's civic life best studied through history and political science or in an integrated way?
- Are morality ethics and social justice to be considered as abstract concepts or are they to be related to specific content, issues and contexts?
- Is education for active citizenship a strand in the curriculum or does it provide an

overarching framework for studies of society and environment?

Answers to these questions will provide an indication of the directions studies of society and environment is meant to take in Australian schools. At the same time, an exploration of the questions will reveal that what *The Adelaide Declaration on National Goals for Schooling in the Twenty-First Century* appears to take for granted is, in reality, highly *contested*. Views about which knowledge is of most worth are neither neutral nor value free—they are deeply rooted in beliefs about the nature of reality and the needs of individuals and society to grow and develop in fulfilling and rewarding ways (Thornton, 2000). Since the *Goals* have adopted a position on what are essential knowledge and skills for all Australian students, it should be expected that there will be critiques of this position and the development of contrary views. Teachers need to be able to contribute to these

critiques as they go about the task of developing specific educational programs for studies of society and environment. Before such programs can be developed, there are decisions to be made about the premises and assumptions on which such programs should be built.

The remainder of this chapter will explore these assumptions by addressing, both directly and indirectly, the questions raised above.

■ Role of the Social Science Disciplines in Studies of Society and Environment?

History and geography have always played an important role in general education, and in the minds of some people these disciplines continue to have a role to play. It is of some interest to note that at the political level there appears to be a rare bilateral agreement on the importance of history. In a speech to the

Australian Teachers Union early in 1993 the then Prime Minister, the Hon. P.J. Keating, outlined a vision for Australian education from which it could be inferred that the study of history was to play a significant role:

> Our education system should serve the interests of each and every individual—and it should serve the interests of Australia.
>
> It should be truly relevant: meaning it should instruct young people in those values we hold as universal and unchangeable, and in the skills and knowledge they will need if they are to play a rewarding role in modern society.
>
> It should be both humanitarian and utilitarian: meaning it should have a moral core—it should encourage belief and trust in institutions, values and traditions of Australia and in liberal democracy; and it should equip students with knowledge, including historical knowledge, of Australia and the world. (Keating, 1993: 2).

In 1997, the Commonwealth Minister for Employment, Education and Training, the Hon. David Kemp, had this to say about the importance of history:

> The Commonwealth Government is committed to ensuring that all Australian students have an understanding of the history and operations of Australia's system of government and institutions, and the principles that support Australian democracy. (Kemp, 1997: 9)

Support for the disciplines as part of the core of studies of society and environment is not confined to politicians or to Australia. In the USA, the National Commission on Social Studies in the Schools recommended 'that history and geography form the centre of the social studies curriculum' (Parker, 1991: 85). At the state level in the USA, California's History and Social Science Framework (California State Board of Education, 1988) has 'return[ed] history, the great integrative discipline, to the core of the social studies curriculum' (Alexander and Crabtree, 1988: 10). In the United Kingdom, history and geography have been given a special place in the legislated national curriculum (Morris, 1992; Medley and White, 1992). Politically, there seems to have been in recent times an international movement that has given specific recognition to the role of the disciplines in the school curriculum. Is there a single explanation for this phenomenon?

While recent political decisions appear to have carved out a special place for the disciplines it is important to note that educational philosophers have argued for a long time over the issue of forms of knowledge in the school curriculum. Hirst (1974: 40), for example, argued that there are fundamental forms of knowledge that are the 'basic contributions whereby the whole of experience has become intelligible to man, [*sic*] . . . the fundamental achievements of mind'. It follows from this premise that if there are such forms of knowledge then they should be the basis of the school curriculum. It was on this basis that a social reconstructionist such as Skilbeck (1979) argued that historical knowledge represents a fundamental form or mode of knowledge that should form part of the school curriculum, thus lending support for Hirst's general position. Wilson and Litle (1992: 199), while not endorsing Hirst's position, also singled out a particular role for history and geography in relation to the California framework so that 'the other disciplines in the social studies are not subsumed by history but rather history, remarried to geography after a much too long divorce, becomes the organiser and enhancer of meaning and scope . . . History as a catalyst for the other social sciences incorporates and relates these disciplines' major concepts, themes and generalisations in a clear, ordered manner'. For some educators, therefore, the current emphasis on the disciplines is by no means new—it simply represents a re-emergence of long-standing philosophical arguments concerning the disciplines of knowledge as the foundation of the school curriculum.

That the debate is an ongoing one has been attested to by Eisner and Vallance, who identified five conflicting conceptions of curriculum, one of which was academic rationalism:

> Those embracing this orientation tend to hold that since schools cannot teach everything or even everything worth knowing, their legitimate function is that of cultural transmission in the most specific sense; to cultivate the child's intellect by providing him with opportunities to acquire the most powerful products of man's intelligence. These products are found, for the most part, in the established disciplines. To become educated means to be able to read and understand those works that the great disciplines have produced, a heritage that is at least as old as the beginning of Greek civilisation. The curriculum, it is argued, should emphasize the classic disciplines through which man inquires since these disciplines, almost by definition, provide concepts and criteria through which thought acquires precision, generality, and power; such disciplines exemplify intellectual activity at its best. (Eisner and Vallance, 1974: 12)

An **academic rationalist** curriculum perspective highlights the cultural transmission function of schools. A cultural transmission approach applied to studies of society and environment would certainly place a great deal of emphasis on the established disciplines of history and geography. The views of people like Bloom (1987) in the USA and Moore (1988) in Australia would conform strongly to a cultural transmission approach to studies of society and environment. It would be focused on disciplinary content, especially in history

and geography, on great lives, on the progress of Western civilisation and on the consensus-making processes in society that admit neither of conflict nor disruption. Environmental issues in this approach would be resolved by governments acting in the national interest rather than by individuals who have discerned that the future of the planet is under threat unless they act to do something about it. In terms of curriculum organisation, studies of society and environment would be studied through history and geography studied as separate school subjects.

The characterisation of a cultural transmission approach to studies of society and environment presented above ignores the work of people like Bruner (1960) and Schwab (1962) that resulted in what Eisner and Vallance (1974: 13) referred to as a restatement of 'the traditional academic rationalist approach by examining the logical and structural bases for the division [between the disciplines]'. While this approach maintained the importance of the disciplines, it tended to highlight processes that were at the heart of a discipline's logical structure rather than content as the essence of an education in the disciplines.

The **structure of the disciplines** approach had a fundamental impact on studies of society and environment in the 1970s. This approach has often been referred to as the 'new social studies' and Fenton (1991: 85) has described it thus:

> the new Social Studies focused attention on two issues: helping students to learn the inquiry techniques used by scholars and identifying a structure of the disciplines that could be taught to students in the schools . . .

An important outcome of this approach was that it moved attention away from history and geography as the exclusive sources of knowledge for studies of society and environment and included other disciplines such as sociology, anthropology, economics and political science. In projects such as *Man: A Course of Study* the emphasis was more on the processes of inquiry that students were expected to use in the course of their investigations than on any specific content that had to be learned. This approach had a significant impact on studies of society and environment in Australia. Syllabus documents and curriculum statements in most states/territories from the 1970s onwards reflected a **process approach** to teaching and learning, based on a multidisciplinary or inter-disciplinary perspective incorporating history, geography, anthropology, economics, political science and sociology. It is important to keep in mind that for the most part this was an outcome of a revised cultural transmission perspective on the curriculum that saw the structure of the disciplines rather than specific disciplinary content as the foundation of the school curriculum.

A summary of the arguments provided by the supporters of the academic disciplines is provided in Table 1.1.

Whether it is being proposed that the disciplines are used for cultural transmission purposes or to promote the processes of intellectual inquiry, the emphasis on the disciplines has not been without its critics. It is important to understand the debates that have arisen for they emphasise directional thinking in studies of society and environment and highlight the simplicity of political prescriptions for the school curriculum.

■ Critiquing the Academic Disciplines as the Basis for Studies of Society and Environment

Smith (1986: 147) has argued that the emphasis on the traditional academic disciplines of history and geography is a reflection of conservative values that have sought to use the disciplines 'to establish the bases of social order and its values'. He sees as part of this conservative social order an emphasis on academic excellence, public examinations, support for free-market capitalism and the contribution of Western

Table 1.1 *The academic disciplines as the basis for studies of society and the environment*

Tradition	Focus	Description
Academic rationalism	1. Cultural transmission	History and geography provide the main sources of content for social and environmental education. The emphasis would be on the lives of great people, the progress of Western civilisation and the consensus-making processes that so often provide Australians with a single identity and admits of no societal conflict.
	2. Processes of intellectual inquiry	All the social science disciplines are used to provide an integrated and conceptual approach to designing social and environmental education programs. The emphasis is on the process of inquiry rather than on the selection of specific content. Questions are posed and answers sought across the full range of disciplines, using methods of research and inquiry.

civilisation to the Third World and for a system of values derived from the Judaeo-Christian tradition. In this view, a return to the disciplines, as evidenced by events in the USA and the United Kingdom, is seen as part of a broad political agenda that seeks stability by appealing to established traditions and ways of knowing. Smith's critique refers specifically to the cultural transmission approach that he, along with Eisner and Vallance (1974), characterise as the most conservative model for use in the construction of the school curriculum.

Another critic, but from a different perspective, is Richard Gross. A long-time supporter of the new social studies referred to previously, Gross admits that mistakes were made in attempting to promote the use of social and environmental curriculum projects using the structure of the disciplines as their foundation. Yet he is not convinced that a return to traditional discipline content will correct the situation. He describes the objectives of groups seeking such a return in the following way:

> A small but vocal, highly motivated, well funded, and very visible interest group is promoting the primacy of history and geography in the school curriculum. This group believes that such studies will ensure that the young appreciate myths, know their national history, understand their environment, develop civic skills, and practice patriotic actions. (Gross, 1988: 49)

As a social studies practitioner for over 40 years Gross (1988: 49) comments that 'there is little evidence from the past, when history and geography held sway, that the study of these subjects produced the results that today's proponents desire'. Yet the new social studies also failed to deliver in important areas. Gross (1988: 48) describes these failures as 'the lack of connection between many programs and the real world (including the local community), between the programs and the emerging concerns of young learners and between the programs and the human needs and societal problems and issues of the day'. These views are supported by those of Fenton (1991: 85) who graphically describes the events that overtook the disciplinary emphasis of the new social studies:

> By the time the New Social Studies projects were available to the general public, however, a different performance gap had emerged. In trip-hammer succession, the assassination of the Kennedys and Martin Luther King, civil rights marches, anti-war protests, student sit-ins, and the sex and drug revolts brought an insistent demand for the schools to focus attention on values, civic education, minorities and societal problems such as the environment . . . Inquiry and the structure of the disciplines seemed archaic in this social context. (Fenton, 1991: 85)

The tension referred to here seems to characterise the current state of studies of society and environment in Australia as we enter the first decade of the twenty-first century. Educators still appear to be caught between demands for an emphasis on disciplinary knowledge and on the genuine educational needs of society and individual students. Evidence that has been reviewed in this chapter so far tends to suggest that discipline knowledge and the processes of intellectual inquiry in themselves are not a sufficient basis for studies of society and environment. Educators must go beyond the different manifestations of an academic rationalist perspective of the curriculum if the real needs of students are to be met. This should not mean discarding the contribution that the disciplines can make to studies of society and environment. Rather, it should mean incorporating what the disciplines have to offer in a broader con-ceptualisation that can meet both personal and societal needs (Evans, 2000). How this might be done will be the focus of the next section.

■ A New Direction for Studies of Society and Environment

A number of writers already referred to have proposed alternatives for studies of society and environment to those suggested by an academic rationalist approach to the curriculum. It will be important to review these along with other views that suggest a way ahead for the future.

Smith (1986: 151) talks about the need to reconstruct the discourse of social studies education so that it can more readily meet the criticisms that are often levelled against it. He argues that social studies needs to assert and to celebrate its plurality. This means discarding traditional debates about 'content' and 'process' and constructing a new discourse located 'in the social, political, economic and cultural conditions of Australian society and the already existing liberal-democratic ideology'. That is to say, studies of society and environment should contribute to discussion and articulation of mainstream societal values rather than articulate a separate set of values that social educators conceive to be important. For example, a liberal democracy like Australia values freedom, equality and social justice. How might studies of society and environment place these values at the heart of the curriculum so that students will be involved in educational programs that are central to the maintenance of liberal democracy rather than marginal to its main concerns and interests? Such an approach, although only tentatively outlined here, wards off criticism about diluted academic standards because it highlights generally held societal values. It does not prevent detailed scrutiny and investigation of those values.

Indeed, such investigation can be upheld as a basic tenet of a democratic society. In this view, studies of society and environment become the means by which young people gain access to basic premises and assumptions underlying their society, culture and environment. At the same time, studies of society and environment come to be seen as central rather than peripheral to the purposes of education.

Gross, speaking from a US perspective, sees the future of social studies in terms of motivational content drawn not only from history and the social sciences but also from the humanities and the sciences. Programs would focus on 'local, state, regional, national and global problems'. Underpinning these programs there would be a study of cultural ideals and values to assist young people develop not only personal value systems but also citizenship responsibilities: 'We must move toward the frequently cited but seldom accomplished aim of making our schools workshops for democratic living' (Gross, 1988: 49). For Gross (1988: 49), the great challenge for the social studies was to 'establish the social studies as a central element in a true civic apprenticeship for children and young adults'.

A somewhat different perspective comes from another US educator, Giroux (1980: 340). He has argued that both the cultural transmission approach and the structure of the disciplines approach 'are trapped in a problematic that separates facts from values and by so doing canonizes the very knowledge that it should be questioning'. He questions the legitimacy of inquiry methods by claiming that they do not enable students to question the social construction of knowledge or to investigate the relationship between knowledge and social control. He is supported in his views by Popkewitz who, after analysing one of the 'new' social science curriculum packages, concluded that:

The test of inquiry is whether student definitions coincide with knowledge in the text. The purpose of instruction is to have children master the statements and ideas as one would fill a hat with items. The certainty projected in curriculum makes it difficult for children to understand the limitations inherent in the knowledge of social science . . . The authority of the teacher as knower is maintained. (Popkewitz, 1977: 57)

For Popkewitz, there is an alternative: children must be exposed to conflicting perspectives within disciplines. They must come to appreciate not only that knowledge is socially constructed but that it is personally constructed as well—their own history is as important as that which they read in the textbook. It is only when knowledge can be questioned that children will be empowered to learn.

The views of Giroux (1980) and Popkewitz (1977) are representative of educators who take a critical stance towards both society and the knowledge it constructs. Their views

have roots in critical theory and increasingly in poststructuralism. They question both the cultural transmission approach and the structure of the disciplines approach to studies of society and environment. For them, knowledge is more tentative and is mediated through individuals and social processes. Education, in this context, must alert students to the tentative nature of knowledge, empower them to create their own knowledge and question whatever knowledge is presented to them.

A summary of these alternative conceptions of knowledge and their implications for studies of society and environment is shown in Table 1.2.

■ Theory and Practice: Blending Theoretical Perspectives to Meet the Needs of Practice

Both Tables 1.1 and 1.2 might seem to suggest that there are hard and fast divisions between different approaches to constructing

Table 1.2 *Alternative conceptions of knowledge and their implications for studies of society and environment*

Focus	Description
Social values	Social rather than academic constructs are placed at the centre of the social and environmental curriculum. In an Australian context long-held social values such as justice, freedom and equality would become the organising concepts for the school curriculum as it relates to social and environmental education.
Citizenship	Content in social and environmental education would be selected on the basis of its potential to confront significant problems facing global and local communities. The curriculum would seek to resolve these problems by using teaching strategies consistent with processes that characterise democratic societies.
Critical/poststructuralist	The social and environmental curriculum would be designed to question all knowledge and would focus on the conflicting knowledge-claims made by different groups in society. Valued knowledge would be seen as personally constructed knowledge. There would be no attempt to impose the same knowledge on all students.

studies of society and environment programs. Yet the theoretical divisions are not always so apparent in practice. This can be demonstrated from particular examples in New South Wales and Victoria.

The apparent emphasis on the cultural transmission approach is reinforced in New South Wales secondary schools where from 1999 onwards students have been 'required to study 100 hours each of History and Geography in Stage 4 and 100 hours each of Australian History and Australian Geography in Stage 5' (Board of Studies, NSW, 1999a: 5). Yet does an emphasis on the traditional disciplines necessarily imply a conservative view of cultural transmission? You will recall that this view was argued earlier by Smith (1986) and Giroux (1980). Recent approaches to the study of the disciplines themselves seem to suggest that the so-called 'traditional disciplines' may no longer be quite so traditional.

Segall has provided a summary of the latest trends in what he has called 'critical history':

> In the last twenty years, developments in historiography, intellectual history, and philosophy of history—both influencing and influenced by literary theory, postmodernism, poststructuralism, deconstruction, feminism, postcolonial theory, hermeneutics, phenomenology, anthropology and psychoanalysis—have redefined the boundaries of history, of historical accounts, of what counts as 'historical', and how (and what) history counts. (Segall, 1999: 358)

The implications of these influences on history as a discipline are significant. History can no longer be a single story told by one historian since this single story comes to be seen as the story of a dominant group—it is but one story. History is about stories. Not just a single story of the rich and the powerful but the story also of those on the periphery of society, those traditionally

excluded (the poor, minorities, the powerless). History is not so much about a search for 'the truth' as it is about searching for the different ways in which 'the truth' has been constructed:

> Always positioned to tell a particular story from a particular time, place and perspective historians story the past in ways that promote certain understandings and interpretations over others. Meanings given to the past are never objective or neutral; they are always positioned and positioning. (Segall, 1999: 364)

What kind of history can be found in New South Wales? Is it critical history or traditional history? The recently released *History Stages 4–5 Syllabus* seems to have drawn from both types of history for its rationale. On the one hand, history is seen as 'a process of inquiry' and 'it allows students to gain historical knowledge and skills'. At the same time, the changing nature of the discipline is recognised inasmuch as the perspectives brought to bear on the past by 'different cultural, ethnic, geopolitical, social and economic groups' are highlighted and 'students and teachers are encouraged to consider these different viewpoints about the past held by these groups'. And overlaying all of this is a quotation inserted into the *Syllabus* and taken directly from the History Department at the University of Sydney:

> History furnishes students with a liberal education and provides them with a sense of the past, an appreciation of context, continuity and tradition, an understanding of the processes of change, and a perspective on present culture. History is intrinsically interesting as well as providing an understanding of the nature of values and institutions of the world in which we live. (Board of Studies, New South Wales, 1999b: 5)

Thus the rationale draws on both traditional and critical approaches to the teaching of history and attempts to blend them—it is not a case of 'either or' but 'both and'. Based on Young's (1993) analysis of the history syllabus that preceded the present one, it might be the case that the attempt to blend is simply part of the politics of syllabus making in New South Wales. This means that much will be left to teachers to decide since warrant can be found in the present syllabus for multiple approaches to the teaching of history.

A final point that can be made here for both history and geography in New South Wales is the explicit link between these disciplines and civics and citizenship education. In geography, 'teachers have opportunities to develop units of work that encourage students to form positive attitudes towards Geography and their responsibilities as citizens' (Board of Studies, New South Wales, 1999a: 6) and in history 'students should develop commitment to informed and active citizenship' (Board of Studies, New South Wales, 1999b: 6). The linking of these disciplines to civics and citizenship education is a recognition that the study of the disciplines is not necessarily an end in itself—but a means to the important end of developing informed and active citizens.

The approach documented here for history (and it could equally be documented for geography) means that the disciplines can be aligned with a view of cultural transmission that interprets 'culture' much more broadly and inclusively than the more conservative approach referred to earlier in this chapter. Whether it goes far enough to satisfy critical writers such as Smith (1986) and Giroux (1980) is another question. It is important to realise that the traditional disciplines themselves have been subject to change and transformation in recent years and teachers should be able to take these changes on board in designing new programs of studies of society and environment.

Reference to history and geography might

seem to be particularly applicable to secondary school approaches to studies of society and environment in New South Wales (where it is referred to as Human Society and Its Environment). Yet it should be noted that there is an expectation that the *Human Society and Its Environment [HSIE] K–6 Syllabus* will articulate with the discipline-based secondary syllabuses:

> The subject matter selected for this syllabus forms part of the K–10 continuum for Human Society and Its Environment. The focus in the K–6 syllabus on events and people in Australia's history up until Federation, for example, provides a basis for learning about people, events and consequences until present times, which is undertaken in Years 7–10. (Board of Studies, New South Wales, 1998: 7)

> Two pivotal questions ensure that students in Stages 2–3 develop a sense of shared history:
> What did the British do to establish their citizenship in Australia?
> What impact did this have on Aboriginal citizenship in Australia?
> (Board of Studies, New South Wales, 1999b: 27)

Thus primary school teachers in New South Wales will need to think carefully about their attitudes to the teaching of the disciplines of history and geography and to ways in which genuine interdisciplinary programs might be designed. The secondary history syllabus appears to offer an alternative approach to the conceptualisation of disciplinary knowledge and therefore might provide some useful guidelines for the inclusion of geography and history in the K–6 syllabus statement.

It is perhaps important to point out here that while there is an expectation that there will be prior disciplinary learning covered in the *HSIE K–6 Syllabus*, the syllabus itself represents a totally integrated approach to curriculum organisation. The syllabus is built around four interrelated strands: Change and Continuity, Culture, Environment and Social Systems and Structures. It is expected that these will be taught in an integrated way but at the same time the knowledge from the disciplines will need to be incorporated into this integrated approach. From a curriculum perspective, there is not the hard and fast division between integrated and disciplinary approaches to teaching.

Another example of the blurring of theoretical perspectives can be found in the Victorian *Curriculum & Standards Framework* (CSFII). *The Studies of Society and Environment Curriculum and Standards Framework* (Board of Studies, Victoria, 1999) differs from the New South Wales approach inasmuch as it attempts to bring together a Years Prep–10 approach without the divisions of K–6 and 7–10. The framework is built around strands of History, Culture, Civics and Citizenship, Geography and Economics.

In the first years of schooling (levels 1–3), the emphasis is upon the social experiences of families and cultural groups; the development of communities; the study of the environment and how people and their environments relate to each other. This is all incorporated under the one strand of *Society and Environment*.

From level 4 onwards there is a specialisation so that the single strand divides into three strands which are discipline-based, namely, *History*, *Geography*, *Economy and Society*.

At levels 4–6 knowledge, values and skills are to be planned based upon these three strands (see Table 1.3). Thus, within the History strand, key concepts are time, change, continuities, cause and effect and leaders. Skills to be developed include using primary and secondary sources, developing a range of interpretations to historical processes and events and appreciating the rights and responsibilities of growing up in Australia as citizens.

Within the Geography strand, the key concepts are location/distance/distribution; region/scale spatial change over time; movement; and ecologically sustainable development/conservation. Skills to be developed include applying geographic techniques, interpreting maps, and doing field investigations.

The key concepts included in Economy and Society are decision making, social organisation, citizenship, employment, commercial systems, career paths and globalisation. The skills to be developed include analysing outcomes of decisions, preparing plans, using

Table 1.3 *Overview of Key Concepts in Strands (CSFII)*

Levels 1–3	**Society and Environment**
	History, Geography, Culture, Citizenship, Conservation
Levels 4–6	**History**
	Time, Change, Continuities, Cause and Effect
	Geography
	Location, Region, Movement, Conservation
	Economy and Society
	Decision Making, Social Organisation, Citizenship, Employment, Commercial Systems, Career Paths and Globalisation

evidence to predict technological change, and explaining governmental processes.

Also included in the structure is essential knowledge which is outlined for each level and each strand. For Society and Environment it includes Australia's people and places; local community and places; and self and family. The essential knowledge for the History strand includes Modern, Australian, Medieval and Ancient History; and the History of Australian Cultures. For Geography the essential knowledge includes geography of Australia and the world, resources, economic activities and settlement patterns. For Economy and Society the essential knowledge includes innovation and enterprise, vocational education, Australia's legal and political systems and Australia's resources and social institutions.

Although it might be gleaned from the above that this new structure is highly discipline-focused, implementation guidelines include topic-based, integrated approaches as well as courses built on disciplines. Does this represent a return to a more academically rationalist curriculum in Victoria? Only time will tell, but it is of interest to note that theoretical dispositions do not go away: they are simply recycled, depending on the times and those in positions of power.

While it might seem that New South Wales and Victoria have taken different paths in constructing studies of society and environment, they do have one major feature in common: an emphasis on student learning outcomes. In New South Wales, the *HSIE K–6 Syllabus* (Board of Studies, New South Wales, 1998) focuses on expected student outcomes across the three stages of schooling represented in infants/primary school/ secondary school. This process is repeated both in the history and geography syllabuses. In the same way, the Victorian *CSF* takes up outcomes from the earliest stage of schooling through to Year 10. Seven levels have been

described in the *CSF* (corresponding to the years of schooling) and exit learning outcomes are described for each strand across these levels (Board of Studies, Victoria, 1995: 17–18). This focus on outcomes is common across Australia and it highlights what students are expected to know and be able to do at different stages of schooling. For teachers the main issue is how to use these learning outcomes: should they be the basis for constructing school programs, for assessment or for reporting on student progress? How are these outcome statements related to more traditional forms of curriculum organisation? The syllabus statements in both New South Wales and Victoria do not deal with these issues, but increasingly they will be issues confronting teachers as they go about the task of school-based program development.

■ Defining Your Own Approach to Studies of Society and Environment

It has been shown how curriculum theorists advocate different approaches to the curriculum and also how education systems tend to adopt or modify one or other of these approaches. Yet the task for individual teachers is to decide what their own approach might be to studies of society and environment.

The first point to note is that a particular school community will in all likelihood have developed its approach based on system guidelines or frameworks or even based on national curriculum frameworks. In this context, individual teachers must be aware of what the values of the school community are in this regard. This can easily be ascertained by reviewing the school's curriculum documents for studies of society and environment. In reviewing those documents you could ask the following questions:

- How are the disciplines incorporated into studies of society and environment? Is the emphasis on single disciplines like history and geography or on a range of disciplines including anthropology, economics, sociology, psychology and political science?
- What is the main emphasis of the disciplinary foundation: the structure of the disciplines (e.g. concepts, generalisations and broad understandings) or facts, events and individuals?
- What form of curriculum organisation is recommended? Is it single subjects such as history, geography or politics, integrated studies, social studies or social science?
- Is there a recommended pedagogy? Is the emphasis on inquiry learning processes and related skills, on a range of teaching approaches or on a direct instructional model of teaching?
- Is there a broader emphasis than the acquisition of skills and knowledge? Are there references to social and political action, to citizenship education, to democratic values, to broader social purposes of studies of society and environment?

Answers to these questions can help you to locate the values embedded in a school's documents. For example, a school's documents might reveal the following:

---

cultural transmission

a disciplinary emphasis exclusively on history and geography; these disciplines are also the actual school subjects with a curriculum emphasis on facts, events and individuals: there is no recommended pedagogy and no reference to broader social purposes. It would be fairly safe to assume that the school community has adopted a cultural transmission approach to studies of society and environment.

Alternatively:

---

academic rationalist

the scenario might be varied with the disciplinary emphasis remaining but with an emphasis on the structure of the disciplines of history and geography, a commitment to an inquiry learning process, and a strong statement on citizenship education. Such a combination of elements could be classified as academic rationalist with a commitment to citizenship education.

The important point to note here is that 'ideal' models rarely apply. It is more likely that schools and their communities will be eclectic—taking bits and pieces from different approaches to suit local needs and demands. But where does this leave the individual teacher?

You, as the individual teacher, can always influence your communities and, in turn, can be influenced by them. It will be important, then, to work out exactly where you stand. Having asked a series of questions about a school's curriculum documents, ask the same questions of yourself. Compare your own answers with those you derived about the school. Are they compatible? Are there any glaring differences? How might any differences be resolved or how might you set about the task of convincing the school community that your particular views deserve some consideration?

These are important professional issues and are at the heart of good curriculum decision making. As a professional educator, you are entitled to hold your own views but you must always consider the needs of the whole school community. Their views may be changed over time as may yours. Schools will always benefit from a full and frank exchange of views on significant issues such as the purposes of studies of society and the environment. In the end, everyone shares a common objective in relation to students: ideas that lead to better programs, better teaching and better outcomes deserve to be widely discussed. Students can only benefit from such a process and studies of society and the environment can only be improved.

■ **Concluding Comments**

Teachers need to be aware of different perspectives about the nature of studies of society and environment. As described in this chapter, the perspectives can be very different. Furthermore, in actual curriculum documents used by education systems, they can be modified greatly.

QUESTIONS AND ACTIVITIES

1. How do your own school experiences of studies of society and environment compare with the different approaches that have been outlined in this chapter?
2. As a new staff member in your first school appointment, how would you explain to your colleagues your rationale for teaching studies of society and environment?
3. At your first parent–teacher night you are asked to explain why you are teaching studies of society and environment. What would you say?
4. The school to which you have been posted has a very traditional program for studies of society and environment based largely on history and geography. In what ways might you ensure that such a program was relevant to the needs of your students?
5. How might a school policy on studies of society and environment draw on the different theoretical approaches outlined in this chapter? Draw up a draft policy for discussion by a school staff.

2 Planning for Learning

Introduction

Successful teaching involves being able to prepare, and use, well-planned lessons. It is possibly one of the most difficult tasks for beginning teachers. Although it might appear to an observer to be a relatively simple task, this is far from the case. Teachers have to consider a number of variables and to combine them together in ways which are meaningful and fulfilling for all parties.

■ Why Plan?

Most would agree that planning is one of the key aspects of effective teaching. The very successful lessons produced by experienced teachers may appear to be spontaneous and unplanned but in fact they represent careful planning, trial and error and reflective analysis over the years.

Some teachers argue that planning should be resisted—that it encourages rigidity and prevents them from taking advantage of unexpected instructional opportunities. Serendipity is, of course, always welcome and it is important to use any recent happenings or opportunities as appropriate. But it is also worth noting that Murphy's Law always seems to operate when a person is least prepared—the school principal always seems to appear when planning has been insufficient. Students' behaviour often seems to deteriorate on occasions when a teacher tries to get by with *ad hoc* activities.

A major reason for planning is that it develops confidence in teachers. If teachers have thought through what will be attempted in specific lessons then they are psychologically prepared to handle any other problems which might occur, such as management and control dilemmas (Chapin and

Messick, 1999). Perhaps it is not so much the slavish detailing of what will be taught but the development of a 'mental script' for each lesson—teachers know where they are going in each lesson and can therefore respond to unexpected events and still return to the lesson with minimal discontinuity.

An equally important reason for planning is to ensure that a preferred approach to teaching in the studies of society and environment actually occurs, and that the teacher has thought about why he or she wants to adopt this approach. Consider the following:

- What should be taught? This is sometimes referred to as scope or breadth. There is an enormous amount of knowledge available but what do you include and what do you exclude?
- When should something be taught? This is often referred to as the sequence. It involves consideration of developmental needs of students and organisational priorities such as expanding environments. The level of maturity of students is relevant in teaching some topics. Many educators argue that students should study nearby environments before studying more distant ones.
- How should something be taught? This is often referred to as synthesis. It involves bringing together topics into a meaningful whole.

Every teacher has to consider his or her approach to teaching. Some common approaches, as described in Chapter 1, include structure of the disciplines and academic rationalist, citizenship, and reflective thinking approaches. By undertaking planning, teachers are able to reflect upon, and put into action, the frames of reference and general value positions with which they identify.

Planning is therefore a most worthwhile activity because:

- it helps a teacher think about what and how he or she will teach and why;
- it gives direction to a teacher and his or her students so that all participants know the purposes and the desired destination;
- it empowers a teacher in terms of his or her decision making;
- it can greatly enhance a teacher's self-confidence;

Planning time and a planning area are crucial for busy teachers

- it provides a framework for evaluating the success or otherwise of a teacher's teaching.

■ Sources to Assist with Planning

A major source is of course the education system's curriculum framework. All states and territories have detailed frameworks, namely:

- *Human Society and its Environment Syllabuses* (NSW)
- *Curriculum and Standards Framework II: Studies of Society and Environment* (VIC)
- *R–10 Studies of Society and Environment* (SA)
- *Outcomes and Standards Framework: Society and Environment* (WA)
- Studies of Society and Environment Planning Grid; A Studies of Society and Environment Reference Book; Studies of Society and Environment Website
- Studies of Society and Environment: Queensland School Curriculum Council Website (Q)

These documents provide detailed guidelines on outcomes, learning experiences and forms of assessment.

In addition to official statements about curricula for specific year levels, there are a variety of student textbooks which can provide useful background information for planning, for example R. Barrett's *Australian Environments*. Although these sources are important, it must be realised that they are generic in nature and are not targeted at specific classes and particular contexts. A teacher breathes vitality into planning by reorganising material from these sources in ways that are meaningful and exciting to him or her and to students. This may involve accessing other printing materials such as reference books, pamphlets and brochures, 'trade' books, newspapers, multimedia materials such as CD-ROMs, videotapes, computer materials and Internet data and community resources such as museums and resource visitors (see Chapter 3).

By putting together material from all these sources, teachers are able to personalise their planning. They are able to put their personal stamp on a planning approach which has the potential to be exciting and fulfilling for them and targeted especially to develop students to their highest potential. If a topic is not exciting to teachers, their lack of interest will surely be conveyed to their students (Chapin and Messick, 1999).

Notwithstanding, it may be desirable for beginning teachers to gradually extend their range of sources for planning and not to be too wide-ranging in their first few years of teaching. It may be desirable to use the plans created in departmental publications and textbooks, or minor modifications of these, rather than moving too quickly to original creations.

■ Levels of Planning

A common classification is to divide planning up into long-range and short-range planning. Long-range planning involves planning the outline for an entire semester or year-long curriculum. It is impossible to cover all topics listed in curriculum guides in great detail. Choices have to be made given the number of teaching weeks available.

Topics, themes or units may be chosen for the semester or year-long curriculum. Typically, teachers will make their selections based upon the following:

- system-level curriculum guides and syllabuses;
- system-level student texts (if available);
- commercial texts;
- state tests (required at specific year level in some states);
- directives/suggestions from the school principal;

- what other teachers at the school are doing;
- pressures from parents;
- potential management problems;
- personal teaching strengths and areas of expertise.

Short-range planning is about lesson planning, either daily or weekly lesson plans. These plans are quite specific and tend to include a common set of headings even though titles may vary. Such headings usually focus upon objectives and outcomes, introductory activities, major learning activities, concluding activities and assessment.

Planning model based upon time

As depicted in Figure 2.1, planning can be conceptualised in terms of a continuum ranging from global, long-term planning to specific, short-term planning. The effective teacher needs to keep both perspectives in mind. Clearly it is essential that individual lessons are successful but it is also important to be aware of the long-term goals in teaching the subject.

Planning model based upon level of teacher independence

Another way of considering planning, apart from the time dimension described above, is to conceptualise it in terms of degrees of teacher and student freedom. Planning can be considered in terms of heavy reliance upon external sources or an emphasis upon classroom or school-level planning. Figure 2.2 depicts some major positions on a continuum with regard to levels of teacher independence.

At both primary and secondary school levels, it is quite common for teachers to depend heavily upon textbooks. There are good reasons for this, such as:

- they are written by professional writers who have the time to do background research and develop and test materials;
- they are up to date and revisions occur every 2–3 years;
- they typically include teachers' manuals including questions for teachers to ask and test questions;
- they include supplementary materials, such as work books, overhead masters and computer disks;
- material is appropriate for specific grade levels because readability formulae have been used.

However, there are many problems for teachers if they depend too heavily upon textbooks. A major concern is that textbooks are mass distributed and cannot satisfy the specific needs of a local area. They can also stifle teacher creativity. If a decision is made to use a textbook as a major source of teaching then the teacher should take note of the following caveats:

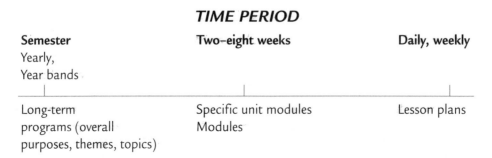

TIME PERIOD

Semester Yearly, Year bands	Two–eight weeks	Daily, weekly
Long-term programs (overall purposes, themes, topics)	Specific unit modules Modules	Lesson plans

Figure 2.1 Continuum of planning based upon time

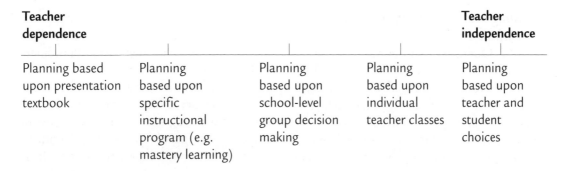

Figure 2.2 *Continuum of planning based upon amount of teacher independence*

- try to vary the textbook routine (read, discuss, write down answers) by using other activities such as simulations, debates, small-group discussions;
- don't try to cover the whole book—skip sections or even whole chapters;
- motivate students for each new chapter or section;
- teach skills in using the table of contents, index, outlining and note taking.

As noted in Figure 2.2, forms of mastery learning can also require high degrees of teacher dependence. For example, the Hunter (1982) model requires teachers to follow a multiple-step approach and this often involves using tightly developed materials. The steps include:

- pre-instructional planning—specifying objectives, analysing and sequencing tasks;
- planning strategies and activities for each objective;
- checking students' understanding;
- giving students guided practice;
- allowing students independent practice.

In some education systems, teachers within a school are encouraged to do their planning in small teams (see Figure 2.2). This usually occurs during school hours, but on some occasions special funding is provided for it to be done during out of class hours. It

can be especially useful when new sequences are being developed across a band of school grades (for example Years 4–6 or Years 7–10). Although it is very fulfilling for the participants, it can also be a very time consuming process.

A number of writers, such as Nelson (1992), argue that planning is predominantly a creative activity and should involve teachers working independently on what is of interest to them. After all they are the ones who have to keep their students interested in a particular topic. In all probability they will teach the same topic again next year. They need to reflect upon what interests them. What topics do I find challenging and exciting? How can I get my students interested in these topics?

Finally, in terms of planning based upon the amount of teacher independence, it should be noted that there are occasions when it is profitable for a teacher and students to be jointly involved in planning. Students can produce a wonderful range of creative ideas for topics (e.g. 'hot-air balloons', 'wheels', 'ice-cream'). By inviting students to participate in the planning they are really taking responsibility for their own learning. Students will then begin to realise the significance of resources and how to access information. They will also be able to work closely with other students.

Planning model based upon knowledge transmission

Figure 2.3 indicates that the transmission of knowledge can also take many forms. With the explosion of knowledge over recent decades it is now virtually impossible for teachers to attempt to teach isolated facts. There are just so many facts—they rapidly become out of date and they have limited application. Although there are some teachers who still persist in teaching a litany of facts ('capes and bays') to be memorised by all students, their number is fortunately declining.

The majority of planning approaches used in preservice teacher education courses and in textbooks are based upon a *conceptual* approach—either based on separate disciplines or an interdisciplinary approach. As detailed in Chapter 5, concepts are an extremely valuable aid for learning because they transcend time and space and have transfer value to new situations. Concepts enable students to organise data in a logical and coherent manner. Examples from specific disciplines include 'scarcity' (economics), 'space' (geography), 'culture' (sociology) and 'time' (history).

'Concept webs' are commonly used to develop concept teaching in a unit (Hyerle, 1996). Near the centre of the web are the broad topics and the most important ideas. The peripheral layers depict the subordinate ideas.

Some educators argue that it is the interdisciplinary concepts that are the key ones for planning (see Figure 2.4). Some of these might include 'causality', 'conflict', 'cooperation' and 'interdependence'. It is possible to revisit these interdisciplinary concepts in succeeding years using more indirect experiences with students, as part of an expanding environment approach.

Then again there are educators who contend that concepts can best be learned by *inquiry* methods (see Chapter 10). Using inquiry problems, students are encouraged to gain conceptual knowledge and also an understanding of the methods used by social scientists. Valuing activities will also invariably occur in these inquiry units.

■ Units

A unit is a collection of related lessons which have been organised around a particular theme, topic or issue. Usually a unit covers some major concepts but it also has provisions for the teaching of skills and values and social participation.

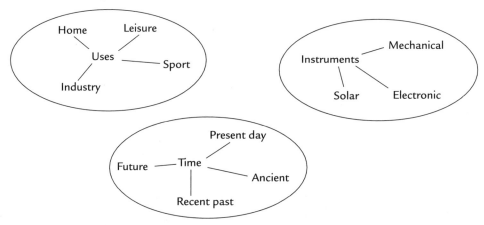

Figure 2.3 *A concept web*

Facts from the disciplines	Concepts from the disciplines	Integrated/interdisciplinary approaches	Inquiry/valuing approaches
Example · Major cities in Australia are located close to the coast · Fresh water supply was a major factor in the location of cities	*Example* Key concepts in geography include: · location · spatial interaction	*Example* The family, using examples taken from: · interdependence · scarcity · sanction · role	*Example* Local road safety issue affecting the community

Figure 2.4 *Continuum of planning based upon knowledge transmission*

In some circumstances a teacher may have complete freedom in choosing a unit but in most cases choices are limited by:

- education system curriculum guides;
- availability of textbooks;
- needs, interests and abilities of students being taught;
- availability of resources.

Teaching in units is widely recommended because it provides students with a focus, rather than their just experiencing isolated lessons.

The use of units can also be very rewarding and stimulating for teachers. It enables teachers to select materials from a variety of sources and to be able to produce dynamic, creative lessons.

Units in the primary school are planned typically to be completed in 2–3 weeks whereas those at secondary school level can last 6 weeks or longer. The length of time is partly dependent upon the extent to which the unit is integrated. If a number of different subject areas are included then the length of time needed will be much greater. Many schools have a curriculum policy about the selection and sequence of units in teaching studies of society and environment.

A distinction is often made between resource units and teaching units. Resource units provide a multitude of activities and

materials from which a teacher has to choose. Teaching units are more focused and are designed for specific classes.

Experienced teachers will modify teaching units as they become involved in teaching them. They will make decisions on some occasions to extend particular activities and on other occasions to terminate them sooner than planned. On subsequent occasions they will make further refinements to these units. In specific classes they may need to make a number of modifications to allow for the needs of students with impairments or for gifted and talented students.

The planning of units is a personal activity and there are many different approaches, but the general phases can be characterised as:

1. unit title;
2. description of the grade level and student population;
3. rationale for the unit;
4. goals, objectives, outcomes;
5. content;
6. selecting and sequencing learning activities;
7. evaluation;
8. resources.

No set format exists for writing units. Some teachers prefer to use columns so that they can be more aware of the inter-relationships between the major headings

Team planning of a unit can greatly enhance teaching

while others prefer to put each heading on a separate page.

Furthermore, there is no special starting point for developing a unit. Although it might be logical to start from the beginning there may be benefits in starting off with areas that have greatest appeal, such as forms of assessment (point 7) or a consideration of specific learning activities (point 6).

With the current interest in outcomes and standards it could be useful to turn the planning sequence upside down. That is, a teacher could list the standards/outcomes desired, then devise appropriate assessments to determine whether students have achieved them and from there devise appropriate learning activities and resources.

1. Unit title
The titles should be succinct and, where possible, challenging and interesting. Examples in the *primary* school might include:
    'Travel day to Bali'

'Ways that each of us is special'
'Treasure hunt'
'My family and I'
'Protecting our wild life'
Examples in the *secondary* school might include:
    'What is prejudice?'
    'Living in cities'
    'Pollution of our environment'
    'Planning a new community'

2. Description of the grade level and student population
Brief details need to be included about the intended age/grade details, to ensure that diverse student needs are accommodated (Fuller and Stone, 1998). Many of the outcome-based planning documents refer to academic levels rather than grade levels.

3. Rationale for the unit
This is an important element and a number of issues should be considered by a teacher

intending to use a new unit. These might include:

- What contribution does the unit make to the studies of society and environment field?
- Does it relate to system-level curriculum guidelines?
- Is it likely to be interesting and challenging to students?
- Is it feasible in terms of time, available materials and students' abilities?
- Does it have more potential than the unit it replaces?
- Are there any possible negative effects of including the unit, in terms of other classes and teachers and parents?

Reflecting upon why a particular unit is being developed is of course an important matter. There must be a close relationship between assumptions and beliefs about content and learning activities and the actual format of the unit.

4. Goals, objectives, outcomes

Goals are general statements which provide teachers and students with a vision—the big picture. They tend to be medium to long term and are usually directed to student achievement. Such goals as 'students will study important figures in Australian history' provide a broad focus for planning but are not sufficiently specific to guide detailed planning.

Objectives are typically a statement of intent about anticipated changes in learners. An objective identifies how students should change their behaviour as a result of certain learning experiences.

Behavioural objectives require explicit statements about expected student behaviour, conditions under which the behaviour will occur and acceptable standards of performance. Except for the teaching of some skills, it would seem that behavioural

objectives are too demanding and that they have limited application to the studies of society and environment field. For example, given a standard Australian atlas, the student will be able to use the index to locate and place on a blank map the location of five regional cities.

Instructional objectives are objectives which are relatively specific, which describe desired learning outcomes in terms of student activities or behaviours, but which do not reduce all classroom activities to behaviourist outcomes.

Instructional objectives are very useful in planning a unit because they provide a specific focus and a basis for evaluating the effectiveness of students' learning. If strong action verbs are used in the objectives (see Table 2.1), this helps provide a very specific guide to the activities required.

In a teaching unit several major instructional objectives are likely to be listed, or at least examples will be included. Examples of instructional objectives which provide specific guidance include:

1. After viewing the videotape, students will be able to write, in order, the four steps in the production of iron ore.
2. After reading pages 10–15 of the text, students in small groups of five will be able to construct an early farming (squatter's) cottage, using ice block sticks, cardboard and blu-tac.

The terms 'outcomes-based education', 'outcome statements' and 'educational outcomes' are being used frequently in the literature (Willis and Kissane, 1997; Forsters and Masters, 1996b; Cumming, 1998). The emphasis is placed on outputs or outcomes attained by students rather than on inputs to be applied by teachers. To a certain extent, the approach represents a recycling of earlier movements, especially in the USA, such as mastery learning and competency-based

Table 2.1 *Some strong action verbs for instructional objectives*

Knowledge objectives	Skills objectives	Attitude objectives
· to describe	· to draw	· to choose
· to identify	· to illustrate	· to relate positively to
· to list	· to construct	· to respond to
· to compare	· to measure	· to approve of
· to contrast	· to locate	· to disapprove of
· to solve	· to translate	· to believe in
· to match		· to acclaim
· to label		· to question
· to recognise examples		· to dispute
· to interpret		

education (Eisner, 2000). However, it does not incorporate specific behavioural statements. Rather, the emphasis is upon broad outcome statements to be achieved—typically, 8–12 statements per subject per year or per level.

The outcome statements incorporate concepts which have been categorised into progressive levels of difficulty. In terms of the outcome statements developed for the Australian Collaborative Curriculum Project, these were complemented by more concrete examples ('pointers') and by work samples. An example follows.

Outcome statement

Identify ideas, issues, people or events that have contributed to national identities and heritages.

Pointer

This will be evident when the student:

- *describes people, issues, events that have contributed to understandings of what it means to be Australian;*
- *identifies some of the influences of historical change and continuity which have contributed to understandings of what it means to be Australian (Anzac legend, bush image);*
- *describes the contributions women have made to Australian political, social, economic and cultural life;*

- *identifies some of the reasons for the changing relations between women and men in Australian history.*

(Curriculum Corporation, 1993: 21)

5. Content

To develop quality units a lot of thought must go into the selection of content based upon some of the considerations raised in Chapter 1. Some criteria to use when selecting content include:

- Does the content assist students to identify and reflect upon societal issues?
- Can the content be developed in such a way that each student will have opportunities for success?
- Is the content suited to the developmental levels and abilities of students?
- Can this content be developed in the classroom with the use of a variety of teaching strategies?

As noted above, concepts are an extremely important tool for teaching in studies in society and environment and typically provide the basis for selecting content (Banks and Banks 1999). Concepts vary in their scope and difficulty. Those that are related to a student's concrete, observable experiences are easier to understand than abstractions. The building of concepts from easy to complex is a difficult task and must be carefully planned (see Chapter 5 on concept building).

Generalisations are statements relating two or more concepts. For generalisations to be understood, the concepts need to be grounded in concrete factual cases. Thus facts do have a role in providing concrete examples for concepts and generalisations. Consider these examples:

Concepts
scarcity—needs—wants—goods—services—markets—competition

Generalisation
In a competitive market, an increase in supply of a particular good or service will result in a lower market price.

Facts
Australian spending on specific consumer items such as video recorders in 1986 and 1996 was $xx and $yy respectively.

The content for a unit therefore is likely to include factual information across time, cultures or periods, which has been carefully sampled to illustrate particular concepts and generalisations. The factual content selected will also be dependent upon system-level guidelines and syllabuses.

A wide range of materials are available from which appropriate content can be selected. In addition to textbooks a variety of print and multimedia materials are available (see Chapter 3).

6. Selecting and sequencing learning activities

A teaching unit needs to include a variety of learning activities. One way to ensure a wide range is to plan for particular teaching techniques and to link these with the teaching of specific concepts. For example, the following teaching techniques (as detailed in Chapter 4) have considerable potential:

- lectures/presentations;
- practical demonstrations;
- inquiry/problem solving;
- simulations and role plays;
- questions/discussions;
- mapping projects;
- model building;
- multimedia presentations;
- library research;
- community-based research;
- individual and group projects;
- self-instructional activities.

Unless mindful of it, teachers will tend to use a small number of techniques with which thay have had direct experience. Although it is more stressful to experiment with new approaches, these need to be incorporated into teaching units because students have very different learning styles (Tomlinson and Kalbfleisch, 1998). By providing a variety of learning activities, teachers keep not only their students stimulated but also themselves.

Teacher-directed instruction is of course not the only approach. There are a number of student-directed approaches which can develop students' independence and motivation. Individual projects and library research projects are useful approaches to develop student skills and to provide a variation from the regular teacher-directed forms (Saye, 1998).

Banks and Banks (1999) assert that it is activities which are the heart of units. Each teacher needs to develop a range of interesting and useful activities that link the unit together. They can be generated from a variety of sources including newspapers and television. The trick is to find particular topics and then use a little creativity to develop them as integrated units, spanning a number of teaching areas.

A simple way to develop each activity is to put the basic details on a separate palm card (see Tables 2.2 and 2.3). All that is needed is

Table 2.2 *An activity example (primary)*

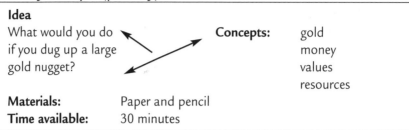

Idea		
What would you do if you dug up a large gold nugget?	**Concepts:**	gold money values resources
Materials:	Paper and pencil	
Time available:	30 minutes	

Table 2.3 *An activity example (lower secondary)*

Idea—choosing between options

Students are to establish reasons for choosing why five of the following projects will each receive $50 million in government funding:

1. project on 'wave power' to see if action of the sea can generate 'power';
2. project on 'test tube babies';
3. project on car safety;
4. project on space flight equipment;
5. project on weather control;
6. project on new weapon system;
7. project on retarding old age;
8. project on turning sea water into good drinking water;
9. project on producing abundant quantities of enriched food;
10. project on rat control

a brief, one-sentence description, an allotted time and the necessary materials. Not all activities will turn out to be useful and a number may need to be eliminated eventually.

As noted earlier, it may be desirable for teachers to commence planning their unit by concentrating first upon activities, that is, to devise activities that students might enjoy doing and then work backwards to formulate appropriate objectives.

7. Evaluation

Evaluations are undertaken to determine the relative effectiveness of teaching units, in terms of the teacher activities and the learning accomplished by students.

In terms of student performance there are a range of assessment strategies that should

be included in a unit. They need to be varied and, above all, they should provide feedback about students' development as reflective, competent and concerned citizens (Worthen *et al.*, 1999). A number of useful assessment strategies are listed in Table 2.4. Many of these are described in detail in Chapter 9.

During the running of a unit and after its completion it is most important for teachers to evaluate its effectiveness. This can take the form of self-evaluation questions as listed in Table 2.5 or more formal approaches as depicted in Table 2.6.

8. Resources

A teaching unit typically includes a comprehensive listing of resources. Not only should this include textbooks and reference

Table 2.4 *Some commonly used assessment strategies to obtain data about student achievement*

· autobiographies	· cooperative learning outcomes	· rating scales
· activity records	· interviews	· role-play enactments
· attitudinal measures	· observation records	· teacher interviews
· checklists	· questionnaires	· teacher-made tests
· class projects		

Table 2.5 *Self-evaluation questions about a unit*

1. Is the theme and content appropriate for the age group?	activities that lead to a satisfactory culmination in the unit?
2. Is there a variety of activities for the students?	5. What are the overall strengths and weaknesses of the unit?
3. Is there integration with other subject areas of the curriculum?	6. What skills might a teacher need to enable that unit to be taught effectively?
4. Is there a progression of experiences and	

Table 2.6 *Some commonly used evaluation strategies to obtain data about the effectivness of a unit*

· External ratings	· Portfolio samples
· Group discussions	· Student questionnaire
· Peer ratings	· Student ratings

books but also the ever-increasing range of non-print materials such as videotapes, CD-ROMs, computer software packages, and the Internet and the World Wide Web (see Chapters 3 and 12).

In addition, there are many other potentially useful resources available in children's literature, music and art. These sources enable students to travel vicariously to other times and places. They add important dimensions to student learning and, in the process, provide further opportunities for students to develop listening, speaking, writing and reading skills.

Every teacher is able to build up his or her range of resource materials using appropriate storage boxes and folders (see Chapter 3). Students can be encouraged also to collect relevant resources and to assist with 'learning centre' tables in their classrooms.

■ Lesson Plans

The focus in the first part of this chapter has been on long-range planning and especially the development of units. Lesson plans refer to the daily instructional experiences which comprise a unit.

There needs to be a careful match between lesson plans and the teaching unit. That is, the overall goals of the unit should be kept in mind when constructing daily lesson plans.

Producing lesson plans is an art form. Teachers need to be able to produce lesson plans that will enable meaningful learning to occur. To do this they also need to capture students' interest and involvement.

Beginnings of lessons are most important. They are a major factor in shaping the motivation of students. There needs to be a smooth transition from what students know and what they have already studied. The lesson plans need to be sufficiently detailed so that the procedures are clearly recognisable. During the running of lessons it may be necessary for a teacher to make changes to these procedures because of unforeseen developments. It might also necessitate changes to the proposed closure to a lesson.

So daily lesson plans are important because:

- they help teachers to build up confidence in their teaching;
- they enable teachers to be better prepared for instruction;
- they enable teachers to consider different options and to be more flexible;
- they assist with evaluating instruction.

The format of lesson plans depends upon the topic and the resources to be used. For example, different formats might be expected for lesson plans based upon:

- videotape presentation;
- textbook and charts;
- simulation experience;
- class discussion;
- demonstration lesson;
- field trip;
- visit by a guest speaker;
- model/construction lesson.

Notwithstanding, some of the typical headings used in a variety of lessons include:

- objectives/outcomes;
- time available;
- materials needed;
- learning activities
  —introductory
  —developmental
  —concluding;
- evaluation.

Each lesson should have a small number of objectives or outcomes. These are derived from the teaching unit and the relevant system-level syllabus or curriculum guide.

The time available for lessons is never sufficient! Where units are integrated in nature, it is possible to spill over into other subject times, especially at the primary school level. Double periods are needed for some activities, such as simulation games.

It is necessary to list all the materials needed and to ensure that they are available at the appropriate time. This is especially the case with audio-visual materials.

Learning activities are the centrepiece of each lesson. The introductory activities are used to motivate students and to present new ideas/topics. This often involves showing items (charts/pictures), or posing questions, or raising an issue based upon a current event in a newspaper.

Developmental activities grow out of the introductory, opening activities. They may involve using a range of resources involving class discussions, individual reading, group viewing and many other approaches, as described above.

The concluding activities involve some closure for the lesson or for a series of lessons. They may involve some reporting back by small groups or individuals or a concluding summary by the teacher.

Evaluation activities, in terms of specific data collection, do not necessarily occur with every lesson. If it is a culmination of a number of lessons then a student assessment may be included (for example, a multiple choice test). Informal evaluative data may be collected by the teacher based on conversations with students or general observations of the class in action.

The production of lesson plans involves personal choices about the amount of detail and the format. Some teachers use a column format for each teaching week so that they can ensure they are using a variety of approaches and resources (see Table 2.7). Others tend to use a full page format. A lesson plan example is included in Table 2.8.

Table 2.7 *A summary of lesson plans for the week*

Monday	Tuesday	Wednesday	Thursday	Friday
Videotape on Japan	Mapping activity	Small-group activity using literature audiotapes	Reading and written assignment	Guest speaker to visit

Table 2.8 *A sample lesson plan on Japan*

Objectives/Outcomes	1. Students are able to describe the location of Japan and major natural resources. 2. Students are able to describe how people's use of natural features has changed over time.
Time available:	1 hour
Year level:	Year 6–8
Materials needed:	· wall map of Japan, hand-out outline maps; · videotape on Japan; · news stories, clippings, photographs of Japan's natural environment; · section in students' textbook on Japan.
Learning activities	
Introductory activities	· show large photographs of scenes in Japan; · compare with Australia; · what are the main features of Japan's natural environment? · list students' responses on white board.
Developmental activities	1. Show 10-minute videotape on the natural resources of Japan. 2. Ask students to read textbook and consult atlas and then locate major features on the hand-out outline map of Japan. 3. Read out excerpts from literature/books about Japanese culture and the natural environment. 4. Ask students to write a paragraph about how the Japanese have adapted to their natural environment.
Concluding activities	Select three students to read their paragraphs out to the class.
Evaluation	1. Observe students in doing the mapping activity. Collect completed maps to be marked and returned during the next lesson. 2. Observe students writing the paragraphs. Provide individual feedback as required.

However, it is up to teachers to develop lesson plans that suit their organisational preferences and which enable their creative strengths to blossom!

■ Concluding Comments

Well-planned programs are essential for good teaching. It is only by detailing intended teaching that teachers can monitor and reflect upon their level of success.

The unit approach is a useful organising device for providing effective and interesting learning experiences for students. Ideally, lesson plans need to be sufficiently detailed so that sequences can be developed and a variety of learning experiences can be included.

QUESTIONS AND ACTIVITIES

1. Examine the curriculum guide for social studies/environment studies in your education system. Critically analyse the information included for developing units and lesson plans.
2. Select a key concept and develop a lesson plan using the headings included in this chapter.
3. List five resources that you commonly use in your teaching units. Why do you prefer these ones? What others might you use? What are some impediments to widening your selection?
4. Think about a grade level you would like to teach. For this grade level identify a unit and provide a summary of how you would teach it, using appropriate headings.
5. Some educators argue that planning takes away from the creative aspects of teaching and that it inhibits spontaneity in learning. What are the arguments for and against planning lessons in studies of society and environment?
6. Produce a concept web based upon water. Try to include such related concepts as 'personal use', 'industrial use', 'consumption', 'production', 'transport'.

3 Resources and Information Literacy

Introduction

Resources are a critical element in effective teaching of studies of society and environment. Unfortunately, teachers tend not to use a wide range of resources and the limited number they do use are recycled year after year. Creative teachers access a wide range of resources because not only do they have the information literacy skills, but they realise the need to accommodate the diverse range of interests and learning styles of their respective students.

Curriculum cannot be implemented without resources. Resources are a critical element in the interactions which occur between teachers and students in classrooms. In fact, it could be argued that the teacher, students and resources comprise the three major elements of classroom learning, even though wider contextual factors of school environment, community, state and nation also influence the learning process.

According to Hunt (1997) resources are changing at a rapid rate and schools will continue to move to the use of resource-based instruction, especially telecommunications technologies. Without doubt, learners of the twenty-first century will be exposed to an information-rich and culturally diverse environment—they have the opportunity to be actively involved in constructing their own personal knowledge rather than serve as receptors of knowledge (Poe, Ford and Dobyns, 1998).

To enable learners (students and teachers) to be able to maximise their use of resources will require well-honed skills in information literacy. Learners will need to be able to choose the information required, and develop the skills to extract it and the confidence and self-esteem to use the information to solve particular problems

(Department of Education, Queensland, 1992).

In this chapter the focus is upon resource-based teaching, although there may be opportunities in some schools, and especially for upper primary and secondary school students, for independent student learning situations (see especially Chapter 10).

The increased availability of computers and associated software (CD-ROM, World Wide Web and Internet, email, on-line bulletin boards, videoconferencing) expands the range of resources available for use in the classroom. Although cost is certainly a major factor, many schools have the finances available to purchase an array of resources, if teachers make the effort to systematically select suitable materials. Herein lies a major problem. Resources are valuable to a school only if they are carefully and continuously used, up to the point at which they are judged to be obsolete and no longer appropriate. Teachers tend not to use a wide range of resources and the limited number they do use are recycled year after year.

This chapter tries to provide some solutions to the problem of resource selection and the establishment of a wide repertoire of resource materials for use in classrooms. Various questions will be posed throughout; for example:

- Who should be responsible for selecting resources in schools?
- What are some reliable criteria to use when selecting resources?
- What are the respective merits of material resources (e.g. computer software) as against human resources (e.g. guest speakers)?
- What are some of the problems in using community resources and visiting community venues?

■ Resources Available in a School Setting

The range of resources available for use in the classroom is constantly growing, and each type has particular merits for teachers and students in specific learning situations.

Any attempt to classify resources is always fraught with problems.

The listing included in Table 3.1 is partly based on print/non-print but not entirely. Some of these resources are promoted vigorously at present (e.g. the Internet) while others have been largely forgotten (e.g. film strips) but yet are still used in a number of schools.

Textbooks

Textbooks in studies of society and environment in Australia have tended to follow the US example of being colourful, eye-catching hard-cover volumes covering a wide range of topics and including numerous colour illustrations, photographs, maps and charts.

With the growth of colourful WWW pages and CD-ROM software, textbooks have to be comprehensive to retain their market appeal. A problem currently facing WWW users is that material on the Web cannot be authenticated and may not be accurate (Laughlin and Haas, 1997).

It can be argued that textbooks are an extremely valuable tool for students and teachers because they provide:

- a core of important learning;
- up to date and accurate information;
- instruction on basic skills; and
- an introduction, a summary or an overview of particular topics.

Textbooks are usually very popular with teachers because good textbooks bring together a massive amount of important material in the one volume, thus saving the busy teacher a considerable amount of time (Orlich *et al.*, 1998). For teachers lacking adequate background on certain topics, a comprehensive textbook can be a very useful stepping-off point—a springboard from which they can get their students to follow up particular ideas, issues and problems (Fan and Kaeley, 1998; Schug, Western and Enochs, 1997).

There is also considerable evidence available to indicate that textbooks are misused by teachers and that the content of the textbooks is often bland, poorly organised and inappropriate for many students (Nelson 1992). Venezky (1992) contends that textbooks have been a barrier to educational progress, a millstone around the neck of educational reform.

Thompson (1996) notes that many textbooks do not reflect current gender

Table 3.1 *A classification of resources available in studies of society and environment.*

1. Material resources	· Television and videotapes
· Textbooks	· Interactive videodisk
· Reference books	· Films
· Trade books (literature books)	· Radio
· Project kits	· Slide-tapes and filmstrips
· Pamphlets	· Overhead projectors
· Study prints and posters	
· Simulation games	**2. Human resources**
· Maps, globes and models	· Persons in specific occupations
· Computers	· Retired persons
· CD-ROM	· Groups, associations and organisations
· Internet, World Wide Web, email	

developments and that they endeavour to be politically correct.

Too often, teachers tend to rely on the textbook as the sole basis for organising a teaching unit, even to the extent of requiring their students to complete each exercise as listed in the textbook (see also Chapter 4). For example, a research study of 10 textbooks conducted by Elliott *et al.* (1985) concluded the following:

1. Most of the textbooks sampled did not have an integrated sequence of topics that built on concepts, skills and generalisations from one level to the next.
2. Few of the textbooks drew on examples taken from a wide range of countries and cultures.
3. Most of the textbooks assumed that teachers would use recitation, reading and simple exercises when teaching content.
4. Many topics were covered superficially.
5. Representations of women and minority groups were unrealistic and generally lacking.
6. Skills sections of the textbooks sampled tended to emphasise map and globe skills only.

Studies undertaken at Stanford University by Calfee and Chambliss (1988) and Chambliss, Calfee and Wong (1990) have also been very critical of studies of society and environment textbooks, noting that there is little conceptual basis for the topics included and few linkages between topics. A study by Laughlin and Haas (1997) of 10 US textbooks noted that information presented was often fragmented and flawed.

These studies highlight several important points. The selection of appropriate textbooks is clearly a very important task and one which must be undertaken very conscientiously by a teacher or groups of teachers at a school (see 'Checklists for evaluating and selecting print materials' on page 42). It is also evident that textbooks must not be over-used in the classroom situation and that teachers and students should consider them as only one of the many resources available.

Further, to use a textbook effectively it must be supplemented, enriched and updated (Banks and Banks, 1999). The content about major political figures, world issues and problems can soon become outdated. It is necessary to supplement textbooks with local, national and international news sources, such as from newspapers or from the Internet.

Charts and tables in textbooks can also become outdated. Statistics, such as census data statistics, need to be updated and they need to be replaced by the latest hard copy statistical bulletins or by information from websites of the Pathfinder Network (http://www.pathfinder.com/welcome/) or *The Economist* (http://www.economist.com/) on the Internet.

Reference books

A myriad of reference books is available in most libraries ranging from world encyclopedias and Australian encyclopedias to specialist volumes dealing with topics such as industrial development, environment and Aborigines.

There are a number of government publications which provide valuable information and statistical data. Examples include publications of the Australian Bureau of Statistics, yearbooks (state and federal), and social security, education and employment statistics. Practically all encyclopedias and government publications have produced CD-ROMs and/or have Web pages which can be accessed on the Internet. For example, Britannica and Grolier encyclopedias have interactive CD-ROMs available which include full-colour photographs, animation, sound and movie clips. Students can search for material by using title, subject, keywords and a number of different indexes (Gardner, 1997). Australian census data is available on CD-ROMs (for example, 1996 Year Book Australia) and on the Internet (http://www. statistics.gov.au).

Trade books

A book designed for use in classrooms is generally considered to be a textbook. However, books that are intended for sale to the general public, including fiction and non-fiction, are considered to be *trade books*. Literature books can greatly enrich teaching in studies of society and environment. Savage and Savage (1993) contend that children's literature plays an important part in conveying the affective dimension of human experience—it stirs the imagination of the readers and helps them to identify with the topic being studied. Koeller (1996) suggests that literature helps students feel empathy towards other ethnic groups.

There are literally hundreds of children's books with good potential, according to the Children's Book Council (1991). They range from classics such as Grahame's (1929) *The Wind in the Willows* to historical fiction such as Park's (1978) *Come Danger, Come Darkness* and Aldridge's (1986) *The True Story of Spit MacPhee*, to contemporary Australasian issues such as Thiele's (1974) *Albatross Two* and Southall's (1965) *Ash Road*. Ethnic trade books, such as Donkin's (1979) *Nini* and Wheatley's (1984) *Dancing in the Anzac Deli*, have a special value to this teaching field (Pugh, Garcia and Margalef-Boada, 1994). As noted by Welton and Mallan (1987), trade books can be used as supplementary readers for students, as background reading material for teachers, as reference material for students, and as the basis for specific teaching units or lessons. Davis and Palmer (1992), Savage and Savage (1993) and Ferrett and Traill (1994) maintain that trade books are more lively

than textbooks and provide a vehicle for humanising and adding personal components to the teaching program. Bean, Kile and Readence (1996) have developed activities such as polar opposites and small-group discussions to encourage critical thinking about selected trade books.

A major difficulty relates to choosing appropriate trade books from the enormous array available. McGowan (1987) suggests that the following criteria should be followed:

1. Is the book developmentally appropriate? (For example, are the setting, plot and themes relatively familiar to students?)
2. Has the book literary value? (For example, is it meaningful and has the author developed characters and imagery?)
3. Does the book present valued information? (For example, is the story told in a realistic way?)
4. Is the book's message of value? (For example, does the author examine issues worthy of the reader's attention?)

Library staff are more than willing to select trade books for particular teaching topics and will either provide boxes on loan to a classroom or will set aside particular shelves in the library to permit easy searching by students. More and more books are now being included on the Internet. This enables interaction between students using the same books in different parts of the country (Poe *et al.*, 1998). Few teachers would miss using some of A.B. Paterson's poetry such as 'The Man from Snowy River' or Henry Lawson's stories such as 'The Loaded Dog' to convey impressions of life in outback Australia. At the secondary school level, there are numerous examples available, such as a German soldier's letter written during the invasion of Stalingrad in 1944 in *Last Letters from Stalingrad* by Schneider and Gullans (1962) or accounts of the atomic bomb being dropped in Japan in Hachiya's *Hiroshima*

Diary: The Journal of a Japanese Physician (1955), or post-World War II scenarios such as Forman's *Doomsday plus Twelve* (1984).

Project kits

Project kits first appeared on the commercial market in Australia in the late 1950s with the advent of Science Research Associates (SRA) kits on reading skills. During the 1960s, many national projects were developed in the US and UK and almost invariably their products were broadened from the hitherto traditional textbooks to kits containing numerous photographs and pictures, work-cards and various audio-visual aids.

The Social Education Materials Project (SEMP) was developed by the Curriculum Development Centre during 1975–77 for secondary school students. Although the topics, entitled Family, Social Control and Conflict, Aborigines and Europeans, and People and Shelter, were of a high quality, the uptake in schools was very limited.

Project kits continue to be produced by publishers but the number and range is quite limited. For example, a Social Education kit (Collins Dove, 1992) for primary students contains books and audiotapes on the four strands of Justice, Transport, Communication and Environment.

Some recent project kits have been developed and funded by organisations and agencies not directly associated with the studies of society and environment field. For example, a number of road safety kits which deal in general terms with studies of society and environment topics have been produced by road traffic authorities in Victoria and New South Wales. *Surveys* (1986), produced by the Road & Traffic Authority of Victoria, consists of a teacher's book and a student book and teaches survey techniques by using a traffic safety theme. *Are You in Control?* (1988), produced by the Traffic Authority of New South Wales, uses statistics and discussion

topics to present problems associated with drink-driving.

Law societies have also been active in producing kits and materials, and the Departments of the Senate and the House of Representatives have taken initiatives with the production of *The Parliament Pack Guide* (1987).

The Australian Dairy Corporation has produced a range of posters, computer disks and books on dairying and dairy products. For example, the New South Wales Dairy Corporation (1988) produced a project kit *Food: Your Choice*, comprising a programming guide, syllabus-link charts and units of work on four themes—Food Facts, Diet and Performance, Diet and Appearance, and Consumerism, Health and Controversies. The Australian Bureau of Statistics (1996) has produced a *Census: School Resource Kit*, including posters, student activities, puzzles and inquiry topics.

The 'Discovering Democracy Project' is a mega-project initiated in 1997 and funded by the Commonwealth Government. It is due to be completed by 2000. The kit has been distributed free to all schools and consists of units of work, three CD-ROMs, website anthologies and professional support manuals. The focus of the kit is to provide students with a thorough knowledge and understanding of Australia's political heritage and to develop skills to participate in civic life (Carter, Ditchburn and Bennett, 1999). Although considerable attention is being given to training and professional development, there are other problems to be resolved such as perceptions that a 'teacher-proof curriculum' is being delivered to schools (Finch, 1999).

The dilemma for busy teachers is to decide whether a particular kit will enhance their teaching or not.

It is unlikely that a national kit will be able to supplant an existing teaching program as there are state-level requirements. A kit is more likely to complement other parts of a program. It is important for teachers not to be seduced by the eye-catching colours, range of materials and technology contained in these kits. The only reliable way to make an informed decision about a kit is to use a materials analysis checklist, as described later on page 42.

Pamphlets and inexpensive materials
There are various inexpensive pamphlets available from commercial companies and government agencies dealing with such topics as mining, community services, pollution and animal killing. These are produced by such organisations as BHP, Hamersley Iron, UNESCO and Greenpeace. Quite often they present up to date information and colourful photographs on topics for which it is difficult to obtain appropriate teaching materials. They do provide a very attractive alternative to traditional textbooks which can often go quickly out of date. Furthermore, the pamphlets are often available in bulk so that they can be used individually or in small groups by a class of students.

A recent development in the USA has been the development of a television channel for schools (Channel One) which includes daily news and feature stories but also advertising. Some critics argue that the acceptance of Channel One in many schools has delivered a youth audience to advertisers and blurred the distinction between the marketplace and the schools (Rank, 1994).

It is important, therefore, to remember that all inexpensive materials (including audio-visual materials providing financial incentives for schools) have been sponsored by an individual or firm and they will be emphasising a particular value orientation. Although it might be expected that the majority of firms have high ethical standards,

organisations will include their viewpoints, sometimes overtly but usually covertly, in their publications.

The wary teacher will, of course, be alert to obvious examples of prejudice and propaganda, and these materials can sometimes be supplemented by alternative publications which provide opposing points of view. To heighten awareness of bias in materials Haas (1985) suggests that the following checklist of questions might be used:

1. What organisation produced the materials?
2. Do the materials teach any unstated objectives?
3. Is the identification of the product or brand necessary to teach the objectives of the lesson?
4. Are the sources of the facts in the materials identified?
5. What important facts are omitted from the materials?
6. Do the materials use half-truths to support their viewpoints?
7. Do the materials use emotionally loaded words or pictures?
8. If you use the materials, what feelings about the sponsors and their goals might you expect the students to express?

Such checklist questions are an important source for teachers, especially at the primary school level. However, in upper primary grades and in secondary schools, such checklist questions might also be used by students. Inexpensive pamphlet materials can provide concrete examples for students to sharpen their critical thinking skills. Examples of bias can be located and discussed by students. They can compare accounts of a topic given in a pamphlet with those rendered by authors in reputable textbooks. There are many possibilities for both teacher and students to share important insights into controversial issues and the use of propaganda and emotive advertising.

Study prints and posters

A file of photographs and posters is a valuable resource for every teacher. Students' concepts of 'pollution', 'inequality' or 'urban blight' need to be explored by using all senses, especially the visual sense (Du Plass, 1996). Prints and posters provide students with graphic illustrations so that they can verify or correct their concepts as they develop them. Study prints have the ability to portray reality with impact.

A variety of large, colourful posters and photographs are available, usually for nominal amounts, from such sources as overseas consulates, travel and tourist agencies, airline companies and some government offices. Once they have been obtained it is necessary to protect them from damage with a suitable plastic covering (preferably a laminating process) or a cardboard backing.

Commercial publishing firms now produce a variety of study prints and photographs, usually covering particular themes and sometimes including follow-up questions. Useful Australian examples include 'You Are What You Eat' (Australian Dairy Corporation, 1991), 'Communities and Ecosystems' (Educational Media Australia, 1988) and 'National Habitats of Australia' (Educational Media Australia, 1991).

Reprographic facilities have improved remarkably over recent years and it is now possible for a teacher to get small snapshots enlarged into poster prints relatively inexpensively. Photocopying machines are also available which provide a variety of enlargement and reduction options, and many machines can also produce colour copies.

Personal collections of study prints and posters are a boon to the teacher in preparing lessons but only if they are readily accessible. An appropriate filing system is usually essential, whether it is a simple card index or a file stored on the school's computer (see Chapter 12). For safety, the study prints and posters should ideally be stored horizontally in large metal chart drawers, but unfortunately the cost of these is often prohibitive for the small school with limited finances.

Simulation games

Details about the creation and use of simulation games are given in Chapter 11, so this information will not be repeated here. Simulation games are a most valuable resource for the teacher, whether they are teacher-made examples or elaborate commercial versions. The evidence from teachers using simulation games suggests that:

- they can modify students' attitudes, usually in terms of a more positive appreciation of the real-world persons whose roles they played;
- they are popular with students; and
- they seem to be as effective for teaching cognitive skills as other teaching techniques.

A wide range of commercially produced simulation games is available. Some examples include 'SimEarth' (Wright and Haslam, 1990), 'Black Christmas' (Cunningham and Teather, 1990) and 'Farm Development and Simulation' (Learning Development Unit, 1990).

Maps, globes and models

Maps, globes and models are essential resources for the studies of society and environment teacher. Maps can portray a tremendous amount of information and students enjoy adding information to large pinboard and whiteboard maps. Small maps are a valuable way for students to summarise information in projects and assignments.

Recent studies have demonstrated that students learn more effectively when verbal materials are augmented with visual-spatial

Large maps can provide valuable information

Creative model-building

means such as maps (Webb, Saltz and Kealy, 1996a) and concept-trees/semantic maps (Antonacci, 1991). Webb *et al.* (1996b) note that when icons are included on maps student learning is enhanced considerably. Kulhavy *et al.* (1993) conclude that students recall more factual information from a textbook or lecture when they are also able to study a related map.

Globes are an essential item in every classroom because they provide the only accurate representation of the earth's surface. Primary school students need to see the relative size of continents, the distribution of oceans and major surface features. Directions and time between different places can be best understood by reference to a globe, which is also a major teaching aid in demonstrating such concepts as rotation, revolution and seasons to upper primary grades (see also Chapter 4). Secondary school students can use more elaborate physical-political globes as an aid to studying migration patterns or exploration routes and to examine global problems (Chilcott, 1991).

All kinds of models can be used to good effect, including model relief maps made from such materials as paper strips and paste, papier-mâché, plaster, clay and plastic starch and detergent. Depending on the project, model maps can be protected and maintained for a long period by painting over the surface with a clear varnish or shellac.

Dioramas are three-dimensional models used to depict particular activities. Although students might not be able to rival the high-quality dioramas available in museums, school model-building can be a very worthwhile group activity. Cardboard figures suitably painted and an appropriate background scene are usually all that is needed to create dioramas of historical events, once students have researched the necessary details about the period or action. A creative teacher can add impact to

dioramas by using various 'junk' materials to highlight figures and backgrounds. For example, Maxim (1983) suggests that all kinds of oddments, such as cloth, straw, seeds, gift wrap, leaves and sand (see Table 3.2), can be used.

The use of art can enrich lessons and heighten student interests (Banks and Banks, 1999). Art materials can be produced by students in class. In addition students can access great art by visiting famous art galleries on the Internet (for example, the Louvre Museum (http://www.paris.org/Musees/Louvre)).

■ Checklists for Evaluating and Selecting Print Materials

The previous examples are just a few of the numerous articles available for use in the classroom. Marketing strategies dictate how these products are packaged, so it is possible for various combinations to be sold. These can consist of wholly printed materials, a combination of models and printed matter, or printed matter and audio-visual materials, to name just a few of the combinations.

All teachers involved in the process of purchasing new materials for their classrooms have somehow to discriminate between useful and unsuitable resources. Although intuition, recommendations from others and subjective reactions to physical appeal are some of the criteria which might be used, the importance of the selections warrants a process which is more rigorous and soundly based.

A number of educators have produced checklists which can be used to select print materials, ranging from relatively simple (e.g. Piper, 1976; Gall, 1981) to comprehensive ones requiring prior training (e.g. Eraut, Goad and Smith, 1975). Most checklists involve examining the print materials in isolation, although some include categories

Table 3.2 *Junk art materials which can be used in creating dioramas*

Textured materials		
Fur scraps	Sandpaper	Feathers
Leather	Velvet	Cotton
Felt	Corduroy	Pipe cleaners
Burlap or sacking	Seeds	Acorns
Corrugated paper	Twigs	Shells
Egg carton dividers	Pebbles	Styrofoam
Carpet scraps	Dried flowers or weeds	
Patterned materials		
Wallpaper samples	Linoleum scraps	Catalogues
Magazines	Patterned gift wrap	Greeting cards
Seasonal stickers	Candy bar wrappers	Stamps
Transparent and semi-transparent materials		
Net fruit sacks	Lace	Metal screening
Onion sacks	Plastic wrap	Coloured cellophane
Crêpe paper	Thin tissue paper	Paper lace doilies
Sparkling or shiny materials		
Sequins	Ribbon	Christmas tinsel
Glitter	Seasonal wrapping paper	Mica snow
Aluminium foil	Paper from greeting cards	Metallic paper
Shapes		
Buttons	Cork	Rubber bands
Drinking straws	Bottle caps	Toothpicks
Wooden applicators	Keys	Beads
Spools	Tongue depressors	Fluted candy cups
Scrap sponge	Cup cake cups	Gummed stickers
Paper clips	Heavy cotton rug yarn	String
Metal washers		Old jewellery
Scattering materials		
Sand	Tiny pebbles	Twigs
Sawdust	Wood shavings	Vermiculite
Yarn	Kitty litter	Coloured aquarium
Gravel	Eggshells	pebbles

for also examining them in actual use in classrooms. Clearly the former involves less of the teacher's time and can be undertaken without disruption to other people.

Piper's scheme is based on four major components and ten subcomponents. A summary of these components is given in Table 3.3 (see also Boxes 3.1 and 3.2). Teachers are required simply to give a yes/no answer to each of these questions. The

Table 3.3 *Piper's materials analysis scheme*

Goals	Processes
1. Aims and objectives	6. Student activities
2. Rationale	7. Teacher procedures

Format	Outcomes
3. Practicability	8. Student outcomes
4. Design	9. Teacher outcomes
5. Content	10. General outcomes

Box 3.1 *Goals and outcomes—
sample questions*

1. Are the aims and objectives
   realistic?   yes/no
2. Is the rationale clearly and
   convincingly argued?   yes/no
3. Are there benefits/gains for the
   student in terms of:
   (a) knowledge/understanding?   yes/no
   (b) skills?   yes/no
   (c) attitudes/values?   yes/no
   (d) perceptions?   yes/no
   (e) interests?   yes/no

Box 3.2 *Format and processes—
sample questions*

1. Is the material 'practical' in terms of:
   (a) school facilities/
       organisation?   yes/no
   (b) equipment?   yes/no
   (c) convenience of handling?   yes/no
   (d) class size/age/ability range?   yes/no
2. Are there special skills/demands
   required of the students?   yes/no

categories include a number of specific questions which an analyst should be able to answer quite readily by scanning the curriculum materials.

The Piper scheme is recommended because of its simplicity, ease of use and flexibility.

The format of the analysis also enables the results to be communicated easily to others. However, it should be noted that the scheme does have deficiencies. The scheme is predominantly teacher directed and highly structured. It might not be appropriate for analysing non-prescriptive curriculum materials. Furthermore, the yes/no answer categories do not appear to be appropriate for all the questions included in the checklist.

■ Multimedia Resources

In addition to print forms, information can be delivered by any one of a large number of means such as a slide-tape sequence, a videotape or videodisk, a computer program or by a combination of these. The manner in which the message is packaged is referred to as 'software' and the specialised equipment for it to be presented to learners is termed 'hardware'. Thus a slide-tape sequence is 'software', and so too is a videotape, a videodisk or a computer program. Each requires hardware to bring the message to the student, such as a synchronised slide-tape player, a videotape player, a videodisk player or a computer.

Computers head up the list because they offer enormous opportunities to teachers now, and will offer even more in the future (Dede, 2000). According to Stonier (1985), 'No technology to aid learning, from prayer wheels and medieval stained glass windows, to overhead projectors and videotapes, approaches the potential effectiveness of computers. Not even books.'

In particular, the World Wide Web is developing into a powerful resource. According to Barron and Ivers (1998), never before has the educational community had such an inexpensive, easily accessible method of communicating and distributing information.

Tapscott (1999) asserts that students are wholly engrossed in the Net Generation. They are surrounded by digital technologies and they are learning, developing and thriving in this digital world. Yet it is necessary to be cautious and practical. There are numerous financial, equity and morality issues (Carey, 1998).

Northup, Barth and Kranze (1991) argue that minimum standards are needed for adequate support of technology including:

- a technology plan—each school should have a technology utilisation plan for current and intended technology;
- technology training—all teachers must be trained to use current and emerging technologies (including Internet and World Wide Web);
- preparation of materials and management of records—all teachers must have easy access to a computer for the production of teaching materials, creation of tests and management of records.

Personal computers

Although computers have been available for several decades (see Chapter 12), personal computers are a more recent phenomenon. Due to microchip technology advances, schools are now able to use desktop computers and lap-top computers at minimal cost.

The use of personal computers in the classroom is expanding rapidly. Although there are logistical problems in organising computers for use by students, it is evident that students perceive them as fun: they never put a child down, they can provide privacy and they can give answers instantly (Stonier, 1985). More information about computers and especially the World Wide Web is given in Chapter 12.

Television and videotapes

Television is an inescapable part of our culture and therefore, as teachers, we must consider positive ways of using this resource. Television programs currently available to students on national and commercial stations can be used to link up with various topics in studies of society and environment. In fact, the various documentaries, plays, round-table discussions, interviews and news reports are admirably suited to use in this teaching area.

Television in the classroom is at its best when it is used to pose a problem, introduce an idea, awaken curiosity and excite the emotions. Research studies (Morgan, 1984) indicate that television is not very appropriate for communicating facts and figures. In fact, it is possibly less effective than traditional methods of teacher instruction when used for this purpose. However, brief televised segments of 10 to 15 minutes to introduce a topic or issue are very useful. Because of the problems of synchronising advertised times of educational television programs with classroom lessons, it is far easier to videotape desired programs so that they can be used later, in whole or in part, as required.

Teachers can also take advantage of the television viewing undertaken by students in their out-of-school hours. At the primary school level, a forum group of four or five students can be asked to watch a particular television program and then to give their reactions and opinions to the remainder of

Reading and listening resource skills

An enormous range of programs are now available for use on personal computers

the class, who are encouraged, in turn, to react to the forum group. Secondary school students can profit from watching movies and documentaries on television depicting particular cultures or historical periods. These television viewing experiences can greatly enhance students' appreciation of particular teaching topics and perhaps help to break down their alienation towards school and school work (Edwards, 1993).

Of course, videotaping need not apply merely to the copying of regular transmission programs. Camcorders are available in most schools, thus enabling teachers and/or students to videotape classroom happenings such as a play or simulation activities (Berwick, 1994). The replaying of these events on videotape enables students and the teacher to get instant feedback about their behaviour. Used on a regular basis, video feedback to students can be a powerful tool for getting students to improve their physical movements, style of speaking and many other facets of their behaviour (Stroschein, 1991).

Videotaping, especially by groups of students, is of special importance for recording projects which take students out of the classroom and into the local community (Berwick, 1994). This enables students to develop their special creative talents in deciding what a videotape should be about and how it is to be presented. Special events occurring in the community and local identities involved in particular occupations are just some of the potential topics for videotaping (see 'Resources available beyond the school setting', page 50).

There are, of course, potential dangers in over-using television as a resource. In the classroom, constant use of television programs limits students to the role of passive learners (Flanagan, 1996). Viewing videotapes is very time consuming, and careful decisions need to be made to set limits on how frequently and for what length of time videotape replaying is to occur in the classroom.

Videotaping equipment is expensive, so care must also be taken with its use. Careless use of camcorders, such as pointing them at the sun, can cause damage. Careless dropping and bumping of a videocassette recorder can also lead to costly repairs. Nevertheless, the development of commonsense rules of handling usually enables quite young primary schoolchildren, as well as secondary school students, to use the video equipment very competently and successfully.

Interactive videodisk

The merging of computer and video has led to the creation of the interactive videodisk— Laser Videodisk or CD-ROM (see also Chapter 12). The rich source of data on a single disk (textual, visual, animation, auditory) provides enormous possibilities for teachers and students (Kanning, 1994). The Internet and especially the World Wide Web is developing rapidly as a major source of data (Risinger, 1996; Wilson and Marsh 1995, Betts, 1996).

As an example, the Board of Studies, New South Wales (1992b), released a CD-ROM disk entitled 'Flashback', designed specifically for the Years 7–10 Australian History Syllabus in New South Wales. Hardware needed to operate the CD-ROM disk includes an Apple Macintosh computer, a monitor, a hard disk and an Apple-compatible CD-ROM drive. The disk enables users to explore a myriad of items from the past including photographs, newspapers, posters, music, famous speeches and radio broadcasts, movie clips, magazines, maps, letters, cartoons and paintings. Other recent additions on CD-ROM include 'Invasion and Resistance: Untold Stories' (Board of Studies, New South Wales, 1996a), 'Bush Tucker' (Arrernte Community, 1996) and 'Convict Fleet to Dragon Boat' (National Archives, 1998).

Interactive videodisk use is gaining momentum as an educational tool. An enormous amount of visual and auditory material can be speedily and accurately accessed by users, either in a set way or in random ways nominated by the users. The quality of simulated situations can also be enhanced by the use of interactive videodisk.

Interactivity, according to Mui (1993), enables students to respond to programs and to control their own learning paths. Multimedia, with its ability to integrate text, still images, graphics, audio and full motion video, promises a total sensory learning experience for students. Notwithstanding, the costs involved in producing software and hardware are considerable, and interactive videodisk is not the solution to every learning problem.

Films

Films as a resource in the classroom have clearly been overtaken by television and especially by video cassettes. Yet there continues to be a place for the 10-minute 16-millimetre film. Most education systems have an audio-visual centre through which educational films (and videotapes) may be borrowed free or for a nominal charge.

Over the years, numerous films, most of them in colour, have been produced on topics relating to studies of society and environment. These enable students to experience more fully what they have been reading about in their textbooks. In many cases, the viewing of a short 16-millimetre film can be an excellent introduction or an added stimulus to studying a topic.

As with all audio-visual aids, careful planning is needed when using films. Films often have to be booked up to three months in advance, and there are often special ordering procedures in a school that need to

be followed to ensure that the films arrive on schedule. Any teacher intending to use films needs to plan carefully to ensure that the topics to be taught in class coincide with the subjects to be covered by the films and that they are not used as fillers or merely to entertain (Banks and Banks, 1999).

Previewing a film is an essential preparation (as it is for videotapes). The summary statement accompanying a film typically provides very limited information, so it is only by previewing a film that teachers can make decisions about whether or not it is suitable for a particular class. The preview also provides valuable advance information to the teacher about the content and difficult words or concepts which might need to be explained to a class before they view it.

Radio

Educational radio programs also have a place in studies of society and environment lessons. Listening skills are critical ones for students to develop, especially since the presence of uninterrupted background noise is common in many homes, and tends to deter students from developing listening awareness skills.

Radio programs can provide provocative and stimulating introductions to a topic. Listening to a radio program compels students to form their own special mental images of what is happening (Chapin and Messick, 1999). This can lead to very productive discussion sessions as students relate their impressions of what they have heard. There is more scope for imaginative student reactions to radio programs than to television or videotape programs, as the latter tend to produce particular visual stereotypes. Students can also become involved in preparing their own class radio programs, complete with appropriate sound effects. Short programs on a particular topic can be tape recorded and replayed on higher quality radio sets or on the school public address system. These small-group student activities can be a lot of fun and are worthwhile educational activities. Radio programs do not require the elaborate 'dressing up' required for making class television programs using camcorders.

Slide-tapes and filmstrips

Slides and filmstrips have a major advantage over the motion picture in that a student can study and analyse each slide or frame for as long as required. Although video cassettes often have a 'still' or 'pause' control to freeze a particular frame, it is not possible to use this repeatedly because of the time it would take to complete the cassette. Also, slides and filmstrips are much cheaper to purchase than motion picture films or videotapes, so the expenses in establishing a class or school library are considerably less.

Commercially produced slides and filmstrips are available on a wide range of topics, especially those that relate to special events in the past, distant places or controversial issues. Slide sets have a greater flexibility than filmstrips in that they can be regrouped in various ways to suit specific topics and occasions. For example, Chilcoat (1991) describes some of the advantages of planning illustrated song slide shows. Nevertheless, there are disadvantages—for example, it is very easy to lose a slide or get slides out of sequence. This can be a problem if the slides are linked via magnetic cues to a cassette tape.

Filmstrips tend to be produced about topics which will not need to be updated in the near future. Topics ideally suited to filmstrips include voyages by early explorers and other historical topics. Filmstrips can be linked magnetically to a cassette tape or they may be available singly with only a brief set of explanatory notes. Recently the tendency seems to have been for audio accompaniments to concentrate on real-life noises

rather than narrative statements. This is a welcome emphasis, as students are encouraged to reflect more on visuals if they are not plied with a barrage of information from an audio cassette.

Both filmstrips and slide-tape sequences can be used effectively in small-group situations. There are a number of inexpensive filmstrip projectors available, which can be used by quite young children in small groups. They can provide an ideal supplementary source of ideas for individual and group projects and can be reused whenever required. Slide-tape sequences require more bulky and expensive carousel projectors, but can also be operated very successfully by groups of students. Students can also be encouraged to produce their own slide-tape sequences and filmstrips. Many students either own or have access to a 35-millimetre camera.

As part of an individual or group project, students may want to present particular items on film and include visuals in the project as either prints or slides. At the secondary school level, many students have access to media classes where they can acquire the necessary skills in filming and processing slides and producing their own filmstrips.

Overhead projectors

Overhead projectors are a common resource in most classrooms. A major advantage of the overhead projector compared with whiteboards is that the teacher can face the class in a normally lighted classroom and can thereby be aware of all ongoing class activities.

Overhead projectors are a special boon to studies of society and environment teaching because they make it possible for the teacher to prepare difficult maps and diagrams, often in colour, in advance. These can then be reused whenever needed. There are enormous time savings here, as will be appreciated by those readers who have laboured over coloured blackboard maps in the past!

The transparencies needed for overhead projectors can be produced in various ways. A wide range of sophisticated, highly colourful commercial transparencies is available, especially on such topics as earth movements, the water cycle, distribution of minerals and many others. A teacher can also make transparencies on most photocopying machines (subject to normal copyright regulations), so any item in a book or magazine (chiefly black and white) can be reproduced in this way. Various soluble coloured marker pens are also available so that a teacher can produce a transparency (e.g. a summary) as an ongoing process during a lesson.

According to Davidson, Rowland and Sherry (1982) some basic principles to remember when preparing classroom transparencies include:

- visibility—use large writing, printing and typing. Letters should be a least 0.5 centimetres high;
- clarity—everything on a visual chart should be instantly recognisable. If it is not, it should be labelled. Colour can be used to emphasise certain points;
- simplicity—keep it crisp and uncluttered. Use a maximum of six or seven lines per transparency.

In studies of society and environment teaching, overlays (i.e. succeeding transparencies applied on top of the preceding one) can be a useful way of explaining particular patterns. At the secondary school level, for example, the population distribution of a specific country can be more readily understood if preceding transparencies (to the same scale) depict physical features and climate. Another useful teaching device is the use of a sheet of paper as a 'blind' so that details on a transparency are released progressively.

The use of overhead projectors, as with all audio-visual aids, can easily be overdone. They are not a substitute for the chalkboard or whiteboard. Transparencies on the overhead projector should only be used when particular visual impacts are needed and when the nature of the material makes it too complicated or too time consuming to be placed on the whiteboard.

Powerpoint projectors (LCD)

Although overhead projectors continue to be used in many classrooms, more sophisticated diagrams, charts and headings can be presented in dazzling colours by using LCD projectors linked to powerpoint programs on a personal computer.

Elaborate graphics can be projected in full daylight conditions and the teacher can direct the projections by remote control.

■ Resources Available Beyond the School Setting

Studies of society and environment has one major advantage over most other subjects. Its focus is on people and the environment and there are countless examples of these social interactions all around us. Teachers should take advantage of these 'live' examples and not limit their teaching to textbooks and in-class examples.

There are many interesting local community studies which can be undertaken by students in the local community and in communities further afield (Hickey, 1991). The types of investigation carried out by students can vary tremendously in scope and purpose: they can be formal or informal, in school time or non-school time, in large groups, small groups or individually, or with students as observers or participants. The range and scope is limited only by the initiative and resourcefulness of the teacher and the students. Examples range from highly structured field trips (see Chapter 4) to informal camping hikes, attendance by students at public meetings as reporters, or student service as aides in a nursing home on a Saturday morning (Rugen and Hartl, 1994).

People in specific occupations

Most local communities contain segments of retailing and wholesaling, light industry, transport and market gardening, as well as various levels of residential land use. All kinds of resource personnel are usually available, but there are possibly two main categories of people who are most useful. There are a select few who are well known for their general knowledge of and interest in the local community. Often these people have held the same positions for a considerable period and have been involved in most of the community action over the years. In this category, one normally finds the local newspaper editor, librarian, shire or city councillor and garage operator. The second category consists of personnel who

may not have lived in the community for a long period and may not be well known but who possess specific skills and knowledge about the industry of which they are specialised members—for example, a bank manager, union secretary and a supermarket manager. Both categories of personnel have useful contributions to make and may, in various ways, enrich and broaden the interests of the students (see also Chapter 4). However, these persons need to be selected with care as they need to be good communicators in front of groups and they should be able to relate to students (Freeland, 1991).

Beery and Schug (1984: 8) provide some useful alternative formats for guest speaker sessions, depending on the topic and the age of the students:

- press conference—speaker opens with a brief introductory statement and then takes questions from the group;
- student questions—class provides written questions for the speaker which he or she can respond to in the presentation;
- guest lecturer—speaker should break frequently for questions, bring visuals and use dramatic and well-thought-out examples.

People now retired, but previously in specific occupations

These are the local 'delights', the World War II veteran and the collector of dolls, who have time to explain and reminisce about their particular hobbies or interests. Then there are the octogenarians who can describe in remarkable detail the social, economic and political activities of the local community in years gone by (Hickey, 1991). These people are the ones who give colour to local community studies and who, if they are carefully sought out (and kept to the topic), can be very useful sources of information. One highly promising way of capitalising on the experiences of older community members is to record on audiotape or videotape their recollections of former times. A collection of such recorded remembrances can bring life to the study of history and can provide students with first-hand experience in collecting and analysing primary data.

Groups, associations and organisations

Local associations are often available and willing to provide specific information to students. An examination of the yellow pages in the telephone directory will reveal that they run the whole gamut, including religious, recreational, sporting, business, cultural, political and social welfare groups. Again, discretion must be used by teachers and students in only contacting groups which have information specifically related to the topic under study. Also, as mentioned above, students need to be aware of indirect (and sometimes blatant) propaganda manoeuvres by these organisations!

Some examples of specific associations found in a local community or nearby town are included in Table 3.4.

Materials and artifacts
Newspapers

Local newspapers are often an important source of information about a community,

both for present-day happenings and historical events. They are often the diary of the community, recording events as they take place and in considerable detail. Daily newspapers often contain local community supplements, flashback columns and, most importantly, special issues covering centenaries and other momentous events. All these newspapers are usually readily available from either the head office of the newspaper or from libraries and historical societies. Depending on the interests of the students (and especially the exigencies of storage space availability), a search of the community can often bring rewarding results. Parents and friends searching through spare rooms may find all sorts of historic newspaper editions and are sometimes willing to donate to schools complete sets going back many years.

Documents and reports

The satisfaction that students gain from working with primary data has been noted by many educators and is elaborated on in some detail in Chapter 10. In the local community, a wealth of documents is available, although head offices in larger centres may have to be visited to actually pick up the data. Data from government offices may include:

- census data on population and industries;
- data on water supply, sewerage and health services;
- land deeds;
- court records;
- vital statistics (births, deaths, marriages); and
- city directories.

Data from private firms may include:

- annual reports; and
- booklets on the historical growth of a particular company.

The availability of relatively inexpensive forms of photocopying enables important

Table 3.4 *Examples of groups, associations and organisations of potential interest to students and teachers of studies of society and environment*

Business
1. Timber Advisory Service
2. Australian Chamber of Commerce and Industry
3. Solar Housing Interest Group
4. National Safety Council of Australia
5. Real Estate Institute
6. Retail Traders' Association
7. Market Gardeners' Association
8. Australian Conservation Foundation
9. Greenpeace Australia
10. Energy Management Centre
11. Planet Care

Recreational
1. Scout Association
2. Senior Citizens' Association
3. YMCA and YWCA
4. Police and Citizens Youth Club
5. Western Walking Club

Social welfare
1. Epilepsy Association
2. Meals on Wheels
3. Red Cross Society
4. Rotary Club

5. Aboriginal Advancement Council
6. Amnesty International
7. Australian Teenage Cancer Patients' Society

Religious
1. Christian Welfare Centre
2. Asia-Pacific Christian Mission
3. Bible College
4. Specific denominations, sects and organisations

Political
1. Equal Opportunities Resource Centre
2. Specific political parties

Cultural and educational
1. Vintage Automobile Association
2. International Friends and Families Reunion Association
3. Latin American Association
4. Debating League
5. Oral History Association of Australia
6. Arts Council
7. Ethnic Hotline
8. Australia–China Friendship

documents to be reproduced in their original form, with a minimum of time and effort. However, two caveats need to be stated. Students should only embark on the examination of documents and reports if they have a specific objective in mind, otherwise the exercise becomes an interesting but wasteful use of student time. Documents must only be obtained by using the appropriate permissions and approval procedures. Obviously the above activities apply mainly to secondary school students.

Photographs
In a local community, a whole wealth of photographs is available—historical and

current, of good and poor quality, relevant and non-relevant. Historical photographs can be very useful for depicting social customs and town life (Kirman, 1995). They are usually available as discards from newspaper offices, business firms and professional photographers or available from state libraries. If asked, parents and local citizens will often provide schools with many old photographs. The major problem is culling out the few really useful ones. Many schools now have photographic facilities where small photographs can be enlarged to a size suitable for teaching.

One of the major advantages of photographs is that they can be used to show scenes

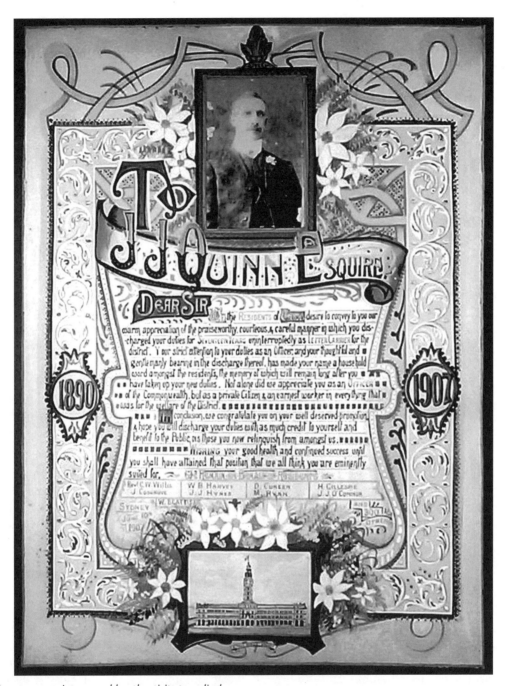

Old posters or prints can add authenticity to a display

at different periods, especially before and after major changes have occurred. Consequently, local community enthusiasts have to be continually on the alert for changes that are imminent so that they can record the present situation for posterity. Such instances might include the demolition of an historic landmark or the pulling up of the tram tracks that run right down the middle of the main street.

Recordings

Photographs provide authentic visual records of events. In much the same way, tape recordings provide authentic auditory evidence. For example, a tape recording of the reminiscences of a notable local resident might be of great value, as might the recording of local folk songs, important public meetings or even sounds of a past era. It is up to the students to record the sounds of objects or persons that might be unavailable in the near future. Modern technology makes it relatively easy to obtain good-quality reproductions of tapes from radio stations or from private and public companies. It is now possible to reproduce high-quality records of past and present-day events by using audiotapes and videotapes and CD-ROM disks.

Miscellaneous personal items

For specific school displays in conjunction with a local community study, parents and citizens are often willing to lend a miscellaneous array of personal items, sometimes of considerable historical interest. Such a display might contain samples of tools, utensils, weapons, crockery or even clothing and toys pertaining to particular groups.

Local museums and historical societies often have a great number of items that can be viewed by students (Field *et al.*, 1996; Mabry and Stake, 1998). In some instances, museums provide boxes of contemporary and historic artifacts on loan to schools for short periods of time. However, most teachers (and cleaners) would be rather reticent, if not appalled, at the idea of collecting miscellaneous personal items for permanent storage!

Some precautions

At regular points in studies of society and environment courses it is both appropriate and effective to give students an opportunity to do studies of their local community or region, either as an introductory stimulus/springboard to a theme or topic, or as a culminating integrative exercise. A steady diet of local community studies might become just as nauseating as regular programs to many school students. However, on occasions, they are able to provide students with realistic first-hand experiences which can be extremely valuable. For example, students in a class can become involved in ongoing community projects where they are not only acquiring information from others but giving information or support. Cumming (1992) documents recent examples of where this has occurred in a number of Australian states and territories.

To some students, local community studies might have too wide a focus, so that they cannot see past an array of undigested, unrelated facts. Training over a period of time is often required so that students can adjust to purposeful searching for relevant material.

Local community studies do not just happen. Very careful planning is required by teachers to ascertain the resources available, the personnel to be contacted, travel details to be arranged, fields of emphasis, follow-up activities and reference materials, just to mention a few aspects. In particular, attention needs to be directed to teacher responsibilities and liabilities for student travel, especially the provisions for student travel insurance.

At the primary school level, additional planning arrangements may need to be made, especially for the junior primary grades (Barton, 1996). As indicated in Chapter 4, there are a number of prior considerations which a teacher must assess before embarking on a visit to the local community or region.

■ Concluding Comments

Improvements in technology and marketing have produced a bewildering array of resource materials over recent years. Print materials have improved greatly in quality. Most books now have colour-coded sections, interesting variations in typeface and a range of colourful prints and maps. Multimedia resources continue to improve, as do the various pieces of hardware which are needed to view the software. Over recent years, the resources with the greatest potential for use in schools have clearly become the computer, videotapes and CD-ROMs. Of these, the Internet revolution is the most significant (Doyle, 1999).

The problem for the teacher is to make informed choices from the wide array of resources available. In some cases, the finances of a school will severely limit the range of choices. Notwithstanding financial constraints, it is up to each teacher to devise an appropriate and systematic way of appraising resources. In this chapter, reference was made to several materials analysis checklists. If these do not adequately cover the type of resources to be selected,

then the teacher should add to and improve on these procedures. The selection of resources must not be relegated to last-minute, capricious purchases.

Pressures of classroom routines often cause teachers to forget about the enormous potential of local community resources. There are numerous individuals and groups available who are willing to share their skills and interests with students. Implementing short community visits and extended field trips can provide very meaningful learning experiences for students. At the same time, they help immeasurably in the development of positive community–school public relations.

Schools of the future are likely to have library/media facilities closely integrated with classroom instructional programs. Resource-based teaching and learning will inevitably lead to greater levels of information literacy on the part of students and teachers and cooperative teamwork between library and teaching personnel.

QUESTIONS AND ACTIVITIES

1. Examine one or more free or inexpensive curriculum materials produced by an external firm or organisation. Appraise the items in terms of the eight criteria listed on page 39.
2. Identify two community resources you might use in a teaching unit. Justify why you would use these resources. What do you perceive to be the likely advantages? Would there be any potential problems in using them?
3. Visit a local school other than the one you teach in or with which you are closely associated. Note the following:
   (a) library resources for use in studies of society and environment including encylopedias, references, literary selections, periodicals and other resources;
   (b) personal computer and video resources and how they are used.
4. Examine a textbook you use or may decide to use within the studies of society and environment field. How inclusive is it in its treatment of gender, minority and disadvantaged groups?
5. Textbooks have a major role in cultural and social reproduction (Apple and Christian-Smith, 1991; Shen, 1994). Compare two textbooks published in different countries and comment on the ideological variations that are evident.

4 Teaching and Learning Techniques

Introduction

Teachers tend to use teaching and learning techniques on the basis of familiarity— they use a small number of conventional methods and disregard a wide range of alternatives. No single technique is better than another. Obviously some techniques are more efficient in teaching certain content or skills than others. Furthermore, not all students learn most efficiently using the same technique. In this chapter a variety of techniques are analysed to alert teachers to the potential use of a variety of teacher-directed and student-directed techniques. After all, teachers have a moral responsibility to improve the life chances of their students (Fullan, 1999).

■ Getting Variety into Teaching

Studies of society and environment as a teaching area has enormous potential because:

- it focuses directly on people and their surroundings;
- it enables primary source data to be collected;
- it builds on current affairs;
- it deals with topics that directly affect a person's livelihood.

Yet, students do not seem to have a very high opinion of this subject. It is often described as being boring, dull and of little relevance.

Perhaps one of the reasons is that teachers prefer to use only a limited number of teaching techniques—ones that they have experienced or with which they are most comfortable—and these may not be very challenging and exciting to students. Further, teachers may believe that they are varying their teaching but their students see it as stultifying routines (Wasley, 1999).

The matter of preferred teaching techniques is dependent to a large extent upon teachers' value positions. If teachers' priority is basic skills this can lead to lessons which are repetitive and routinised. Banks (1995) exhorts teachers to be transformative in their approach and to challenge mainstream knowledge. He states that knowledge is not neutral, but is influenced by human interests, that all knowledge reflects the power and social relationships within society, and that an important purpose of knowledge construction is to help people improve society.

Collinson (1999) concludes that excellent teachers are recognisable by their high level of competence, their skilful interpersonal relationships with students and their well-developed character. Capel, Leask and Turner (1999) have produced a similar list when referring to teacher styles. They consider that successful teachers have developed professional knowledge, understand the environment in which they teach and have special personal qualities.

Students differ considerably in their preferred learning styles. Some students prefer teacher-talk presentations while others gain most from doing their own research. Woolever and Scott (1988) and Dunn, Beaudry and Klavas (1989) contend that it is crucial for teachers to match up their styles with students' learning styles. Every person has a learning style—it's as individual as a signature. Knowing students' learning styles, teachers can organise classrooms to respond to their individual needs.

Yet it can be very difficult to diagnose learning styles of students. What criteria does a teacher use? For example, is a student's actual performance in certain subjects more important than his or her potential performance? How does a teacher take account of students' needs and interests? Although it might be laudable to argue that teachers should match learning tasks to the needs, interests, abilities and previous experiences of students, how do they do this in practice?

Fraenkel (1973) provides one possible solution. He suggests that teachers select from 'organisational', 'demonstrative' and 'creative' activities in providing a mix of learning activities which best suit the needs and interests of students in a class (Table 4.1). For example, some students will enjoy doing organisational activities such as chart-making and summarising; others might gain most satisfaction from demonstrative activities such as role playing or sketching; others might be most positive about creative activities such as solving problems or creating a mural. A teacher needs to plan for a range of activities in each lesson and there is a need to include examples from each of these three categories.

Variety does appear to be a key element of effective teaching and it can be brought about by:

- including learning activities that span the range from teacher directed to student directed;
- using groups of different sizes ranging from whole group to small group;
- including a range of teaching techniques.

■ Teacher-directed–Student-directed Continuum

Teacher-directed activities are commonly used in schools and occur when a teacher is engaged in direct instruction with students. Information is personally delivered and the teacher controls both the pace of classroom activity and the pattern of classroom interaction. Research evidence indicates that direct instruction can be very effective for increasing student achievement on tests of basic skills (Good and Brophy, 1984; Rosenshine and Meister, 1995). It is especially effective for teaching basic skills to low-achieving pupils. Typically in direct instruction:

- the teacher is actively involved with the class for the entire class period;
- the pacing of the lessons is brisk;
- there is a high percentage of academic learning time;

Table 4.1 *Providing variety in student activities*

Organisational	Demonstrative	Creative
outlining	role playing	solving problems
chart making	discussing	inventing new uses
graphing	writing	for things
mapping	drawing	composing songs
time-line building	question forming	or poetry
diagramming	reporting	writing essays or stories
arranging	explaining	role creating
note taking	analysing	miming
filing	generalising	painting
question answering	building	writing fiction
question asking	singing	question asking
stating	dancing	cartooning
re-stating	modelling	hypothesising
building	describing	predicting
summarising	debating	singing
writing	reacting	drawing
identifying	story-telling	dancing
categorising	preparing murals	proposing
choosing	applying	building
recording	sketching	
experimenting	choosing	
ordering		
sorting		

- interaction between students is minimised;
- mastery learning is emphasised.

There are a number of teaching techniques which emphasise direct instruction, for example lectures, directed reading and demonstrations. Although there are situations when these techniques can be very effective, they can also be monotonous, regimented and uninteresting for students.

At the other end of the continuum, student-directed activities involve minimal teacher supervision. Students work alone or in small groups. Woolever and Scott (1988) and Banks and Banks (1999: 218) argue that student-directed activities are especially valuable in the field of studies of society and environment where 'they serve to develop students who are independent and self-motivated rather than dependent on an authority figure to stay on task or achieve'. Recent studies have demonstrated the value of student-directed activities based upon constructivist pedagogy—where students' actively participate in constructing meaning from their activities (Rainer, Guyton and Bowen, 2000; Olsen, 2000).

Examples of teaching techniques which are student-centred include inquiry activities, simulation games, individual and group projects, cooperative learning and individual student contracts.

Effective teachers will endeavour to use a range of teaching techniques that span the continuum from teacher-centred to student-directed—the choice should revolve around the 'mix' of students in a class and their specific needs and interests.

Students with handicaps who are in mainstream classes will have particular needs. As a consequence, some teaching techniques such as the viewing of films or video cassettes would be a poor choice for students with sight impairment or hearing impairment.

Gifted and talented students often complete their work very quickly. They need special enrichment activities that challenge them—not the assignment of more work just to fill in time!

◼ Teaching Groups of Different Sizes

Variations in teaching can be achieved by changing the size of the teaching group (Emmer, Evertson and Worsham, 2000). The whole class as the teaching group is most common and may often be the most effective group size to use. Yet small groups can also be most effective. In deciding whether to use small groups or not, a teacher needs to consider the following:

- What are my intended objectives and to what extent will they be achieved by using small groups?
- Is the lesson content conducive to being learned by group activities?
- Is the time allocated sufficient for group activities to be undertaken satisfactorily?
- Is the teaching setting appropriate for undertaking group activities?
- Are specific materials/resources available for each group to undertake specific group tasks?
- What information do students need to know and what responsibilities will be delegated to the groups?

These are important questions and it may be that group work is not appropriate for many lessons and subjects. Where group work is undertaken, the following categories or types are most common:

- groups of students with a similar achievement level;
- groups with the same skill level;
- friendship groups that allow friends to work together;
- interest groups.

In the field of studies of society and environment, small-group activities are most important as they create opportunities for students to develop personally and socially. In ideal situations, group work should enable all students to be challenged (Killen, 1998). This may involve having high-ability students working together in a small group and lower ability students working in separate groups, or it might be advantageous for individuals of different abilities to be located within each small group (see 'Cooperative learning' on pages 74–75).

◼ Teaching Techniques

Before examining particular teaching techniques in detail a distinction should be made between 'strategies' and 'techniques'. Most teachers will have an overall strategy (or strategies) about how to promote optimal learning in students, keeping in mind their need for classroom discipline and organisation. This may cause individual teachers to be disposed towards a particular point on the teacher-centred—student-directed continuum described above. Some may reject a strategy which is strongly teacher-centred or student-directed and accept a 'mixed' position, reflecting a blend of the two. A major consideration for teachers is to develop a teaching strategy which doesn't rely too heavily on a particular technique (Duck, 2000).

The following section provides details on

a range of techniques. It behoves every teacher to widen his or her repertoire to ensure that students in a class are given a variety of learning opportunities in terms of their needs and interests. There are increasing pressures from parents and the wider community to do so (Dinham and Scott, 2000). A wide-ranging list of teaching techniques categorised into teacher-centred and student-centred are included in Table 4.2. Some of the relative merits and demerits of each are included in the following section.

■ Teacher-centred Techniques

Lectures/teacher-talks

A lecture is an oral presentation usually by the teacher. It can also be given by a guest such as another teacher or a parent (Cruickshank, Bainer and Metcalf, 1999). It can be a formal lecture, which tends to be long, uninterrupted and highly structured, or an informal lecture, which tends to be brief, uses multimedia support and includes some student participation. At primary and secondary school levels, most would agree that informal lectures of up to 20 minutes are the preferred version out of the two forms. They are very commonly used by teachers teaching within the field of studies of society and environment.

Topics for lectures have to be chosen very carefully. If topics can be presented in an interesting way, possibly with the use of audio-visual aids, then they are likely to be successful using a lecturing mode. But there may be better techniques for presenting a topic. A teacher needs to consider the following aspects when deciding whether or not to use a lecture mode:

- the vocabulary to be introduced;
- the seating arrangement in the room;
- the attention span of students.

As a variation on lectures, Hill (1994) and McGuire (1996) note that the teacher as storyteller is a very important role. They argue that a strong, dramatic story is a powerful technique to enable students to experience vicariously the life stories of other people.

A good lecture is one that incorporates the following important characteristics. The teacher should:

- keep his or her voice at an interesting pitch, use expression, make sure all students can hear;

Table 4.2 *A range of teaching techniques*

Teacher-centred	Student-centred
· Lectures/teacher talks	· Inquiry
· Skill practice	· Library research
· Directed questioning	· Simulation games
· Directed reading/directed assignments	· Role plays
· Class discussions	· Learning centres
· Demonstrations	· Computer activities
· Media-based presentations	· Independent study
· Construction activities	· Cooperative learning
· Aesthetic expression	
· Map and globe activities	
· Field trips	
· Guest speakers	

- at the beginning, state the key points to be made and use advance organisers;
- use a number of multimedia aids, models, hand-out sheets and whiteboard drawings (to focus the attention of the student, serve as a reference point and to make the subject more concrete);
- present the lecture in a lively, vibrant manner;
- demonstrate his or her intense interest in the topic;
- limit it to 20 minutes; the content must be appropriate to the interests and abilities of the students;
- encourage students to ask questions;
- follow key statements and questions with strategic pauses;
- interject students' names into the lecture and relate content to areas that interest the students;
- use notes sparingly to ensure optimum dramatic effect.

There are of course many potential problems in using lectures. Some of the disadvantages of lectures are that they:

- do not allow for student creativity or problem solving;
- can become an 'ego trip' for the teacher;
- can lead to student boredom;
- don't provide opportunities for students to practise/apply certain principles;
- provide minimal opportunity for social development.

Skill practice

There are many skills in the field of studies of society and environment which require practice throughout the grades, ranging from cognitive skills to social skills. According to Rosenshine (1995) it is important for students to have extensive and successful practice. Skills of special significance which need to be presented at increasing levels of difficulty include:

- reading skills;
- writing skills;
- map, globe, graph and time skills;
- study and reference skills;
- computer literacy skills;
- valuing skills;
- social interaction and group skills.

The practising of these skills needs to occur within the context of the topics being taught (see Chapter 6). Skill practice tends to be most effective when:

- students understand why it is necessary to gain mastery of specific skills;
- there are frequent opportunities for group practice and immediate evaluation feedback;
- students are encouraged to record and diagnose their performance;
- games are used to practise the skills;
- the skills being practised are varied in terms of amount and type, according to the needs of the students.

Directed questioning

Questions are a crucial element of a teacher's repertoire. For every question that a teacher asks there is some underlying purpose although some of these purposes may not be related directly to student learning! It is important to note that questions can be used by teachers:

- to pose a problem for solution;
- to get immediate feedback during a demonstration;
- to focus a discussion;
- to help students sharpen their perceptions;
- to attract a student's attention;
- to get a particular student to participate;
- to diagnose a student's weakness;
- to allow a student to shine before his or her peers;
- to build up a student's security to an extent where the teacher is quite sure the student will respond correctly.

The questions that teachers ask are often related very closely to their overall strategy. For example, teachers who pose questions that begin with 'Who?' or 'What?' have an orientation to studies of society and environment which gives a high priority to learning facts. By contrast, the three-question sequence developed by Taba (1967) of 'What?', 'Why?' and 'What does it mean?' gives a high priority to cognitive mapping.

The pace at which questions are asked by teachers is also important. Questions can be used in rapid-fire succession or they can proceed more slowly with time for thoughtful responses. The types of questions teachers ask will determine the kind of thinking they want their students to do. Various writers have provided different classifications of questions. Some of these include:

- high- and low-order questions: low-order questions mainly recall facts and specifics; high-order questions mainly cover application, analysis;
- convergent and divergent or closed and open questions: convergent/closed questions lead to expected answers; divergent/open questions allow new directions in answers;
- what, when, how, who and why: a useful

range to use which proceeds in sequence from the low order to high order.

Considerable practice is needed in framing appropriate questions. A useful starting point is for the teacher to choose an appropriate topic and then write down a range of questions which cover the sequences listed above. He or she should ensure that the questions are concise and at an appropriate level of difficulty for students and eliminate questions that appear to be ambiguous or vague. Table 4.3 provides some useful beginnings for questions based upon the purposes teachers may have in mind.

Planning good questions is only part of the exercise. Knowing how to present the questions to the class and responding to their reactions is of major importance. Using eye contact, distributing questions around the room, giving students plenty of time to answer (wait time of three–five seconds) and extending thinking by using further probes such as 'are you sure?' or 'give me an example' are just some of the techniques to ensure successful use of directed questioning.

Directed reading/directed assignments
Directed reading and assignments are typically associated with using the student textbook.

Table 4.3 *A range of question beginnings*

Purpose	Use questions that begin with:
To check understanding	How do you know? Explain, Compare, Contrast
To assess knowledge	Define, Describe, Tell, List, Who? When?
To identify	Where?
To help analyse problems	What causes? How? Why?
To explore values	How do you feel? Why do you prefer? Why do you feel?
To encourage creative thinking	What if? How else? Just suppose
To evaluate	Select, Judge, Evaluate
To apply knowledge	Demonstrate, Use the information to, Construct

Source: Roe, Ross and Burns (1989: 169).

Directed reading involves careful checking by the teacher

There are advantages in setting directed reading from the textbook because:

- it is common reading material for all students;
- the material is up to date and authoritative;
- it is relevant for particular curricula and grade levels.

Notwithstanding, students are generally not very positive about directed reading associated with textbooks. It can become very monotonous and boring. It is up to the teacher to enliven directed reading assignments so that they have real meaning to students (Capel, *et al.*, 1999). This can be achieved by the following procedures:

- use the textbook selectively and present chapters in the order that suits your teaching;

- use other reading materials such as trade books to enliven assignments (see Chapter 3);
- ensure that students understand why specific assignments are being set;
- motivate students—arouse interest and curiosity in a topic before giving the reading assignment;
- ensure that students have the reading skills needed such as acquiring new vocabulary, recognising topic sentences and identifying main ideas, bringing meaning to reading and being able to read critically.

Class discussion

Teacher-directed class discussion is a very popular mode of instruction, especially for controversial topics within studies of society and environment. Some of the advantages of class discussion are that it:

Presentation and discussion with a small group

- encourages students to think critically and to express their views;
- develops students' speaking and listening skills;
- develops students' tolerance of and empathy with other points of view.

However, it should be noted that this technique is of less value with young children who do not have the levels of reasoning required.

To be effective, it is important that the physical layout of furniture is conducive to group discussions. Chairs arranged in circles, horseshoes and other configurations are usually the most effective.

When using this teaching technique it is essential that the teacher is willing to relinquish some authority and to tolerate various directions (and dead-ends!) that a discussion might take. Accepting low degrees of structure and organisation can be difficult for some teachers and may require considerable adjustment.

A variation of class discussion that is most successful is brainstorming (Savage and Armstrong, 1987) whereby students are invited to generate and share as many ideas as possible about a topic. The ideas are recorded without comment until the flow has dropped off noticeably and then each idea is discussed in detail by the class.

Demonstrations

Demonstrations can be an extremely valuable teaching technique in studies of society and environment for illustrating landscape processes (e.g. stream table demonstrations of erosion and deposition), settlement patterns (e.g. the location of towns and cities) and solar system processes (e.g. rotation and revolution of the earth). Demonstrations can range from elaborate, involving the whole class, to the demonstration of a skill to a single student.

Demonstrations can be especially appealing to students and not simply because they represent a change from the usual classroom routines. However, it is important that the teacher is not only knowledgeable about the topic but uses a variety of aids to ensure that students understand what is being demonstrated.

To ensure successful demonstrations the teacher should:

- make sure that it is kept simple and focused—don't try to teach too many concepts and ensure that the demonstration is at an appropriate difficulty level;
- ensure that all students can see and hear the demonstration;
- check frequently during the demonstration to ensure that students are following;
- make sure that a wide range of objects or models are used to aid the demonstration;
- where appropriate, encourage students to also demonstrate the activity or process;
- use a lively, enthusiastic style;
- ensure that all safety considerations have been met.

Media-based presentations

'Teacher-talk' as a common form of instruction to students can be extremely dull and boring. Students need opportunities to use all of their five senses rather than simply being passive listeners.

There is an ever-increasing range of media available for teachers as described in Chapter 3. In addition to the well-established range of projectors (overhead, slide, 16 mm), video recorders and charts and pictures, there are the rapidly developing CD-ROM and Internet resources. The teacher should ensure that:

- material is appropriate for a particular class of students by previewing it in advance;
- the equipment is operating properly before the lesson commences;
- all students can see and hear the presentation;
- the topic has been introduced thoroughly

(with appropriate motivation) prior to commencing the presentation;
- there are appropriate follow-up activities.

Construction activities

The potential for using construction activities in the field of studies of society and environment is very high. Construction provides students with opportunities to make objects that are models, replicas or facsimiles of original objects. Examples might include:

- building a model of the Eureka Stockade or a squatter's dwelling;
- weaving a blanket with strips of coloured paper;
- using Lego blocks or plasticine or wood to make agricultural tools.

Before undertaking construction activities a teacher needs to consider the following questions, to ensure that this is the appropriate teaching technique to use:

- What teaching objectives can be achieved by this construction activity?
- How practical is it in terms of available materials and time?
- Do students have the necessary skills?
- In what ways is it more effective than using other teaching techniques?

There are a variety of materials and items available for construction activities and many of them are inexpensive (see Table 3.3 in Chapter 3), including:

- constructions using paper and cardboard—examples include collages, mobiles, puppets, dioramas;
- constructions using wood—examples include farm machinery or buildings;
- constructions involving the processing of materials—examples include making cottage cheese, dyeing fabrics, churning butter, candle making.

For all construction activities it is essential

that safety precautions are well established. Students must be careful when using tools such as scissors, saws and knives, and all construction activities must be closely supervised. Parent assistance is often sought with construction lessons to ensure that there is adequate adult supervision.

Aesthetic expression

There are a range of works of beauty in all cultures that provide opportunities for students to gain an appreciation of beauty. To a large extent, multimedia presentations may be a major source for presenting the visual/auditory images to students but colourful 'trade' books (see Chapter 3) can also be most useful.

Activities involving aesthetic expression should be incorporated into the major teaching topics. This can be achieved by careful planning and searching out sources of materials. Field trips such as visits to museums and art galleries are also an important resource for aesthetic expression activities.

Map and globe activities

In the subject area of studies of society and environment, a basic understanding of maps and globes is essential. According to Nelson (1992), without a basic geographic frame, students' studies of economic conditions, historical events and political events become muddled. The study of maps and globes is an essential element therefore in almost all lessons. In terms of teaching techniques, it is important to incorporate maps and globes whenever possible.

It should be noted that understanding maps and globes is difficult for students because the symbols used are abstractions of the real world. Typically students acquire these understandings and skills developmentally, as they mature. Teachers need to provide meaningful activities at an appropriate level to students' developmental awareness.

The examples included in Tables 4.4 and 4.5 provide a sample of the map and globe skills needed by students as they progress from primary to secondary school. It behoves teachers to include map and globe resources/examples in a number of their lessons to ensure that students acquire these skills and to have them adequately reinforced.

Globes should be available in all classrooms. In primary classrooms, globes should ideally be available for students to handle or play with informally. A diverse range of maps also needs to be available in classrooms and displayed appropriately on pin-up boards or around special topic tables or learning centres. Hand-out sheets involving mapping activities (e.g. map puzzles, preparing own maps, interpreting a map) should be regularly used by teachers.

Table 4.4 *Map skills*

1. Making a classroom map using butcher paper.
2. Drawing maps of local areas, using sand tables, blocks.
3. Using simple map symbols and terms.
4. Drawing maps of routes to school, to friends' houses, to recreational activities and using appropriate symbols.
5. Orienting a map to direction.
6. Making a trip map and using a legend.
7. Reading a map and understanding scale.
8. Using travel maps.
9. Introducing special-purpose maps.

Table 4.5 *Globe skills*

1. Use of simple globes depicting land masses and oceans; finding one's own country.
2. Students build wire mesh and balloon globes.
3. Use of globes to locate North Pole and South Pole.
4. Use of globes to find vacation destinations.
5. Use of globes to examine relative and cardinal directions.
6. Use of globes to examine air routes of the world.
7. Use of a globe in a cradle to depict angle of rotation and seasons.
8. Use of globes to demonstrate how latitude and longitude is measured.
9. Use of globes to demonstrate rotation of the earth and day and night.

Field trips

Field trips can be used very effectively to integrate theoretical models with real world practical examples. As noted by McElroy (1984), teachers can use field work to introduce a topic or to reinforce it, as revealed by the following three examples:

- model → field work;
- field work → model;
- model → field work → model.

Field trips can add a major dimension to students' learning and they have tremendous potential within the field of studies of society and environment. There are numerous opportunities for field studies within walking distance of a school as well as further afield.

Field trips that are carefully organised by the teacher are likely to be very successful. They provide enriching, hands-on experiences for many students. Yet there are many horror stories about things that can go wrong with field trips. The reminders included in Table 4.6 give an indication of the range of planning activities that need to be undertaken by the teacher.

At secondary school, a variation of field experience which is proving to be most worthwhile is work experience. Students are attached to a local firm or industry for one day per week where they are involved in

Table 4.6 *Reminders for planning field trips*

1. Are you satisfied that the proposed visit is appropriate for the age and developmental level of students?
2. Have you visited the site personally and noted possible outcomes and potential problems?
3. Have you obtained administrative approval before announcing the field trip to students?
4. Are advanced bookings needed? Who needs information about the planned schedule (school principal, other teachers, parents)?
5. Have you considered liability and safety precautions?
6. Will guides be available at the site or will you be responsible for providing explanations and answering questions? Will you require additional parent helpers?
7. What pre-field and post-field activities are planned? Do the students understand why these activities have been chosen?
8. Prior to leaving for the field trip have you divided students into task groups and distributed relevant worksheets?
9. Have you sent parental permission slips home to ensure that you have full parental approval?

observing and participating in a range of work-related activities. It can provide opportunities for students to acquire important practical skills and to be more focused on their career needs. Of course, the planning of these placements is crucial and the teacher has to make a number of visits to each firm to ensure that students will gain maximum experience.

Guest speakers

Guest speakers can provide students with valuable information or can demonstrate special skills (see also Chapter 3). Among other things guest speakers:

- can demonstrate skills not possessed by the teacher;
- can serve as role models for career aspirations;
- can serve as models of non-stereotyped or non-traditional roles;
- have charismatic qualities in areas of interest to students.

As noted in Chapter 3, it is essential to select guest speakers carefully, ensuring that they are effective and have had some experience in speaking to students, and that they understand the specific purpose of their presentations. Students need to be prepared for guest speaker presentations. Thank-you letters need to be organised and students need to follow appropriate courtesies with these visitors.

■ Student-centred Techniques

Student-centred or independent learning occurs when each student has the opportunity to work alone or with a small group of students, with minimal teacher supervision. There are a number of advantages in using student-centred techniques in the field of studies of society and environment. The examples listed below provide for varying levels of student independence but are conducive to developing student creativity and problem-solving skills.

Inquiry

A number of approaches have been developed over recent decades which collectively are termed 'inquiry' (Olsen, 2000). It basically involves a different pattern of instruction whereby students decide what information they need; they use the teacher as a resource person, gather data individually or in small groups and proceed to develop solutions to specific problems or issues.

Inquiry situations provide problems for students to solve. Each inquiry activity should assist students to develop their thinking processes. Students are often highly motivated to examine novel problems and to have the opportunity to formulate possible solutions (Killen, 1998).

The inquiry process and its purported advantages and disadvantages are discussed in detail in Chapter 10.

Inquiry learning can be very rewarding for teachers and students. Successful learning occurs when:

- all materials needed are carefully prepared/made available in advance;
- the approach is appropriate to the subject area and to the needs and interests of the students;
- sufficient attention is given to elaborating the initial problem/dilemma to engender sufficient motivation;
- the activities are feasible within school routines (including out-of-school activities).

Library research

Library research is a common technique used in studies of society and environment and can involve students in searching out information from the school library or public libraries. Access to Internet and the World Wide Web (see Chapter 12) is a more recent and extremely valuable, international library source.

Library research is likely to be of most value to students if:

- the focus is on questions/problems which have arisen in class;
- it arouses their curiosity;
- they have some choice in selecting topics.

From time to time it appears that teachers assign library research that is little better than mindless copying of material from encyclopedias (Murray, 1984). Unless carefully monitored, it is quite feasible for students to do the same mindless copying of information from the World Wide Web.

Library research involves students in acquiring specific skills. At primary and secondary school levels they need to know how to acquire and interact with data and information. It involves practical searching and recording, structured note taking and report writing. The main elements can be summarised as:

- locating and collecting data;
- retrieving data to solve specific problems or providing information about particular topics;
- interacting with the data to seek out additional information or possible solutions;
- preparing and presenting reports.

Simulation games
Simulation games are a very effective and motivating learning technique and of special value in studies of society and environment. The processes involved in developing and running simulation games are detailed in Chapter 11. An examination of computer-based simulations is included in Chapter 12.

Role plays
Role playing, socio-drama or creative dramatics are examples of where students act out a specific situation or event where there is no prepared script and it is usually unrehearsed. It can be teacher structured or

relatively open ended and initiated by students.

There are various springboards that can be used for role plays such as large photographs, cartoons or sketches that depict problem situations. Unfinished stories are also a useful source. Examples of problem situations suitable for role plays include:

- taking your pet on public transport;
- finding a snake in the garden;
- explaining to parents how your bicycle went missing;
- comforting a young child who is lost in a crowd at a show.

Role playing enables students to explore people's feelings, thoughts and behaviour. However, role plays must occur in a supportive, 'safe' class climate. Having an attentive audience is critical—the class needs to listen carefully and not to judge the performance or make disparaging comments about the role players.

Debriefing is also needed whereby students have an opportunity to share their feelings about what happened and why.

Learning centres
A learning centre is typically a table or countertop or bulletin board where a wide selection and variety of teaching materials and associated learning activities are located.

The materials in a learning centre can include:

- task cards with directions to be followed;
- artifacts (tools, clothing, etc.);
- worksheets;
- folder activities;
- teacher-made books;
- library books;
- multimedia;
- materials (computer and software, film strips);
- bulletin board containing headings, visual displays.

A role playing activity

A learning centre can cater for a wide range of interests

The purpose of a learning centre is to allow an individual student or a group of students to carry out their own learning. This means usually that exercises of differing levels of difficulty need to be included. Learning centres are able to cater for different needs and interests of students and to allow them greater choices.

Learning centres have to be planned very carefully. The teacher needs to plan which concepts, skills and values are to be learned, reinforced and experienced. Consideration also has to be given to students' needs and interests—what types of activities are likely to appeal most and yet achieve the desired objectives.

Activities can vary in their attractiveness to students. Directions need to be clear and completion requirements have to be realistic (see Table 4.7). The questions included in Table 4.8 illustrate some of the points that a teacher must consider in planning learning centres.

There are a myriad of possible topics or themes that can be developed in learning centres. Some examples include:

- *Task cards*—ideally placed on brightly coloured posterboard. 'How much can you buy with a dollar?', 'Where we live'; 'How I've grown'.
- *Games*—teacher-made board games, for example variations of 'Concentration', shooting a rocket to the moon.
- *Bulletin board*—brightly labelled activities such as 'Life in our neighbourhood', 'Travel in our community', 'Signs for safety'.
- *Worksheets*—single sheets with activities involving writing, drawing, colouring, for example 'Occupations', 'Who am I?'.
- *Teacher-made books*—usually task cards bound together with coloured wool, for example 'The story of cotton', 'Our State', 'Travelling through space', 'Community resources'.

Table 4.7 *Examples of materials included in a learning centre for studies of society and environment*

- Several copies of texts and reference books providing a range of reading levels
- Trade books, cookbooks and songbooks
- Maps of all shapes and sizes
- Magazines and newspapers
- Artifacts (coins, stamps, etc.)
- Study prints, pictures or travel posters
- A box of costumes for role playing
- A box of 'building' materials (Lego, wood, clay, wire)

Table 4.8 *Questions to consider when planning learning centres*

- Do the learning centre activities relate to specific teaching objectives?
- When is the learning centre to be used?
- Can the students perform the activities independently?
- Are there activities that can be achieved successfully by students with different abilities?
- How will student activities be recorded and assessed?
- Do students know what is expected of them on a daily or weekly basis?

Computer activities

Teaching involving the use of computers has reached new heights and all sorts of further advances are likely. Consider the following claims:

- Challenging interactive software, dramatic narrative conveyed through electronic media, beautiful art and animation, and the rythmic force of music all have a strong appeal in our culture (Becker, 1998: 20).
- The World Wide Web has emerged rapidly to become the premiere electronic medium. Its attributes match those of print, audio, video and computer, but with the addition of vast scope (content and geography) (Hackbarth, 1997: 59).

Effective teachers are now using the computer in a wide array of situations. They have no choice because students, parents and the community expect nothing less. It is inevitable that new uses will become available such as videoconferencing over the Internet to provide face-to-face feedback to students located in isolated regions (Fetterman, 1998).

However, there are problems associated with this teaching technique and some have only surfaced recently. For example, Zinberg (1998) reports that a research study at the Carnegie Mellon University in the USA concluded that students and adults who spent considerable periods of time on the Internet had increased feelings of loneliness and depression and a loss of friendships.

Couture and Dobson (1997) provide a fascinating account of how email and the Internet have produced new opportunities for students, many of which might be counter-productive to teacher interests. For example:

- students perceive email as a glorious, high-tech way of passing notes;
- students actively seek out ways of looking busy and duping the teacher;
- students use Web pages to troll for new friends;
- students develop adversarial positions to the teacher if surveillance techniques are used to monitor their computing activities.

There are clearly major opportunities, developments and a number of pitfalls associated with computers. Details about instructional uses of computers are included in Chapter 12.

Independent study

Independent study activities can take various forms but the common element is that the focus of responsibility for learning changes from the teacher to the student (Sizer, 1999). 'Independence' is the key term although the amount of independence given to students will depend upon their level of maturity, commitment and ability.

The key purpose is to match up individual students' needs and interests with appropriate teaching materials and learning activities. Students can differ markedly in terms of:

- cognitive development;
- language development;
- social development;
- presence or absence of handicapping conditions;
- ethnic background;
- socioeconomic background;
- family environment;
- learning style;
- right-brain and left-brain modalities;
- time needed to learn.

Clearly, a teacher cannot provide an individualised program in each subject area for each of 25 or more students. A small-scale approach is needed. The teacher should select three or four students who would gain most from an individualised approach and set them specific contracts or projects. The need for extensive planning should not be underestimated (Williamson, 1995). Once a successful pattern of operation has been established with a small group of students, it may then be appropriate to extend it to more students and to a wider range of activities.

Within studies of society and environment there are many opportunities to develop contracts and projects for individual students—they can last over several days or even weeks. The tasks included in learning centres (as described above) are often very suitable for individual contracts. Computer software programs now include a range of individualised and self-instructional activities (see Chapter 12).

Cooperative learning

As noted by Killen (1998) cooperative learning is both an instructional technique and a teaching philosophy. Its philosophical basis is that learners can gain by working together in small groups and that they can be rewarded for their collective accomplishments (Cruickshank *et al.*, 1999). The procedure is especially valuable in studies of society and environment because it enables students to develop skills in working together in groups as social beings.

Cooperative learning is a special form of small-group work. Students can work successfully in small groups by being very competitive! Cooperative learning in small groups is different because there is a cooperative incentive structure in place.

A number of different approaches to cooperative learning have been developed but most share the characteristics listed in Table 4.9. Cooperative learning is a technique where a group is given a task to do that includes efforts from all students. Students need to interact with and support each other in completing the overall task and the subtasks.

Not all lessons are conducive to cooperative learning. Ideally, topics are used which require the searching out of answers and exploring alternative solutions. The teacher also has to make organisational decisions which may only be possible in certain circumstances—for example, rearranging the room furniture and organising materials. There can also be difficulties in assigning students to groups; the intent is to form truly heterogeneous groups (see Table 4.9) but personality conflicts will still occur.

To overcome some of these difficulties, and especially with lower grades, it may be

Table 4.9 *Characteristics of cooperative learning classrooms*

- Most classroom activities involve using small groups of 3–5 students.
- Each group is as heterogeneous as possible in terms of gender, ethnicity and knowledge and ability.
- The teacher and students set clear, specific individual and group goals.
- Each student has to achieve certain individual goals as well as being accountable for group success.
- The teacher provides worthwhile group rewards on the basis of group members' individual achievements.
- Each group divides up group work into individual tasks.
- Each group member soon learns that interdependence is needed for the group to function effectively—this involves a considerable amount of face-to-face interaction.
- Each group member learns effective listening and communicating skills and group-processing skills.

necessary for the teacher to assign roles. Chapin and Messick (1999) suggest the following:

- one student as chairperson to organise the group's work;
- one student as recorder or secretary to write down the group's answers;
- one student as check person to check that everyone can explain and agree with completed answers;
- one student as encourager to keep participants interested and excited.

The research evidence on cooperative learning is extremely positive and includes literally hundreds of published studies (Ellis and Fouts, 1993; Stahl and Van Sickle, 1992; Barry *et al.*, 1998; Emmer and Gerwels, 1998; Zehnder and King, 2000). Some of the major findings are:

- achievement effects of cooperation learning are consistently positive— experimental groups have significant positive effects over control groups;
- positive achievement effects occur across all grade levels from 2–12, in all major subjects, and the effects are equally positive for high, average and low achievers.

A number of different cooperative learning models have been developed and used in school settings, including Student-Teams Learning (Slavin, 1978) and Jigsaw (Aronson *et al.*, 1978). The Student-Teams Learning approach involves the following:

- the teacher divides the class into teams with 4–5 members;
- each team is heterogeneous in ability levels;
- new content is introduced by traditional large-group instruction;
- each team is then given study worksheets describing tasks to be done and problems to be solved;
- team members tutor each other and interact to ensure that all have completed their tasks;
- when all tasks have been completed the team members take individual tests.
- The scores of the individual team members are combined to yield a team score.

The Jigsaw method involves the following:

- the teacher divides the class into teams of 5–6 students and there is a mix of abilities in each team;
- the assigned team activity has subtasks so that there is one task for each team member, which is variously labelled as A, B, etc.;
- the persons assigned to do task A in each team come together and form a new team. New teams are also formed for B, etc.;
- the newly formed teams (A team, B team, etc.) work on completing their task by discussing issues and then working individually or collectively;
- when the tasks have been completed the students reassemble in their original teams. Each team member (for example A, B, etc.) shares his or her information and this is compiled into the overall assignment which is then submitted to the teacher. It should be noted, however, that there are limitations to using this technique, namely:
  - peers need to be able to teach and nurture low achievers. Not all high achievers will want to help less able students;
  - students in a group must get on with each other. If this doesn't happen, some students will work less hard;
  - some students may object to their assessment being dependent on the learning of others in the group;
  - it takes time for students to develop the skills of group interdependence.

■ Concluding Comments

There are numerous teaching techniques available to the teacher to enhance learning in the field of studies of society and environment. The competent teacher needs to be skilled in a range of teacher-directed and student-directed approaches. A varied range should be part of the repertoire of every teacher to accommodate the diverse needs of students and the material being studied.

QUESTIONS AND ACTIVITIES

1. What factors do you think are responsible for the teacher-talk (lecture) and discussion as teaching techniques in studies of society and environment? How can a greater variety of approaches be encouraged?

2. Cooperative learning is one of the most researched teaching strategies of recent years. The plethora of information about cooperative learning is testimony to its versatility and effectiveness (Killen, 1996). What are some advantages and limitations of using cooperative learning?

3. Tape record or videotape yourself running a class discussion or delivering an informal lecture. What do you consider are your strengths and weaknesses in leading these kinds of activities?

4. Prepare an outline for a teaching topic based upon a lecture mode and then try to think of ways it could be presented using alternative teaching techniques such as inquiry or small-group discussion groups. Which approach best suits the topic, students and you? Why?

5. Teaching is hazardous—there is so much at stake . . . so much is contested . . . the futures of children and of young adults are at stake . . . the teacher is also at risk . . . (Richardson, 1990). Do you accept this stance? What are some implications for the teaching techniques you select and use?

6. Some teaching alternatives foster competition, others cooperation. With reference to a class with which you are familiar, outline a technique which you consider is most appropriate and explain its degree of cooperation or competitiveness.

7. How might you combine cooperative learning with computer-assisted instruction? Outline a topic/project which could be used to achieve this end.

5 Concept Building

Introduction

Concepts are of fundamental importance because they enable us to make sense of a very complex world. They enable us to categorise, identify and recognise objects and processes. Concepts enable us to communicate effectively with each other.

We live in an amazingly complex and changing world. During the course of our lives, we encounter huge numbers of ideas, things and people. 'One way to simplify a complex world full of variation and individuality is to group objects and events together on the basis of some similarity between them' (Lee and das Gupta, 1995: 116). When we do this and give them a collective name, we are conceptualising.

Apart from helping to save our sanity by simplifying the vast amounts of data we sense every day, concepts help us to understand what we experience and to also communicate with others.

Concepts help us to generalise by acting as collective names for groups of specific items sharing common features. *Factory*, *machinist* and *manufacturing* are all concepts. People agree that a factory is a building equipped to fabricate, process or assemble goods, that is, manufacture them. If we speak in particular of the Acme Furniture factory, we can infer that materials are used to produce such things as chairs and tables in this place. Similarly, machinist is the term identifying the people who operate the machines to process and fabricate products of factories. Machinist and manufacturing are concepts related to but different from factory. Our understanding is refined as we learn to discriminate between related concepts.

This chapter addresses aspects of teaching and learning concepts in studies of society and environment. We shall begin by considering some characteristics of concepts and go on to their place in frameworks of knowledge. This is our basis for a discussion of approaches that might be adopted by teachers intending to help their students build concepts.

We use concepts when we communicate with others. Effective communication requires that the people involved give the same meaning to the word used to name a concept. Given this, using concepts helps us make sense of the varied and complex world we live in. Actually, we use concepts whenever we use language, as is illustrated in Table 5.1. Fluency with language is crucial to students building concepts.

It is not always easy to use concepts because, quite often, there are public meanings of, technical definitions of, and personal responses to words signalling concepts. This idea may be illustrated by reference to the word *sophisticated*. A dictionary definition of the original meaning of this word (late middle English) is 'Mixed with a foreign substance, adulterated, impure.' (*New Shorter Oxford English Dictionary*, 1993: 2949). But in a living language, usage has allowed other meanings to emerge, and they include: experienced, worldly, cultured and discriminating in taste. These are the meanings currently intended by many people using the word. Listeners/readers encountering it react in varied ways to someone so described—with admiration, respect, warily and perhaps with derision. Our personal meanings for concepts are often coloured by particular experiences and associations.

Teachers who wish to help their students build concepts are in effect concerned with the growth of understanding and with the development of their language. So, language used in classrooms is important and this is particularly true in relation to language used by peers because the language of one pupil is much influenced by the language of others. Expression of ideas should consistently be vivid and precise. Teachers have special responsibilities because much of our acquisition of language is based on modelling.

Many teachers also believe that some concepts must be taught or learned specifically and directly. Quite often these concepts are part of the technical vocabulary of the subject being taught. For example, a history teacher working with the explorers Blaxland, Lawson and Wentworth is likely to decide whether such concepts as *exploration*, *direction*, *ridge-top*, and *inland rivers* should be taught directly. Teachers' decisions are influenced by knowledge of their students' achievements.

Suggestions about approaches to teaching and learning are made later in this chapter.

■ An Example of Concepts in Use

Table 5.1 is an extract and analysis of text that might be read by upper primary school students preparing a project on the topic of communications.

■ Concepts: Definitions and Explanations

A concept is a class of specifics sharing like characteristics.

This traditional definition indicates that all of the instances of a concept should share at least one attribute.

Definitions by educationists include: 'A concept is a set of objects, symbols, or events that share common characteristics (defining attributes) and thus can be referenced by a particular name or symbol' (Good and Brophy, 1995: 249), and 'Concepts [are]

Table 5.1 *Concepts in use*

The text, with emphasis on *selected* concepts	Analysis of concepts
Modern means of communication such as fax, email and the Internet have developed from *earlier* inventions. They are vastly *different* from other methods of communication that preceded them in history; for example, *cave painting* (as early as 30 000 *years BP*), picture *writing* (hieroglyphics), the alphabet and printing, typewriters, *telephone* and radar. The new ways of communicating are *changing* our lives; for example, by enabling messages to *reach mass* audiences across the world in text, sound and picture. This has *deeply* affected human awareness and aspiration.	*Modern, earlier:* concepts involving time, and chronology. *means, communication:* terms representing abstract ideas. *different:* contrast/comparison. *cave painting, writing, telephone:* simple concepts for tangible objects. *years BP:* a convention, used for indicating considerable periods of time (BP = before present). *changing, reach:* concepts involving action. *mass*; a way of quantifying. *deeply:* concept indicating intensity.

mental abstractions that characterise sets of objects, events, or ideas' (Eggen and Kauchak, 1999: 298).

These definitions of concepts are useful in that they identify what distinguishes the concept of *concepts*, but are limited because the instances of a concept seldom have all its defining features. A more general 'definition' is 'a term's use in the language'. This is more appropriate for such concepts as *activity* which do not appear to have a clear attribute shared by all instances. It also signals contemporary thinking about how people learn. 'Distinctions that used to be made between thinking and learning, between language and thought, between the individual and the social, have all become problematic' (Nuthall, 1995: 1). Knowledge acquired at school is now regarded as the outcome of how a student's mind is engaged by student talk, teacher talk, classroom environment and learning resources. Knowledge is acquired as the student seeks to make sense of these experiences. New experiences are interpreted in the light of old and help develop the existing ideas. Many concepts grow in the minds of students in this way and rarely are

they static because continuing use and experience refine and elaborate the concept in the mind of an individual.

Given that learning—including concept building particularly—takes place in this way, it might reasonably be accepted that:

1. language in the classroom is important; and
2. interactions with other students are also important.

Language is thought to be important in learning concepts because a particular characteristic of learning by people is that it involves making meaning. 'Language is not the transparent or neutral medium through which preordained knowledge is transferred from the mind of the teacher to the minds of the students. Curriculum knowledge, and the conditions for thinking about experience and acquiring knowledge, are created in the process of using language' (Nuthall, 1995: 46).

Interactions with other students are also important to concept building because of the distinctive relations that exist between learners as contrasted with those between learner and teacher. There is less certainty about just how teachers can train/help students to contribute effectively in cooperative learning experiences, but the importance of peer interactions is well established.

Learning a concept involves grouping things which share characteristics, that is categorising (see Lee and das Gupta, 1995: 119–123). The product of categorising is a concept. But categorising can rarely be cut and dried, as the forthcoming example of rivers demonstrates.

The traditional definition of concept may be useful to teachers seeking to help students learn the technical vocabulary of their discipline. These terms usually require tight definition for accurate use.

Let us consider aspects of the concept, *river*. *River* is used as a label for a group of features on the earth's surface. Most people would probably agree that the following definition is adequate. 'A river is a natural stream of water of considerable discharge, flowing to the sea.' Examples or instances of rivers are the Nile, Amazon, Mississippi, Yenisei, Darling, Wanganui and Jordan. But let's now consider some features of the sample rivers.

- There are times when the Darling stops flowing along part of its course. (Does it cease being a river when it is not a stream of water?)
- The Yenisei freezes hard along a substantial part of its northern course each winter. (Can ice be regarded as water?)
- Parts of the Mississippi and its tributaries are dammed or contained by artificial levees. (Is it then natural or modified?)
- The Wanganui does not have 'considerable discharge' by world standards. Certainly the discharge of the Amazon and Wanganui are hugely different. (Should it be called a creek?)
- The Jordan flows to an inland sea (or

lake?). (Should the phrase 'flowing to the sea' be dropped from the definition?)

It becomes apparent that identifying the *necessary* features of a concept is not always simple. So, how would you define 'river' accurately and precisely? What would you consider to be an adequate understanding of the concept by a child in mid-primary years, or by a student in the final year of secondary schooling? These questions raise the idea that concepts are not fixed, but that the concepts we hold as individuals are likely to develop as we live and learn, though the essence of a concept is similar in the minds of children and adults. Building concepts involves the development of our thought processes through the use of language.

When people conceptualise, that is, engage in concept building, they classify specific instances (examples) and they group the instances consistently. Classes or groups are built from distinguishable features of the concept. These features are both necessary for identifying the concept and are shared by instances of the concept. The emphasis is on recognising elements common to the whole class while features belonging to just a few instances are omitted as one forms a concept.

It helps us to know what concepts are and how our minds use them if we think of them in three ways, as follows:

1. The first is that **instances** of concepts can be given.
   (a) Instances of the concept *government revenue* include:
     - taxes;
     - fines;
     - earnings from government-run business;
     - conscience money;
     - stamp duties.
   (b) Instances of the concept *home* include:
     - houses;
     - caravans;

- home units;
- flats;
- yurts (look up yurt in a book about the anthropology or geography of Asia).

2. The second way of thinking about concepts is that their **features** can be identified.

   (a) Features of the concept *government revenue* include:
      - monies received by the government;
      - payments for services provided by the government; and
      - voluntary and compulsory transfers of items of value to the government by citizens and aliens.

   (b) Features of the concept *home* include:
      - a shelter;
      - a place to eat and sleep;
      - a place that is shared with other members of one's family;
      - a place for which we have feelings.

Generally, several features are required to define membership in a concept. The properties often refer to size, value, texture, shape, weight, material component, beauty and morality.

3. The third way of thinking about concepts is that their features may have a **specific form.**

   (a) In relation to the concept *government revenue*, taxes may be levied on:
      - income (tax);
      - imports (tariff);
      - spirits (excise);
      - gifts (duty).

Tax, tariff, excise and duty are specific forms.

   (b) Specific *homes* are, for example:
      - the apartment in which John Thompson lives;
      - the Cox family home;
      - number 84, High St, Oxenbridge.

The instances of the concept *government revenue* make it clear that some features are necessary descriptors of this concept. Other features are possessed by only some instances. The concept *street* may be used further to illustrate this point. The

Instances of the concept 'home' . . .

Macquarie Dictionary (1985: 1677) defines street as 'a public way or road, paved or unpaved, in a town or city, sometimes having a pavement, and having houses, shops or the like on one or both sides'. All streets may be described by such features as: linear shape; use by traffic (including vehicles and perhaps pedestrians); lined (more or less densely) by buildings (of various kinds); and a smooth, made surface. Streets may have other characteristics, for example a limited number of access points (freeway), low capacity for traffic (alley, lane), require payment for use (tollway), be tree lined (avenue), be broad and tree lined (boulevard), and closed to through traffic (cul-de-sac). Streets possess most of these features in varying degrees, but the necessary descriptor is that they are public ways for the movement of traffic.

Summary

Concepts involve characteristic uses of terms in our language. Instances of concepts share similar characteristics.

A concept:

1. may have many examples;
2. has distinctive features though these are often hard to identify;
3. may possess other features not shared by all instances;
4. may vary in the specific form of its features.

■ The Place of Concepts in Frameworks of Knowledge

Ideas may be expressed in varied forms with different degrees of generality and verification. These forms include percepts and facts, concepts, generalisations, theory and law. They are related to each other as shown in Figure 5.1. Facts are readily verifiable items of information, while percepts are ways in which individuals have perceived things. Language provides a way of communicating facts and percepts and a means of describing them. Thought enables the process of generalisation,

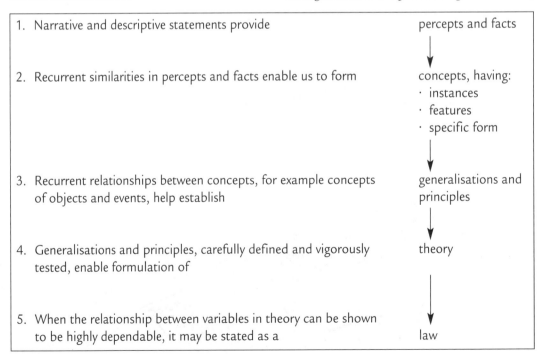

1. Narrative and descriptive statements provide — percepts and facts

2. Recurrent similarities in percepts and facts enable us to form — concepts, having:
   · instances
   · features
   · specific form

3. Recurrent relationships between concepts, for example concepts of objects and events, help establish — generalisations and principles

4. Generalisations and principles, carefully defined and vigorously tested, enable formulation of — theory

5. When the relationship between variables in theory can be shown to be highly dependable, it may be stated as a — law

Figure 5.1 Keystones in frameworks of knowledge

that is, recognising similarities between specific instances or consistent links between events. These, in turn, enable formation of concepts and principles, the elegance of which is related to the level of cognitive development achieved by an individual. A principle is a statement of relationship that is too tentative to be regarded as theory or law. Theory is 'a set of propositions that are syntactically integrated and serve as a means of predicting and explaining observable phenomena' (Snelbecker, 1974: 31). Law is a 'statement about a relationship between variables whose probability of occurrence is so high that the relationships can be counted on as being highly dependable' (Snelbecker, 1974: 34). The forms of knowledge in Figure 5.1 are so arranged that each develops from those preceding. The development involves greater generality and/or tighter verification. The key place of concepts in the framework is apparent in the figure. Concepts represent the very essence of our thinking, so concept building is vital to learning. The figure helps us to discriminate between the forms, but does also suggest greater separation than really exists between them. It tends also to mask how diverse concepts are. Different concepts are based on quite varied criteria, as exemplified by the concepts in Table 5.1.

Relations between the forms of knowledge shown in Figure 5.1 may be illustrated as follows. Facts and specifics are particular and disparate. 'Arthur Phillip was the first Governor of the NSW colony' is a fact; 'I find Christchurch a charming city' is a percept. While facts can be verified, percepts contribute to the formation of concepts. Generalisations are related to concepts in that they indicate links between concepts; for example:

- *Parents raise families* (three concepts)
- *Taxes* are *necessary* but *unpopular* (three more concepts)

The most inclusive generalisations involve many concepts and may be developed into theories. Theories serve to relate major concepts of disciplines of knowledge. In doing so they offer potential for explanation and prediction.

The distinguishing character of concepts and their place in a framework of knowledge point to their utility, particularly in the activities of curriculum development and teaching. This is illustrated in Table 5.2.

Concepts are particularly useful to learners because they allow the use of past experiences. Indeed, it has been suggested that curriculum producers and teachers 'rarely credit young children with the ability to understand issues on a complex level and thus tend to belabor the obvious, the cheerful and the stereotypical' (Martin, 1990: 306). Encouraging children to use their own real experiences at school or in their neighbourhood fosters the study of community in primary classes. In return, this approach pushes the development of concepts (such as community, friendship, courage, liberty, ownership) because features and instances of these concepts are drawn from the lived experience of the children. They 'are no longer passive recipients of knowledge but actively think, talk, pursue information, and evaluate their own experience and knowledge' (Martin, 1990: 307).

Not only may concepts be built from experience, they also facilitate the use of language as a means of expression and communication. Without some means of using our experience we would find all first-time encounters quite unfamiliar and we would have to relearn on each encounter. This may be illustrated in the following way:

Wellington is the capital city and centre of government of New Zealand.

Knowing this, we reasonably infer that Wellington has a parliament house (or a seat of government), public servants, effective

Table 5.2 *The use of concepts in learning and teaching*

Use of concepts	Example

1. Concepts reduce the complexity of the environment through the process of categorising.	There are times our purposes are best served by using the term *vegetation* rather than by a lengthy tabulation of plant types, including:
	 (a) trees:
	   (i) dedicuous (e.g. oak, elm);
	   (ii) evergreen (e.g. eucalypt, acacia);
	   (iii) conifer (e.g. pine, spruce, fir)
	 (b) scrub;
	 (c) grass;
	 (d) moss, etc.

2. We use concepts to help us identify things.	Houses, tents, igloos, offices, etc. provide sheltered places in which humans can live and work. A multi-storeyed apartment building lived in by many people is another form of housing. Shelter is a more inclusive concept than housing.
3. Using concepts helps us to ease the burden of learning. A concept is based on necessary similarities recurring in all instances of its class. Knowing that a new instance is a 'such and such' enables us immediately to attribute certain features to it.	Pineapples are edible fruit, so we know that they may be eaten without harmful effects, though their taste may not be enjoyed by all.
4. When we are told that some specific item with which we are unfamiliar is a member of 'such and such' a class, we may be able to identify a range of possible uses for the new item.	Knowing that computers are electronic machines that can make rapid calculations and control operations by changing the commands in the light of what they find out as they work, we may use them for such operations as calculations, word processing, control systems, navigation, health monitoring and as personal organisers.
5. The essence of conceptualising is orderly organisation and recognition of relatedness, not only of individual features but also of classes of features. This facilitates explanation and prediction.	Mountains (a class of things) may produce orographic uplift of warm, moist air which condenses and precipitates given certain atmospheric circumstances. Knowing this enables us to explain why it has rained or to predict that it will do so at some location.

means of communication with other parts of the country and other features used in the process of government.

The statement that concepts are useful may be further developed. Inventors get a hunch that an idea may work because of the way in which they have conceptualised it. Researchers guess, or hypothesise, on the basis of their conceptual understanding of their study topic. Concepts help focus attention in both cases. Another example can be drawn from the following statement:

> The president was widely regarded as a benevolent despot. There was evidence of his benevolence in newspaper reports from his own country at the time and in the range of welfare programs begun during his regime. Yet he was overthrown in a military coup. It seems we shall have to search for other causes of the revolution than the character of his rule.

Knowing about instances, features and specific forms of the concept *revolution* helps us realise that causes of revolution do not lie exclusively in the rule that is overthrown. *Inter alia*, the aspirations, power, eloquence and cunning of those leading the revolt should also be considered.

Summary
Concepts help:

1. people organise their area of knowledge;
2. people make sense of their lives;
3. researchers and inventors to gain new insights;
4. the development of language and communication.

■ Key Concepts

Concepts vary from those which are simple and factual to those which are abstract and inclusive of many subsidiary ideas. During the 1960s and early 1970s, curricular attention was focused on the key organising concepts belonging to disciplines, because the key concepts are basic to the substantive structure of the discipline. The term substantive structure refers to the framework of concepts which serve to relate information used in the discipline. Key concepts of disciplines are

related and these relationships between concepts contribute to the structure of a discipline. Those who know the structure of a discipline can use it to explain ideas and so improve their understanding of the world.

There have been effective uses of the key organising concepts in the development of courses of study in the individual disciplines, for example in geography, economics and anthropology. However, welding the key organising concepts from individual disciplines into an integrated course has been less successful. Integration has been elusive. Yet the curricular task of providing a course conferring individual sensitivity and civic consciousness on learners remains urgent in a world characterised by their scarcity.

Perhaps this integration or reconciliation is emerging through the developing maturity of the individual disciplines, especially as evidenced in their conceptual structures and syntaxes. The word syntax is used here to refer to the methods of inquiry used by scholars in the discipline. Examples of developing integration are:

1. Some of the basic assumptions of rationality in economic behaviour are being reappraised in order to admit psychological ideas about variability of human behaviour affecting economic decisions.
2. Contemporary approaches to history include psychological interpretations of motivation and a focus on social history which is concerned with the human condition of ordinary people, rather than on constitutional history or the dates and causes of major events. Historians are also using the concepts of location, distance, environment and resources (more commonly associated with geography) to amplify their interpretations.

Indeed, specialists are extending the breadth and explanatory capacity of their disciplines by recognising and exploiting their interdependence. History, geography, economics, government, psychology, sociology, anthropology, environmental science and ethics are growing together.

As the separate disciplines gradually converge and constitute the bases of school studies of society and environment, it is likely that concepts will function as the links between academic rigour and the personal and social relevance of the school studies. For example, location is a key concept in geography and is inescapable in any statement of where things are in the world. However, individuals and groups of people perceive places in different ways; for example, imagine how differently Jerusalem is perceived by Jews, Christians and Moslems. Strengthening the links referred to above will enable the improvement of studies of society and environment in schools. In turn, the formation and development of concepts by school students assumes considerable importance.

The curriculum profile for studies of society and environment, as used in several states, includes strands, that is, groupings of content, process and conceptual understanding, as major organisers of learning areas. While they are somewhat different from the key concepts of disciplines, many of the teaching/learning procedures recommended for concepts can also be applied to the strands of studies of society and environment. The strands are (Australian Education Council, 1994: 10–18):

- Time, Continuity and Change
- Place and Space
- Culture
- Resources
- Natural and Social Systems
- Investigation, Communication and Participation

There are variations in the expressions of these between states and territories.

Most of the strands draw on the concepts of the disciplines; for example, Place and Space makes reference to spatial pattern, location, distribution, association, region, spatial interaction and natural and built environments (from the discipline of geography).

■ Concepts: Their Formation and Development by School Students

Most of us engage in forming and developing concepts as we try to make sense of our world and manage our daily lives. Essentially, *forming* a concept involves identifying necessary features of the object so that we can categorise it. Forming a concept involves the reaction encompassed in the phrase, '*Aha! So that's what it is, a . . .*'

Developing a concept is a rather different process in that we analyse examples and gradually broaden and deepen our basic understanding of the concept. Some features recur in the instances and we accept them provisionally as necessary features of the developing concept. For example, a gardener may have developed a concept of *ideal growing conditions* for dahlias after several seasons of growing them. The features of the gardener's concept of ideal growing conditions are likely to include: friability of soil, amount and timing of watering, fertilising, planting time, pruning and cultivation, and control of pests. Each of these features also possesses a specific form.

It helps educators to plan the learning experiences associated with concepts if they know which concepts students find easy or hard to learn. However, it is virtually impossible to list concepts in any order of difficulty. What people find difficult to form into concepts varies with the effects of past experiences (for example, a child living in Renmark in South Australia is likely to find it easier to understand the concept of *irrigation*

Developing the concept of transport

than many other children; a child living in Queenstown, New Zealand, may understand the concept of *mountain* more readily than a child who lives an isolated life in the outback of Australia). There are, however, many experiences that might condition the attainment of both concepts. Factors likely to make some concepts harder than others for the majority of students include:

1. Direct and previous experiences (as illustrated above) generally help concept formation more than vicarious experience, especially among children.
2. Sensitivity to the environment, for example the oft-cited 'heightened sensitivity' of poets or artists, can be enhanced by learning experiences. The sensory walk (see Chapter 11) is one such activity developed for just this purpose.
3. Characteristics of concepts may be used as

criteria for listing them in some order of difficulty; for example:
- Some concepts represent specific, tangible things (e.g. *tree*). Presumably this concept is more readily formed than the more inclusive concept *forest* and more readily than *woodland*, which has more subtle distinctions to do with the size and spacing of trees.
- Processes are more difficult to grasp than objects (e.g., *lumbering* and *timber*).
- General abstractions are more difficult than specifics (e.g. *international balance of payments* and *buying a bus ticket*).
- Tightly defined concepts are more readily grasped than those which are open ended (e.g. the distinguishing features of *elector* are more limited than those of *responsible government or republic*).

■ Introduction of Concepts in Year Levels of Schooling

The factors affecting the relative difficulty of concepts are useful for teachers, but they do little to guide the year level of schooling at which a particular concept may be introduced. Indeed, most concepts can be learned to different degrees of precision and refinement. This suggests that a spiral curriculum is appropriate in helping students acquire meaningful concepts, especially about difficult or abstract ideas. The concept may be acquired in an early year of schooling in a simple form which does not contain inaccuracies to be corrected later. It may be developed in later years when other concepts necessary to the development have been formed. Table 5.3 is an example, using the concept of *distance*.

Teachers sometimes object to the spiral curriculum on the grounds that their students, on being reintroduced to a topic, complain,

'Oh! We did that last year', and show scant interest in the work. The extension and application of concepts (as illustrated by *distance*) is quite different from the repetition of content, and reduces the chance of an unfavourable reaction from students.

■ Organising Concepts for Learning

When teachers ask the question 'What concepts should my students know to help them learn the topic?', they are indeed addressing:

1. the key concepts in the subject; in this case studies of society and environment; and
2. the main concepts in the topic they are planning to teach and the necessary features of these concepts.

Teachers need to analyse their topic to identify the main concepts from the two

Table 5.3 *Grade placement of a concept*

The concept of distance	Supporting concepts
1. Distance is the length of the straight line between two places. A tape may be used to measure the distance between a child's desk and the board. The straight-line distance between two towns shown on an atlas map may be measured with the help of a rule and the scale.	· length; · units of measurement; · locations (of desk and board); · maps; and · scale.
2. Distance as the length of a bending line between places (e.g. road distances, the length of a river).	Similar supporting concepts to (1) but increased difficulty in the process of measuring.
3. Other measures of distance (e.g. time taken, cost and personal perception*).	· time; · money and value; · emotions; and · familiarity.
4. Applications of the concept of distance (e.g. social distance, as between racial groups in an American city, or as used in the phrase 'the tyranny of distance').	· society; · race; · urban social stratification; and · metaphorical language.

* Personal perception of distance refers to whether an individual regards travel between two places as arduous or easy. The perception is influenced by subjective reactions.

categories above and then to recognise the distinctive features of the concepts. These approaches are exemplified in the following examples:

Example 1   *The topic* work

1. Key concepts from relevant disciplines contributing to the topic *work* in the subject studies of society and environment include:
   - chronology (history); changes in types of work as new technology has been developed;
   - price, market (economics); wages for work; opportunities for work;
   - labour legislation, unionism (politics); regulation of work practices, membership of collectives;
   - location of work, local and global (geography); types of work in rural and urban areas, variations in work practice from one country to another.
2. Concepts specific to the topic *work* may include:
   - types of work; for example, primary, secondary, tertiary and information-based;
   - paid and unpaid;
   - specialisation and the division of labour;
   - work and technology;
   - productivity of labour and capital; and others.

Example 2

The concept map for *city* (Figure 5.2) identifies distinctive features of this concept and some instances. Such a figure is a useful way of clarifying the features and instances of a complex concept.

Example 3

This example deals with the concept *location* in geography. The location of something may be stated in several ways:

- as a point on a grid system (e.g. by using parallels of latitude and meridians of longitude);
- in terms of adjacent areas (e.g. Sydney is located to the east of the Blue Mountains on the central coast of eastern New South Wales);
- in terms of distance and direction from other locations (e.g. Wellington is approximately 500 kilometres SSE of Auckland).

Cities are large settlements (simple definition) that have:

Features (attributes), such as	and	Instances, as in
· Many people	These necessary features of the concept *city* take the form of objects in the city and are reflected in:	· Mexico City
· Buildings		· Paris
· Urban land uses		· Sydney
Urban landscapes		
Other features include:		
· Movement and contacts	These necessary features are processes, comprising	· Los Angeles
· Economic activity		· Singapore
· Power		· New York
· Ideas		

Urban activity, leading to links with hinterland and change.

Figure 5.2 *Concept map—city*

To be able to use the concept *location* effectively students require some understanding of:

- what *where* means;
- distance, and the meaning of terms such as *nearby* or *remote* (these are supporting concepts);
- direction, and the cardinal points;
- grid systems, as on road maps;
- precision, that is, stating locations in ways that have different orders of accuracy.

■ Teaching and Learning Concepts

Teachers find that as students progress through school years their capacity to work with concepts develops quite considerably. In general, young and less able students are more at ease with factual than with abstract concepts. Teachers regularly offer these students many instances of concepts and give examples of their attributes. Careful attention is required to the vocabulary used by students expressing concepts. Sometimes they use terms (perhaps quoting textbook definitions) without being able to recognise an example of the concept involved. At other times students may possess a concept for which they do not have an appropriate name.

Concepts may be acquired: (1) by reception from expository teaching in class; or (2) through discovery as students engage in inductive inquiry. It is possible to achieve some combination of these in a sequence of learning activities aimed at helping students acquire concepts.

The steps in traditional concept teaching through exposition are listed in Owen *et al.* (1978) as:

1. Present a definition of the concept, including its label and attributes.

2. Provide positive examples, emphasising attributes.
3. Provide negative examples, helping to distinguish irrelevant attributes.
4. Provide positive and negative examples, requiring students to identify the positive examples.
5. Provide feedback, giving reasons for errors.

Eggen and Kauchak (1999: 300–1) generally reinforce these steps in their '*rule-to-example*' approach which involves the following steps:

1. Define the concept; link it to a super-ordinate concept (a larger class it fits into); and identify essential characteristics.
2. Clarify terms in the definition.
3. Provide positive and negative examples.
4. Provide additional unlabelled examples asking students to identify and justify their choices of true examples.

The customary steps in discovery learning commonly follow a pattern such as:

1. Arousal of interest, motivation, a need to know.
2. Exploring the idea/question, familiarisation.
3. Gathering data, learning about the topic.
4. Considering possible answers; testing them for accuracy and relevance.

Eggen and Kauchak (1999) apply these procedures generally to concepts in their *examples-to-rule* approach as follows:

1. Provide several examples.
2. Ask students what patterns they see in the examples, that is, what are the recurring distinctive features.
3. Give it a name and form a definition.

The two approaches to acquiring concepts are illustrated in the following sections.

■ Developing Concepts from Expository Teaching

Developing a concept requires that we build the concept in our minds after being presented with a definition. We analyse examples and find that some features recur in each instance. They become the essential features of our developing concept.

Five steps in direct, expository teaching are suggested: introduction, definition, analysis, presentation of examples and practice. These steps are based on ideas in the previous section. Each step is illustrated by reference to a different concept to illustrate concepts within several content areas of studies of society and environment. The diverse examples also reinforce the importance of developing concepts in students at all year levels of schooling.

1. Introduction

Purposes: To inform students of the concept to be learned; motivation; assure student readiness.
Concept/topic: The puzzle of the rivers (NSW nineteenth century); primary school class.

The puzzle of the rivers was faced by Governor Darling in the Colony of New South Wales in the early 1820s. Oxley and Evans had discovered the headwaters of the Lachlan, Macquarie and Castlereagh rivers but they appeared to end in marshes. Did they flow into an inland sea? Darling commissioned Sturt to undertake explorations to solve the puzzle of the rivers. Introductory teaching activities may include:

- the construction of a time line showing explorations and settlements in eastern Australia since Cook;
- a description of daily life in the young colony;
- given a map showing the incomplete courses of the three rivers in 1820, the students are asked to complete the map to show where they think the rivers might flow;
- a short essay written by the students. They are asked to try to see the explorers through the eyes of Aboriginal people at the time. The title of the essay is 'My feelings about these explorers'.

2. Definition

Purposes: To provide a concise statement identifying attributes
Concept: Democracy. Political studies; senior secondary.

The concept is a form of government in which citizens of a community or country vote directly to make the laws that govern their community or country. This means that the majority of the people decide what their laws will be like without anyone else interfering with them. A government is a direct democracy if and only if it has all of the following:

1. citizens of that community or country vote directly upon the issues and/or laws that can influence the way their government operates; and
2. citizen decisions will be put into action without any person or any group of people interfering with the will of the majority of citizens.

This definition is presented to and discussed by the students.

3. Analysis

Purposes: To examine the definition to note its essential features.
Concept: Weather; primary class.

Weather has been defined as 'What the air is like at one time and at one place'. The teacher stresses three essential features of the concept: (1) what the air is like, by referring to temperature, moisture and wind; (2) one place, by referring to the local area contrasted with a familiar but very different place (e.g. the South Pole); and (3) one time, for example now. The weather now can be contrasted with the weather at the same time yesterday.

4. Presentation of examples

Purposes: Familiarisation with essential features.
Concept: Republic; primary class.

A definition of the concept has been established earlier in the series of lessons. Instances of the concept are now required. The following examples are suggested:

- How the government of France changed in 1789.
- What the phrase Republic of Eire means.
- Why American colonists fought the War of Independence from 1775 to 1783.
- What changes would occur if Australia became a republic.

Attention should be drawn to the ways in which each example represents the distinguishing features of the concept.

5. Practice

Purposes: To reinforce learning and correct errors.
Concept: Home; primary class.

Examples are presented to students who are required to decide which are true and which are not. Young students can profitably be asked to write the name of the concept on true examples and all students should be asked to give their reasons for acceptance or rejection of each example.

After the concept *home* has been taught to primary school students, practice in recognising the concept may be provided by showing them an illustration and reading a brief description of the following: a suburban house in any Australian or New Zealand city; a block of flats; an Eskimo igloo; a central Asian yurt; a caravan; a bird's nest; the interior of a business office; a cabin on a passenger ship. Practice in making use of the concept can be provided by daily oral activity in class; for example, the oral composition required by 'Tell me what you know about . . .' greatly helps concept development.

■ Forming Concepts by Guided Discovery

Forming concepts involves identifying the essential features of something specific so that it may be classified.

It is largely a form of discovery learning in which students identify the essential features of a concept by studying an extended example of it. Table 5.4 illustrates this process. The tasks of the teacher are summarised by the four points in the table.

The approach through guided discovery is particularly effective when technical vocabulary is being introduced, for example diminishing marginal utility (economics), colonialism (history), plantation agriculture (geography) and preferential voting (government). The Churchill example draws attention to the importance of language and interactions between students in forming concepts. This applies both in primary and secondary classes.

■ Summary of Teaching/Learning Activities

Two approaches to helping students acquire concepts have been described: (1) expository teaching, and (2) guided discovery. The teaching/learning activities are:

Expository teaching of a concept

1. Select the concept or generalisation. Seek to identify the crucial attributes.
2. Identify prerequisite knowledge and assess students' readiness.
3. Introduce the definition to students.

Table 5.4 *Classroom activity for forming concepts*

1. Teacher presents the scenario in written form so that students can the read and analyse it carefully.	*Scenario:* Winston Churchill became British Prime Minister during World War II. The year 1940 was one of grave crisis for the British Isles, due to heavy bombing and threat of invasion by Nazi Germany which had already occupied much of Europe. Churchill's bold personality, great skill in public speaking, knowledge of military tactics and political guile helped him act as a rallying figure for the British war effort. His ever-present cigar and V-for-Victory sign made with two fingers opened became familiar across the country. At times his generals disagreed with his war plans but he usually prevailed over them with reasoning, coaxing, encouragement and the exercise of authority.
2. Teacher seeks to ensure understanding of the scenario. Comprehension exercises.	· Who needs specific words explained? · Who is the story about? · What is it about? · How do you know this? · What theme underlies the story?
3. Teacher stimulates a search for the essentials of the concept which the story illustrates.	· What do you think this story is all about? (Replies vary: 'Winston Churchill'; 'the War'; 'England'.) · Can you name any other people who have also done things similar to Churchill? (Several replies. They are probed). · Read the scenario again. What is it about?
Teacher records on the board those answers which are essential features of the concept being sought.	Replies include: · the actions of one man; · his personal qualities; · the way he used these qualities; and · events in England during World War II.
4. Continued discussion	It may be suggested that the underlying idea of the story is *human character*, but some of the story describes *actions* taken by Churchill, so this is rejected. The teacher categorises Churchill's actions as *leadership* and notes the necessary features of leadership as being: · rallying the support of associates; · acting towards the achievement of purpose.
and consolidation of understanding of the concept	Churchill's activity as described is consistent with these essential qualities. A student may suggest military leadership as the concept which Churchill's actions exemplify. It would be necessary to decide whether the scenario referred to kinds of leadership exhibited peculiarly by military persons (e.g. combat tactics planned by generals). It is probably safe to conclude that Churchill's activity is an exemplar of the more inclusive concept, *leadership*.

4. Introduce examples and non-examples as needed, usually three or four.
5. Introduce examples and non-examples randomly.
6. Provide practice.

Guided discovery

1. Select the concept or generalisation and identify the crucial attributes.
2. Identify prerequisite knowledge, arrange varied learning resources and assess students' entering knowledge.
3. Provide a hands-on activity that offers experience with crucial attributes. Purposeful small group discussion is valuable.
4. Use questioning to analyse the experience.
5. Use a combination of questioning, presentation and student discussions to identify the crucial attributes.
6. Identify the symbol or symbols used to present the concept or generalisation.
7. Provide spoken and written practice in the use of the concept in social settings.

■ Building a Complex Concept

There is a wide range of complexity in concepts. Such concepts as *city*, *economic* *welfare*, *standard of living* and *historical causation* are complex ones. Some can be taught in simplified form to young children (e.g. a *city* is a place where many people live and work). Spiral teaching over successive years can be used to amplify and refine the concept.

Let's now take the concept *city* to show how instances of its features can be used to broaden and deepen a person's understanding of *city*. Defining *city* is hard but a useful statement may be made by identifying the distinctive features of the concept.

Figure 5.2 attempts the difficult task of providing a framework of distinctive features of the concept *city*. These features are illustrated by the following limited descriptions of six world cities. Each description focuses on one feature well illustrated by that city. Possible alternative resources for learning are noted at the end of each description to promote the idea that concept development may be fostered not only by comprehension of expository text but also by such activities as picture interpretation, map reading, problem solving, gaming and analyses of numerical data.

Complex concept: City

Example 1:	*Mexico City*
Feature:	Many people.

Aspects:

• numbers	The crush of people in Mexico City is intense—over 20 million and rising. This number enables Mexico City to claim the doubtful honour of being the world's most populous city.
• growth	The growth is promised by the yearly influx of 400 000 from the Mexican countryside and by the youth of the city's population (half are under 18).
• effects of growth	The population growth is evident in almost all aspects of living in Mexico City. The peak-hour crush into subway trains is so severe that women and children are given separate carriages to reduce the risk of injury; 30 per cent of families (average size is five) sleep in a single room; people live in 'caves' in the garbage at the city dumps.

Aspects	Mexico City (continued)
• problems related to such overcrowding	Mexicans come to their capital city searching for work and a livelihood. The problems they find are related to the numbers of people. Thirty-thousand factories and 3 million motor cars pollute the air over the valley in which Mexico City stands. Water is scarce and has to be pumped in over the fringing Sierra Nevada Mountains; sewage has to be pumped out. Jobs, housing and services do not keep up with this wildfire growth of people in Mexico City.
Alternative resources:	Series of photographs highlighting aspects of life in Mexico City described in the preceding paragraphs.

Example 2:	*Paris.*
Feature:	Buildings.
Aspects:	
• construction materials	Paris is a city for people and this feeling comes from many things, notably the buildings, with the sandstone fronts which give them a warm appearance in the sunshine, the broad tree-lined avenues and outdoor cafes.
• arrangement of buildings	There are few skyscrapers in a city where six-to-eight-storey buildings are more typical.
• notable buildings	There is beauty too. Some of the famous buildings are hundreds of years old, magnificently designed and constructed. Notre Dame Cathedral, the Louvre Art Gallery, the Sorbonne University, the Eiffel Tower, the Palais de Justice and the Arc de Triomphe are some of the examples.
Alternative resources:	A series of brief personal statements made by visitors to Paris about their reactions to Parisian lifestyle and buildings.

Example 3:	*Sydney*
Feature:	Urban land use.
Aspects:	Sydney, city of 3+ million people, extends from surf-side and harbour-side suburbs to the fringes of the Blue Mountains 60 kilometres to the west.
• variety of urban land use	The regional diversity of land use in this metropolitan area is striking. Consider, for example: • the central business district—Martin Place, central city (a financial core with tower offices of banks and insurance companies). • residential—Vaucluse and Wahroonga (exclusive, leafy residential areas on the south head and the north shore). • commercial—North Sydney, Chatswood, Parramatta (important business districts). • manufacturing—Campbelltown (manufacturing on the outer fringe of the metropolitan area).

Aspects	Sydney (continued)
	Generally, these uses of the land reflect the capacity of the users to pay for space. Pleasant scenery, as on the waterfronts, and central locations with good access to other areas command high rents and are used by the people/firms who can afford to pay.
Alternative resources:	Sydney; land use planning map for the early twenty-first century. Map of Olympic Games 2000 sites.

Example 4:	Los Angeles
Feature:	Movement.
Aspects:	
• motor car commuting	Los Angeles is a motor car metropolis. Satellite cities within metropolitan Los Angeles are spread widely across a coastal plain and into the mountains and canyons inland. Public transport is poorly developed; there are millions of motor vehicles on the roads and millions of people make a daily commuter's trip to work, as far as 150 kilometres each way.
• freeways	They travel an elaborate system of freeways. These are multi-laned and high speed except when traffic jams occur in peak hours. Freeway cross-overs are intricate webs of ramps and lanes of concrete and steel.
• land used for transport	A third of the land in Los Angeles is used for transport—traffic noise is loud; exhaust fumes create the smog which frequently affects all of Los Angeles but is poisonous to people living beside the freeways; gas stations, fast-food shops and motels, all with garish signs, cluster at the on/off ramps; factories are built near the main freeways.
Alternative resources:	Problem solving. What alternatives to the present systems of transport should be considered as ways of reducing the effects of smog? What are the practical difficulties of introducing vehicles powered by electricity?

Example 5:	Singapore
Feature:	Economic activity.
Aspects:	
	Its modern growth began in 1819 when the British established a base there to protect their trading interests in South-East Asia.
• Entrepot trade	Entrepot trade grew in Singapore which then developed connections with Java, Sumatra, the Malay Peninsula, Philippines, Celebes, Borneo and Bali. It served as a centre for the exchange of products of Europe, India and China with products of the Malay Archipelago and South-East Asian countries.
• Singapore as manufacturing centre	Singapore's wealth comes from its trade which has flourished because of geographic location and stable government. However,

Aspects	Singapore (continued)
	Singapore is also an important manufacturing nation with some emphasis on high-technology industries, although it is also one of the world's largest oil refining centres.
Alternative resources:	Statistics showing recent trade and manufacturing information.

Example 6:	*New York*
Feature:	Power and ideas.
Aspects:	
• head offices of corporations	New York is at the centre of North American big business. A hundred of the United States' biggest corporations have head-quarters in New York; dozens of overseas firms run their North American business from that city.
• business decisions	There are also thousands of small commercial and manufacturing businesses. Many of these cater for the needs of New Yorkers. However, a decision in the board room of a multinational corporation can close a factory and throw thousands out of work in one country and open a factory in another country providing work and resource markets there. Trade on the New York Stock Exchange affects and reflects many business decisions.
• advertising	The advertising campaigns mapped out in Madison Avenue shape the tastes of North Americans; the success of a new play or musical on Broadway probably means worldwide success.
• mass media	Decisions in the New York headquarters of radio and television stations affect the very news that Americans hear and see; newspapers, magazines, novels, references (all fundamental means of spreading ideas) pour from the productions of New York publishers.
• dynamism	The emergence of information technology industries has led to some devolution of New York's power.
Alternative resources:	Role play of a simulated meeting of the board of a big corporation making a major business decision.

Summary

These profiles of the six cities do not present a comprehensive picture of any one of the cities. All cities possess all of the features focused by the profiles in varying degrees. So, it is suggested that the six features of:

• many people;
• buildings;
• areas of urban land use;
• movement;
• economic activity; and
• power and ideas

are all necessary to the complex concept *city*. The six examples also refer to many other typical but non-essential features of cities (e.g. rapid change, racial diversity, smog problems and freeways).

Teaching about cities in primary or secondary school is a major task requiring many lessons.

Complex concept: **city**

Cities are densely settled, built-up areas of intense human activity. They are multifunctional and provide services for and are dependent on their hinterlands. Cities are characterised by distinctive opportunities for human lifestyles not available in rural areas, and many are affected by urban problems associated with overcrowding, traffic, anomie and crime.

■ Concluding Comments

A concept is a group of specifics sharing like characteristics. Concepts are important because they help us to make sense out of the complexity of the world in which we live and because they are basic to communication between people.

Established views about learning and thinking in classrooms are currently being challenged by the view that the close links between the growth of understanding, use of language, and interactions between students are significant influences on concept learning. As a consequence, teachers aiming at concept learning would do well to take a broad view of lesson planning in which they 'see teaching as the management of the classroom as a community rather than simply as instruction in specific curriculum areas' (Nuthall, 1995: 74). Everything that happens in classrooms affects student learning, but just how teachers should manage the class is uncertain.

So, two proposed sets of teaching/learning procedures have been offered in this chapter. The expository approach may be well adapted to helping students acquire the technical vocabulary of subject disciplines, while the guided discovery approach may be well adapted to learning a wide range of concepts in classrooms where teachers judiciously manage the many influences on learning.

Some concepts are complex, and understanding them well depends on understanding several simpler concepts. This reference to simple and complex concepts emphasises the key place of concepts in organised bodies of knowledge or disciplines.

The ideas in this chapter are related to other chapters. For example, many of the skills discussed in Chapter 6 may be used to help students build concepts, while the concepts built in ways outlined in this chapter contribute to studies involved in values and issues (Chapter 7). Careful thought should also be given to concepts in the planning activities referred to in Chapters 2, 3 and 4; and special concepts should be recognised in relation to the issues considered in Chapters 13, 14, 15 and 16.

QUESTIONS AND ACTIVITIES

1. Name three environmental concepts. Give at least three examples of each one. What features are common to all examples of one of the concepts?
2. State as precisely as possible a definition for each of the concepts you named in question 1.
3. Choose any one of the social sciences. Name three or four of the key concepts that pervade much of the chosen discipline. What links are there between these key concepts?
4. Why are some concepts harder to acquire than others?
5. Choose any concept relevant to the study of society and environment. Outline a teaching/learning episode that you might implement when seeking to build this concept in the minds of either:
   * primary school children; or
   * students in the middle years of secondary school.
6. Devise an ingenious learning resource that you might use in the episode in question 5.

Skills Teaching

Introduction

Skills and competencies are used in a wide range of human activities. They can be simple or complex; they can require related knowledge, and they can all be improved by practice. Skills are typically acquired because they are needed to fulfil a purpose.

Driving a car . . . drawing a map . . . diving from the high springboard . . . estimating distance . . . dancing . . . constructing a pie graph . . . playing a video game.

Skills are organised and coordinated activities that people develop during repeated experiences. Skills are found in many of the activities in which people engage as they go about their day to day living. Being skilful at something involves a person in many things, such as thought, physical coordination, commitment, habit and practice. Skills may be taught directly by teachers who present demonstrations of and commentaries on the skill, and then arrange for practice by their students. Skills may also be learned by students who become knowledgeable about the particular skill and monitor their own progress in acquiring it. In classrooms, teachers may adopt a sequence of procedures which help their students acquire a skill, or they may create settings which foster more independent learning by the students. In either case, learning a skill may well be linked closely with the need for it by students as they go about their learning.

Skills-in-action: Making a social survey

An effective way for students of society and environment to learn about aspects of the community they live in is to make a social survey. This involves the students in original data gathering from members of the community. To do this, they need skills in techniques of making a social survey (see Table 6.1). The surveys may be linked to issues relating to social justice.

Throughout any social survey, the key activities of students are observing, recording and describing. These can be achieved by numerous methods, such as notes, maps, sketches, photographs, audio tapes and traverses. Field activities can normally be extended later in class by interpretation and critique aimed at identifying injustices experienced by individuals or groups. This work may lead to student action seeking social justice.

■ Characteristics of Skills

Skills have several characteristics (as outlined in Table 6.2), which influence

Table 6.1 *Skills in techniques of making a social survey*

Techniques	Examples
1. *Observing and describing* Qualitative descriptions of social institutions and their operation can be made by student observers.	· Observing a day's activity at a law court, the stock exchange, a fête or other case studies. Recording observations by photos, descriptions.
2. *Making a tally* A simple form of quantitative description. It is precise and can lead to the recognition of trends and sequences. Tallies can be made with little intrusion by students into the lives of other people.	· Counting the number of vehicles of different types passing through a busy intersection. · Counting the number of people entering selected shops in a mall.
3. *Field sketches* Useful in recording the typical assemblage of features in an area/place.	· Panoramic sketch of a village or urban scene, made from a vantage point.
4. *Interviewing* Useful in discovering multiple viewpoints on some matter. Replies can be quantified. Practises students' social skills. Helps students judge the value of testimony.	· Simple questionnaires seeking opinions about matters of current interest, or people's habits. For example, opinion about a council proposal to introduce a new form of waste disposal; or where people do their shopping and why.
5. *Service learning* Learning while doing something for someone else enables skills development in purposeful activity; affects values.	· Students visit people in a home for the aged. See the example in Chapter 7.
6. *Combining techniques* Making a social case study.	· Cases include: a shopping centre; a churchyard; contents of a newspaper; a long-standing resident.

Table 6.2 *Characteristics of skills*

Characteristics of skills	Examples
1. Skills are processes, that is, sets of operations leading to some achievement. We learn skills because they make it possible for goals to be achieved.	· A map summary of Europe in 1848 may be drawn so as to convey the impression that major events happened in that year at several different locations in Europe. · Children may be shown how to use shading and symbols to show highlands on a map.
2. Most skills require related knowledge which improves our mastery of the skill. However, it is possible to possess knowledge without proficiency in the skill.	· We can pass a written driving test without having practical proficiency in driving the car in traffic on a highway. · It is also possible to drive a motor car without understanding how the engine works (e.g. not knowing what the generator generates or what is the function of the carburettor). Understanding these things is one way of improving our driving.
3. Skills can be improved by practice, but as we become more skilful, we do them without thinking. Indeed, a self-conscious approach to using a skill will probably impair our performance.	· You can test this by walking down a staircase twice. First, walk down normally. Second, start at the top of the staircase, lift your right leg, put it forward over the first step, put it down; pause, lift the left leg, move it forward over the second step, put it down, etc. Note how your performance is impaired—and be careful not to fall down the steps!
4. Many activities which are regarded as skills are complex combinations of subskills.	· Drawing a map is often regarded as *a skill*, but it is comprised of many skills including: —pencilling a first draft outline; —lettering—choosing appropriate placement of words on the map, choosing appropriate lettering for different features, actually making the letters by hand or with some mechanical device; —inking lines on the map; —applying colour and/or other symbols; —other contributing skills in the overall drafting of the map. Computer-generated cartographs require quite a different set of skills in their production.

both the way they are used and the approaches that teachers might adopt when helping students to learn them.

Table 6.2 identifies several characteristics of skills but a more systematic overview of the range of skills is offered

Table 6.3 *Taxonomy of psychomotor skills*

Level	Outcome	Example
Reflex movement	Involuntary actions	Blinking
Basic movements	Innate movements	Eating, running
Perceptual abilities	Movement made after interpreting stimuli	Skipping over a rope; writing letters of the alphabet
Physical abilities	Endurance, strength and flexibility	Push ups, distance cycling
Skilled movements	Efficiency in complex tasks	Serving in tennis, bowling an offbreak
Non-discursive communication	Body language	Facial gestures, movements of hands

by Eggen and Kauchak (1999: 507) in their psychomotor taxonomy. The levels in the taxonomy refer to the increasing complexity of skills that humans are capable of achieving as they grow and develop. This increasing complexity demands more coordination and interpretation in association with the skills at each level. Knowing about the taxonomy may well help teachers enhance the guidance they offer to students learning skills.

Acquiring skills

A person acquiring a skill normally passes through the three phases outlined in Table 6.4. The three phases are not entirely separate and they do not always operate in the same sequence. Being aware of the three phases, however, is useful to teachers designing learning experiences aimed directly at developing and improving students' skills. This will be considered later in the chapter.

Table 6.4 shows that skills, as organised and coordinated activities, have both affective (feelings) and psychomotor (practical) components, and also a cognitive (understanding) underpinning.

We know about the skill and may reflect on our own performance with a view to improving it.

■ **Highlighting Two Themes**

Students need skills as they learn any of the subjects in studies of society and environment. Two themes are developed in this chapter. The first theme is that *there is no great merit in teaching or acquiring skills unless they are used for some purpose.* Skills should be taught to enable further learning and action. In relation to studies of society and environment, the further action may well be decision making for effective living in Australian or New Zealand society. This is quite a broad statement: obviously specific skills have specific applications. The first theme requires definition of skills and a rationale for including skills in relevant school curricula. It may also be related to the impact of the back-to-basics movement on studies of society and environment, and to the continuing drive for enhancing employment-related competencies.

Table 6.4 *Phases in the acquisition of skills*

Phase	Example
1. Information about the skill is gained. This may be the motive for becoming proficient; however, the need to use the skill is usually a more powerful motive.	A potential skill learner (i.e. any of us) sees computers in operation in several aspects of daily life; we are aware of advertisements featuring computing in the media; we may learn about computing in formal courses of study where the teachers inform us of the advantages of becoming skilful in the use of computers. We thus become convinced that we should acquire keyboard skills and other skills in the use of computers in order to achieve some of our daily tasks.
2. The learner begins to apply the information needed to gain the skills, thinking carefully about correct procedure while practising.	We learn how to use a computer keyboard—that is, how to hold our hands and use our eyes, which letters are assigned to each finger and so on. Our learning may be coached by a teacher and/or based on the use of a computer manual. We also learn to refine our skills while actually practising them.
3. The new skill becomes part of our behaviour; it may be some process of reasoning or some physical activity.	We practise typing until the appropriate fingers hit the keys automatically.

The second theme is that the *actual learning of skills is fruitful if undertaken when needed by students as they learn by making decisions*. The second theme focuses attention on learning experiences needed for the acquisition of skills and on the links between different objectives and skills. It supports the contemporary emphasis on teachers providing direct instruction showing their students how to learn a skill before they make use of it. The instruction may well continue while the students are using the skill.

The first theme
Skills should be learned so they can be used for some purpose.

A rationale for the development of skills
We need skills in order to live effectively in our society, and the arguments supporting skills learning are undeniable. They include:

- Day to day activities demand skills for effective living in our culture. The skills include those associated with communicating, cooperating, manipulating (implements), deciding, planning, and using technology. We also make frequent reference to time and location in daily living ('Let's meet in the library at noon on Thursday') because they help define the context of our activities. Knowing prior events and the character of the place where something happens helps us organise our lives. Helping students understand time–place settings is a crucial task for teachers.
- Concern has been expressed about the effectiveness of teaching and learning social skills, especially in secondary schools (Iannaccone *et al.*, 1992; Kain

Acquiring creative and manual dexterity skills

et al., 1988). Various forms of interpersonal violence (mugging, discrimination, slandering, gang wars, drug abuse, rape) offer evidence of social skills deficit in Australian and New Zealand societies. Remedying this deficit is one of the most important tasks of contemporary schooling in general and of society and environment classes in particular. The need for educators to enhance their students' humaneness was a clear focus of the competencies movement in Australia in the 1990s, and is represented by Mayer's (1992: 8) 'working with others and in teams involving learning to equip individuals to participate effectively in a wide range of social settings and adult life more generally'.

- Skills in communicating include reading, writing, listening and speaking, computing and the drafting and interpretation of maps, diagrams, tables and charts. These skills can be acquired with varying degrees of mastery by students of all ages.

- The use of skills acquired in society and environment lessons and developed while making social surveys should (sooner or later) lead to social action which may take many forms. Social action is behaviour aimed at having some influence on public matters. Simply knowing about and reflecting upon an issue may be regarded as one form of social action because the knowledge will probably affect the way we vote in elections. Other forms of action are extensions of our critique of some activity or policy and reflect our informed commitment to the views we hold. These are hallmarks of active citizens in a democracy and the actions may include writing letters to members of

Parliament, canvassing, fundraising, protesting and using mass media.

Achieving competence in the use of skills drawn from the above groups helps students make progress in their studies of society and environment. Our theme that learning skills should focus on making decisions leading to effective living in our society is defensible in that social action requires decisions based on the following values:

1. Valuing government, elected by informed citizens and acting to secure the welfare of the community at large.
2. Valuing individual rights (to life, liberty, justice, peace) and freedoms (to worship, assembly, inquiry, expression) and responsibilities (to respect human life and the rights of others).
3. Valuing environments as finite sources of the resources we require to sustain life.

Skills in studies of society and environment

Three ways of grouping the skills supporting studies of society and environment are reviewed in the following section.

1. Basic skills

The skills used in making effective social and personal decisions are arguably those which are basic to studies of society and environment in primary and secondary schools. The word *basic* may mean 'necessary for survival', in which case the context of the action becomes important. It is obvious that certain skills are necessary for survival in emergency situations such as when one has just been bitten by a venomous snake or has been dragged offshore by a rip in the surf. However, first aid and swimming may

not be basic to the curriculum because the two situations are only possible emergencies rather than certain experiences. The Curriculum Development Centre (1980: 4) has attempted to clarify the issue with the use of the terms 'basic' and 'essential'. They are defined as follows:

* Basic learnings are 'those which provide a base or foundation necessary for other study and learning, and for continuing personal development'.
* Essential learnings go beyond basics to include what is needed for effective living in our culture, such as 'knowledge of political processes, skill in interpreting simple scientific data or understanding environmental issues'.

2. Skills in the social studies

National Council for the Social Studies Task Force (1984) identified the following as the general range of skills required by students engaged in social studies in schools.

(a) *Skills related to acquiring information*:
  (i) reading skills;
  (ii) study skills;
  (iii) reference and information-search skills; and
  (iv) technical skills unique to electronic devices.
(b) *Skills related to organising and using information*:
  (v) intellectual skills; and
  (vi) decision-making skills.
(c) *Skills related to interpersonal relationships and social participation*:
  (vii) personal skills;
  (viii) group interaction skills; and
  (ix) social and political participation skills.

The task force's work may reasonably be regarded as an important statement of skills. Their summary of essential skills (1984: 260–261) elaborates sub-skills in each category and indicates the year levels (K to 12) where attention to each skill may be given.

The task force has focused clearly on skills as means to learning, identifying as they do skills related to acquiring information, skills related to organising and using information and the skills needed when people learn together. Their classification might be criticised as being deficient in two respects:

1. The task force does not identify basic content. Perhaps it is unreasonable to expect this in a statement about *skills*. However, it is maintained in this chapter that skills are best developed when needed in learning. It would have been useful to teachers holding such a view had the task force at least identified criteria guiding the selection of basic or essential content.
2. The task force does not include suggestions for action that students might take as a consequence of their social learning. Becoming aware, reflecting and acting (doing something) are near-concurrent phases in studies of society and environment. Skills in social action could well have been added.

3. Lifeskills
'Lifeskills' is a term used to describe the mix of knowledge, processes, skills and attitudes that are considered necessary for people to function adequately in their contemporary and changing life roles and situations. Demonstration of lifeskills takes place in two overlapping dimensions: practical performance of and critical reflection on those skills.

It is possible to identify at least four sets of lifeskills which enable students to participate in life roles. The lifeskills and related life roles are:

1. personal development skills—growing and developing as an individual;
2. social skills—living with and relating to other people;
3. self-management skills—managing resources;
4. citizenship skills—receiving from and contributing to local, state, national and global communities.

Studies of Society and Environment 'develops lifeskills in a number of ways, by applying the processes of investigating, creating, communicating, participating and reflecting, which enables students to function in, critique and improve the world in which they live now and in the future.' (Queensland School Curriculum Council, 1999: 10).

The three groups cited above (basic, social studies and lifeskills) provide useful emphases in thinking about skills. Table 6.5 is based on an arrangement of skills that help effective decision making in Australian society. The list of six skill categories may appear somewhat unfamiliar but it has been devised because it is consistent with the first theme—that skills should be generally acquired for purposeful use. The six groups also illustrate the second theme—that learning skills should be integral parts of the work of students. Two other comments on the decision-making skills are worth making:

1. The column of examples reveals the inclusion of many conventional skills with which teachers are comfortable.
2. The sequence of the six groups suggests an order of activities in lessons. However, many other ways of arranging them are open to teachers.

Table 6.5 *Decision-making skills in studies of society and environment*

Elements	Processes involved
1. Recognising the context, that is, the occasion, situation, issue or problem requiring some decision prior to action.	· Observing people and events (e.g. as reported in the newspaper) · Analysing the situation · Interacting with others (e.g. by asking questions about or discussing the matter)
2. Acquiring knowledge on which to make the decision, and awareness of the value bases of the information.	· Finding information · Reading and comprehending books, journals, newspapers, etc. · Interpreting graphs, diagrams, numbers, cartoons, maps, etc. · Using the resources of the community · Analysing values
3. Establishing values and priorities associated with the matter requiring a decision.	· Devising criteria · Ordering the alternative decisions · Probing for values premises of alternative courses of action · Considering who decides and for whom
4. Studying, reflecting on and ordering the possible decisions, either individually or as a member of a group.	· Using logical and critical thinking skills · Recognising consequences · Accepting responsibility · Applying criteria to make judgments · Considering several viewpoints on the topic · Cooperating with others making the decision
5. Deciding, and acting on the decision.	· Feeling confident about the decision · Taking appropriate action
6. Reviewing consequences of the decision and the action(s) after the event (where practicable).	· Finding out about the effects of the decision and actions on others · Reviewing the effects on self

Table 6.5 outlines the skills required for decision-making activities in studies of society and environment.

■ Stage and Sequence in the Introduction of Skills

Skills are vital to meaningful learning. There is a place for the development of skills at all stages of the curriculum from Years K to 12. Questions of stage and sequence may be raised at this point. Is there an optimum time for the introduction of specific skills to students as they progress through primary and secondary years? Is there an optimum sequence? Little definitive research has been recorded on these questions, so two possible criteria are noted here.

The first is 'expanding environment'

which is regularly cited in the literature. This criterion suggests that the ordering of content and of skills, especially in the primary years, should progressively expand the environment familiar to the students. It is based on the principle of working from the known to the unknown and using what is presently known as a basis for learning new material. The principle of expanding environment may be interpreted in three ways:

1. in a geographical sense of moving from home/school/local area to remote locations;
2. in a psychological sense of moving from self to familiar groups (family, school class), to more formal and remote associations of persons; and
3. as referring to learning which expands the student's environment by enabling him or her to probe it in greater depth and generate deeper insights.

The second criterion, that might be applied to the sequence in which skills are developed by school students, centres on how learning experiences are organised. A unit of study involving students in an inquiry will encompass somewhat different skills and a different order in their introduction from a unit organised for expository learning. While the first criterion (expanding environment) may well be applied to several years of schooling, the second criterion is more effective within the major topics making up a course.

The second theme

The second theme is that the actual learning of skills is fruitful if undertaken when needed by students as they learn by making decisions. This second theme focuses attention on the learning experiences needed to help students gain skills and on the links between different objectives and skills.

Approaches to teaching and learning skills

Students learning skills need to pass through the stages of:

- understanding;
- organising; and
- perfecting the skill.

Teachers can help students in many ways at each stage, notably through fostering:

1. *Understanding* Students need to know about the skill, what it is, what

Skills teaching should involve practical experiments by students

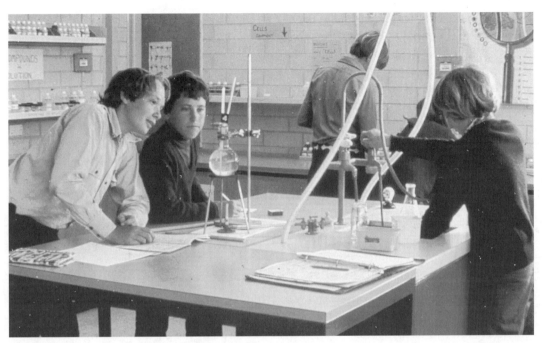

Repeated use of a skill until high levels of performance are attained

it achieves and who is good at it. They can find out about these things by observing someone practising the skill, listening to a description of the skill, reading about it or watching a film or video clip about it. However, it is difficult to improve on direct observation of the skill as a first step in knowing about it; for example, student surgeons frequently watch and assist at operations in hospitals. It is also desirable that school students understand what underpins the skill; for example, students drawing time lines need some sense of chronology. They need to be able to distinguish between yesterday, last week, last year and a century ago. They also need to understand scale and how symbols can be used to represent things.

2. *Organising* Early practice sessions give learners opportunities to try out the skill, find out how to coordinate their actions, make mistakes and try

again. Students drawing the time line will learn how to use a rule to make straight lines, how to measure subdivisions of time along the line and how to draft lettering clearly. Coaching by teachers is important at this stage.

3. *Perfecting* This involves repeated use of the skill until manual dexterity is nearly automatic. Perfecting also involves improving on understanding and on organisation as ways of enhancing performance. Sometimes several specific skills are linked in any composite activity; for example, gear changing, steering, braking, etc. combine to become driving. Our students drawing the time line will profit from (assigned) work where the use of the line helps the study in hand.

Models for teaching and learning skills

The three phases may be linked in models guiding teaching and learning of skills. The principles come from theory and research in education. The procedures are practical applications of the principles. Steps 1, 2, 3 and 4 in Table 6.6 can be used to contribute to student *understanding* of the skill, steps 4, 5, 6 and 7 contribute to *organising*, while steps 6, 7 and 8 contribute to *perfecting* skills. The overlap between understanding, organising and perfecting is clear.

■ The Anatomy of a Skill: Teaching Upper Primary Students to Draft a Map

Principles and procedures associated with teaching skills are outlined in general terms in Table 6.6. This section, on the other hand, presents a detailed application of these principles and

Table 6.6 *Principles and procedures for teaching skills*

Principles	Teacher's procedures
1. Many educational skills are complex and require several abilities in people practising them.	Analyse the skill to identify its components.
2. The overall set of activities making up a complex skill should be related to the known abilities of students.	Find out about the ability of individual students to undertake the activities involved in the skill, by testing them, by reviewing their past achievements and by watching their early attempts to use the skill. Use remediation where necessary.
3. Students should see competent demonstrations of the skill.	Demonstrate the whole skill, its parts, then the whole again. Closed circuit television can help give close access to demonstrations.
4. The demonstration is enhanced by a commentary and/or by guiding notes.	Provide a commentary and/or guiding notes. Encourage students to record their own notes.
5. Supervised practice soon after the demonstration helps to perfect the skill.	Time lessons so that practice can follow demonstration. The demonstration plus practice should be of each part of highly complex skills.
6. Comments on performance during practice help minimise errors.	Comments should be made to students as they practise a skill, that is, provide coaching.
7. The application of a skill to diverse learning tasks makes it meaningful and transferable.	Plan for different ways of using the one skill and build it into complex activities such as problem solving.
8. Evaluating one's own performance leads to improvement in the skill.	Help students find out how to judge a competent performance and encourage them to judge their own.

procedures. The ubiquitous task of drawing a map is selected. The procedures recommended are relevant to upper primary students though they also work well with students in their first year of secondary school (see Figure 6.1).

Context Students have worked with maps in the past, using atlases and globes to find places and become familiar with the distribution of major features of the world. They have also used simple maps of the local area. Maps for recording information have been completed from outlines distributed by the teacher. These activities have given them some familiarity with distance and how scales represent it, with shape and area and with direction and the cardinal points. The teacher then decided it was time to develop in the students the skills needed to devise and draft their own maps to make a reasonable record of their current studies. These studies were about characteristics of the population of Australia and the map was to show the distribution of population. The teacher and the class discuss the map and decide to:

1. shade areas of dense, medium and sparse population;
2. add vertical bars scaled to the population of each state and of New Zealand; and
3. divide the columns to show how much of the population of each state and of New Zealand is in the capital city and how much is in the remainder of the state or country.

The activities in Table 6.7 are then carried out by the teacher and the students.

Following activities   These are useful:

1. comments by the teacher on the set of skills involved in drawing a map, that

is, the sequence of drafting operations, decisions about shading and types of lettering;
2. reading and interpreting the map to further the students' understanding of the topic 'Population in Australia';
3. thinking about some of the things related to the population in Australia but not shown by the map.

Comment This example has been included as a detailed illustration of an approach to teaching and learning a skill. It is obvious that many skills are complex and have numerous components. A type of task analysis is a useful way of breaking down a complex skill as a prelude to teaching it. The elements of understanding, organising and perfecting are readily recognisable in the map-making example. The series of activities as presented takes for granted the need for having students develop such a skill. Before undertaking it in a classroom, teachers will have considered its place and utility in their program of lessons.

■ Skills in Making Meaning from Maps

Tables 6.6 and 6.7 detail suggested procedures that might be used to help school students acquire fairly simple practical skills. There is little element of critique in these activities. But critique may be used to:

- enhance performance by self-review (see later section entitled 'Skill development with self-monitoring');
- enhance understanding derived from the exercise of skills. Enhanced understanding involving critique is illustrated in the following section on map meaning.

Table 6.7 *Skill development through direct teaching. Drafting a map*

Teacher activity	Student activity
1. Rules a chalk framework on the board while commenting carefully (see Figure 6.1).	Watch the teacher's demonstration on the chalkboard. · Note the measurements on the figure. · Rule lines lightly in pencil in the following order: · the top horizontal line; · the middle vertical line; · the bottom horizontal line; · join the ends of the top and bottom lines; and · rule the mid-horizontal line.
2. Supervises student work; offers comments to individuals.	Use pencils, rules and erasers to draw the framework in their books.
3. Demonstrates how to draw the coastline of Australia in the top-right part of the frame; names coastal places as he or she proceeds (e.g. starts with Cape York).	Watch teacher's demonstration.
4. Supervises.	Draw the northeastern coastline in pencil on the frameworks in books.
5. Draws students' attention to an atlas map of Australia, especially the northeast coast.	Make comparisons between the teacher's outline on the board and the atlas map.

(Steps 3, 4 and 5 are repeated in turn for the southeast, southwest and northwest parts of Australia and for the two major islands of New Zealand.)

6. Draws two lines on the chalkboard map to show the limits of dense, medium and sparse population.	Observe the teacher working on the board and listen to the commentary. Ask questions for clarification.
7. Shows how to draw a vertical bar scaled to the population of Victoria.	Observe and listen. Questions.
8. Leads class discussion on where on the map to place the bars for each state.	Join in discussion.
9. Marks these places on the chalkboard map.	Observe and listen. Questions.
10. Supervises individuals.	Draw in pencil the vertical bar for Victoria followed by those for the other states.

Table 6.7 *Skill development through direct teaching. Drafting a map (continued)*

Teacher activity	Student activity
11. Shows students how to use atlases to locate capital cities.	Observe and listen. Questions.
12. Supervises.	Mark points for the location of capital cities and their maps.
13. Demonstrates and comments on shading of three areas of population density.	Ink (biro) all names on map. Observe and listen.
14. Supervises.	Shade their maps.
15. Demonstrates and comments on inking coastline and dividing lines between areas of different population densities.	Observe and listen. Questions.
16. Supervises.	Complete their linework in ink so as to avoid 'crossing out' words.
17. Completes map scale, title, key to shading and scaling of bars on chalkboard.	Observe and listen. Questions.
18. Supervises.	Complete the activity.

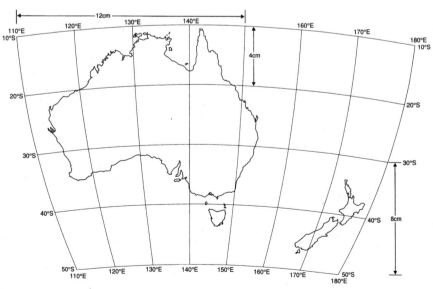

Figure 6.1 *Skills teaching (drafting a map of Australia and New Zealand)*

People live in places and organise the use of the land they inhabit. In doing so they give the places a character reflecting their culture. Many aspects of place, as occupied space, can be represented on maps, which are documents of crucial importance to all teachers of society and environment, not just the geographers. Reading and interpreting maps are vital skills to all.

An earlier section in this chapter offers practical suggestions for teachers showing students how to draw a map (as distinct from generating it on a computer). This section is focused on suggested procedures that students/ teachers might adopt in making meaning from maps. The procedures: (1) are readily adaptable to students at different year levels; (2) seek to combine effective methods from direct teaching and from student inquiry guided by metacognition; and (3) proceed to an (optional) deconstruction of maps, as means of communication, to expose assumptions and messages underlying the symbolic representations on the maps.

Student activities developed from ideas in the 'Examples' column in Table 6.8 will be more effective when the kind of map relates well to the abilities and ideas of the learners using the map. For example, a pictorial map-sketch is likely to be more appropriate to young readers than a topographic sheet using many conventional signs.

Table 6.8 *Making meaning from maps*

Procedures	Examples
1. Making meaning from the map symbols by using the map legend to learn the meaning of each symbol.	Map reading, that is, direct translation of the symbols; for example ● represents a building.
2. Making meaning of perspective, scale and direction requires activities to help students understand the map's frame of reference.	Activities requiring orientation of maps; the meaning of plan perspective; comparison of distance on the ground with distance on the map; use of the cardinal points.
3. Making meaning of spatial patterns shown on maps. This requires students to go beyond reading to interpretation.	Studying the amount of overlap (covariation) between distributions shown on the map, e.g. between climate and plant life, and making inferences about their relation.
4. Giving purpose to the map study by relating the data obtainable from the map to the current topic or inquiry.	Learning how to draw a map showing intervisibility when planning the location of a tourist lookout.
5. Beyond competence—being critical of the map. Finding underlying meanings. Considering reasons for the inclusion or omission of related data.	The Peters map projection elongates the continents, distorting their true shape. It was developed to provide greater focus on Third World countries in intertropical areas.

Skill development with self-monitoring

The steps in a model guiding the teaching of skills are detailed in Table 6.6 and illustrated in Table 6.7. The learning by students is clearly directed by the teacher. Though the students are not passive, they take little initiative in or control over their learning. Learning theorists (Flavell, 1979; Forrest-Pressley, MacKinnon and Walker, 1985; Reynolds and Wade, 1986; Davidson, 1987) have explored the possibilities of **metacognitive** principles as guidelines for people wishing to learn how to learn. Planning, remembering and self-monitoring are aspects of meta-cognition that can be applied to the acquisition of skills such as those used by students of society and environment. These metacognitive principles emphasise making descriptions of one's own processes of learning and using these descriptions to help make decisions about how to proceed with the learning.

Students may enhance their development of skills when they are encouraged to ask themselves such questions as:

- Why have I chosen to acquire this particular skill?
- How will it help my studies?
- Where should I begin?
- What have I done so far?
- I find this part of the task easy (or hard). Why is this so?
- Do I need to go back over that step to check it?
- How can I summarise the sequence of steps I have undertaken?
- How does my own evaluation of my performance compare with the teacher's evaluation of it?

Such questions reflect the self-monitoring, self-planning and remem-bering activities emphasised in the metacognitive approach. A sustained example of teaching and learning guided by metacognitive principles in a geography class is reported by Neighbour (1992). The roles of teachers at these times are mainly:

1. making students aware of these questions and of the value of asking them, and
2. observing the students at work and offering comments on progress, especially when asked by the students for them.

The sequence of procedures and underpinning principles by which students might learn a skill (as distinct from being taught by the teacher) is shown in Table 6.9.

Contrasting the teaching model (Table 6.6) with the learning model (Table 6.9) shows the shift in responsi-bility to the learner. Learning how to learn is the focus of the second approach, which is based on meta-cognitive principles. The meaningfulness and motivation usually associated with finding out for oneself are strengths of the discovery approach. The teachers' roles shift from exposition, demonstration and commentary to encouragement and facilitation. The two approaches are contrasted in Table 6.10.

Skills in making an environmental study

The school subject, studies of society and environment obviously has the dual interests in society and environment. Inquiries into both are encouraged in syllabus documents. Early in this chapter, guidance was offered in techniques that students might use in making a social survey. To complement this work in Table 6.1, guidance is

Table 6.9 *Principles and procedures for learning a skill*

Principles	Procedures
1. Motivation is crucial.	Ensure that the skill is needed in studies that follow.
2. Learners should know about the principles on which the skill is based.	Teachers should provide access to this knowledge.
3. Understanding practical aspects of the skill is essential.	Teachers might provide this by demonstration and commentary.
4. Learners should consider different ways of acquiring the skill, and choose one.	Teachers provide access to this knowledge.
5. The learner should try one way; make own commentary on what is being done and how the learning is happening.	Implementation is by the learner; teachers provide encouragement.
6. Self-monitoring is the key to improvement.	Learners question their own performance as part of a process of reflection.
7. Repeated rehearsal, self-commentary, self-questioning and reflection contribute to perfecting the skill and making it transferable.	Learners are encouraged to undertake these activities.

offered here in making an environmental study.

The skills that students need to engage in environmental studies are largely extensions/adaptations of the skills used in making social surveys (see Table 6.1). A general approach to making an environmental survey is suggested in Table 6.11.

■ **Case Study: Signs in Orchard Avenue—A Teaching Unit which Incorporates Many Skills**

The following example illustrates the incorporation of many skills in a teaching unit which can be adapted to a wide range of students in primary and secondary schools.

Introduction

An outline of a teaching unit, called Signs in Orchard Avenue, is presented in this section as a way of illustrating the general ideas about teaching skills that have been developed throughout the chapter. The unit applies the two themes presented earlier. The skills used by students working on Orchard Avenue all extend their study of the topic; what they find out from the use of a skill enables them to go on with the unit. Some of the skills are new to students, so the teacher has planned demonstration–organising–perfecting sessions for these.

Outline of the unit: Signs in Orchard Avenue

1. *The students:* Upper primary–lower secondary.

Table 6.10 *Procedures for learning skills: through guided inquiry, or directly from teachers*

Direct teaching	Guided inquiry
Preliminary: Teacher analyses the skill to identify its component tasks.	1. Anticipatory set for readiness and motivation.
1. Questioning or practice to identify student readiness; motivation.	2. Learners acquire the knowledge base on which the skill rests.
2. Demonstration of overall task, then of its components in sequence.	3. Learners familiarise themselves with practicalities associated with the skill.
3. Teacher commentary accompanies demonstration; summary (e.g. lab manual) is provided.	4. Learners review alternative ways of attempting tasks requiring the skill.
4. Student practice straight after the demonstration.	5. Independent practice, with self-commentary, describing the what and how of their own learning.
5. Teacher coaches individual students working with the skill.	6. Continue self-monitoring against self-devised criteria during sustained practice.
6. Practise wider applications of the skill.	7. Modify the learning process in the light of self-evaluation.
7. Teacher and students formulate criteria to judge performance, and apply the criteria.	8. Reflection on the process of learning the skill so that it transfers readily to other tasks.

Table 6.11 *Making an environmental study*

Student focus	Examples
1. Acquisition of skills needed for making studies in the community and environment, prior to and during the fieldwork.	1. See the range of skills suggested in Table 6.1. Also needed, simple techniques for making scientific measurements, e.g. of water purity.
2. A feeling of concern for the local environment and its sustainability.	2. Note the range of procedures for fostering values as suggested in Chapter 7.
3. Recognition that there are often political decisions affecting environmental issues.	3. Skills in scrutinising documents, speeches and viewpoints of participants in decisions about the environment; values analysis techniques.
4. Commitment to responsible action toward a sustainable future for the environment.	4. Skills involved in negotiation, making submissions and public statements.

2. *The unit topic:* Environmental studies in the local area.
3. *Theme of the unit:* Visual aspects of the environment, especially advertising signs, road signs and others.
4. *Purposes of the unit:*
   (a) to observe and describe visual aspects of the environment;
   (b) to find out who cares about them;
   (c) to decide what might be done to improve the environment; and
   (d) to act appropriately.
5. *The structure of the unit:* Signs in Orchard Avenue (Table 6.12).

Samples of the skills and supporting resources are presented on following pages. Use Table 6.12 to see how each sample slots into the unit.

Outlines of some of the skill activities built into the Orchard Avenue unit

This section includes possible ways in which several of the skill activities (outlined in Table 6.12) may be developed in class.

1. *Picture analysis* Questions need to be devised for specific pictures, that is, those taken in the avenue itself. Questions based on photographs often:

(a) draw attention to specific features in the photograph;
(b) require estimates of the scale and size of these features;
(c) help students observe which features are associated; and
(d) ask for tentative conclusions about the time (year) when the photograph was taken or about what has happened in the scene.

The questions related to the cartoon in Figure 6.2 present some guidance to devising questions which aid the study of a photograph.

2. *Comprehension exercises* This activity is based on a 'letter' to the editor of a local newspaper (see Box 6.1). Such letters do appear from time to time and some teachers find it useful to clip and file them for reference.

Questions to help students understand the letter might include:
(a) What do the following phrases mean?
   • 'express my concern';
   • 'advertising fast food';
   • 'mid-city nightmare';
   • 'blot on the landscape'.

Table 6.12 *The structure of the unit: Signs in Orchard Avenue*

Sequence of major teaching/learning activities	Supporting resources	Skills
1. Planning and advance preparation by the teacher, including putting photographs of Orchard Avenue on display, preparation of 'letter to the editor' and contacts with some residents of Orchard Avenue.		
2. Introducing the unit via the photographs and the letter.	Phototgraphs, letter	Reading and interpreting photos; comprehension exercise.

Table 6.12 *The structure of the unit: Signs in Orchard Avenue (continued)*

Sequence of major teaching/learning activities	Supporting resources	Skills
3. Students express their opinions on the appearance of the avenue.		Logical thinking exercise; distinguishing facts from opinion.
4. Valuing activity; an index of student commitment to the topic.		Values questions.
5. Brief field excursion. Purposes: familiarise students with Orchard Avenue, enable students to meet with some members of the local community (shopkeepers, residents, local councillor) who might express an interest in the students' work and give it a service learning quality.	Orchard Avenue Local persons	Direct observations; sensory walk. Social skills; asking questions.
6. Students gather information about visual pollution.	Library	Where-to-find-information exercises.
7. Gathering several points of view about visual pollution.	Reference books and persons	Interpreting a cartoon; recognising value positions.
8. Class debate; leads to recognition of the need for more information. Is the visual pollution in Orchard Avenue restricted in extent? Is it becoming progressively worse?		Verbal skills; social skills; reasoning skills; analysing political decisions e.g. of town planners.
9. Fieldwork.	Orchard Avenue	Field mapping; devising a time line.
10. Proposing a range of possible decisions for the future of Orchard Avenue.		Establishing criteria for ranking the decisions; discussion skills.
11. Making the decision and writing the report.		Social group skills; writing, mapping and drawing a diagram.
12. Presentation of the report in class and to other interested parties (shopkeepers, local council)		Social skills.

Old lady: *Things have changed a lot since our street became one-way to progress!*
Young man: *Aren't there any other ways?*

Figure 6.2 *Signs on Orchard Avenue*

Box 6.1 *Letter to the Editor*

Dear Editor,

I am writing to express my concern about the change that has come to Orchard Avenue. I grew up in a home on this avenue over 30 years ago. Then it was quiet and it was safe for us to play on the footpaths after school. There was no television in those days. Now it has become a one-way street and the shopping centre has been built on the corner with the highway. Some of the trees have been cut down to make way for street signs like: One Way; Keep Left; and No Parking after 4.00 p.m. Perhaps these are necessary but there are also many signs advertising fast food, petrol and even one advertising a hotel nowhere near this area. A pretty street has been turned into a mid-city nightmare, because the place no longer looks nice. I recognise the need for traffic signs but the others are just a blot on the landscape. It is important for places to look nice. I wonder if people stop being nice to each other when their neighbourhood stops looking nice. Won't someone do something about this mess?

Yours sincerely,

Mrs Myrtle Tree

(b) Does Mrs Tree give good reasons for her complaint?

(c) What do you think she regards as a nice pretty place?

(d) Do you agree with her? Why?

(e) Did Mrs Tree suggest who could improve Orchard Avenue?

(f) What is the point of view of the writer?

(g) What kind of person do you think Mrs Tree is?

3. *Skills in thinking critically: distinguishing facts from opinions* The teacher noted the following statements (shown in Box 6.2) made by different students during the course of discussions in class and asked students to decide which were statements of fact and which were opinions.

4. *Valuing activity* Students can profit from undertaking simple activities designed to build skills based on values. Some of these skills enable effective cooperative work in groups; other value-oriented skills enable students to 'know their own views' better. The exercise built into this phase of the Orchard Avenue unit is aimed at testing student commitment and at strengthening their motivation for the study. So it is aimed at students individually and personally.

(a) If you had the power to pass a law for Orchard Avenue would you make the avenue:
   • greener?
   • cleaner?
   • quieter?

(b) Fill in the scale presented in Box 6.3, twice, using X for Orchard Avenue as you think it is now, and O for how you would like it to be. Put the Xs and Os on each line at the place that is right for you.

(c) There are several different kinds of pollution. Air pollution (i.e. a reduction in the purity of the air) is one of the worst. Many things pollute the air, for example exhaust from cars, smoke from factories, cigarette smoke, gas from spray cans, smoke from burning rubbish in back yards and dust.
   • List three things you do which pollute the air.
   • Which of the three would you be prepared to give up if you were shown how they pollute the air?

Box 6.2 *Student statements*

Piang Chin: Wide streets always look prettier than narrow ones.

Thomas: Orchard Avenue is just 22 metres wide, including footpaths.

Aaron: I like the signs; they make the place look alive.

Gina: Some of the signs are needed to direct traffic.

Tim: That's true, but the same sign has been put up in three different places. That's the Go Slow sign.

Ailsa: You've just got to have signs.

Box 6.3

quiet _____ noisy
no traffic _____ much traffic
no advertising signs _____ many signs
few road signs _____ many signs

5. *Field study skills: A sensory walk* A sensory walk is an excellent way of sensitising students to the quality of an environment. It consists of activities that focus students' perceptions through one or a limited number of their senses; for example:

(a) Have students walk in pairs down Orchard Avenue. One should be blindfolded. The other assures the safety of the 'blind' person. The person with sight also records the impressions of the blind one walking down the street.

(b) Have students record different signs they can see in Orchard Avenue and classify them later on.

(c) Students may make a count of:
   • cars;
   • trucks; and
   • bicycles
   they see in Orchard Avenue over a 15-minute period.

(d) Students can be asked to count the different smells in Orchard Avenue and identify their sources.

6. *Exercises designed to build skills in finding information* These are designed to help students find sources and make effective use of them. Examples of such exercises are:

(a) If you wanted to know what Orchard Avenue looked like 30 years ago, which of the following sources would be the most useful?
   • An atlas of Australia including a map of this city
   • A book on the history of this city
   • A street directory printed 30 years ago

• A person who has lived in Orchard Avenue for 35 years
• Old copies of the local sub-urban newspaper
• The Internet

(b) Use the computerised catalogue in the library, the table of contents in a book, and the index of a book and ask questions promoting skill in their use, such as:
   • Put the following words in alphabetical order: citizen, government, civics, mayor, law, ceremony, parliament.
   • Name three library books which should give information on the history of part of Sydney such as Orchard Avenue. How did you find out?
   • Which pages of the book entitled *City Development in Australia* might have information on areas like Orchard Avenue? How do you know?
   • If there is no index entry for 'Orchard Avenue', suggest other words you might look for in the hope of finding out something about streets like Orchard Avenue.
   • What key words would you enter in the library computer to find information about Orchard Avenue?

7. *Interpreting a cartoon* Cartoons show persons and events from a particular viewpoint and are often exaggerated to make this obvious. Studying cartoons in old newspapers is one way of finding out what opinions were held about people and events in the past. However, one needs some skill to be able to read

the interpretations made in cartoons. The following activities are designed to help the development of these skills:

(a) Cartoonists often use symbols to show ideas, for example a dove represents peace and scales represent justice. Can you see any symbols in the cartoon shown in Figure 6.2? What do they mean?

(b) Draw the symbol that you would use to show great wealth.

(c) Cartoonists tell you about the character of persons by making a special feature of their personal characteristics. In your opinion, what kind of person is the woman in the cartoon?

(d) How do you know that the man is puzzled?

(e) What do you think that the cartoonist is trying to tell us?

(f) How well does the caption convey the message?

8. *Recognising value positions* Often different people see the same event in different ways. There are many reasons for this; a point of view is likely to reflect a person's character, education, occupation and other personal characteristics. Table 6.13 shows some comments made by different people about the signs in Orchard Avenue. The students' task is to complete the third column.

9. *Field mapping* Developing skills in making and using a map relevant to the Orchard Avenue study. The students are given a base map of Orchard Avenue showing its junction with the highway at the northern end. The following activities are aimed at fostering skills in making and using maps.

Cartoonists often use symbols to show ideas

(a) Class discussion about different types of signs, prior to the fieldwork. Students name as many as they can remember; they are listed on the chalkboard and a simple classification of them is made. The types of signs recognised are:
  • traffic (e.g. Stop);
  • local information (e.g. street names, house numbers); and
  • advertising (e.g. 'Burgers are beaut!').

Three different symbols, one for each type of sign, are invented.

(b) What is the purpose of each type of sign?

(c) What is the distribution of each type of sign in the Orchard Avenue area? Comment on this distribution.

(d) Who can see each type of sign: pedestrians, motorists or both?

Answers to (b) and (d) are made with the aid of field observations. Students walk along Orchard Avenue and the highway. They mark the location of each type of sign on

Table 6.13 *Comments about Orchard Avenue signs*

Statement about the signs	Person making the statement	Why do you think that was said?
1. 'The signs are necessary to direct the traffic.'	Highway engineer	
2. 'Well, at least they've cleared the trees out of the way—you *can* see the signs in this street.'	Taxi driver	
3. 'We have to use signs to attract customers, especially passing motorists.'	Local shopkeeper	
4. 'It pays to advertise. Our rivals would take our sales if we did not advertise. I don't care what Orchard Avenue looks like so long as we sell. My job depends on it.'	Executive of very big firm	
5. 'The place is an eyesore: a disgusting mess. All done for the dollar.'	Keen conservationist	
6. Mrs Tree's letter.	Local resident	
7. You write in a statement here.	You	

_____

_____

_____

their maps, using the symbols decided on in class.

10. *History study* Finding out what Orchard Avenue used to be like as a way of understanding its present character and why some residents are unhappy about the recent developments. Time lines are used to assist this study (see Figures 6.3 and 6.4).

The following questions are used to assist the development of skill in interpreting the time lines:

(a) How long ago is it since Orchard Avenue was a quiet two-way street?

(b) What event led to its becoming a one-way street?

(c) Which of the three types of signs

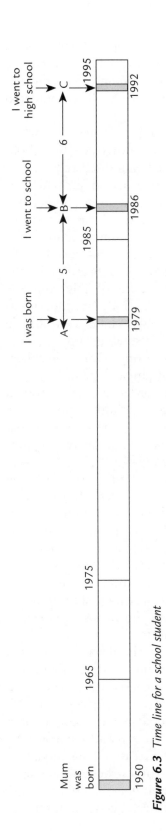

Figure 6.3 Time line for a school student

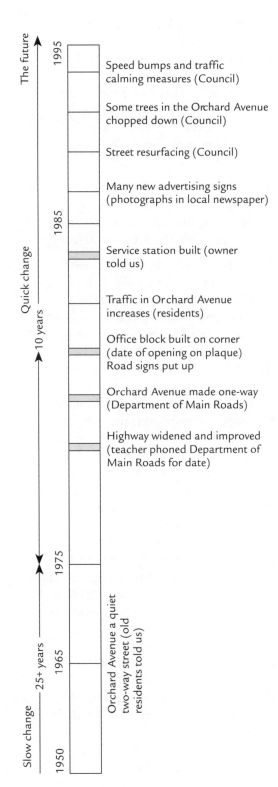

Figure 6.4 Time line for Orchard Avenue

have always been there? How do you know this?

(d) When did advertising signs begin to appear?

(e) To what events can we give exact dates? What other events happened over a period of time?

(f) Do you think Orchard Avenue is changing quickly? Why?

11. *Making decisions in small-group discussions* Obtaining a range of possible solutions and devising criteria to guide the decision making.

Comment This section suggests a possible way of concluding the unit on Orchard Avenue. There may well be some doubt among teachers about including decision making in this unit for school students. A rationale for decision making as a legitimate activity in school classes is elaborated in the early part of this chapter. Students at work on the Orchard Avenue unit might be moved by the question at the end of Myrtle Tree's letter. They might feel that they should come to some conclusion at the end of their study to make it really meaningful. Towards the end of the unit, students are likely to have:

(a) become reasonably well informed about the matter of visual pollution in Orchard Avenue, both through secondary sources (school libraries, other persons) and primary sources;

(b) reviewed the opinions of various interested parties; and

(c) considered the values held by themselves and others toward the matter.

Thus, students are well placed to participate in small-group discussions. Teachers who organise discussions among such groups of students in their classes probably realise the potential for learning offered by this learning experience. This potential includes:

(a) intellectual stimulation when peers are knowledgeable about the topic being discussed;

(b) cooperative learning, which is fostered in a non-competitive environment, so the experience of failure is minimised; and

(c) the development of social skills, refinement of expression in the give and take of talk and the accommodation of individual differences, which can all be fostered in small groups.

Organising group work Teachers should organise group work carefully in order to avoid pooled ignorance and desultory talk in the groups. The following steps make up one approach to effective organisation of group work:

(i) Teachers should stimulate the interest of students in the topics to be discussed. Different topics should be assigned to or devised by each group. The topics may arise from the experience of students or from current affairs/current learning, and may be posed in the forms of question or hypothesis.

(ii) Teachers should help students acquire information about the topic. This is easy when the small-group discussion is embedded in an ongoing topic in the society and environment subject that they are studying.

(iii) The topics/themes/questions emerge and are highlighted by the teacher in classroom talk.

(iv) Groups are formed. They may be semi-permanent groups meeting from time to time in the class. Membership of groups may be decided by teachers mindful of student preferences, but ensuring balance and diversity among members. The optimum number of students in a group is 3 to 5, so that all students are readily involved in the activity and all can experience such roles as group leader, discussion recorder and reporter over the school year.

(v) The discussions and preparation of reports take place in small groups regularly visited by the teacher who encourages and facilitates.

(vi) Reports are presented to the class at large and responses are invited.

(vii) The work of all groups in the class is synthesised by the teacher, who also decides what record of the groups' studies should be kept by all students.

Student discussions and decisions
Students in one group suggested some possible solutions. These included:

Tom: The local council should just tear all the signs down.

Melissa: As long as they're kept freshly painted and tidy, the signs should be allowed there.

Suek Yin: Why not move the residents of Orchard Avenue who object to a noisy neighbourhood? There's no way of stopping progress.

Lauren: The council should limit the size of signs and the height of the posts they stand on and remove all neon lights so that the signs are not a nuisance at night.

Jan: We should be like that group of people who deliberately mess up signs by painting over them.

Students realise during discussion that it would be difficult to arrive at some reasonable decision unless it was guided by agreed principles. The following criteria could emerge from the debate in the group:

(a) The solution should be reasonable. (At first students were enthusiastic about this criterion but they quickly realised that the word 'reasonable' meant different things to different people.)

(b) The cost of making the changes should be limited to what the local council could afford.

(c) The solution should attempt to respect each of the main viewpoints.

(d) Public signs should be consistent with the type of neighbourhood. Only traffic and local information signs should in future be allowed in streets like Orchard Avenue.

Skills used during the course of such small-group discussions include:

- social skills (e.g. speaking in turn, listening to other points of view);
- logical thinking skills (e.g. avoiding *non sequiturs*); and
- making the final decision (e.g. by voting).

Presentation and action The final presentation may be made in the form of a short written report including:

(a) why we studied this topic;

(b) what we found out;

(c) a map, a time line, some quotations from people interviewed, photographs of Orchard Avenue; and

(d) the decision we came to and why.

Skills used in the presentation include:

• preparation of a clear written statement;

• map and graph drawing; and

• communication with people in and outside the classroom.

Finally, students might decide to send their report to the local council, and lobby members of council to support their submission.

Comments on the use of skills in the Orchard Avenue unit

The unit illustrates the implementation of the two themes of this chapter. Skills are learned to be used and they are well learned when used for a purpose. The skills involved in the Orchard Avenue unit are practicable in that they do not demand very many or difficult to obtain resources. Certainly, the unit does suggest some time outside school and some communication with persons in the local community. Sometimes work outside school is seen to be difficult to fit into the school organisation. However, it is eminently defensible in any society and environment course because it enhances both contacts between school and community and also the reality of learning. The short periods of time needed outside school (a half-day or three consecutive periods) are not normally difficult to organise either in primary or secondary schools.

The purpose of encouraging some interest by the local council or shopkeepers in the work done by the students is to infuse a service learning quality into the study. Service learning takes place when people learn as they provide a service for someone else who genuinely wants that service provided. Students put into a service learning situation generally show increased motivation and purposefulness.

The Orchard Avenue unit offers varied opportunities for students to learn and also enables them at the same time to take some appropriate and reasonable action based on their learning. This should contribute to the social relevance of the study.

■ Concluding Comments

The terms 'skills' and 'competencies' are used for a wide range of human activities including those associated with the acquisition and application of knowledge (both general and vocational), those associated with feelings and those associated with manipulation or dexterity. All are used by students of society and environment, so teaching skills becomes meaningful when guided by ideas in the two themes of this chapter. In essence, the themes are that skills are taught to be used and that skills are learned best when they are needed.

Many of the decisions teachers have to make about skills depend on the characteristics of the particular students in their classes, including such characteristics as ability, experience and zest for learning. Teachers' knowledge of their students will guide their decisions about the range and sequence of the skills they hope their students will develop. The suggestions made in this chapter about teaching skills will be most effective when adapted to the particular needs of a class.

There are also more contentious matters concerning skills which may be decided in the light of school policy and teachers' philosophies of education. For example, some skills (such as making decisions) have significant affective and personal elements. Many teachers will approach teaching for such skills with professional caution because of concern over possible indoctrination of their students and out of respect for the distinction between personal and public issues (see Chapter 7). This example may be extended to consideration of the propriety of having school students engage in socially critical actions as a consequence of their inquiries in studies of society and environment.

Ultimately much of what is learned is included in the curriculum both for primary and for secondary schools to help students make decisions about effective living in Australian and world society.

QUESTIONS AND ACTIVITIES

1. Give examples of skills that students of society and environment might commonly use in their investigations.
2. Discuss ways in which skills complement content knowledge.
3. How did you learn to drive a car? Identify the main steps in your process of learning.
4. When would you introduce skills into your university program of studies of society and environment? Why?
5. What do you regard as the basics of studies of society and environment?
6. Choose one teaching skill in which you are quite proficient. Describe the organising phase you experienced while acquiring this skill.
7. Now assume that you are teaching the skill referred to in question 6.
   * What understanding do your students require?
   * How would you organise their skill development?
   * What practice would you arrange?
8. What are the main questions students should learn to ask if they want to know how to monitor their own progress in acquiring a skill?
9. Refer to some lesson notes you have prepared, for example during practice teaching. Identify:
   * the skills used by school students during the lesson;
   * the teaching skills you used during the lesson; and
   * the ways in which both sets of skills are linked to other aspects of the lesson.
10. Accessing data from the Internet requires particular skills in using a PC.
    * Identify these skills.
    * What procedures would you use to find Web pages about teaching skills as part of studies of society and environment?
    * What do you regard as an effective method for teachers to show school students how to access Internet data?

7
Studying Values and Controversial Issues

Introduction

In terms of teaching studies of society and environment it is impossible for teachers to avoid imparting values in one way or another. The basic question with regard to values is not whether they should be taught but how best to carry out the teaching.

People in many communities are increasingly calling for schools to become active in moral and values education.

'In recent times, a stridency has developed because of the increasing lack of civic values exhibited by young and old alike' (Levitt and Longstreet, 1993: 142). Mass media frequently report acts of inhumanity, crime, irresponsibility of public figures and behaviour consistent with the Biblical 'seven deadly sins'. Calls for moral education and the inculcation of values may in part be a response to these ills affecting our society. Certainly some of the calls are for a more positive delineation of 'good' living than

offered by the attempts of value neutrality and clarification without comment on their ethical worth.

The identification of widely acceptable values is complex in multicultural societies, but those supporting human rights are widely endorsed. They are becoming manifest in school curricula through the contemporary emphasis on civic education and on teaching and learning about issues, particularly in social education subjects such as studies of society and environment.

Issues emerge when people have different views on some matter and the views are not only opposed but supported by reasoned arguments. The essence of issues is debate or controversy.

The issues are part of daily living in Australian and New Zealand societies. They may affect the lives of many people or they may be personal to individuals; some are long standing while others are quickly resolved. Some examples of issues are:

- Should private ownership of automatic firearms be banned in the interests of public safety?
- What actions should Australia and New Zealand take to help reduce conflict in the Balkans?
- How can crimes of violence against persons be curbed?
- Should Aboriginal land rights take precedence over mineral development in northern Australia?
- How ought people to be treated and how should disputes between people be resolved (Wright, 1993: 149)?
- Should Australia and New Zealand become republics?
- What overall system of taxation is fairest for Australian society or New Zealand society?
- What is the 'fair treatment' of boat people refugees to Australia?
- Should I study this chapter or go to the beach/snowfields today?

These questions/assertions provoke contrary opinions or controversy. They are issues because there is no unanimous opinion on consequences or courses of action they present. Notice that the word *should* is often used in the expression of an issue. This indicates that issues often require moral and ethical decisions. Stevens (1996: 155) regards moral decisions as those arising out of 'rightness or wrongness based on what a community believes to be good or right in conduct or character', while ethical decisions arise from 'more universal standards and

codes or moral principles'. The central ethical question is: What should I (or we) do? Ethical questions involve attitudes and values.

Opposed values are at the heart of the controversy inherent in issues. The first eight examples are of public issues of concern to many people, while the last is an example of a personal issue.

Mounting concerns about public morality and civic literacy and the need to work towards the resolution of issues have stimulated moves toward citizenship education in Australia in recent years (see Chapter 14). Civics education encompassing 'the multiple ways in which citizens are encouraged to pursue their roles in democratic society' (Kennedy, 1997a: vii) is clearly inseparable from values. For example, for more than the first half of the twentieth century, citizenship in Australia was not for all, was focused on Christianity, the English language and capitalism (Musgrave, 1994)—premises clearly indicating values underlying Australian citizenship at the time.

The thrust of civics education is to highlight to students not only what Australians share collectively, including their values, but also the importance of protecting the interests of individuals. The rights of individuals are balanced by their responsibilities and by the collective rights of groups. Translating these ideas into educational practice leads to recognition of multiple viewpoints, to controversy and to the emergence of issues in which, as usual, the contrary views rest on opposed values.

The development of citizenship education in Australia was catalysed by the *Whereas the People* report by the Civics Expert Group in 1994. Issues emerging as citizenship education programs formulated include: What constitutes appropriate curricular expression of citizenship education? How should we educate about Australia's emerging republicanism? What are effective approaches to values-based education as issues are discussed in schools? Current studies of society and environment developments in Australian states incorporate aspects of citizenship education and the study of values in school curricula.

Values play a part in studies of society and environment in three important ways (Australian Education Council, 1994: 5):

1. values are an object of study;
2. values influence what is selected for study;
3. certain values are the result of study.

Four clusters of values are regarded as significant in studies of society and environment, notably:

1. *democratic process:* 'The key value of democratic process is based on a belief in the integrity and rights of all people, and promotes ideals of equal participation and access for individuals and groups' (Queensland School Curriculum Council, 1999: 6);
2. *social justice*, which includes concern for the welfare, rights and dignity of all, empathy with people from different cultures, and fairness;
3. *ecological and economic sustainability:* 'A sustainable environment is one in which the natural environment, economic development and social life are seen as mutually dependent—and the interaction between them contributes to the sustainability and enhancement of the quality of people's lives and the natural environment' (Fien, 1996: 2.1);
4. *peace* 'is based on the belief that to promote life is to promote positive relations with others and with the environment' (Queensland School Curriculum Council, 1998: 6).

Now let's consider the nature of values and ways of working with them in class, as a prelude to our study of issues.

■ Values and Attitudes

Values and attitudes relate to affect—the feeling component of human behaviour—but they are not wholly separate from thinking. Values are more stable guides to our behaviour and decisions than are attitudes, which are predispositions to reacting in a particular way to some stimulus.

'The act of valuing places an estimate of worth or priority on some object, feeling or idea' (Hill, 1994: 264). Expression of opinion, attitude, interest, appreciation and empathy may well contribute to the process of value formation and to the use of values in establishing priorities. All of these are expressed by people as they debate issues, and decisions reflect the priority given to certain values.

Values are reasonably enduring throughout a person's lifetime and are formed under the influence of parents, knowledge, experience and peers. However, they may be changed. Rational analysis can change values; for example, a person might be influenced by the respective arguments of feminists and right-to-life campaigners in adopting a viewpoint about abortion. Traumatic experiences can also change a person's values. Some people adopt a new lifestyle after recovering from a severe heart attack. They exchange stressful, busy and economically profitable activity for a way of life less likely to produce burnout. Such a change indicates a shift in values from a premium on success and power to cherishing life itself with good health.

The values of individuals are rarely displayed consistently in all their actions. Indeed, it may be suggested that values are relative (not held absolutely) and vary with the situations in which people find themselves. Nevertheless, values are more highly esteemed and less flexible than attitudes. Our attitudes sometimes impel us to seek out or to avoid things; for example, an individual may prefer a red car to a yellow one of the same model. The cars' mechanical performances are identical but there is a preference for the red colour. Indeed, people's reactions to many things are coloured by attitudes. Knowing that attitudes affect behaviour is important to anyone designing an educational program, including schooling (Campbell, 2000). Knowing about ourselves is also crucial in education. This is a major reason for including analysis of and reflection on our own and others' attitudes in school programs. Attitudes are often held towards self, society and environment and are arguably proper inclusions in social studies in schools.

Everyone has values, for several reasons:

- things appeal to our taste through our senses, for example paintings, clothing style, food and wine;
- things are valued because of their monetary worth, for example sculpture, land, diamonds;
- qualities affecting lifestyles affect values, for example freedom, peace, excitement;
- ways of dealing with other people affect values, for example compassion, equity, reliability.

These examples make it clear that we might reasonably regard values as criteria which we use in making judgments about goodness, beauty and truth.

Clues about the values held by people are provided by their words and actions. Shakespeare wrote that action is eloquence, while modern educationists regard action as an indicator of commitment. Consider these examples:

- Restricting TV violence and sex (e.g. by installing V-chips) during children's viewing hours suggests that the community values the protection of children from these influences. It also reflects moral values proclaimed by the community and its decision makers.
- 'Cheating is forbidden in the examination room.' Such a rule reflects ideas about equity and fair play. It may also provide a commentary on the relations between examiners and examinees.

Activity
Take a piece of paper and rule three columns, headed respectively: 1 Value; 2 My words; 3 My actions. List the following values (or actions reflecting values) in column 1: personal freedom, responsibility, street violence, proclaiming beaches for nude bathers, euthanasia, the 'Buy Australian-made' campaign. Record your comment on each in column 2. Describe any action you have taken in relation to this value in column 3. What does the range of your responses tell you about the values you cherish? Are you entirely consistent in exhibiting these values in your daily life? Why or why not?

■ Values Education

Education as an intentional process is based on the assumption that what is taught and learned is deemed worthwhile by those responsible for curriculum decisions. Carbone (1991: 290) stressed that 'Since teachers cannot avoid imparting values in one way or another in the normal course of their activities as teachers, moral education in some sense is unavoidable. Thus, the basic question is not whether, but how it should be carried on.'

Values education is particularly important in studies of society and environment because of its central focus on individuals and groups of people and on the decisions that affect the quality of human life and environments.

Teaching involving values: some guiding principles

Teachers have to make crucial decisions about values education as they seek to answer the question 'How can I implement effectively the aims of my teaching (of a value-laden study)?'. Several principles may be used to inform the decisions. They are:

- the degree of complexity and/or abstraction of values and issues should be related to the needs and abilities of the students;
- using specific examples and those relating to the lived experience of the students maximises comprehension and interest;
- students should be actively involved in the learning process; and
- values are difficult to study without a context and this may admirably be provided by the study of issues in which the values are embedded.

We turn next to the range of teaching strategies which may be used in the process of values education.

■ Teaching Strategies

Since the 1970s several strategies for teaching values have been proposed, implemented in some schools and have been subject to critical review. They are summarised in Table 7.1. Some of the limitations of these strategies have become increasingly apparent as multicultural development has occurred in Australian and New Zealand populations (see also Chapter 15). Hill (1994: 58) proposes 'critical affiliation' as an approach to recognising 'the rights, needs and contributions of all groups in the present cultural mix'. The central focus is on the 'empowerment of the social and political self, resulting in a person critically loyal to the democratic society' with commitment to both private and common good. Classroom activities contributing to the achievement of

this include: helping students become aware of and knowledgeable about values through discussion; analysis of ways in which values are communicated through speaking, writing and actions; critique of values underpinning social institutions and as exhibited by public figures; student representation on school councils; and action to sustain and enhance human rights and environmental quality.

Moves for the restoration of strategies for positive teaching about values are illustrated by the proposal of Ryan (1986) who suggests value formation guided by:

- example, provided by teachers acting as role models;
- explanation, in which the rationale supporting lived values is carefully analysed;
- exhortation, that is, by preaching and inculcation led by teachers;
- environment, or a classroom milieu framed by the moral principles adopted in the school; and
- experience, that gives the students opportunity to put values into action.

Strategies that have been tried since the seventies are summarised in Table 7.1.

Inculcation

Teachers universally engage in inculcation, either intentionally or unintentionally, as they provide models which their students may emulate. Inculcation occurs when teachers (seek to) instil values usually deemed desirable by society; for example, by habitually treating students fairly they provide a model of equity and create the impression that they value it; by arriving in class on time regularly, they indicate their approval of punctuality.

Inculcation is differentiated from indoctrination in that the latter is much more coercive. While indoctrination involves systematic and sustained efforts to implant

Table 7.1 *A range of procedures for teaching and learning about values*

Approaches	Purposes	Methods
Inculcation	· Teachers seek to instil chosen values in students · To change student values so they more nearly reflect socially accepted, substantive values	· Providing role models; reinforcement; praising; chastising; selecting alternatives; providing incomplete or biased data; gaming and simulation; role playing
Moral growth	· To help students develop more complex approaches to moral reasoning · To encourage students to talk about their value-based decisions, not only to share with others, but to encourage growth in their own moral reasoning	· Moral dilemma activities e.g. discussion in small groups, carefully structured by teachers · Making ethical decisions. Structured by teachers. Ideas, motives, reasons are tested against evidence and precedents
Values analysis and reflection	· To show students how to think logically about value-based questions · To help students use systematic analysis in order to refine their values	· Thoughtful discussion structured by teachers. Ideas, motives, reasons are tested against evidence and precedents
Clarification of values	· To encourage and enable students to know their own values and those of their classmates	· Values clarification activities; simulation; gaming; acting roles
Service learning involving direct experience	· To provide students with opportunities to learn by doing things for others who benefit from the services · To encourage students to view themselves as members of a community or society	· Service activities at school and in the community (see text). Organising groups and relating to others

a particular viewpoint (perhaps without a supporting reason), inculcation is usually associated with information about viewpoints and the learner has a choice of accepting or rejecting the offered viewpoint.

Inculcation is not without its critics. The title of Rich's (1991) article focuses on one of the conflicts in moral education, 'Teaching Principles or Virtues?'. *Principles* suggest guidelines helping students make decisions about their moral behaviour, while *virtues* suggest the kinds of good behaviour to be inculcated. Inculcation is a form of values transmission which faces particular problems in multicultural societies. Such societies are dynamic in that values are frequently challenged and reconsidered, so that mere transmission has inherent obsolescence sometimes leading to the charge that schools lag the society at large. How would you resolve this issue?

Furthermore, inculcation needs to be complemented by moral reasoning.

Moral growth through reasoning

This approach is based on psychological theories that humans can and do grow morally, and that this growth can be stimulated by teachers. People do not all grow morally in a uniform way, though stages in moral growth have been suggested (Kohlberg, 1975).

The teaching strategy for moral growth is often based on presenting a moral dilemma. For example, should destitute parents steal costly, life-saving medicine for their critically ill child after conventional ways of obtaining the medicine have failed? Students are encouraged to probe this moral problem and associated issues, and asked to justify the choice they would make.

One of the problems with this approach is that it is hard to create appropriate dilemmas. Taken out of cultural context, the dilemma stories can become morally dubious and have little educational value (Kirman, 1991: 33–34). Stevens (1996: 156) suggests that moral dilemmas can be operationalised through:

- the use of literature, especially drama, and
- court cases,

both associated with active class discussion of the dilemma. These settings facilitate the adoption of the following as guiding values:

- respect for persons;
- beneficence (seeking to keep people from harm and injustice); and
- justice (what is fair and deserved).

When teachers show their students how to engage in moral reasoning applied to everyday life, teachers' work can be considered to be moral action based on

reflection. Otherwise it remains largely unproblematic and uncritical inculcation.

Values analysis

Values analysis may proceed in class when teachers help students think clearly about values by identifying one at a time the components of a viewpoint toward an issue. The process of analysing values is guided by logic and has much in common with reflective thinking. So the process involves:

- identifying and clarifying one's value position on an issue (it could be any issue, for example those noted in the introduction to this chapter);
- assembling and organising relevant information;
- testing the truth of the assembled information;
- clarifying its relevance;
- arriving at a tentative values position;
- testing the value principle. This may be done with a universal consequences test. Such a test requires that we envisage the results if everyone in such a situation were to act according to the value being tested. Then we should decide whether we can accept these consequences (Superka *et al.*, 1976: 55–59).

Values analysis has the merit of focusing on substantive knowledge as a vehicle for the values. Soley (1996: 10) stresses how important it is to have knowledge as a basis for learning 'for it is useless . . . to learn how to think unless there is something important to think about'.

Nevertheless, moral reasoning, a cognitive process, should not be overemphasised at the expense of affect, such as caring (Kohn, 1997: 435).

Values clarification

Values clarification is achieved by participation in practical activities such as those reported in Simon (1972), in the Focus series (Braithwaite *et al.*, 1973) and in SEMP material (Curriculum Development Centre, 1977, *Teachers' Handbook and Workshop Leader's Handbook*) and Banks and Clegg (1990). The practical activities are aimed at enabling students to become more keenly aware of their priorities, that is, at clarifying their feelings towards a person/event/issue as part of proceeding with the study. For this reason it is contended that the usefulness of values clarification is greater when it is associated with some study rather than undertaken *in vacuo*. Adverse assessments of values clarification have been sustained for some time now (Kaplan, 1990: 228; Kohn, 1997: 435). Those seeking restoration of positive moral values object to the clarification view that all values are equally important and that students can be left to realise their own values. Values clarification understates the importance of power and political decision making as underlying causes of issues in society. Another weakness is that the outcome of clarification exercises is uncertain; for example, an exercise centred on racial hatred may have the (presumably unintended) outcome of strengthening the hatred.

Some teachers using values clarification seek, with difficulty, to remain neutral in classroom discussions by offering comparable respect to student expressions of opposed values. In doing so, teachers, fail to discriminate between the ethical substance of the various value stances. Value neutrality is 'an oxymoronic phrase' (Hamberger, 1997: 301).

Rank ordering is sometimes used as a practical activity to help students clarify their values. The teacher tells students that they will be asked to make choices which they must consider very carefully. The teacher then places on the board three or four words or statements. The students are asked to rank

the items in terms of their value preferences from most desirable to least desirable. Some examples are given in Box 7.1.

Another application of the technique is to consider a *value issue*. Students, or the teacher, may identify the extreme viewpoints about it. Each student may then mark his or her position on the line. Discussion may ensue as each student explains what his or her position means (see Box 7.2).

The values grid (Figure 7.1) is also used to help students clarify values. It serves to highlight the extent of personal commitment to an issue. Participants are asked to put check marks in whichever of the seven columns apply to themselves. A key to the numbers is provided beneath the table.

The seven numbers heading the columns on the right-hand side of the grid in Figure 7.1 represent the following seven questions:

1. Are you *proud* of (do you prize or cherish) your position?
2. Have you *publicly affirmed* your position?
3. Have you chosen your position from *alternatives*?
4. Have you chosen your position after

Box 7.1 *Ranking items in terms of value preferences*

A If you could improve your community, would you make it:

———————— more peaceful and law abiding?
———————— more multicultural?
———————— with wider individual rights?

B The rural council has purchased the two vacant lots adjacent to your school. How would you like to see the land used?

———————— housing for teachers
———————— a school tuck shop
———————— a playing field for use by the school

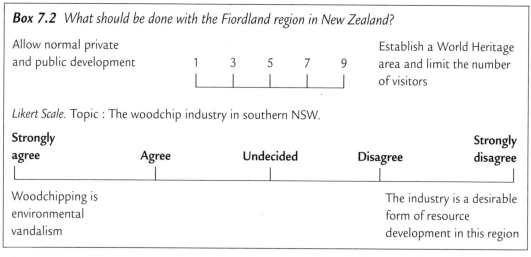

Box 7.2 *What should be done with the Fiordland region in New Zealand?*

Allow normal private and public development	1 3 5 7 9	Establish a World Heritage area and limit the number of visitors

Likert Scale. Topic : The woodchip industry in southern NSW.

Strongly agree	Agree	Undecided	Disagree	Strongly disagree

Woodchipping is environmental vandalism

The industry is a desirable form of resource development in this region

Issue	1	2	3	4	5	6	7
Urban crime							
Mining in national parks, e.g. uranium, beach sand minerals							
Promiscuity							

Figure 7.1 *Values grid*

thoughtful consideration of the pros and cons and consequences?

5. Have you chosen your position *freely*?
6. Have you *acted* on or done anything about your beliefs?
7. Have you acted with *repetition*, pattern or consistency on this issue?

What does the profile show about your commitment to these issues?

Aesthetic association

Techniques for developing feeling for landscapes through associating the landscape with some beliefs or values rely heavily on values clarification (see Figure 7.2).

Service learning

Commitment to a value position and to the resolution of an issue can be made evident in

action. What actions can school students take, learning as they do most often in vicarious ways? Indeed this vicarious quality of school learning has been both condemned for its lack of reality and also praised for the protection it affords immature students from the world outside the school.

Some educators (Graham, 1975; Ball and Ball, 1973) propose action or service learning as a way of helping students grow morally and also as socially responsible action that can be undertaken by students. Service learning occurs when students learn in the course of doing something for someone who really wants the service they are providing. An example follows.

The senior geography class was engaged in settlement studies and had undertaken several

Scales

1	Graceful	☐	☐	☐	☐	☐	☐	☐	Awkward
2	Wild	☐	☐	☐	☐	☐	☐	☐	Tame
3	Boring	☐	☐	☐	☐	☐	☐	☐	Exciting
4	Unique	☐	☐	☐	☐	☐	☐	☐	Common-place
5	Full	☐	☐	☐	☐	☐	☐	☐	Empty
6	Disturbing	☐	☐	☐	☐	☐	☐	☐	Restful
7	Colourful	☐	☐	☐	☐	☐	☐	☐	Drab
8	Beautiful	☐	☐	☐	☐	☐	☐	☐	Ugly
9	Weak	☐	☐	☐	☐	☐	☐	☐	Powerful
10	Active	☐	☐	☐	☐	☐	☐	☐	Passive
11	Artificial	☐	☐	☐	☐	☐	☐	☐	Natural
12	Hushed	☐	☐	☐	☐	☐	☐	☐	Loud
13	Good	☐	☐	☐	☐	☐	☐	☐	Bad
14	Primitive	☐	☐	☐	☐	☐	☐	☐	Civilised
15	Delicate	☐	☐	☐	☐	☐	☐	☐	Rugged
16	Alive	☐	☐	☐	☐	☐	☐	☐	Dead
17	Turbulent	☐	☐	☐	☐	☐	☐	☐	Tranquil
18	Barren	☐	☐	☐	☐	☐	☐	☐	Fertile
19	Simple	☐	☐	☐	☐	☐	☐	☐	Complex
20	Cold	☐	☐	☐	☐	☐	☐	☐	Warm

How much do you like or dislike this scene?

21	Like it very much	☐	☐	☐	☐	☐	☐	☐	Dislike it very much

Tick your response for the scene depicted in this slide.

Figure 7.2 *Semantic differential (for a chosen landscape, represented on a poster or photographic slide)*

field trips to a dairy-farming area in a coastal valley. One of the field studies centred on flows of commodities, people and services between the farms and the towns in the valley. The collection points at farms for milk carried by road tanker to a co-operative factory were plotted on a map as part of a pre-field practical exercise. Economic aspects of milk production were discussed during the course of a subsequent visit to the co-operative factory. During the visit, one of the young geographers who had plotted the map of pick-up points, remarked that his group thought that costs of collection could be reduced if the tanker took an alternative route. The factory manager's reply was reasonably enthusiastic, 'Show us a better route and we'll use it'.

This was something of a challenge to the pupils. They spent a weekend of their own time measuring distances, checking road surfaces and grades of hill climbs and timing the runs between various points. Back home, the pupils plotted and replotted trips always attempting to reduce the overall distance of the round trip and the distances to be travelled uphill on poor road surfaces when the tanker was heavily loaded. Eventually they devised a route that compared favourably with the presently used journey. It was sent to the co-op manager who tried it, found it to be good and had it adopted.

The geography pupils had learned a great deal about linear distance, and other things, like community service, in the course of an activity that engaged them in doing something that someone else really wanted done. (Bartlett and Cox, 1982: 193)

■ Controversial Issues

Issues can arise from events, results or consequences. Essentially they are unresolved. Some examples of issues are:

- Union membership should be compulsory for all workers.

- Is the Big Bang theory an accurate explanation of the origin of the universe?
- Does violence on television have a harmful effect on viewers, especially children?

Most issues are characterised by:

- divisions of opinion between groups in the society and in the school over the issue or the way of resolving it; for example, ethnic conflict in southeastern Europe;
- division of opinion resting on conflicting value stances toward the issue; for example, sustainable environments and sustainable development;
- conflict resulting from the use of power in its various forms (legislation, finance, unions of workers, military forces) to the advantage of some groups at the expense of others; for example, the right to strike of workers in public utilities;
- being contemporary, and this contributes to their lack of resolution.

Let's reflect on these ways of characterising issues. Mere division of opinion is necessary but insufficient to identify controversiality because some divided opinions (e.g. 'I think it is 10 kilometres from A to B.'; 'No, it is only seven.') can easily be resolved by reference to a generally agreed authority. So, the essence of issues is that controversy results from the different views which are both opposed and reasonable. Note the following:

- 'A standard tax on goods and services bought by consumers will benefit most Australians.' This is controversial because there really is insufficient evidence at the present time to decide, and opinions differ.
- 'The wood chip industry in Tasmania should be expanded.' This is controversial because opponents and proponents place different stress on otherwise agreed criteria that can be derived from environmental protection or from economic development.

- 'Striking workers in public utilities should be sacked.' This is controversial because it is hard to get consensus on which criteria should be used to help solve the issue.
- 'We should strive to achieve conditions fostering individual opportunity and welfare rather than the collective welfare of people in the community.' This is controversial because the implied viewpoints are supported by irreconcilable ideologies.

It is issues such as these that are discussed in this chapter. Examples of matters which have controversial aspects in many societies, including Australia and New Zealand, are:

- relations between ethnic groups;
- forms of discrimination on the basis of sex or age;
- operations of multinational companies;
- exploitation of natural resources;
- birth control and euthanasia;
- urban sprawl; and
- management of water in farming areas.

Many others could be cited. Sometimes it is specific instances of these issues that are controversial. For example, the economic use of national resources is not universally controversial, but mining uranium in Kakadu, irrigation in salt-affected areas, the allegedly premature damming of the Clutha River gorge near Cromwell, New Zealand, and the flooding of the Franklin River in Tasmania all became controversial when groups in the community argued from opposing premises (often value positions) about the merits of one or another course of action. Humanitarian ethics and ecological distinctiveness are very important to protagonists of some viewpoints in relation to these specific issues.

What might be at issue in a society tends to change as time passes. This variability results from several factors. Political sensitivity, new technology, mass media of communication and social reforms can raise or resolve matters at issue in society. They are summarised and exemplified in Table 7.2.

The nature and examples of issues presented in this section illuminate their importance in the lives of individuals and societies. This importance is a compelling case for their inclusion in social and environmental education. The National Council for the Social Studies (NCSS) in the USA (1991: 13–15)

Protesters resort to a street demonstration

Table 7.2 *Factors affecting the emergence and resolution of issues*

Factors	Examples
1. Sensitivity to some issues varies between political parties. A change in the government may raise or resolve an issue.	Conservative political parties in Australia tend to favour vigorous utilisation of natural resources and find themselves in conflict with conservation groups.
2. Changes in technology increase the impact of human activity, for example on environments and lifestyles.	Very large earth-moving machines have enabled the economic development of open-cut mining and have raised the issue of environmental degradation; irrigation schemes have caused serious problems of soil salinity in parts of the Murray River basin.
3. Modern mass media of communication have affected the global diffusion of information and the general level of public awareness.	Television satellites have enabled many people in different parts of the world to see action and share ideas almost instantly. Examples are: 'video wars' in Iraq and the Balkan Peninsula; and the near-global use of the Internet.
4. Social reforms produce new issues, particularly when attention is drawn to forms of structural violence which discriminate against groups of people in society.	The women's movement has drawn attention to sexist implications in some language structures, and in some practices in employment. The land rights movement has focused attention on indigenous peoples.

stated that the study of controversial issues should develop in students the wish 'to make intelligent choices from alternatives'; willingness to value differing viewpoints, skills in evaluating information, and readiness to participate in democratic decision making. These desirable outcomes apply also in Australia and New Zealand.

The National Council's support for teaching issues is extended in their 1996 *Handbook*, and by Simpson (1996) and Soley (1996). Simpson (1996: 5) writes 'Countries where controversial issues are swept under the carpet, or where individuals who bring such issues to the fore are regularly subjected to violence, cannot establish healthy and stable democracies'. Soley (1996: 9) extends the case in the following way: 'The *raison d'être* for the social studies is to teach students the kind of

substantive knowledge that will promote a deeper understanding of their social world. This means instilling the capacities to make thoughtful decisions and judgments . . .'. The NCSS noted: 'It is essential that schools and communities foster a reasoned commitment to founding principles and values that bind us together as a people' (1997: 225).

■ Problems Associated with Teaching Involving Values and Issues

Support for the inclusion of curricular experience of values and issues is not unqualified.' Limitations become apparent usually when teaching involves a particularly sensitive instance of a generally tolerated issue (e.g. the context of some schools may make it hard to present multiple viewpoints about Aboriginal or Maori land rights). Several things limit the possibility of teaching issues and undertaking valuing activities. These include:

1. *Beliefs about the readiness of students to learn about particular issues* Readiness may depend on possession of knowledge and on the emotional maturity of students. It is likely in many cases that these will affect the treatment rather than a teach/not teach decision in any particular year level of schooling.
2. *Formal directives from employing authorities* These may result from religious beliefs, from the political ideology of a government or from the actions of a government influenced by electoral considerations or by lobby groups.
3. *Covert influences* These include the views of a school's administrative staff, the views of colleagues and the many standards in the community which contribute to lack of consensus and polarisation of opinion.
4. *The expertise of teachers* Teachers sometimes make disclaimers about their being insufficiently informed to work with an issue in class. This appears to be a specious argument because most have the skill to find out (if not the time). A more serious objection lies in the need for teachers to adopt roles that are somewhat different from those they use in didactic settings. The new roles may not relate comfortably with their teaching style. The teacher's stance is examined later in the chapter.
5. *Issue-specific factors* Issues of the present are necessarily unresolved. Students are likely to gain views about them from sources outside school (such as the media and parents) and these views are seldom uniform. Mining and export of uranium may, for example, be considered against

such divergent criteria as maximum trade gain, world security and pollution hazards. Measures against these criteria are not readily verified. This example shows the importance of proceeding carefully, devising learning experiences compatible with the particular problem and with the students, rather than excluding controversial issues and attendant values from the teaching program.
6. *Lobby activity by groups in the community* Some groups vigorously pursue political activity aimed at having their viewpoint adopted by the community at large. Examples of such groups include the gun lobby and animal liberationists.

These difficulties notwithstanding, it is both difficult and educationally unsound to disdain valuing and issues in class because of being influenced in any of the following ways:

1. There are unresolved questions debated in all subjects. It is bad curricular practice to divest any subject of its controversial elements because such a practice denies part of the structure of the subject and its problems to learners.
2. Omitting controversial elements limits students' opportunities of trying ways of testing truth commonly used with that subject.
3. The fact that many formerly controversial ideas (e.g. 'The earth is flat') are no longer so illustrates the progress of human knowledge. School students are not to be denied the insights into human inquiry that may be gained from knowing about the development of human knowledge, that is, knowing that many new ideas are controversial before they are criticised, tested and verified.

Perhaps readers will regard these arguments supporting the inclusion of controversial topics in school lessons as being themselves controversial!

■ Making Decisions about which Issues are Included in Studies of Society and Environment

What issues should be included in studies of society and environment designed for primary and secondary school students? Two criteria may be used to help make these decisions. The first is that some issues are of sufficient significance to the community or nation that they should be taught, at least during the time that they are of public concern (see Chapter 1). The second involves how people react to issues. It can be argued that people need to know about issues to be good citizens. Obviously the word 'good' raises the question of what goodness is in this context. It is likely to include elements of rationality, participation in decision making, morality and being informed if it is being considered in the context of a liberal democracy. Thus the content of some issues may be used to justify their inclusion in school programs.

Controversial issues may arise in classroom discussion in most subjects, especially studies of society and environment, English and science. Explicit provision is made in some syllabuses for discussion of environmental issues (e.g. in the senior geography syllabus in Queensland, in the economics syllabus for Western Australian schools and in the New Zealand Social Studies Syllabus). It is likely that there are regional/state variations in handling issues because of the local operation of various constraints.

Constraints that might affect the selection of issues for study in schools include:

1. Limitations in the knowledge and skills of teachers. The debate on many issues (e.g. those based on economic principles) is enhanced when teachers can infuse specialist knowledge. Skills in classroom management are also important and handling controversial issues often requires roles for teachers other than those associated with recitation.
2. Constraints arising from school, parish or departmental policy. These constraints may arise from religious or political sensitivity and not uncommonly are indirect rather than explicit embargoes. Other constraints arise from the composition and attitudes of people in the class (e.g. the ethnic composition) and parents.
3. Some constraints relate to particular issues at particular times (e.g. issues relating to sex, or issues relating to a war in which the home country is presently engaged).

Another approach to selecting issues for study in class centres on the ways in which people know/reflect/act on issues. Many issues arise and then fade from public prominence (e.g. the Falklands War, the sinking of the Greenpeace vessel *Rainbow Warrior* in Auckland harbour). Their 'life' depends on changes in the cultural context of the community and on the success of efforts to resolve them. Some issues do persist for a long time, for example the problems of Northern Ireland. They persist because of the irreconcilability of the contenders and their values, and because of the serious consequences of the conflicts. However, schools have a responsibility to help students become proficient in approaching the study of issues. This proficiency extends to knowing, reflecting and acting. Each of these three overlapping aspects of learning about issues can be taught and learned. Each requires the development of a range of skills in the learner. A real difficulty with this process approach is that no single process of inquiry is appropriate to the study of all issues. This is because of the importance of the context and the character of the issue, as outlined in the earlier section on constraints.

The different achievements of students, their cultural backgrounds, the ethos of particular classrooms, school rules and the style of the teacher are among the influences which make it impracticable to propose a standard process for the study of controversial issues other than in such general terms as:

* students need a framework of ideas including those derived from ethics about the issue;
* this should be associated with reflection and action; and
* the reflection will include elements of analysis and criticism.

■ Procedures for Teaching and Learning about Values and Issues

There are controversial elements in all school subjects. As teachers, we communicate with our students—words are part of being human, as are the non-verbal gestures and expressions we use. Our patterns of thought are revealed to our students in our words, our approach to the subject and the ways in which we regard our students. It is futile to believe that teachers can sustain neutrality. Our modelling contributes to the inculcation of values in students.

Neutrality as an absolute is unattainable but there *are* degrees of partiality in the position we may adopt on an issue. Teachers, among others, may be committed advocates, be devil's advocates or may welcome ample and varied evidence. Thus, an answer to the question about how controversial issues may be brought into the school curriculum is that they are integral parts of subjects and can be

considered as they arise during the course of studies. The special lesson on controversial issues is to be avoided because it takes the issue out of context.

An example of the way in which controversial issues may be incorporated into lessons is provided in Table 7.3, which presents a summary of a topic that might be taught at primary school level. A series of lessons and activities for students may be based on the topic summary. The learning experiences in which the questions are considered may vary from whole class discussions, small group brainstorming sessions, discussing issues in pairs, and individual reflections.

Teaching procedures
The special circumstances of individual classes and the distinctiveness of particular issues make it undesirable to recommend a standard approach to the study of issues. However, some combination of:

* inculcation
* knowledge
* reflection
* action

will provide an effective approach to studying controversial issues. These four are neither mutually exclusive nor to be used in an invariable sequence (see Figure 7.3).

Inculcation
This is used as a teaching procedure to achieve the purpose of instilling values in students. All of us engage consciously or unconsciously in inculcation. Table 7.4 includes some of the ways by which we inculcate ideas in our students.

Inculcation should be distinguished from indoctrination, which involves the presentation of one viewpoint (derived consistently from an ideology) on all issues

Table 7.3 Topic summary

The election of a school council

Developed from: *Studies of Society and Environment,*
                Queensland draft syllabus, June 1999, Level 3,
                Core learning outcome 3.3 in Systems, Resources and Power strand.
                'SRP 3.3   Students apply the principles of democratic decision making in
                co-operative projects.' (p. 29)

1. The purpose of our school:
   · Should the school program emphasise good citizenship more than good scholarship?

2. Members of the school community; e.g. students, staff, parents, others.

3. The school as a system; how it works:
   · inputs; materials and ideas
   · effort; teaching and learning, administration
   · results; knowledge, skills and values.

4. Decisions that make the system work; e.g. class size, staff allocation, spending the budget.
   · Should high achieving students be drafted into special classes to accelerate their learning?

5. Who makes the decisions? And for whom? Rights and responsibilities of participants.
   · Should students who neglect their school responsibilities be denied the right to vote for
     candidates for school council?

6. Student representation in school government; the supporting case; limitations on student
   power.
   · Should the school principal have the right to veto student resolutions on council?

7. The mechanics of an election; frequency, voting rights of students and staff, preferences,
   counting.

8. The role of council; advisory or policy formulation; relations with the school executive.
   · (Indicates issues that might be woven into this topic.)

considered in a class. Australian parents have little to fear about indoctrination of their offspring *in* schools if only because influences *outside* schools (media, peers and parents themselves) have a more potent influence on the values and attitudes held by young people.

Knowledge

The study of issues requires a base of information and consideration of what is good from which students and teachers may draw during their discussions. The 'How do you feel about . . .?' type of values-clarifying activity is almost pointless unless students have some knowledge of the subject in question. For example, 'How do you feel about the former Soviet Union's withdrawal from Afghanistan?' requires the illumination provided by knowledge of the then political system of the Soviet Union, its foreign policies towards southern Asia, the rightness of military intervention in another country and the geopolitical location, people, culture and history of Afghanistan. Would we necessarily feel the same way about the NATO bombing of Serbia in 1999?

The ways in which students acquire

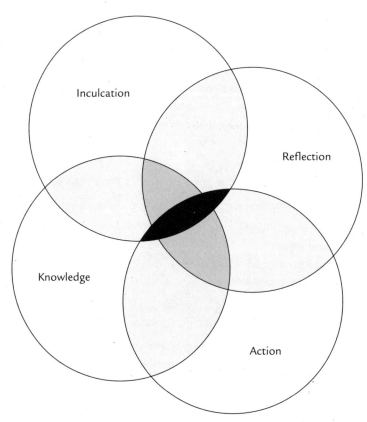

Figure 7.3 *Links between inculcation, knowledge, reflection and action*

Notes: 1. All four activities may initiate or conclude learning about an issue.
        2. Different combinations of the four may occur concurrently.
        3. Any one of the four learning experiences may predominate at a given time.
        4. Inculcation and gaining knowledge often begin before reflection and action.
        5. Ethical matters are often associated with reflection.

Table 7.4 *Forms of inculcation*

Method	Example
1. Modelling	The teacher's work on the chalkboard is invariably neat, shown in coloured chalks and carefully set out.
2. Positive and negative reinforcement	'Excellent work, Mary.' 'I don't like it when you interrupt, John.'
3. Sarcasm and nagging	'You *are* a smart fellow, aren't you, Dimbleby?'
4. Using biased or incomplete data	The story of Florence Nightingale working by the light of her lantern to tend the wounded of both sides is told to demonstrate the humanitarian ethic of modern medical orderlies during combat. In reality, her actions are said to have been rather less altruistic.

knowledge are manifold and need no repetition here (see Killen, 1996). However, it is claimed that the processes of reflection and action are well sustained by students who possess knowledge and extend it while engaging in these processes.

Reflection

The process of reflection done individually or in association with a few others is central in working to resolve issues. Technically, reflection means looking back, even mirroring, but it also means the ways we use our minds to deal with ideas received by sensation or perception. Reflection, in the latter sense, involves persistent and careful consideration of an idea in the light of the tributary ideas or evidence supporting it and ethics framing it. Two considerations emerge:

1. Reflection enables us to recognise the consistency of the set of related ideas. Knowledge both provides data for reflection and may also be the product of reflection.
2. Reflection helps us to become aware of and reconcile the multiple realities with which so many things or events are perceived by different people.

Box 7.3 illustrates one way in which reflection about controversial ideas may be set into a framework of learning experiences.

This class episode makes it clear that people see objects and events in different ways. Teachers need to be aware of this and to make allowances for it in their teaching.

Reflection is a particularly important part of teaching and learning about issues. It may be enhanced by two complementary sets of learning experiences, notably:

1. the acquisition of related knowledge and of skills in thinking carefully about issues;
2. analysing, clarifying and acting on one's own values with a view to promoting a moral approach to living.

Both sets of learning experiences merit some elaboration.

1. The acquisition of related knowledge and skills may be brought about in the following ways:
   (a) Knowing the history of the person or the event. This helps develop understanding of how the present situation acquired its character.
   (b) Making an analysis of the present situation. This can be done by identifying internal and external characteristics of whatever is being studied. It might be a school, taxation, a country—virtually any of the studies of society and environment. Internal characteristics derive directly from the subject being analysed. They may include such things as cost, technological complexity, personnel and political power. The external characteristics come from the setting of the subject and refer to things around it. The analysis contributes to the depth of our understanding.
   (c) Making an inquiry into one instance or example as it takes place, that is, a case study. It is possible to generalise within the case that is studied (perhaps it is a particular farm) but not from it, for example to all farms growing the same crops. Many things make suitable cases for study including:
   - a ship on a trade route;
   - a factory at work;
   - an historic building;
   - a day in the life of the Prime Minister; and
   - commercial activity in the city of Perth.

   These can readily be adapted to students in primary or secondary schools.
   (d) Making statistical analyses of

Box 7.3 *Example: Class activities in lessons about taxation*

Setting the scene	'Many people work a third or more of their typical working day just to pay tax on what they earn.' This can be said in another way if you remember that the tax year runs from 1 July to 30 June: 'We work from 1 July to the end of October or even further into the year just to pay our taxes! But what we earn for the rest of the year is ours to spend.' There are likely to be many reactions to this stimulus in class, including surprise, disbelief and allegations that it is unfair.
Inculcation (perhaps early in the series of lessons or perhaps throughout)	Statements, mainly from the teacher, such as: · 'It's important that we all pay taxes so that the burden is shared by all income earners.' · 'Taxes are necessary so that the government can run the country.' · 'I always pay my taxes.' · 'Tax dodgers are cheats not folk heroes.'
Knowledge	The students are given access to a range of information about taxes; for example: 1. Types of taxes include: property tax, income tax, sales tax, excise, customs duty and licence taxes. (Provide description and examples of each.) 2. The ways in which governments spend tax monies; for example, on the process of government, defence, welfare, health, education and relations with other countries. (Provide recent statistical information about government expenditure in these areas.) 3. Criteria that might be used to help judge what are good taxes include: · fairness; · easily understood by members of the community; · easily collected; · do not discourage people from working; · citizens know about them well in advance; and · do not have harmful effects, for example a heavy tax on milk and vegetables might cause parents to neglect the health of their children. 4. Tax systems in other countries.
Reflection	What follows is a record of part of the discussion in class.

Peter:	My Dad said that pay-as-you-earn taxpayers are slugged harder than most others. That's unfair, so it's okay to dodge tax if you can.
Jean:	You shouldn't be telling what your father says—anyway what he says doesn't matter.
Peter:	Why not?
Teacher:	We should respect everyone's right to have an opinion. But we should also think carefully about it before we agree. Do you remember the criteria we listed for good taxes? Let's say them.
Khoon Yoong:	Easily collected.
Debbie:	They don't discourage work or make you want to move interstate.
Sharifah:	They should be fair.
Teacher:	Yes. But just how would you decide what is a fair tax?
Larry:	Wealthy people pay the most.

Box 7.3 *Example: Class activities in lessons about taxation (continued)*

Lisa:	Pensioners shouldn't pay at all.
Teacher:	Larry and Trish have given us two useful ideas, but we need to think more about both. Do wealthy people pay the most simply because they have a big dollar income or do they pay more because their rate per dollar is high?
Peter:	My Dad says wealthy people have so many lurks that they hardly pay any tax at all.
Piang Chin:	Yes. I read that in the paper too.
Teacher:	Okay. So we need to decide what income can justly be exempted from tax and how the tax laws can be changed so they can't be abused by some people.

In this way, reflection on the theme of tax burdens may develop in class. Progressively more evidence is brought to bear on the theme. Alternative viewpoints are accepted and examined carefully in the light of rational criteria and of expressed preferences. Student values are clarified. The teacher's role is often one of facilitating the debate, that is, a process role. But at times the teacher needs to give information to students. Inculcation may also enter such discussions.

Action   Two possible consequences of reflection in the class discussion are:
1. Students decide that they need to be better informed about taxation and invite a speaker from the Department of Taxation.
2. Students decide to send a letter to the Tax Reform Society seeking information and expressing their views to the society.

---

numerical data in search of regularities and significance.

(e) Applying logical operations in the reasoning processes used during reflection, for example:
- distinguishing fact from opinion;
- recognising statements difficult to prove right or wrong;
- putting items in some sequence; and
- identifying *non sequiturs*.

Some examples of these are provided in Chapter 6.

The review of the class discussion about tax contributes to the conclusion that reflection requires both the development of understanding and also work with values.

2. The second way in which reflection may be enhanced is by critical analysis of values with a view to promoting the moral growth of students. Moral growth is evidenced by an advance to more complex moral reasoning. Kohlberg (1966) developed and validated six stages of moral development based on numerous cross-cultural studies. Simplified examples of these stages are:

(a) A primary school student can be encouraged to move from an instrumental orientation in which the student's needs are satisfied towards a position in which good behaviour is seen to be that which pleases or helps others.

(b) A secondary school student can be encouraged to move from a law-and-order orientation in which good behaviour is seen to be in accord with law and authority or fixed rules towards a position in which good behaviour is seen as being guided by conscientious decisions made in the light of ethical principles such as justice and equality of human rights.

Teaching strategies that may be used to promote moral growth and help students reflect on values are presented under 'Teaching strategies' earlier in this chapter.

Action

The fourth element of teaching and learning about controversial issues is action taken by the students. Taking action indicates commitment and shows that learning about issues is not simply inert, but has made some difference to the lives of the students. This is fostered in part by students acquiring knowledge about issues that they are able to use, by their developing values associated with justice, truth and beauty, and by giving them skills enabling them to contribute well to the improvement of the society in which they live. Action taken by student-citizens whose individual growth has been fostered in the way just described will ultimately contribute to a just society. Their immediate actions are likely to focus on such things as:

- achieving a high level in school learning, especially about environments and communities;
- learning *in* the environment and community outside school, through such means as excursions and field trips;
- undertaking service learning. This can readily become learning *for* the environment and *for* the community, when these are improved as a result of the students' actions.

Critical theorists regard these actions as minimal as they have limited capacity to achieve reform. There have been many proponents of critical reflection and action on social and environmental justice since the publications by Van Manen (1975) and Kemmis *et al.* (1983). They present cogent arguments for schools to develop in students the capacity to recognise injustices by probing underlying meanings. Understanding so gained is the basis of individual or joint political action to secure reform.

Critical reflection and action as applied to issues may develop through the following stages (developed from Fien, 2000):

1. help students to recognise issues arising from social and environmental injustice;
2. encourage and train students to make studies in and about the community;
3. help students to recognise the political aspects of issues and actions taken to resolve them;
4. students analyse values underlying viewpoints on the issue; and
5. participate in action to achieve a sustainable future.

A range of actions may be taken, including the following:

- writing to persons who are able to influence decision making in the community, such as members of Parliament, business leaders, television managers and secretaries of pressure groups, such as the Australian Conservation Foundation;
- making public statements, in the form of letters to the editor, speaking at public meetings and organising petitions;
- fundraising activity for specific causes; and
- joining organisations.

The possibility of actions contrary to contemporary law is not ruled out. Some actions may be morally good but illegal. An example is protesting against the build-up of nuclear arms by trespassing on military installations. It is self-evident that this idea is controversial and likely to be contrary to the policies of educational authorities, such as departments of education.

■ Roles and Activities of Teachers During Issues-based Lessons

Recognition of the importance of the role of teachers during class discussion of controversial issues has been spurred by:

- growing acknowledgment of the right of students to come to their own (informed) decisions about their stance toward issues; and
- the emergence of increasingly multicultural populations in Australia and New Zealand. Population diversity increases the probability of issues arising, particularly as policy toward migrants has shifted from the post-war assimilation to recognition of multicultural communities.

Teachers may well be challenged by cultural diversity, intensity of feeling and the uncertainty yet inevitability of controversy as issues arise in studies of society and environment. In the past, teachers have responded to the challenges in different ways, including preaching a particular viewpoint, and seeking to maintain a position of neutrality (McNeil, 1988: 435).

A balanced stance is sought by Hill (1994) who both advocates the transmission in school classes of values associated with the many cultures of Australians and urges that awareness of the values be critical. Students in such classrooms can affiliate with democracy, being neither submissive nor subversive, but critically reflective. Hill (1981: 334) calls such a stance **committed impartiality**, and writes of it that 'teachers are encouraged both to foster critical analysis and discussion of the grounds of various beliefs and values, and to exhibit their own beliefs as additional data for analysis, providing that their procedures for testing and assessing remain impartial'.

Neighbour (1995) attempted a sustained application of such an approach with a senior class of economics students. His analysis of the experience led him to formulate the following (abridged) guidelines (1995: 374–377) for teachers wishing to handle controversial issues by adopting a committed impartial approach.

Such an approach is reflected in the language, activities and relationships in classrooms.

- Teachers should encourage the classroom use of language which presents ideas without offending persons. Viewpoints, including those of teachers, should be supported by evidence and logical arguments.
- Learning activities should include those which encourage critical thinking by students and engage them in small-group discussions (see suggested teaching activities in Chapter 6).
- Relationships in class should be sufficiently open for students and teach them to express their views without summary dismissal, though the views may be challenged with contrary arguments.

■ Sustaining Kakadu: Perspectives on an Issue

1. The geographical context

Kakadu is distinguished by the diversity of its tropical landscapes and by the varied perspectives of those seeking to chart its future. Kakadu has areas of stunningly beautiful wilderness which led to its establishment as a national park in 1979 and to its inscription on the World Heritage List in 1981 (and extended in 1987). There are hundreds of species of tropical plants, animals and birds and a succession of landscapes from the Arnhem Land plateau to the coast of Van Diemen Gulf of the Arafura Sea.

The tiered landscapes from the plateau to

the gulf provide a series of habitats for life in the area. Northern Arnhem Land is edged by an escarpment slashed by waterfalls in the wet season. Below the scarp there are woodlands with rocky outcrops, many of which have special significance to the Aboriginal inhabitants. In succession the woodlands yield to open forest and it in turn yields to monsoon forest. Then there are paperbark swamps, floodplains and mangrove coasts merging with the sea.

All of these habitats are home to wildlife. The jabiru (black necked stork) and the salt water crocodile have become popular symbols of Kakadu to the many tourist visitors, as also has the introduced Asian water buffalo. The habitats have also been home to indigenous Aboriginal peoples for at least 40 000 years. The complex ecology is matched by a complex geological history which has produced commercially valuable deposits of uranium ore.

Its outstanding landscapes have led to Kakadu becoming a focus of often competing human interests. The major parties include: the Aboriginal peoples, environmentalists, miners, tourists, ecologist, and the government. Their competing but defensible perspectives have led to the emergence of issues, most of them ongoing.

2. Significance

Aboriginal settlement Kakadu is one of the sites of early human settlement in Australia as people entered from the north. The Aboriginal tradition is that spirits swept across the area establishing the characteristic landscapes during the Dreamtime. Aboriginal people attach special significance to many places, the sacred sites, which have spiritual associations. Aboriginal life over thousands of years is recorded in rock art which abounds in Kakadu. Painted in caves and rock overhangs, some of the art has

Ubirr Rock, Kakadu National Park (photograph courtesy of Dal Anderson)

survived a very long time. Collectively, the art is a remarkable record of an ancient culture and is also of considerable significance in the lives of contemporary Aboriginal people.

Mining Uranium deposits were discovered at Ranger, Nabarlek and Koongarra in 1970, and at Jabiluka in 1973. Ranger and Jabiluka are major bodies of high-grade ore. The Commonwealth Government in 1975: (1) agreed to mining at Ranger, (2) gazetted the National Park, and (3) set up an environmental inquiry. An agreement with the Aborigines in 1979 recognised Aboriginal title to traditional lands. Lands within the national park, proclaimed at this time, were leased for 99 years to the Australian National Parks and Wildlife Service. Mining actually began at Ranger in 1981. A temporary mining town was established in the park at Jabiru, and the park was extended to stage 2 in 1984.

World Heritage status The establishment of the World Heritage list of cultural and natural sites of excellence is an international undertaking to protect such sites from the threats posed by underdevelopment and overdevelopment. It was implemented after an international convention in 1972. There are criteria for selection of cultural sites and also for natural sites.

In brief, the cultural monuments and sites should:

- constitute a unique achievement;
- have exercised a considerable significance at a certain period;
- provide evidence of a civilisation that has disappeared;
- illustrate a significant historical period;
- constitute an outstanding example of a traditional way of life;
- be associated with ideas of beliefs of universal significance.

Nourlangie Rock, Kakadu National Park (photograph courtesy of Dal Anderson)

The criteria for natural heritage are that the site should:

- illustrate a stage in the earth's evolution;
- represent ongoing geological processes;
- constitute remarkable natural formations of areas of exceptional natural beauty;
- contain the natural habitats of endangered species.

Kakadu is one of the small number of sites in the world that have qualified under both sets of criteria.

World Heritage listing is subject to ongoing monitoring. When the federal government took the decision in 1997 to allow the development of the Jabiluka uranium mine within the national park boundaries, representatives of the World Heritage Commission visited Jabiluka and considered declaring that the mine

Ranger Mine, Kakadu National Park (photograph courtesy of Dal Anderson)

development would place the Kakadu heritage listing 'in danger'. The Australian Government disagreed and development work continued at Jabiluka. Further consideration by the Heritage authorities in July 1999 led to the decision not to place Kakadu on the in-danger list. This is considered to be a political coup for the Australian Government.

3. The issues

Matters at issue in Kakadu include:

- the management of the Heritage Area to meet the expectations of growing numbers of tourists;
- protection of the way of life of Aboriginal inhabitants, involving sources of livelihood, sacred and archaeological sites;
- limitation of the negative effects on park ecology of introduced species such as water buffalo, cane toads and salvinia;
- the further development of uranium mining in the new mine to be established at Jabiluka.

These areas of concern have given rise to more specific issues, including:

- What constitutes safe disposal of radioactive tailings after uranium ore processing?
- How can Aboriginal rock art be protected from tourists, air pollution and mud wasps?
- Is the contribution of uranium oxide to Australian export earnings sufficient to justify continued mining in Kakadu?
- What means are there for resolving deep divisions of opinion among Aboriginal groups toward mining?
- What constitutes responsible policy that might be expected of governments toward issues involving Kakadu?

- Given that they choose it, how can it be made possible for Aboriginal people to continue their traditional way of life?
- Does the 1979 deal between the Australian Government and Aboriginal peoples have continuing legitimacy?
- How can cane toads be prevented from reaching Kakadu and causing serious ecological damage?
- What are the most appropriate and effective methods that might be adopted by people protesting against development at Kakadu?
- Do the people in the mining town of Jabiru have a right to their way of life and jobs?
- Are there some issues on which compromise is meaningless (in the same sense that one cannot be 'half dead')?

Teaching and learning about the issues at Kakadu

Approaches to teaching and learning about issues generally have been suggested earlier in this chapter. An application to Kakadu follows.

Inculcation: Achieving a sustainable future for Kakadu

The earth's environments provide the resources that support human life and contribute so much to its quality. The milieu of our lives is inseparable from ourselves. Some areas possess outstanding qualities that meet the criteria of World Heritage listing and add a special dimension to the argument for sustaining them. Achieving a sustainable future demands that the earth's resources be maintained and where possible enhanced. These truths are self-evident and must become part of the learning of school students.

Many Web pages on the Internet provide examples of statements which represent a particular viewpoint. Such statements include:

- Kakadu National Park Management Plan http://www.erin.gov.au/portfol.../manplans/kakadu/contents.html
- Response by Government of Australia to the UNESCO World Heritage Committee http://www.biodiversity.enviro.../kakadu/jabiluka/response.html
- Environmental battle waged in Australia's Kakadu http://www.earthtimes.org/oct/...nvironmentalbattleoct26_98.htm
- Kakadu uranium protested in Belgium http://www.lycos.com/envirolink/news/stories/3540.html
- Kakadu—Australia's Ancient Wilderness http://www.pbs.org/edens/kakadu
- Kakadu National Park. Inscription and extension http://www.unesco.org/whc/sites/147.htm
- Kakadu: Scene, history, management http://www.environment.gov.au/...nea/kakadu/pom/description.htm

Knowledge base and conclusions that might be analysed

The following illustrate statements that might be analysed in critical reflection over issues at Kakadu.

1. The 1997 federal government decision to approve uranium mining at Jabiluka was a 'pro-jobs, pro-development decision' (John Howard). The miner, Energy Resources of Australia, estimates that uranium from Jabiluka will boost export income by $4.5 billion over the next quarter century. Environmentalists and some of the traditional Aboriginal owners believe that economic gain is outweighed by negative impact on the environment and lifestyle deterioration for the Aboriginal people.

2. 'Nuclear power is here to stay. We, as Australians cannot prevent the further development of nuclear power by

denying supplies of uranium . . . Reliable supplies of energy are vital for the economic development and social stability of modern societies . . . Nuclear energy is cheaper than many other energy sources and no new energy source is likely to have a significant impact for at least 25 years . . . Nuclear power is one of the safest forms for generating electricity.' (ERA booklet, *Safeguarding Ranger Uranium*, p. 2, undated, mid-1980s).

3. 'ERA has undertaken to abide by the 1978 Agreement between the Commonwealth Government and the Northern Land Council acting on behalf of the traditional landowners. The terms of that Agreement include detailed environmental safeguards as well as provision to ensure minimal disturbance to the local Aborigines and measures for their development and welfare.' (p. 5) and 'The water management system (at the mine) is designed to operate smoothly and safely regardless of climatic extremes.' (p. 13) (ERA booklet, *Ranger Uranium Mine and the Environment*, undated, mid-1980s).

   John Hallam, from Friends of the Earth, believes that the Ranger inquiry (1977) was just, but the following negotiations with Aboriginal owners were not because the agreement was achieved under duress. 'In 1982, Pancontinental Mining—by a mixture of trickery, bribery and standover tactics—forced an agreement to allow mining from the Mirrar people. The words of the then senior traditional owner, Toby Gangali, "I can't fight any more", were interpreted as "consent".' (Hallam, 1998: 7).

4. Public perception of uranium as a source of energy is different from perceptions of other forms of energy, mainly because

of the military applications of uranium. But these are now controlled by international agreements. Although people are still mindful of the nuclear accidents at Chernobyl and Three Mile Island, the end of the Cold War has reduced the impact of green viewpoints about uranium.

5. Current objections by environmentalists to uranium mining in Kakadu emphasise the hazards of tailings, that is, the dusty residue of crushed ore after extraction of the mineral. The tailings are radioactive and will remain so for about 200 000 years. They could be spread by water or wind or even digging animals over this time. Jabiluka will produce about 20 million tonnes of tailings which are to be dumped in the exhausted pits at Ranger, covered and revegetated.

6. The Gundjehmi Aboriginal Corporation (1998: 23–24) published an 11-point summary of their reasons for wanting to stop Jabiluka. The reasons include: the Mirrar people are unequivocally opposed to this mining; sacred sites are endangered; the agreement with the mining company was obtained by coercion; there are fallacies in the environmental impact studies; mining has brought very little economic benefit to the traditional owners of Kakadu; the radioactive tailings will lead to terrible sicknesses throughout their country; Ranger has not solved water management problems; and the ore at Jabiluka will jeopardise the health of miners because of its radioactivity.

7. One analyst (O'Faircheallaigh, 1991: 11) has pointed out that uranium mining in Kakadu could bring about considerable social disturbance to local Aboriginal people, outweighing their compensation. As Jabiluka will provide

limited numbers of jobs and world markets for uranium oxide are not robust, the economic argument supporting mining is far from unassailable.

8. Feral animals are causing problems for environmental management in Kakadu. Buffaloes were imported from Asia after 1828 to provide fresh meat and draught animals for the settlers. Feral buffalo have been a tourist attraction, but their grazing, trampling, wallowing and tree rubbing had such negative effects on environments that the buffalo have now been almost exterminated to protect environments. Similarly, cane toads introduced to control insects in Queensland's cane fields have expanded far beyond their points of introduction and are likely to devastate indigenous fauna in Kakadu in the next few years. How to control them and how to fund control measures are difficult questions. Proposals for control by the CSIRO require considerable funding to implement them.

9. Environmental disturbance often has unanticipated outcomes. Caves and overhanging rocks provided admirable sites for the Aboriginal rock artists. The legacy of art accumulated over 20 000 years is superb. The same caves are favoured by mud-daubing wasps which build thick nests sometimes directly on top of the art. Physical removal of the nests damages the rock art. Formerly, the mud was available to the wasps only in the wet season. Modern facilities for tourists have given the wasps access to water year round and have exacerbated the wasp problem.

10. The 1999 decision by the World Heritage Commission was considered to be a political coup for the pro-development Australian Government. The Mirrar people, traditional owners of Kakadu, were among those who wrote to the World Heritage Bureau seeking to have Kakadu National Park placed on the list of World Heritage in danger. The decision not to so list it was made after many parties, including the Australian Government, actively lobbied the World Heritage commissioners. This illustrates the significance of politics as well as other criteria in attempts to resolve issues.

A process of critical reflection and valuing
Consideration of issues that have emerged at Kakadu might well proceed through the following steps:

1. Initially students should have direct experience, or at least vivid vicarious experience of the Kakadu area to contribute to their knowledge base of Kakadu.
2. Students should proceed to investigate Kakadu issues, recognising that there are opposed viewpoints, sensitivities and politically motivated decisions.
3. Students should analyse the motives, causes and messages that underlie actions and documents affecting Kakadu, so that relevant statements are teased apart to reveal more than a superficial impression of the issues.
4. The preceding steps should lead to a recognition of the values underpinning the messages and motives of those involved in the issues at Kakadu.
5. Critical inquiries should extend to students taking constructive action on the basis of their convictions about Kakadu. These actions will reflect the defensible values of the students (perhaps respect for participation, belief in democratic decision making, equity and social justice and respect for moves to create a sustainable future).

Action

Very many actions have been undertaken by the stakeholders in Kakadu. The actions have included:

1. Negotiations with Aboriginal peoples; for example, by government, miners and tourism companies.
2. Environmental impact studies.
3. On-site protests in Kakadu.
4. The development of mines and tourist facilities and their supporting infrastructure.
5. Public education programs, propaganda and advertising to influence the public about matters affecting Kakadu.
6. Political lobbying; for example, by environmentalists and miners. An interesting example of lobbying was provided by the way the Australian Government 'courted' the World Heritage people who visited in 1999 to consider whether Kakadu should be declared in danger.

These actions represent and seek to advance the interests of the various stakeholders in Kakadu. Indeed, all Australians are stakeholders, so the initial responsibility of school students is to become well informed about the perspectives toward Kakadu. Other actions that students take regarding Kakadu should be a result of their informed personal decisions made after critical reflection. Teachers who believe in social education for active citizenship should encourage their students to proceed beyond passive acquisition of and reflection on their knowledge.

■ Concluding Comments

Marked differences in values and opinions about many things are held by individuals and societies round the world. These differences lead to controversy and to the rise of issues, that is, matters about which there are alternative viewpoints that are both contrary and reasoned. Schooling for life in contemporary Australian and New Zealand societies cannot neglect the study of values and issues. Studies of society and environment has a particular responsibility because of its special character as a subject in the school curriculum.

Both affective and intellectual capacities are required by students engaging values and issues. These capacities can be fostered throughout schooling by teachers who work with their students to enable learning from inculcation, knowledge, reflection and action. These four may be combined in various ways by teachers having the needs and achievements of their own students in mind. Inculcation of values and attitudes, acquisition of knowledge, stimulus to reflect critically, the conduct of reflection involving intellect and affect and taking action may all be fostered in school through a wide range of specific teaching/learning experiences. These experiences may be enhanced by teachers adopting a stance of committed impartiality toward the issue.

QUESTIONS AND ACTIVITIES

1. Identify the distinctive characteristics of issues. Choose an example of a contemporary environmental issue and show how the characteristics apply to it.
2. What place do you believe there is for personal issues in studies of society and environment? Why?
3. In relation to issue in class, do you believe that:
   * teachers should be committed advocates of a viewpoint, or
   * teachers should provide diverse evidence for their students, or
   * teachers should adopt a committed impartial stance in class?
   Support your viewpoint.
4. Identify the values teaching strategy which you think would work well in your classes. Indicate why you chose the strategy (ies) by referring to:
   * your own style of teaching, and
   * characteristics of the strategy.
5. Devise a set of values analysis activities all related to a chosen issue. Establish an educational rationale in support of the ensemble of activities you have devised.
6. Work the values grid (Figure 7.1) as a personal statement of your commitment to these issues.
7. Conduct a survey of either (a) students in your class at practice teaching or (b) peers in your social education curriculum class to identify the social and environmental issues of most concern to these people.
   How might you use the survey findings in devising a course of studies in society and environment?
8. Read the section entitled 'Problems associated with teaching involving issues and values'. How would you minimise these problems when teaching about society and environment?
9. Devise a learning experience for school students so that their major activity is careful reflection about a chosen social issue.
10. What decisions would you make in resolving the issues relating to mining at Kakadu/Jabiluka? Why?

8 Conceptual Strands of Studies of Society and Environment

Introduction

*Studies of society and environment draws together distinct but related subjects.
It was one of the eight learning areas used to develop curriculum nationally during the
1980s and 1990s. This learning area continues to be widely used in the twenty-first century.
They are not fundamental categories of knowledge but national agreement was reached
on them in 1993 after considerable debate, concessions and compromises (Wilson, 1999).
At the time, the strands (concepts) included in studies of society and environment
were considered to be the key, generic aspects of the field. Since 1993, all states
and territories have received the materials and in the process made modifications.
These modifications have ranged from major (for example, NSW) to minor
(for example, Tasmania). It is important to understand how and why the strands
were developed and to analyse and give reasons for the subsequent modifications
that have occurred.*

■ National Curriculum Planning

During the 1980s federal Ministers for Education (and especially John Dawkins) initiated pressures for change in education—national education was seen as being indispensable to national economic recovery (Reid, 1992).

The means by which the federal minister transformed rhetoric into action was through the Australian Education Council (AEC), a body comprising the federal minister and State Ministers of Education. This strategy could be perceived as inevitable since the federal government has no constitutional responsibility for education.

The AEC progressed and made substantial progress with its national collaborative curriculum project although there were to be significant setbacks ahead. One significant step forward was the Hobart Declaration on Schooling in 1988 in which a set of common goals for education was agreed upon by all state Education Ministers at an AEC meeting in Hobart (Table 8.1). Although panned by some critics as being merely symbolic, the Hobart Declaration was the first public statement about explicit national goals.

It is evident that the pace quickened over 1992–93 as committees of the AEC, especially the Standing Committee (Schools), composed of state chief executive officers, and the Curriculum and Assessment Committee (CURASS), composed of directors of curriculum in state Education Departments and directors of assessment agencies, decided upon an extremely tight schedule to complete the national curriculum project. The motivation to complete the total array of national statements and profiles for the eight learning areas (Mathematics, English, Science, Technology, The Arts, Languages Other than English, Health and Physical Education, Studies of Society and Environment) may have been due partly to frustration about the time taken during 1988–1991 to obtain collaborative support from the states and territories on curriculum matters, but it also appears to have been a strategy to counteract pressures from industry and training groups who had high visibility in policy reports, such as Finn (1991), Mayer (1992) and the Employment and Skills Formation Council (1992).

The AEC Curriculum and Assessment Committee (1992) emphasised four major educational and economic advantages of the national collaborative curriculum project:

1. improved quality of curriculum through the use and sharing of the expertise of officers beyond system boundaries;
2. cohesion through reduction of unnecessary differences and overlaps in curriculum, and thereby remedying present problems for mobile students;
3. pooling of resources and resources savings through adoption of programs and materials;
4. developing a more consistent approach to student reporting.

Some other advantages that appeared subsequently included the following:

- The national statements represent modern thinking about the learning area (Mitchell, 1993). They focus upon what might be, rather than just conserving the status quo.
- The national statements represent a summation of the best available knowledge about the content in the eight learning areas. 'It builds upon some of the best of current practice and provides moral support for the continuance of a range of good practices' (Willis and Stephens, 1991: 4).
- The knowledge (product) base of the national curriculum statements complements the employment-related key competencies (process) recommended by the Mayer Committee (1992). 'Together, the national curriculum statements and the Key Competency strands recognise, in Lawton's (1981) terms, the importance of both "inputs" and "outputs" as essential components of any curriculum' (Kennedy 1992: 35).
- The national statements and profiles reinforce the move towards an outcomes-based education system, in common with many other developed countries. The move towards an outcomes basis is associated with a call for more explicit specification of what should be valued and reported on in schools (Boston, 1992: 30).
- 'The national statements are providing a framework which define agreed common ground but yet are flexible enough to contain diverse, if not divergent, content, methods of learning and means of assessment' (Hannan, 1992: 28). The national statements do allow room for

Table 8.1 *Common and agreed national goals for schooling in Australia (1989)*

The national goals for schooling will, for the first time, provide a framework for cooperation between schools, states and territories and the Commonwealth. The goals are intended to assist schools and systems to develop specific objectives and strategies, particularly in the areas of curriculum and assessment.

The agreed national goals for schooling include the following aims:

1. To provide an excellent education for all young people, being one which develops their talents and capacities to full potential and is relevant to the social, cultural and economic needs of the nation.
2. To enable all students to achieve high standards of learning and to develop self-confidence, optimism, high self-esteem, respect for others and achievement of personal excellence.
3. To promote equality of educational opportunities, and to provide for groups with special learning requirements.
4. To respond to the current and emerging economic and social needs of the nation, and to provide those skills which will allow students maximum flexibility and adaptability in their future employment and other aspects in life.
5. To provide a foundation for further education and training, in terms of knowledge and skills, respect for learning and positive attitudes for long-life education.
6. To develop in students:
    · the skills of English literacy, including skills in listening, speaking, reading and writing;
    · skills of numeracy, and other mathematical skills;
    · skills of analysis and problem solving;
    · skills of information processing and computing;
    · an understanding of the role of science and technology in society, together with scientific and technological skills;
    · a knowledge and appreciation of Australia's historical and geographic context;
    · a knowledge of languages other than English;
    · an appreciation and understanding of, and confidence to participate in, the creative arts;
    · an understanding of, and concern for, balanced development and the global environment; and
    · a capacity to exercise judgment in matters of morality, ethics and social justice.
7. To develop knowledge, skills, attitudes and values which will enable students to participate as active and informed citizens in our democratic Australian society within an international context.
8. To provide students with an understanding and respect for our cultural heritage including the particular cultural background of Aboriginal and ethnic groups.
9. To provide for the physical development and personal health and fitness of students and for the creative use of leisure time.
10. To provide appropriate career education and knowledge in the world of work, including an understanding of the nature and place of work in our society.

Providing a sound basis for a collaborative effort to enhance Australian schooling, the agreed national goals will be reviewed from time to time, in response to the changing needs of Australian society.

Source: AEC (1989a).

states and territories to make their own adaptations (Eltis, 1993).

Yet major concerns were raised, including the following:

• The eight national learning areas lack a rigorously developed theoretical base. It is apparent that the division into eight learning areas is a confusing amalgam of traditional subjects and pragmatic expediency. Hannan (1992: 29) concedes that the learning areas are 'both pragmatic and conservative: this is the break-up nearest to that already in use around the country'.

• There is no research evidence for the profiles approach. Although Reid (1992) concurs that the National Collaborative Curriculum Project 'has been shaped by progressive bureaucrats who are seeking to ward off the worst excesses of the market-driven educational philosophy of the New Right' (p. 15), he argues that it is not clear what learning theory has been the basis for the profiles. If a behaviourist approach is allowed to occur within learning area profiles, it will trivialise learning by focusing only upon learning activities that can be observed.

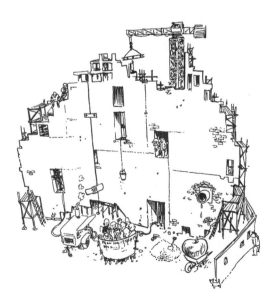

• The professional development implications for teachers are enormous and should not be underrated (Hughes, 1990).

• Consultation with various groups was not a strong point of the National Collaborative Curriculum Project.

• A major priority of CURASS, especially during 1992 and 1993, was to provide uniformity across the eight learning areas by ensuring the same number of levels (eight) in the national statements and profiles, and similar numbers of generic strands, pointers and attainment levels in all profiles. There was concern from some learning areas, for example the Arts (Boughton, 1993), that not all subjects should or can be compartmentalised using this reductionist approach.

Questions can be asked about whether it is possible to develop a developmental set of curriculum outcomes which has validity for all Australian children in all schools; whether school knowledge can be divided up into 'areas of knowledge' and then subdivided into 'strands' (Collins, 1994a).

■ Emergence of Studies of Society and Environment

Studies of society and environment is one of eight learning areas initiated as a National Collaborative Curriculum Project in 1988. The national statement was guided by the Common and Agreed National Goals for Schooling in Australia (AEC, 1989), especially in terms of goals 4, 6, 7, 8 and 10 (see Table 8.1). The national statement also drew upon two mapping studies completed in 1991, Mapping the Environmental Education Curriculum (Australian Education Council, 1991a) and K–12 Studies of Society Curriculum Map (Australian Education Council, 1991b).

Both project teams produced comprehensive information about system policy and subject framework documents (AEC,

1991a, b). The studies of society K–12 Mapping Project was especially complex because of differences in nomenclature between states and territories, different ways in which the field is conceptualised and the range of titles of courses of study included in this curriculum field. In terms of scope, some 19 topic areas were delineated ranging from Aboriginal and Torres Strait Islander studies to community studies. These topic areas tend to be organised in either multidisciplinary and integrated courses (e.g. Asian studies) or in single discipline courses (e.g. history). It is interesting to note that team writers of the mapping project explicitly excluded such areas as business/commerce, career education, LOTE languages, religion, technology and personal development. At a later AEC meeting, a decision was made to include business/commerce within the studies of society and environment learning area.

The project team defined dimensions of learning (knowledge, skills, values and action) and essential learnings. Further, they identified the following conceptual strands covering people in patterns of interaction with:

- environments;
- heritages;
- change;
- cultures;
- systems.

Skills (e.g. research and processing of information, analytical and critical thinking, social participation) and values processes (e.g. clarification, exploration) were made quite explicit in the final report.

The report by the Environmental Education Mapping team was also quite ambitious. The writers, for example, proposed that their recommendations should be considered in all the eight learning area national statements and profiles. They also made a strong case for a separate national statement for environmental education to be developed.

The mapping team argued that a diversity of teaching approaches should be used with environmental education, such as cross-curriculum, a whole-school approach or as a separate subject. The mapping team stated that the following strands should be considered as the major concepts and understandings:

- ecosystems;
- resources;
- growth;
- heritage;
- aesthetics;
- environmental ethics;
- decision making;
- participation.

Process strands should include:

- sensory skills;
- problem-solving skills;
- skills for investigating the environment;
- social/communication skills;
- skills for courses of action (including advice on how students can identify and examine conflicts and problems associated with controversial issues).

At the time they were commissioned, the mapping activities served a useful purpose. They provided an overview of the educational resources currently available, the range and scope of courses and, in some instances, the range of approaches to the curriculum areas as revealed from literature searches.

By early 1991 it was evident that the AEC intended to move faster with curriculum development in the learning areas. For studies of society and environment, the AEC commissioned a 'brief' to be produced within three months. The brief was to consist of a set of specifications and guidelines for the writing team given the responsibility of producing the national statement.

The contract for writing the brief was awarded by CURASS to a consortium team from the Secondary Education Authority of Western Australia (SEA) and the Senior Secondary Assessment Board of South Australia (SSABSA). The team drew upon strands (concepts) identified in the studies of society K–12 Mapping Project (see Table 8.2) but with some differences. Because the learning area had been identified by the AEC as being 'society and environment' it was considered that these broad themes would permeate all strands—there was no need to have a separate 'environment' concept. Also, CURASS required all learning areas to include a 'process' strand, and the one chosen by the team was 'Investigation and Participation' which incorporated:

- communication;
- social and environmental investigation;
- participation.

It should also be noted that CURASS had widened the studies of society and environment learning area to include business and commercial studies. The learning area was defined as:

- single discipline studies which include anthropology, ecology, economics, geography, history, philosophy, politics, psychology, sociology. Some of these combine as studies such as economic geography, political history.

- multidisciplinary studies which include Aboriginal and Torres Strait Islander studies, Asian studies, Australian studies, business and commercial studies, community studies, cultural studies, environmental studies, global studies, legal studies, peace studies, studies in religion, women's studies.
- integrated studies which include social studies/science/education, citizenship education.

The team produced a set of strands which were to become the blueprint for further development in the national statement and profile (see Table 8.2).

Consultations between interest groups proved extremely difficult to arrange within an extremely tight time line of three months. As noted by the co-director of the team:

at the commencement of the brief writing, contact was made with five national professional associations, the higher education forum, two national teacher unions, the ACTU, the Confederation of Industry, two national parent organisations and non-State employing authority peak bodies. By May 1992 and at the completion of the draft, less than a quarter of these groups had been actively involved. Dependent upon the support provided and rapport between liaison officers in government school systems and

Table 8.2 *Evolution of the strands in preparing the brief, statement and profile*

Strands in the brief	Strands in the national statement	Strands in the national profile
· time, continuity and change	· time, continuity and change	· time, continuity and change
· place and space	· place and space	· place and space
· culture and beliefs	· culture	· culture
· natural and human resources	· resources	· resources
· natural and social systems	· natural and social systems	· natural and social systems
· investigation and participation	· investigation, communication and participation	· investigation, communication and participation

members of the writing teams, consultation sessions varied from wide-ranging, supportive and comprehensive to limited, diversive and non-productive. (Marsh, 1994: 74)

A major stumbling block which caused considerable debate at CURASS meetings was whether the strands should represent individual disciplines or whether they should be generic. Various proposals were considered whereby the strands might be reorganised, for example collapsing them into two strands or replacing them with discipline-oriented titles. A special meeting of CURASS members was called for June 1992 to resolve this matter. It was decided at this meeting that a discipline-based approach was not appropriate in terms of providing maximum flexibility for primary and secondary school teachers. For example, it was noted that the discipline focus would not be acceptable for primary teachers. Furthermore, if a discipline approach was used for subjects such as history, inevitably some disciplines would be excluded, such as sociology and psychology.

The contract for writing the national statement for studies of society and environment was awarded to a consortium representing the Queensland Department of Education and the Australian Federation of Associations for the Study of Society and Environment. Within a very tight time frame a first draft was produced, but disagreements occurred between the secretariat officers of CURASS and members of the team, as described in Gilbert *et al.* (1992), Ellerton and Clements (1994), Land (1994) and Marsh (1994). At a CURASS meeting in October 1992 it was decided that the draft national statement produced by the Queensland team should not be released for consultation and that the secretariat should build on the existing statement and revise it where necessary, using curriculum policy

officers and subject associations from a number of states. This draft of the national statement was completed by January 1993 and distributed widely for consultation. The strands included in the national statement are listed in Table 8.2.

Meanwhile, tenders for writing the profile were advertised, and a consortium of members from the SEA, SSABSA and New South Wales Department of School Education, together with additional officers selected from a number of states and territories, and coordinated by a learning area member from the secretariat, were appointed to write the profile.

The profile writing team was able to prepare drafts and have a completed document available by the end of March 1993. During the trialling period (April–May 1993), teachers were asked to comment on the levels statements, the outcomes statements, the pointers, the language style and levels of inclusiveness.

Despite the very tight time line, a large number of responses was received from the consultation/trialling. Although there was substantial support for the profile, a number of criticisms were made, including the following:

- Environmental studies, issues, values and actions were not adequately represented in the profile.
- Particular groups were not well included, namely students with disabilities, students learning English as a second language, girls, students living in poverty and students living in isolated areas.
- There was divided opinion about the sequence of outcomes in the cultures strand with its emphasis on Aboriginal and Torres Strait Islander groups. Some considered that a more generic sequence of outcomes referring to cultures was preferable.
- There was an undue emphasis on Australia in the outcomes, particularly in

the 'Time, Continuity and Change' strand.
- The literacy expectations of level 1 were too high.
- There was a mismatch between the process strand and the other strands. In particular, the process strand failed to capture values and action outcomes pertaining to active citizenship, environmental ethics and action and career education.

The empirical validation of studies of society and environment undertaken by the Australian Council for Educational Research (ACER) revealed that the strands were interpreted consistently and that teachers used the outcomes as intended. However, it was noted that there was insufficient separation between some levels of the profile. In each of the strands, it was noted that the levels increased progressively in their calibrations, although some levels showed insufficient separation, particularly in the higher levels of the strands and typically at levels 6, 7 and 8.

Details of the trialling and validation procedures were reported to the May 1993 meeting of CURASS. There was further discussion about some of the strands in studies of society and environment, especially the systems strand, but after lengthy debate it was considered that it should be retained in the profile.

The project team writers were able to accommodate final revisions based on the trialling and validation reports and to complete these in time for the June 1993 CURASS meeting. At this meeting the profile was approved and submitted to the AEC. The strands approved for the profile are listed in Table 8.2.

■ Cultural Understanding

This concept was debated strongly at state and national levels in the 1990s. Expert training groups such as the Finn Committee

(1991) and the Mayer Committees (1992) argued that it was a fundamental competency.

Cultural understanding was defined as:

- understanding and knowledge of Australia's historical, geographical and political context;
- understanding of major global issues, for example competing environmental, technological and social priorities;
- understanding of the world of work, its importance and requirements.

The whole exercise was a classic case of boundary conflict and subject matter inertia (Goodson and Marsh, 1996). It proved to be extremely difficult to develop appropriate performance levels for cultural under-standing. Furthermore, there was little support from the school sector to include it in the already overcrowded studies of society and environment. Despite considerable federal funding, support for the concept gradually waned.

The Ministerial Council on Education, Employment, Training and Youth Affairs (MCEETYA) discontinued funding for the project in 1996.

For some adherents, the emergence of Civics Education as a new federal government initiative might have provided some solace. However, it is unclear whether cultural understanding will figure promi-nently in the Discovering Democracy materials (see Chapter 14).

■ Analysis of the Strands (Concepts)

Despite the political manoeuvrings by various interest groups, espousing intellec-tual, political and bureaucratic priorities (as described in Marsh (1994) and Wilson (1999)), the conceptual basis for studies of society and environment strands changed very slightly during the national curriculum development phases of writing a brief and preparing the national statement and profile.

The six strands provided maximum flexibility across bands A–D (spanning primary and secondary schooling), in particular the integrated nature of most primary school studies (bands A and B), and the more specialised curricula of senior secondary schooling in band D. It is useful to describe the strands as generic because they provided coherence for the learning area and were flexible in that a broad range of studies was possible. The concepts illustrated in Table 8.3 show the relationship between the generic strands and some illustrative disciplines.

The five conceptual strands and one process strand were the six key organisers (Table 8.4) in the initial national structure. The strands, in total, established the knowledge, understandings, skills, attitudes and values of this learning area. It is instructive to examine these national strands separately, even though some states and territories have subsequently made a number of modifications and deletions.

Time, Continuity and Change

This strand provides a chronological dimension that forms a context within which learnings in the other strands may be developed. Knowledge and understanding of the past provides a useful basis for making decisions about the future, as well as developing understandings of and empathy with past societies and environments. Opportunities are provided to develop a sensitivity to the effects of continuity and change in the natural and social environment, involving an exploration of a range of social and environmental heritages, with particular reference to Australia in a global context.

The central discipline underpinning this strand is history. Other disciplines such as philosophy, anthropology, archaeology and ecology are drawn upon, as are

Table 8.3 *Examples of discipline concepts embodied in the conceptual strands*

	Culture	Natural and Social Systems	Resources	Place and Space	Time, Continuity and Change
History	· tradition · beliefs · values · myths	· societies · subcultures · communities	· people · conflict · causation · evidence	· nationalism · imperialism · colonialism · migration	· era · continuity · change · chronology
Geography	· cultural diffusion	· inter-dependence · energy flows	· distribution · resource management	· location · spatial patterns · regions	· spatial change · physical processes
Politics	· justice · freedom · power	· democracy · communism · government	· authority · equity · representation	· nation–state alliance	· revolution
Anthropology	· ritual · ethno-centrism	· kinship · family	· cultural groups	· sacred sites	· evolution · heritage · adaptation

Table 8.4 *Summary of the six strands*

Time, Continuity and Change focuses on people's experiences, recorded in various ways over time; on the causes and effects of key events; on patterns of change and continuity; on the roles, intentions and motives of individuals and groups; and on traditions and institutions that have developed.

Place and Space focuses on the relationships between people and places; on the spatial dimension of human experiences; and on the importance of scale, location, pattern and process as ways of examining cultural and natural phenomena and their associated landscapes.

Culture focuses on ways of sharing and regulating human experience; on how people identify with cultures through belonging to groups and being part of wider social systems; and on how people's beliefs structure their cultural practices, ideas, symbols and the relationships between groups.

Resources focuses on the nature of resources; on the human abilities, initiative and enterprise; on resource production, distribution and use; on the different values assigned to them; on the processes different groups and societies use to make decisions about resource access, development and management; and on the impact of resource use.

Natural and Social Systems focuses on a systems view of the world, and highlights the interrelationship and integration of its parts.

Investigation, Communication and Participation is the process strand. It focuses on what students do in their studies of society and environment; on how they acquire and make use of information; and how they develop the key processes of investigation, participation and communication. These processes are built into the descriptions of the conceptual strands at each band.

multidisciplinary studies such as Aboriginal and Torres Strait Islander studies, Australian studies, Asian studies, community studies, multicultural studies and women's studies.

The key concepts for this strand are listed in Table 8.5. It can be seen that the key components focus upon students acquiring knowledge about events and people in the history of Australia, its region and the world and to use this knowledge to draw links between contemporary society and its history. A study of the time dimension challenges students to take action to conserve what is valued in their heritages and to act responsibly towards future generations. This includes ideas, beliefs, values and traditions as well as places, buildings, documents, photographs, artifacts and environments. A recognition of

the impact of change over time will better equip students to evaluate the ethical considerations involved in making changes and in placing environmental changes within a framework of ecological sustainability.

The content areas to which the strand can be applied include studies of people in a particular place in the past, movements of major societal change, significant themes that reflect major fields of human concern and activity, and broad chronological studies of particular societies or civilisations. These can range temporally from the remote past to the present, and spatially from Australia to the world.

Place and Space

This strand refers to the location and interaction of phenomena within the social,

Table 8.5 *Strands and key components*

Strands	Key components
Time, Continuity and Change	understanding the past in the world; understanding the past in Australia; time and change; interpretation and perspectives; causation.
Place and Space	features of places; people and places; care of places.
Culture	Aboriginal and Torres Strait Islander cultures; cultural cohesion and diversity; personal, group and cultural identity.
Resources	uses of resources; people and work; management and enterprise.
Natural and Social Systems	natural systems; political and legal systems; economic systems.
Investigation, Communication and Participation	investigation; communication; participation.

commercial and natural environments in which people and all living things exist and interact, with particular reference to Australia in its global context. The strand provides a spatial dimension that forms a context within which learnings in the other strands may be developed.

Geography is the central discipline underpinning this strand, which provides a range of methodologies for studying places and the phenomena, patterns, processes and interactions in them. It also draws upon the disciplines of ecology and anthropology and multidisciplinary studies, such as Aboriginal and Torres Strait Islander studies, Australian studies, Asian studies and environmental studies. There are strong links between this strand and various integrated studies, particularly where they focus on space and location.

The key components for this strand, as listed in Table 8.5, enable students to develop a sense of belonging to places and areas with which they identify, as well as appreciating the characteristics and functions of other places. An understanding of the social and natural processes affecting places and spaces can enable students to make informed decisions and be involved in meaningful participation concerning the future. This will require consideration of the key values of social justice and ecologically sustainable development. This strand also provides opportunities for students to acquire knowledge about places and spaces in Australia, its region and the world.

These concepts can be applied to different contexts with a primary emphasis on Australia and its place in the world. Studies can focus on identifying the location of key physical aspects (such as climate, vegetation, landforms) and of cultural aspects (such as demography, sacred sites, transport, land uses). They can examine the processes responsible for these aspects and study structural and spatial patterns (such as workforce composition or climatic regions) on various scales.

Culture

Culture embraces the beliefs, values, ideals, customs, languages, discourses, artistic products and symbols of a group with particular reference to Australian groups in a global context. The expression of a people's culture can be found in their traditions, memories, treasured materials and artifacts which can create a sense of personal and group identity. The expression of people's culture can also be found in the dynamic aspects of their society, such as their language, the way in which they interact in formal and informal settings and their lifestyles. It should be recognised that all cultures contain diversity and conflict. It should also be recognised that culture is largely socially constructed and subject to change.

The central disciplines underpinning this strand are anthropology and sociology. It draws on a number of other disciplines, such as philosophy, psychology and history, and various multidisciplinary studies including Aboriginal and Torres Strait Islander studies, multicultural studies, women's studies and studies in religion. The strand offers the concept of culture as a significant organiser for integrated studies such as social studies and social education.

The key components enable students to explore their own identity and those of the various groups that exist in society. A closer appreciation of the perspectives of various cultures can enable students to develop understanding and respect for the values of others and a concern for their welfare and dignity.

Broad content areas to which the strand can be applied include the cultures and cultural heritages within Australia, the Asia/Pacific region, the countries of origin of immigrants to Australia and elsewhere in the world.

Resources

The study of resources refers to both human and natural phenomena and how these are managed to cater for the requirements of members of society, with particular reference to Australia in its global context. A natural resource is anything in the geophysical and biophysical environment appraised by people as being useful in satisfying these needs or wants within the geographical and prevailing social, political, economic, commercial and institutional conditions. Human resources refer to all people in terms of the knowledge, skills, values and attitudes they possess, and their ability to transmit these through their membership and participation in society. Manufactured resources include those goods and services produced through the use of natural and human resources. Issues associated with the conservation and development of resources will be investigated to promote a clearer understanding of the key value of ecological sustainability.

The central discipline underpinning the strand is economics. It also draws upon the disciplines of geography, ecology and sociology and various multidisciplinary studies, notably business and commercial studies, environmental studies and global studies. The strand has strong links with various integrated studies, particularly where they focus on the productive dimension, socioeconomic context and the role of enterprise in human affairs.

The key components enable students to better understand how an appraisal of environment varies for different groups and how decisions on ways of using environments depend on prevailing and often highly changeable conditions. The initiative applied to the use of resources to satisfy needs and enterprise is also a key focus. Students should develop an understanding of issues associated with the use of human, manufactured and natural resources, including an appreciation of the need to actively encourage policies associated with social justice and ecological sustainability.

Content areas to which the strand can be applied include: the shrinking of many shared global resources; human resource management practices and access to factors affecting human resource development (e.g. food, health, education and training); and the impact of technology on all resource development and management practices.

Natural and Social Systems

Natural and social systems can be identified by the structures and processes that together make up society and environment. This strand adopts a perspective that involves the study of natural systems, social systems (including business and commercial systems) and the interdependence that exists within and between these systems, with particular reference to Australia in a global context.

The central disciplines underpinning this strand are ecology, politics, law and economics. It also draws upon a number of other disciplines, including sociology and geography, and various multidisciplinary studies including legal studies, business and commercial studies, global studies and Aboriginal and Torres Strait Islander studies. Within integrated studies, the strand enhances systemic understandings of societies and environments.

The key components enable students to recognise some of the organising elements within society and environment, and the processes by which cohesion or equilibrium may be created, maintained or broken down. Analysing, examining and evaluating patterns of organisation within society and the natural

environment should enable students to develop the key values of social justice, ecological sustainability and democracy. Students will be provided with the opportunity to evaluate the changes that may be necessary to maintain and develop a quality of life compatible with ecological sustainability and equity between social and racial groups.

Broad content areas to which the strand can be applied include the nature and diversity of Australian ecosystems and human impact on them; the values and objectives of the Australian economic system, particularly the ownership and allocation of resources; issues of economic development and competitiveness, social justice and ecological sustainability; the diversity of global political systems and their relationships with economic and legal systems; roles, rights and responsibilities of groups within social systems; decision making in the family, school and community.

Investigation, Participation and Communication

The key processes in terms of investigation involve researching the problem, issue or study; processing data; and applying the findings. Researching the problem involves defining, acquiring and organising information. Processing data involves classifying, interpreting, distinguishing between fact and opinion and synthesising information. Applying the findings involves reporting, discussing, drawing warranted conclusions and identifying personal implications.

In terms of participation and action, the key processes involve developing personal skills, interpersonal skills and social interaction. Personal skills include sensory awareness, assertiveness, advocacy, empathy and aesthetic appreciation. Personal skills are an important precursor for the development of effective interpersonal skills.

Interpersonal skills can be developed

through collaborative learning exercises where students are involved in group activities; learning how to participate in various roles; learning how to set goals; assisting in organising, planning, delegating, sharing information and making decisions. Developing skills in persuading, compromising and negotiating in the resolution of conflict are also important.

Social interaction is an important dimension as it provides students with an opportunity to extend and demonstrate their learning in a practical form. Appropriate social action is based on knowledge and understanding of facts and relevant factors, clarification of their own values with an appreciation of various options and a recognition of the possible consequences of alternative actions. Appropriate social action will be determined not only by the students' level of understanding but also their level of skills and commitment to the action strategy.

The key processes in terms of communication involve interpreting, manipulating and producing messages. Processes will include interpreting and presenting information using a variety of forms, empathising with the thoughts and feelings of others, using information technology and the mass media, exploring the value of literature and the visual and performing arts and civic writing and speaking.

■ International Comparisons

Comparisons with overseas conceptualisations reveal some commonalities. For example, in 1994, in the USA, the National Council for the Social Studies (NCSS) produced curriculum standards for social studies teaching based upon 10 themes, namely:

- culture;
- time, continuity and change;
- people, places and environments;
- individual development and identity;

- individuals, groups and institutions;
- power, authority and governance;
- production, distribution and consumption;
- science, technology and society;
- global connections;
- civic ideals and practices.

The first three themes are almost identical with three of the national statement and profile strands but the remaining seven provide discipline-based focii (psychology, economics) and interdisciplinary focii with science and technology. The NCSS curriculum standards are intended to provide 'an integrated social science, behavioural science and humanities approach for achieving academic and civic competence' (NCSS 1994: 365).

It is also insightful to compare individual strands of the national statement and profile with specific discipline conceptualisations developed overseas. For example, the national statement strand 'Time, Continuity and Change' draws heavily upon the discipline of history, but with a narrow focus. The national history curriculum in the UK appears to provide a wider conceptualisation of history by its concentration upon:

- describing and explaining historical change and cause;
- understanding interpretations in history;
- acquiring evidence from historical sources and forming judgments about their reliability and value (Booth, 1993; Foster, Morris and Davis, 1996).

Comparisons can also be made with geography. The national statement strands 'Place and Space', 'Resources', 'Natural and Social Systems' are all directly linked to the discipline of geography (see Reynolds, 1997). These strands appear to include most of the major geographical concepts included in the geography guidelines developed in the USA in 1992 (Boehn and Petersen, 1994). They include:

- space and place;
- environment and society;
- spatial dynamics and connections.

Conceptualisations in curriculum are affected by changing political priorities—which can lead to 'turf wars' (Evans, 1998). Ahier and Ross (1995) describe the growth of social studies as a school subject in the UK in the 1970s and 1980s only to be 'legislated into oblivion' (p. 77) by the imposition of the National Curriculum. The combination of environmental studies and social studies in Australia to form studies of society and environment occurred at a time when some states were lobbying strongly for environmental studies but had not been successful in establishing a separate school subject for it. The inclusion of business studies was also a surprising addition to some educators but not in states where economics and business school subjects were closely linked under commerce. Subsequent variations to the national statements and profiles reveal decisions by some states (especially NSW and Victoria) to reassert the supremacy of specific disciplines.

■ Critiques of the National Statement and Profile

In the 1990s there were a number of authors who criticised the process of national curriculum development, were critical of the limited consultation and questioned some of the highly political decisions (e.g. Reid, 1995; Kenway, 1992; Ellerton and Clements, 1994; Collins, 1994a; Gilbert *et al.*, 1992). However, few provided a critical analysis of the conceptual structure of studies of society and environment.

Collins (1994b) was a notable exception. She critiqued assumptions about the national profiles that school knowledge can be divided up into eight areas and that each of these areas has coherence. Furthermore she

queried whether children typically follow a learning path along each strand to greater knowledge and whether the path is one of continuous development.

Land (1994) presented arguments for the use of the terms 'invasion and settlement' to represent Aboriginal and Torres Strait Islander perspectives in the Queensland primary social studies curriculum. This perspective is helpful when analysing the 'Culture' strand in the national statement and profile, although Land does not refer specifically to these documents.

An Australian Curriculum Studies Association workshop at the Brisbane Biennial Conference in 1993 analysed the treatment of values in the national profile and concluded that 'the contested nature of society's values, beliefs and practices (for example, "social justice", "democratic process", and "ecological sustainability") at any given time should be acknowledged, instead of the consensual view that is emphasised' (ACSA, 1993: 1).

Rather surprisingly, little critical comment has been published about profiles and in particular about studies of society and environment since 1993.

Gough (1997) has criticised the lack of attention being given to environmental education within this learning area. Dufty (1999) asserts that the value of individuals (persons) has been de-emphasised because of the emphasis upon society and culture.

Watt (1998) examined directions and levels of reform in all states and territories and concluded that antecedent conditions, especially in NSW, were critical in determining independent stances against the national profiles.

Wilson (1999), in response to criticisms from a distinguished American visitor, argued that there was a basis for the eight learning areas, and that the national Australian consensus was an extraordinary achievement.

The opportunity for changes to the national profile and statement came as a result of the momentous AEC meeting in Perth 1993 whereby the completed documents were 'referred back to the States and Territories for review and local consultation; the extent, timing and nature of any implementation or adaptation will be determined by each State and Territory' (Marsh, 1994: 161). In some cases the amount of modification which took place to studies of society and environment was little more than political rhetoric, but in particular states major conceptual changes did occur.

■ Modifications to the Conceptual Structure of Studies of Society and Environment, 1994–2001

For the first few years (1994–96) the majority of states and territories largely supported and retained the conceptual structure developed in the national statements and profiles for studies of society and environment. Modifications were indeed minimal. Included within this group were the ACT, Northern Territory, South Australia, Tasmania and Western Australia. Victoria could also be included even though the number of levels has been reduced from eight to seven in that state. New South Wales, as a result of the Eltis Report (1995), appeared to be planning a different structure using syllabus statements and outcomes, without profiles. Queensland, after an inactive period, started to produce new documents through the newly established Queensland School Curriculum Council. This trend continued for most states and territories after 1996.

The ACT continued to use Curriculum Frameworks (statements) and Curriculum Profiles for Australian Schools.

Although ACT officials increased the number of cross-curriculum perspectives, the nationally developed structures have been implemented without modification. Additional support documents for teachers were distributed in 1997.

The Northern Territory commenced using the national statements and profiles, but more recently has undertaken a series of reviews (see Table 8.6). A pilot project in 1995 led to the development of the Northern Territory Outcomes Profiles with a greatly reduced number of outcomes (Watt, 2000). The Learning Area Statement for studies of society and environment included four of the national strands but deleted 'Resources' and added 'Indigenous Perspectives'. A recent proposal is to develop a Curriculum Framework directly relevant for the Northern Territory. This may be aligned closely to South Australia's recent move to develop a Curriculum, Standards and Accountability Framework.

South Australia distributed the national documents to schools unchanged in 1994 and developed a comprehensive implementation support plan for 1995–97. A variety of support materials was developed including newsletters, planning charts and classroom guides for teachers. Considerable emphasis was given to whole-school curriculum renewal. As a result of a review undertaken in 1998, decisions were made to promote greater devolution of decision making to local school communities and to establish essential learnings (Watt, 2000). These priorities will be incorporated in the new South Australian Curriculum, Standards and Accountability Framework. The framework is being trialled in 2000 and will be implemented in South Australian schools in 2001 (see Table 8.6). Details are available on the Web: www.nexus.edu.au\curriculum\pathways and www.sacsa.nexus.edu.au\downloads\writersbrief\documents\attach 15 – society – env.doc.

Tasmania distributed the national documents unchanged in 1994. In this state too a variety of support materials was prepared including Starter Posters (providing a greater emphasis to the three key studies of society and environment values), a Program Planner and an SSE Tool for Integration and Connection. Studies of society and environment was a priority area for implementation in 1996–97.

In 1999 further support materials were provided for teachers including *Taking Action*, a specific reference book for studies of society and environment and the Studies of Society and Environment Planning Grid.

Up to date information is now available on a studies of society and environment website, www.ec.tased.edu.au\las\sose, and a CD-Rom has been distributed to schools.

Western Australia repackaged the national profile document and issued it in 1994 to all schools under the title 'Student Outcome Statements: Working Edition 1994', as part of a two-year trial; the national statement was largely ignored. Only minor changes were included to the national profile in the studies of society and environment working edition—some pointers were rewritten to reflect Western Australia syllabus documents and small changes were made to the Aboriginal and Torres Strait Islander substrand.

The Curriculum Council of Western Australia published a Curriculum Framework in 1998. In terms of studies of society and environment, the five national strands and process strand were retained, but 'Active Citizenship' was added. A subsequent refinement of outcome statements was undertaken by the Education Department of WA to ensure congruence with the Curriculum Framework (Watt, 2000). Implementation of the framework in all government schools is to be fully completed by 2004.

Victoria supported the outcomes-based approach in the national statements and profiles but each of the eight learning areas were reviewed by the Board of Studies soon after the fateful July 1993 AEC meeting.

The minister requested the Board of Studies to develop a Curriculum Standards Framework (CSF) whereby the national statements and profiles would be combined into one document. By reducing the number of levels from eight to seven, it was possible to make explicit links between levels of achievement and school year levels to Year 10.

Although earlier reports had indicated major deficiencies in the national profile in studies of society and environment (a clearer representation of the disciplines, less value-laden learning goals), it is not all that evident in the CSF that significant changes were made. Apart from the reduction to seven levels, as described above, other changes included:

- the Investigation, Communication and Participation strand was removed from the set of six strands and reworked as 'inquiry strategies' identified in each of remaining five strands;
- the strand organisers were removed.

Some trialling of the CSF commenced in 1995 but it became more intensive in 1996 with the release of support materials such as SSE Course Advice (which suggested learning activities, resources and assessment strategies), Course Advice Professional Development Kits, a computer software program, KIDMAP, and companion kits such as the interactive multimedia kit, 'Understanding Australia'.

A review of the first CSF was undertaken in 1998 and this led to a new CSF draft being produced in 1999. Curriculum and Standards Framework II (CSF II) was widely circulated for comment to schools and has been implemented this year (2000).

Some major changes have been made to the studies of society and environment learning area. At the primary school level the five strands have been replaced by a single strand, Society and Environment. At the secondary school level, the five strands have been replaced by the following:

- History
- Geography
- Economy and Society

Civics and citizenship education has also been included.

Overall, the number of learning outcomes in CSF II have been greatly reduced compared with CSF I. The change to a discipline-oriented structure at secondary school level (Wilson, 1999) is an interesting revisiting of the discussions which occurred at CURASS meetings in 1992 (Marsh, 1994).

In NSW, the Board of Studies in 1995 undertook an elaborate process of linking outcome statements from the national profile with existing New South Wales syllabuses. This process was halted by a change of government and a Ministerial Committee of Review, chaired by Professor Ken Eltis. This report, accepted by the state government, recommended the use of an outcomes-based curriculum, reaffirmed the prime role of New South Wales syllabuses in describing curriculum content and as a consequence largely ignored the national profiles (Eltis, 1995).

The Board of Studies is now embarking upon a comprehensive review of syllabuses. 'Human Society and its Environment' is the title used to address studies of society and environment in that state. A primary school syllabus framework, K–6, was completed in draft form in July 1996. It includes some of the national strands:

- Change and Continuity;
- Cultures;
- Environments;
- Social systems and structures.

Civics and citizenship education was incorporated into the syllabus recently. The syllabus is being implemented in 2000.

At the secondary school level (Years 7–10) revised syllabuses have been produced for history, geography, commerce, studies of religion and Aboriginal studies. Each of these syllabus documents contains mandatory outcomes and elective outcomes, which are only partly related to the national strands. As from 2002 all students at the end of Year 10 will sit for external examinations in Australian history and Australian geography incorporating civics and citizenship.

In Queensland new structures for managing curriculum were developed in the early 1990s which led to the establishment of the Queensland School Curriculum Council in 1996. A studies of society and environment draft syllabus was produced in 1999. It is being trialled in 2000. The syllabus includes four of the national strands, namely:

- Time, Continuity and Change
- Place and Space
- Culture and Identity
- Systems, Resources and Power

Sourcebook modules and resource documents have been produced for teachers. The website provides up to date information: http://www.qscc.qld.edu.au. Another exciting development is the conceptualisation and trialling of materials produced by the New Basics Project (Education Queensland, 2000).

Since 1993 it is evident that the national influence on curriculum development has waned. In some states such as NSW and Victoria there has been a major shift away from the national profile in studies of society and environment. It is likely that this trend will also become more marked in South Australia and Queensland. To a certain extent, this might be expected as an obsolescence factor emerges for 1990s materials no longer deemed to be relevant for the twenty-first century.

Yet, it should also be noted that a national influence is still present through the

Discovering Democracy program and through funding provided for specific environment projects such as the National Greenhouse Strategy. The Discovery Democracy program was established in 1997 and involved an input of 25 million dollars by the Commonwealth Government. It is no accident that many of the states and territories have now included a civics and citizenship strand into their studies of society and environment structure (see Table 8.6).

It would appear that some of the problems which occurred with developing the national statements and profiles are reoccurring with Discovering Democracy (Gill and Reid, 1999; Hogan and Fearnley-Sander, 1999; Finch, 1999). Nevertheless, the development of these curriculum materials is having a major impact on all states and territories.

At another policy level it might be argued that MCEETYA's efforts in Adelaide in 1991 to formulate Australia's common and agreed national goals for schooling in the twenty-first century was another attempt to influence the curriculum agenda. Compared with the Hobart Declaration of 1989 (see page 167), it should be noted that there is a stronger emphasis in this set of goals upon employment-related skills, the fostering of enterprise skills (Frost, 2000) and the use of new technologies.

■ Concluding Comments

Studies of society and environment, as a generic learning area, is being maintained in all states and territories even though in one state it is referred to as 'Human Society and its Environment'.

On the one hand, it might be argued that there is an urgent need for critical reviews of the structure of studies of society and environment and the assumptions underlying profiles, strands and outcomes. It would seem that these studies are needed to justify any major changes such as the decision in Victoria to have one integrated strand at primary school level and discipline-oriented strands at secondary school level.

Yet it can also be argued that states and territories have adjusted to local contexts and as a result of extensive consultation with teachers, principals and parents have produced structures which best suit their needs. The decisions have been made based on school data and pragmatic rather than theoretical considerations.

States and territories have used a variety of strategies to introduce teachers, principals and parents to the new outcomes-based approach (see Table 8.7). They have included various trialling arrangements (and subsequent refining); whole-school approaches offering multiple pathways; professional development opportunities; and the provision of clear guidelines, policy and support materials (Francis and Holt, 1997).

During the 1990s considerable progress has been made by all states and territories. Yet, there are still major problems to be overcome. Some of the common difficulties include:

- workload for teachers;
- time allocations for each of the eight learning areas;
- teacher concern about accountability;
- difficulties in reporting to parents;
- difficulties in making valid and reliable judgments about standards defined in outcomes.

Table 8.6 *Modifications to the conceptual structure by states and territories (1994–96)*

	Titles of documents	Modifications to strands	Modifications to national statement	Modifications to profile
ACT	ACT Curriculum Framework in SSE; Profile in SSE Support papers on each cross-curriculum perspective	Nil	Incorporated into ACT curriculum framework; additional band for preschool to Year 1; addition of Broad Outcomes; elaboration of nine cross-curriculum perspectives	Nil
Northern Territory	Learning area statement 'The Studies of Society and Environment' 'Common Curriculum Statement' 'Common Assessment and Reporting Statement' (Northern Territory Board of Studies)	Minor	Minor	Trialled 4 strands: · Investigation, Communication and Participation · Democratic Processes · Social Justice · Ecological Sustainability
South Australia	'Curriculum Standards and Accountability Framework'	Strands reduced to 4: · Societies and Cultures · Time, Continuity and Change · Place, Space and Environment · Social Systems Essential learnings also included	Major	Great emphasis on devolution of standards to schools

Modifications to cross-curriculum perspectives	Modification to outcome statements in national profile	Modification of values	Schedule
Enlarged to include Aboriginal & Torres Strait Islander Education, Australian Education, Environment Education, Gender Equity, Information Access, Language for Understanding, Multicultural Education, Special Needs Education, Work Education	Nil	Some elaborations	Support documents for teachers published in 1997
	Nil	Some elaborations	Plans to develop a draft framework
Currently under review	Currently under review	Currently under review	The draft was completed in 2000. The final version is to be implemented in 2001

continued ...

Table 8.6 *Modifications to the conceptual structure by states and territories (1994–96) (continued)*

	Titles of documents	Modifications to strands	Modifications to national statement	Modifications to profile
Tasmania (Dept of Education & the Arts)	'Studies of Society and Environment Planning Grid', *Taking Action— A Studies of Society and Environment Reference Book*	Includes essential learnings	Minor	Minor
Western Australia	'Curriculum Framework' 1998 (Curriculum Council), 'Society & Environment Student Outcome Statements' (Education Dept of WA)	Addition of 7th strand 'Active Citizenship'	Minor	Annotated work samples and pointers published
Victoria	Curriculum and Standards Framework II (Board of Studies)	1 strand 'Society & Environment' for primary years (levels 1–3); higher levels, five strands reduced to 3: · History · Geography · Economy & Society Essential know-ledge included for every level	Levels reduced from 7 to 6	Major changes (see strands)

Modifications to cross-curriculum perspectives	Modification to outcome statements in national profile	Modification of values	Schedule
Minor	Minor	Minor	
Minor	Minor	Minor	Implementation in all government schools by 2004
Emphasis on civics, environmental education, vocational education	Learning outcomes reduced from 45 to 24	Major changes (see cross-curriculum)	Trialled in 1999. Implementation will commence in 2000

continued ...

Table 8.6 *Modifications to the conceptual structure by states and territories (1994–96) (continued)*

	Titles of documents	Modifications to strands	Modifications to national statement	Modifications to profile
NSW	'Human Society & its Environment' syllabuses (Board of Studies), K–6 Syllabus, 7–10 Syllabuses in: · Geography · History · Studies of religion · Aboriginal studies	Mandatory outcomes for geography and history and elective areas. K–6 syllabuses follow 4 of the national strands (Change and Continuity, Cultures, Environments, Social Systems and Structures); syllabuses for 7–10 include different outcomes	Not used	Not used
Qld	'Studies of Society and Environment' (Queensland School Curriculum Council) · Studies of Society & Environment 1–10 Syllabus · Years 9–10 Civics Optional Syllabus · Years 9–10 Optional Syllabus · Years 9–10 History Optional Syllabus	4 strands only: · Time, Continuity and Change · Place and Space · Culture and Identity · Systems, Resources and Power	Modified	Modified

Modifications to cross-curriculum perspectives	Modification to outcome statements in national profile	Modification of values	Schedule
Minor changes. Civics & citizenship education included in K–6 syllabus	Some inclusion of outcomes in syllabuses	Minor changes	Syllabus for K–6 implemented in 2000. In 2002 all Year 10 students will sit for external examinations in Australian history, Australian geography, incorporating Civics & Citizenship
Minor changes	Modified outcome statements included	Minor changes	Copies made available in term 1, 2000. Sourcebook guidelines and modules trialled in 2000

Table 8.7 *Examples of diverse approaches used by states and territories to implement studies of society and environment curricula*

- Implementation support plans involving teachers, principals and parents
- Folders of exemplars, assessment tasks
- Teams of consultants to visit schools
- School-based projects
- NPDP projects
- Action research groups
- External evaluation studies (for example, by the ACER)
- Case studies by independent researchers
- Newsletters
- Parent brochures
- Whole-school planning workshops
- Student mapping profile sheets
- Planning charts
- Multimedia kits
- Computer software programs for recording assessments (for example, KIDMAP)
- Sample programs

Studies of society and environment has evolved as a distinctive learning area in Australian schools. The next decade will be a significant one to see whether educators can build on current successes and tackle some of the more enduring problems associated with a standards/outcomes approach.

QUESTIONS AND ACTIVITIES

1. To what extent do you consider studies of society and environment to be a viable and distinctive learning area? What are some of the problems of combining social studies and environment into one curriculum area?

2. What are the arguments for representing individual disciplines (e.g. economics) rather than generic concepts or strands (e.g. resources)? If a disciplinary basis was used, what disciplines would you include? Why? Why would a disciplinary focus be unacceptable to early childhood and primary school teachers? Is it feasible to have different curriculum structures for primary schools and secondary schools?

3. What do you consider would be the major concerns for you personally to teach studies of society and environment using a standards/outcomes approach?

4. An attempt to produce a national curriculum started with a flourish in 1988 but was stalled, if not terminated, by events in 1993. Is there any likelihood of a national curriculum being accepted in the near future? What are some major factors? Are there significant advantages or disadvantages in having a national curriculum?

5. 'The levels (in the profiles) do not mark a necessary ordering of any developmental sequence (more accurately, we have no evidence that they do) but are simply a setting out of particular, and likely to change, majority cultural patterns' (Collins, 1994b: 14). Discuss.

Assessing, Recording and Reporting Student Learning

Introduction

Assessment and reporting are important aspects of teachers' work. Assessment information is used to inform decision making about teaching programs and is the integrating factor (New South Wales Department of School Education, 1996c). All students should have regular opportunities to receive and discuss information about their progress. The assessment techniques used in schools must recognise the differing needs of students and address the complexities of Aboriginality, culture, gender, socioeconomic status, disability and geographic isolation (Department of Education and Children's Services, 1995).

■ Some Definitions

Ideally, assessment of students' learning should be:

- fair and honest;
- understandable by all students;
- an integral part of the learning process;
- to enable all students to demonstrate some achievement;
- lively, active, rewarding experiences;
- comprehensible to parents and external groups;
- based on teaching objectives/outcomes.

In practice, assessment can be a very subjective and risky affair (Turner, 1994). Grades can be wrongly assigned and erroneous judgments about students are often made. In the literature there are numerous accounts of the tyranny of tests and the need for assessment reform (Wolfe and Reardon, 1996).

One reason for the negative comments about assessment is that a number of terms are used interchangeably when there are, in fact, major differences. The term 'evaluation' is often used synonymously with the term 'assessment' but there are important distinctions. Evaluation subsumes assessment. It is an omnibus term which describes all the kinds of data which are collected about schooling, including data about students' behaviour, teachers' planning and instruction, and the curriculum materials used. It is possible to do an evaluation of a teacher and his or her classroom, although more commonly evaluations of the total school are undertaken.

Grading is the assigning of a grade or mark (numerical score, letter, grade, descriptive ranking) for work undertaken by students, such as a project or a written test.

Assessment is the term typically used to describe the activities undertaken by a teacher to obtain information about the knowledge, skills and attitudes of students.

Alternative assessment is used to express a very different approach to assessment, largely diametrically opposed to traditional quantitative measurement of relatively low level skills, as illustrated by many standardised achievement tests.

Performance assessment refers to a variety of tasks and situations in which students are given opportunities to demonstrate their understanding and thoughtfully to apply knowledge, skills and habits of mind in a variety of contexts.

Authentic assessment refers to assessment practices that engage students in 'real-world' tasks and where the assessment criteria relate to actual performance in the world outside the school. However, the term 'authentic' is somewhat misleading, because it seems to imply that other forms of assessment are 'non-authentic'. The evidence to date reveals that there are additional costs and some negative consequences of using authentic assessment (Mehrens, 1998).

■ Purposes of Assessment

Assessment practices are often criticised because they may be used for different purposes, some of which can be diametrically opposed. Typically the purposes of assessment include:

- diagnosis of learning/monitoring progress;
- grading students;
- predicting future achievements;
- motivating students;
- diagnosis of teaching;
- informing parents.

Diagnosis of learning/monitoring progress is a major reason for assessment. This information may be gleaned by a teacher asking questions of individual students or by student comments. The diagnosis should help each student understand his or her weaknesses and it also helps the teacher to know where to direct his or her instructional energies.

In most cases, student grades are assigned to indicate achievement at the end of a unit or term, semester or year. Sufficient evidence needs to be collected by a teacher to enable the person to assign accurate grades. Generally, the more frequently and varied the assessments used, the more informed the teacher will be about the grades to assign to students.

Assessment can also be used to predict students' eligibility for selection in future courses. This is usually of importance at upper secondary school levels.

Assessment can often increase the motivation of students even though the teacher may not consciously highlight it as an incentive to work hard. It depends of course on the individual learner, as some students will be highly motivated by an impending test whereas others might suffer excessive stress and/or be demotivated.

Assessment data can provide valuable diagnostic information for the teacher, for example reasons why lessons fly or flop (Eisner, 1993). It may indicate, for example, that aspects of content or processes were not understood fully by students or that the material presented was too difficult or too easy for a particular class.

■ Intended Audiences

There are close links between reasons for assessment and their intended audiences. Possible audiences include:

- *learners*—this should be the main audience, but typically they are not given a high priority. They are rarely involved in planning the assessment activities;
- *teachers*—teachers need feedback about the effectiveness of their teaching. Student assessment data is being used increasingly as a data source for appraising teachers;
- *parents*—parents want regular feedback. Media efforts to publicise school results and 'league tables' of schools has led to increased clamourings for assessment information;
- *tertiary institutions*—universities and technical and further education colleges require specific assessment information from applicants intending to enrol;
- *employers*—employers are demanding more specific information especially in terms of literacy and numeracy and key competencies.

■ Modes of Assessing

Teachers have the opportunity to use a variety of modes of assessment which can range from highly prescriptive to collectively negotiated. The choices are largely dependent upon a teacher's value stances about what is to be taught, how and when. In studies of society and environment there are many opportunities for using a variety of approaches.

Harris and Bell (1994) suggest that modes of assessment can best be analysed by separating them out into separate bipolar constructs, as depicted in Table 9.1.

Table 9.1 *Modes of assessing*

diagnostic/ formative	Summative
informal	formal
norm referenced	criterion referenced
process	product
learner judged	teacher judged
internal	external
inclusive	exclusive
liberal	technicist

Diagnostic/formative—summative

Students come into classrooms with varying backgrounds and interests, and it is inefficient to start a new teaching unit without checking their knowledge and understandings. Some may lack the prerequisite skills needed to undertake the lessons required of them and, worse still, others may have certain negative attitudes to the topic which will present a major difficulty unless the teacher is aware in advance of these emotional attitudes. On the other hand, if the students already have a number of skills or understandings the teacher intended to teach them, their interest and enthusiasm would be reduced if the same activities were repeated.

Diagnostic assessment reminds teachers that they must start their instruction at the level the students have reached. What is more, the teacher needs to be continually aware of students' levels in their progress through the curriculum unit. In this sense, the teacher is undertaking diagnostic evaluation through all the stages of instruction.

Formative assessment provides data about instructional units in progress and students in action. The data helps to develop or form the final curriculum product and helps students adjust to their learning tasks through the feedback they receive. Formative evaluation then is important because it provides data to enable 'on the spot' changes to be made where necessary (Tunstall and Gipps, 1996; Torrance and Pryor, 2000).

Summative assessment is the final goal of an educational activity. Eventually teachers need to know the relative merits and demerits of a curriculum package. Also, they need to have collected appropriate information about the levels of achievement reached by students. Of course, this information may be used in a diagnostic way as a preliminary to further activities, but it must be emphasised that summative evaluation provides the data from which decisions can be made. Table 9.2 lists a range of assessment techniques that can be used as diagnostic, formative or summative assessment.

Informal—formal

Informal observations of natural situations are especially valuable in studies of society and environment for gaining information about student interactions (Gipps, 2000). The less obvious it is to students that they are being assessed, the more natural will be their behaviour. However, this means that careful records need to be kept if the progress of each student is to be recorded accurately.

Formal assessment is planned and is often an obtrusive activity. Thus any weekly tests and planned assignments could be categorised as formal assessments. Parents often want understandable formal tests (Orlich *et al.*, 1998). There are a number of forms of informal and formal assessments that can be used (see Table 9.3). Typically, primary teachers rely on informal evidence and observation, while secondary teachers tend to use paper and pencil tests and other written evidence (McMillan, Workman and Myran, 1999).

Norm referenced—criterion referenced

Norm-referenced measures are used to compare students' performance in specific tests. These measures simply provide comparative age-based data on how well certain students perform in a test (e.g. mapping skills) compared with other

Table 9.2 *Commonly used assessment techniques*

Diagnostic evaluation	Formative evaluation	Summative evaluation
· checklists	· checklists	· checklists
· rating scales	· *rating scales*	· rating scales
· *interest inventories*		
· *projective techniques*		
· *attitude scales*	· attitude scales	· attitude scales
· content analysis	· content analysis	· *content analysis*
· semantic differentials		· *semantic differentials*
· objective tests	· objective tests	· *objective tests*
· essay tests	· essay tests	· essay tests
· standardised tests		· *standardised tests*
· interviews	· interviews	· *interviews*
	· anecdotal records	· anecdotal records
	· log books	· log books
· performance charts	· performance charts	· performance charts
· autobiographies	· group discussions	

(Categories in italics indicate the assessment phase at which the technique is most frequently used.)

Table 9.3 *Commonly used assessment techniques in terms of studies of society and environment goals*

Assessing facts, concepts and generalisations	Assessing skills competence
· anecdotal records	· rating scales
· group discussions	· checklists
· checklists	· creation of a product
· objective tests	· self-assessment
· essay tests	· peer assessment
· samples of student work	· objective tests
· class projects	· performance tasks
· assessment tasks	**Assessing decision making and citizen action**
Assessing thinking skills and reflective thinking	· student logs
· interviews	· attitude scales
· group discussions	· student diaries
· anecdotal records	· anecdotal records
· observations	· checklists
· samples of student work	· interviews
· creation of products	· portfolios
· role-play enactments	· self-assessment
· rating scales	· objective tests
· checklists	
· essay tests	
· objective tests	
· peer assessment	
· assessment tasks	

students of the same age. Of course they are open to misinterpretation. Students who receive special coaching or good teaching are likely to outperform those students who do not have these opportunities. Norm-referenced measures provide valuable evaluative data about the performance of students on specific tasks but does not tell us anything about an individual's potential or attitude toward certain subjects.

Criterion-referenced measures avoid the competitive elements of norm-referenced measures because information is obtained about students' performance in terms of their previous performances rather than in relation to the performances of others (Filer, 2000). They can be used at any point in an instructional experience. Once the skill level for a particular task has been defined (the criterion) then it is presumed that a student will persevere until it is attained (mastered). The difficulty, of course, lies in defining learning activities in terms of tasks to be mastered.

Process—product

Most assessment involves making judgments about products such as an assignment, project or object. Products are often perceived to be the major priority of the course. Yet processes such as thinking skills, working cooperatively in groups and problem solving are very important (Withers and McCurry, 1990). To date, processes have been extremely difficult to measure and, as a result, tend to be overlooked.

Learner judged—teacher judged

At most levels of schooling the teacher does the judging about standards. Typically individual teachers set and mark their tests and other forms of assessment, yet if students are going to become self-directed learners they need to be responsibly involved in setting goals and in assessing their own progress toward attainment of these goals. Developments in outcomes-based learning make the standards more explicit, and provide more opportunities for student input into the planning of assessment tasks.

Internal—external

Internal assessment involves those directly participating in the teaching–learning process. External assessors become involved when 'high-status' assessments are to occur state-wide, typically at the completion of Year 12. These forms of assessment are likely to have major impacts upon teaching but they also have negative effects (Mehrens, 1998). With the exception of Queensland and the ACT, all other Australian states and territories use external assessments at Year 12 because they believe they have greater public confidence and credibility, even though such beliefs are difficult to confirm or refute!

Inclusive—exclusive

The production of forms of assessment should, ideally, provide access to all learners and be inclusive, regardless of gender, ethnicity or disadvantage. Studies have indicated that a number of forms of assessment are exclusive. For example, some multiple-choice tests tend to be biased against females (Salvia and Ysseldyle, 1998; Gipps and Murphy, 1994). Teachers' assessment of ethnic minority students can often be biased, as reported by Cunningham (1998).

Liberal—technicist

A number of writers argue that traditional forms of assessment are technicist and are used to identify and perpetuate the social hierarchy (Blackmore, 1988; Broadfoot, 1979). Many forms of assessment, especially traditional written examinations, concentrate upon a narrow view of student achievement which emphasises the outcomes of the academic curriculum. A liberal orientation to assessment provides a wider framework and takes into consideration economic and political issues of society.

■ Commonly Used Assessment Techniques

A number of assessment techniques are available to teachers and they can be used at various diagnostic, formative and summative stages. Some are informal but the majority are formal techniques. It is desirable for teachers to use a variety of techniques to ensure that the multidimensionality of student performance is adequately explored (Haney and Madaus, 1989). But there is also the danger of over-assessing and collecting vast arrays of data that have limited use.

Furthermore, it is important for each teacher, when selecting specific assessment techniques, to consider major goals in studies of society and environment teaching. For example, Table 9.3 categorises assessment techniques in terms of four major goals or priorities. A number of the assessment techniques are appropriate in each of the four categories but some have optimal use in a particular category.

Examples of assessment techniques from each of the four categories are described below.

Objective tests

As indicated in Table 9.3 objective tests are useful in all of the four categories but they are especially valuable in assessing concept attainment and thinking skills (Worthen *et al.*, 1999).

Teachers commonly use objective tests—they contain items that can be marked quickly by hand or by machine (Clarke *et al.*, 2000). Such tests are deemed 'objective' because all answers can be definitely classified as correct or incorrect and therefore no subjective judgments go into the scoring. Of course, many subjective decisions about what items to include and how items are stated go into the creation of such a test. Well-constructed items are thus a necessity for test results to be valuable, and it is important that the items cover all portions of the curriculum being evaluated.

The most common types of objective tests are the following:

1. Multiple-choice items—each item consists of a question or an incomplete statement followed by three or more possible responses. The correct or best one is the answer, the others are distractors. For example:

Draw a circle around the best answer to end the sentence.

A person who buys goods and services is a

consumer   producer   worker

2. Matching items—these items are used to assess students' ability to associate terms and meanings. It is important to have items in each column that are related and that there are more choices than can be matched. For example:

Match the following countries with the continents in which they are located.

Mexico	South America
Finland	Africa
Chad	Europe
Chile	Asia
India	Asia
	North America
	Australia

Using observations to assess thinking skills

3. Alternative-choice items (True–False, Yes–No)—the items are relatively easy to prepare but students are prone to guess correct answers. Simple recall questions should be avoided. For example:

Mark the following as True (T) or False (F)

East is to the right of someone facing south

       True   False

Villages are larger than towns

       True   False

4. Sentence completion items—these items require students to complete sentences or give examples. A range of cognitive and affective outcomes can be assessed. For example:

Complete the following

A democracy is government by

_____

A dictatorship is government by

_____

Objective tests have a number of advantages:

- they are quick for students to complete, efficient and, when well constructed, reliable;
- a wide range of specific topics can be assessed;
- they are potentially fairer than essay tests because penmanship and neatness are irrelevant.

Disadvantages include:

- they require considerable skill and time to construct;
- there is tendency to include recall items.

Assessment tasks

Assessment tasks are concrete performance tasks designed to be part of regular classroom instruction. The 'authentic' nature of assessment tasks is important to teachers but especially to students—they need to recognise that various aspects of the typical school day can be incorporated as assessment tasks and that judgments based upon them are likely to be far more meaningful than judgments based upon external tests (Darling-Hammond and Falk, 1997). Furthermore, assessment tasks are a promising technique for assessing outcome statements and making judgments about levels (Griffin and Smith, 1998).

Assessment tasks will vary considerably in the length of time needed to complete them. Some can easily be accommodated in a single lesson or period, but others might extend over several weeks. It will depend on the activities being considered. Some may be more appropriate as brief, intense activities (e.g. a role play) whereas others may require extended time for exploratory investigation, analysis and presentations. Assessment tasks are likely to be mainly produced by individual teachers, but as students become more familiar with the activities they are likely to become willing and important planners/developers. In some classrooms, students are being given far more opportunities for self-assessment in regard to assessment tasks. By reflecting on their performances or products, students can understand criteria that need to be established and the goals that they need to set themselves for further learning.

The opportunities for using ongoing teaching–learning activities as assessment tasks are many and varied. For example, Table 9.4 provides 25 classroom activities that can be used most effectively.

Assumptions about creating assessment tasks:

- they must be meaningful to students;
- they must include explicit assessment criteria;

Table 9.4 *Classroom activities which can be used for assessment tasks*

Examples	
1. Portfolios	14. Field trips
2. Journal writing	15. Problem-solving tasks
3. Role playing	16. Concept mapping
4. Imaginative writing	17. Induction/deduction tasks
5. Designing/presenting community projects	18. Panel discussions
6. Team interviewing	19. Dramatic enactments
7. Model-building	20. Computer simulations
8. Surveys involving parents	21. Flow charts
9. Dialogue diaries	22. Songs
10. Mini-investigations	23. Collages
11. Presenting position papers	24. Dances
12. Reports based on reflective/critical thinking	25. Plays
13. Individual and group projects	

- criteria will involve process as well as product.

Questions to consider when designing assessment tasks:

1. What knowledge, skills and attitudes will the students demonstrate?
2. How will this activity enhance the curriculum taught in my class?
3. Will I use formal or informal, structured or unstructured criteria for assessing the task?
4. Will I design the assessment task single-handed and/or work collaboratively on it with other teachers and/or involve my students?
5. What length of time will be available to complete the assessment task?
6. What individual/group activities will be included?
7. What materials and equipment will be needed?
8. Will I assess the assessment task or will other teachers be involved or will students do some self-assessment?
9. How will the judgments be used for further teaching and learning?

The details provided about an assessment task should, of course, be enticing and inviting for the students. The format should be easy to follow. Most especially, the directions for successfully completing the task should be clear and achievable by a large majority of students. If the assessment task is based on ongoing classroom learning and the interests of the students, there should be no difficulty in producing tasks which are appealing and highly motivating to students. As noted by Brookhart and De Voge (1998), assessment tasks involve students in mental effort (persistence, thinking skills) as well as completing overt tasks.

The reality check comes with the criteria to be used to judge performance on the assessment task. By stating explicit criteria in advance, this should give most students sufficient notice about what will be expected of them. To ensure that a multidimensional approach is taken it is important that the criteria include aspects relating to process (e.g. evidence of investigative skills) as well as product (e.g. presentation of models, charts, written materials). Self-assessment and peer-assessment elements could be important aspects of many assessment tasks.

Example
Our Needs and Wants: Assessment Task

1. The context
- To evaluate how a student identifies the events and stages in people's lives.
- To identify that each of us has different needs and wants depending on our life situations.
- At different stages in our lives we have needs and wants which are satisfied by others, within the constraints of particular environments.
- Students need to be aware of life stages and be familiar with reading and making time lines. They will have been introduced to the concepts of basic needs and wants.

2. Strand and Level

Strand	Substrand	Level
Investigation, Communication and Participation	Investigation	1–3
Time, Continuity and Change	Time and change	1–3
Place and Space	People and places	1–3
Natural and Social Systems	Economic systems	1–3

3. The task
Students will be asked to construct a time line to indicate the needs and wants we desire at different stages in our lives.
Suggested time: Two 1-hour sessions.

Preparation
Materials: students' drawings, cut-out pictures, A3 sheets of paper, magazines, glue and scissors.
Worksheet to show how some needs and wants are satisfied (self-assessment sheet).

Procedure
Students are required to:
- construct a time line showing a number of stages in human development;
- place pictures and drawings appropriate to the needs and wants of life stages represented on the time line;
- identify how some needs and wants are satisfied at each developmental stage;
- attempt to define the difference between a need and a want;
- attempt to describe how environmental and economic constraints affect how wants and needs are fulfilled.

4. Making judgments
Level 1 students will be capable of constructing a time line with three developmental stages (say, baby, child, adult) and will place their pictures to represent these life stages. They will be able to identify their own needs and wants and be aware of the people who help provide them. Level 1 students should be able to make their own selections of appropriate pictures and give reasons for their placement on the time line. At level 1 students will be capable of identifying from which source their own needs and wants will be met and will recognise that sometimes needs and wants cannot be provided.

Students will be demonstrating level 2 understandings if they can make their own decisions about which stages will be included on their time line and accurately classify and justify placement of pictures. Students will be aware that some needs and wants will continue throughout people's lives and some will change. Level 2 students will be able to give examples of how people obtain their needs and wants and will identify reasons which might make their acquisition difficult or even impossible.

A typical level 3 will construct a time line including sequence of years or time periods. They may gather information from and clarify ideas through interviews with people currently in a particular developmental stage. Level 3 students will be capable of showing that some changes in needs and wants occur because of changes in technology used in the home, industries and community facilities. They can describe how the natural environment and economic constraints may create barriers to fulfilling needs and wants.

5. Student handouts

(a) A3 sheets of paper on which students draw time lines (sample).

BABY	CHILD	ADULT
Needs Wants	Needs Wants	Needs Wants

(b) Allow level 2 and 3 students to draft own tables (sample).

Life Stage	A Need	Provided By	A Want	Provided By

(c) Self-assessment Sheet

Name: ————————————

What I have learned about needs and wants: ————————————
————————————————

I think a need is: ————————————
————————————————

I think a want is: ————————————
————————————————

Sometimes we cannot have what we need because:————————————
————————————————

Sometimes we cannot have what we want because:————————————
————————————————

One thing I need is:————————————
   I can get it from: ————————————
   It is made from:————————————
One thing I want is: ————————————
   I can get it from: ————————————
   It is made from:————————————

Rating scales

Rating scales have a wide range of uses within studies of society and environment. It is possible for a teacher to rate the level of skill of an entire class, a small group or individual students. Table 9.5 depicts a rating scale.

It is important to bear in mind that use of a rating scale may not create new knowledge for the teacher; it may merely make explicit those judgments that a teacher already holds. However, students' skills may change over time or be demonstrated in new ways, so making explicit judgments may clarify for the teacher how well students are mastering general skills, specific topics or a whole curriculum. Because the teacher rates students on a numerical scale, this approach seems to some people to be more appropriate for rating specific skills than general understandings or even more nebulous items such as values and attitudes. So a teacher may wish to confine the use of rating scales to only what is specific and concrete. For instance, a rating scale might be used to diagnose why a certain student is having trouble learning a particular topic. Information from the scale might also help the teacher focus discussions with a student over a period of time.

An interesting variation is to have a small

Model building can be used as an effective assessment task

Table 9.5 *A Rating scale*

Name:
Date:
Skill being taught:

1. Understood the steps involved

1	2	3	4
Unsatisfactory	Fair	Good	Excellent

2. Willing to be involved

1	2	3	4
Unsatisfactory	Fair	Good	Excellent

3. Mastered each subskill in turn

1	2	3	4
Unsatisfactory	Fair	Good	Excellent

4. Completed the skills activity

1	2	3	4
Unsatisfactory	Fair	Good	Excellent

group of students carry out a task or demonstrate a skill and ask the remainder of the class to rate the group's performance. Comments by peers are often helpful to students and may be accepted more readily than comments made by the teacher. The problem with such activities is that the purpose is sometimes lost in the activity, which becomes an end in itself. Rating scales are helpful to students and teachers only if they provide useful feedback about present behaviour concisely and expeditiously; if they become time consuming and complicated, then their purpose is lost (Cangelosi, 1992).

Here is a summary of the advantages and disadvantages of rating scales.

Advantages

- Rating scales crystallise teachers' judgments about individual students or group of students.
- They can be done quickly and easily.
- They can be used by teachers or students.

Disadvantages

- They provide teachers with no new information.
- They are difficult to compile and to be used other than for specific skills and competencies.

Checklists

Checklists are designed to assess work completed by students but they can also be used for student self-assessment and peer assessment. Checklists are typically used to provide informal assessment and undertaken as part of daily teaching. They can be used to assess mapping skills, group work, reports and projects (see Tables 9.6 and 9.7).

Advantages

- They can measure behaviours that are not easily assessed through paper and pencil tests.
- They are simple to use.
- There is no restriction on who uses them.

Table 9.6 *Example of a mapping checklist*

1. Appropriate title	Very Good	Good	Fair	Unsatisfactory
2. Clear map key	Very Good	Good	Fair	Unsatisfactory
3. Clear compass rose	Very Good	Good	Fair	Unsatisfactory
4. Appropriate symbols	Very Good	Good	Fair	Unsatisfactory
5. Items located accurately	Very Good	Good	Fair	Unsatisfactory
6. Legible printing and headings	Very Good	Good	Fair	Unsatisfactory

Table 9.7 *Example of an inquiry unit checklist*

	Attacks problem in rational manner	Organises data	Gathers information	Grasps principles	Total
Kerry	/	/	X	/	5
Peter				/	1
Kim	X	/	X	/	6
Alan	X	X	X	/	7
Kylie	/	X	/	X	6
Jeff	/	X	X	X	7
Maria	/		/	/	3

No evidence	☐	0 points
Some evidence	/̲	1 point
Good evidence	X̲	2 points

Disadvantages

- They usually only indicate the presence or absence of a given behaviour.
- It is difficult to produce the pre-identified categories.

Portfolios

Portfolios are sources of evidence for judgments of student achievement in a range of situations (see Table 9.8). As noted by Forster and Masters (1996), working portfolios are used to monitor students' day to day progress and to encourage students to reflect on their own learning. They are especially valuable for enabling students with disabilities to record their achievements (Kearns, Kleinert and Kennedy, 1999). They provide an excellent opportunity for students and teachers to undertake ongoing formative and diagnostic assessment because:

- each student can identify achievements and discuss these at portfolio conferences;
- the teacher assesses each student's ability to reflect on and structure his or her portfolio;
- each student's portfolio provides a rich picture about his or her progress in achieving specific learning outcomes (Ross, 1996).

Hebert (1998) notes that students are strongly motivated to select samples of their work and to assemble them into a portfolio. In so doing, they are undertaking a measure of self-assessment. In addition, items can be included in the portfolio which require substantial self-assessment.

For example, self-assessment checklists and questionnaire forms can be a required component; student 'journals' can be required whereby students reflect upon particular activities they have undertaken; 'logs' of performance can be included which indicate dates and details about topics/ projects that have been commenced and finished; a portfolio conference with each student enables the teacher to ask questions about a range of issues.

Forster and Masters (1996a) distinguish between working portfolios and documentary portfolios. Documentary portfolios are assembled specifically for assessment and only include selections of students' best work (final products and evidence of processes used). For documentary portfolios it is crucial that the criteria (rubrics) for assessment and grading are very explicit (Goodrich, 1997). The teacher must ensure that the guidelines about which items to include do in fact cover the instructional goals or outcomes. Students need to know what ratings will apply and what criteria will be used to award particular grades.

Documentary portfolios should provide for open-ended tasks so that students have the opportunity to demonstrate their varying levels of knowledge and understanding. If a task is too focused it may prevent a number

Table 9.8 *What a student portfolio might contain*

· written essays	· team or group efforts
· summaries	· creative expressions
· journal/daily logs	· major projects/products (e.g. dioramas,
· self-assessments, checklists, rating forms	oral history collections, audio/videotapes,
· experiments	charts, cards, time lines)
· demonstrations of specific skills	· tests
· research notes	· teacher comments
· rough drafts and finished products	

of students demonstrating their strengths and interests. Further, it could favour a particular gender or cultural group.

Advantages

- They enable students to be actively involved in constructing their own know-ledge.
- They encourage students to assess themselves.
- They encourage teachers to allow a broad range and variety of student products for assessment.
- They require students to demonstrate thinking and expressive skills.
- They can provide an equitable and sensitive portrayal of what students know and are able to do.
- They enable teachers to focus on impor-tant student outcomes.
- They can provide credible evidence of student achievement to parents and the community.

Disadvantages

- Enormous amounts of time are needed by teachers in helping students select tasks, providing support and assessing portfolios (Hall and Hewitt-Gervais, 1999).
- Portfolio grades have only moderate correlations with other forms of assessment.
- There are problems in storing and display-ing large numbers of bulky portfolios.
- Inter-ratio agreement on portfolio assessments is very low.
- Portfolios may not represent an individual student's work but represent the efforts of several supporting peers, teachers or parents.
- Portfolios cannot provide the same con-trol over skills being assessed compared with multiple-choice tests (Reckase, 1997).

■ Collecting Assessment Evidence

Teachers can collect evidence of student attainment from a range of ongoing classroom activities. The techniques listed in Table 9.2 indicate a range of informal and formal ones that are available.

A most important task for every teacher is to identify which activities or outcomes are significant ones and which techniques provide the most accurate and reliable assessment information. These decisions need to be made carefully—a 'hodgepodge' of activities is of little value to the teacher or his/her students (McMillan *et al.*, 1999).

In terms of the studies of society and environment profile, students will be working at very different rates and so it is necessary to collect evidence about:

- student work in progress (rough notes, progress reports and plans);
- final products (drawings, models, research reports);
- assessment tasks (as described earlier in 'Assessment tasks').

Teachers will use evidence from all these sources in arriving at judgments about the level of a student's achievement. They can be assisted in making judgments by looking at the pointers provided for each outcome and also the work samples.

■ Recording

Good record keeping is essential for teachers because it is impossible to remember a range of data about a number of students. Further-more, recorded assessment data is needed to make decisions about programming and reporting (Moyles, 1995). It is also needed to facilitate communication when more than one teacher is involved with a class, and for whole-school planning.

Every teacher needs to develop an effective method of recording, yet it must not be so time consuming that other important activities are curtailed.

Some important characteristics of good recording systems include:

- they must be easily accessible (e.g. record cards, journals);
- they must be readily interpretable (standard terms or symbols are used);
- they satisfy the school or district requirements;
- they are appropriate and efficient for the class situation;
- they involve students in the process (e.g. keeping a student portfolio, self-assessment records);
- they are meaningful to all users of the records;
- they allow unanticipated as well as planned outcomes to be recorded;
- they provide comprehensive information

about students and enable effective monitoring of student progress to occur.

Yet it is also necessary to raise the caveat that excessive recording can get in the way of good teaching! (Neill, 1998). Teachers need to reflect carefully on what are the essential items to record and why they are essential.

There are very many ways of recording student information (see Table 9.9), many of which are closely tied to the assessment techniques described earlier in this chapter.

The example included in Table 9.10 is based upon recording levels for the process strand, Investigation, Communication and Participation, for an upper primary school class. It is a convenient summary which the teacher can use to compile final levels for students' reports.

It is very easy to get into a routine about recording without stopping to consider some basic points. In addition, there are now available numerous computer software packages (e.g. KIDMAP) for recording

Table 9.9 *Examples of record-keeping techniques*

· anecdotal records	· checklists
· observation sheets	· student self-assessment proformas
· record cards	· peer-assessment proformas
· student portfolios	

Table 9.10 *Year 6 Studies of Society and Environment*

	Investigation	Communication	Participation
Levels available	3 4 5	3 4 5	3 4 5
Student Names			
Example: Ross	Completed a library research project, covering all the headings. 4	Gave a very good oral presentation to class on the research project. 5	Worked in a team of 4 to prepare a follow-up local survey. 4

results. These packages need to be examined carefully to ascertain their respective strengths and weaknesses. The following questions are useful to reflect upon to ensure that your recording is equitable and economical, namely:

- Will any student be disadvantaged by using this recording technique? If so, what can be done?
- Are the records objective or judgmental, or a combination of both?
- Are the students involved in the process? How?
- How frequently should results be recorded?
- Who should have access to the records? (students? principal? other teachers? parents?)
- If you are using a computer software package, does it satisfy the criteria of being economical and equitable?

■ Reporting

Reporting is communicating information about students to parents and caregivers. Over recent years schools have been experimenting with different reporting formats to better inform parents and caregivers about each student's progress (see, for example, Cumming, 1998).

Some of the major types of reporting are listed in Table 9.11. All reporting systems attempt to provide good communication and foster collaboration between schools and parents. Plain English is an essential! (Smith, 1997). Some schools maintain traditional approaches which are no longer effective for

parents in the late 1990s. For example, the Department of Education and Children's Services (1995) note that many parents and caregivers:

- have work commitments that make attendance at meetings difficult;
- speak English as a second language;
- are not literate in English or in their first language;
- find visits to school difficult because of lack of transport or childcare facilities;
- feel alienated by schools.

Using profiles and outcome statements provides a rich source of topics for structuring written and oral reports but also ushers in new problems. Trialling of outcomes has revealed considerable enthusiasm by parents for the new common language but it has caused uncertainty about the amount of information which should be reported to parents (Education Department of Western Australia, 1995). For example, reports might include:

- information about each student's levels only (reporting only once a year because it takes considerable time for a student to progress from one level to another);
- information about students' performance on specific outcome statements;
- information about students' performance on strands and levels.

The completion of the national profiles in 1993 created a need for innovative, computer-based methods of reporting. This has led in a short time to new computer software becoming available such as CSI

Table 9.11   Examples of reporting

· formal and informal interviews	· written numerical reports
· individual subject reports or whole-school reports	· reports of profile levels
	· basic skills test reports
· work samples and portfolios	· key competency reports
· written descriptive reports	· computer-generated reports

Profiles, DUX and KIDMAP (McLean and Wilson, 1995). The ACER has been extremely active in this area and produced 'developmental assessment' packages which can:

- estimate students' locations on a progress map;
- estimate students' profile levels and outcomes achieved;
- estimate students' attainment on specific assessment tasks.

The DART Package (Forster, 1994) provides calibrated assessment tasks and developmental records in the English strands of viewing, reading, listening, speaking and writing. This computer-based package greatly reduces the recording time needed by teachers. Similar formats are likely to be available in the near future for studies of society and environment.

Although there is considerable enthusiasm for new reporting methods, especially those linked with profiles and outcomes (Resnick, Nolan and Resnick, 1995; Waters, Burger and Burger, 1995), there are still numerous, ongoing issues to be resolved, including:

- establishing the audiences for reporting (students, parents and caregivers, other teachers, school, system, employers);
- finding ways to reduce excessive teacher workloads associated with reporting;
- establishing the function of reporting (for example, to inform, to motivate);
- establishing the best format of reporting;
- establishing most appropriate formats of reporting for different levels of schooling;
- establishing when and how frequently reports should be issued;
- establishing how parents and caregivers might respond to reports they receive;
- providing reports that are clear and readily understandable by parents and caregivers.

■ Concluding Comments

In many countries right now new strategies are being used to reform assessment (Eisner, 2000). Some would argue that we are experiencing an assessment culture where teachers and learners collaborate about learning. The focus is upon using assessment to strengthen teaching and learning at the school level by engaging students in more meaningful, integrative and challenging tasks (Darling-Hammond and Ancess, 1996). That is, the teaching is now becoming more performance oriented, in keeping with performance assessments (McTighe, 1997).

Teachers are being encouraged to widen their repertoire of assessment techniques and means of reporting because it is realised that assessment is a powerful lever for school change. It is highly likely that teachers will find that the new forms of assessment will both motivate and sort students more effectively—assessment reform could transform teaching over the next few decades.

QUESTIONS AND ACTIVITIES

1. Does your school (or a school you can visit) have an assessment policy? What emphasis is given to informal and formal techniques? Critique the policy in terms of integration across the grades and recording and reporting procedures.

2. 'A major challenge for teachers is to create viable, satisfying assessment tasks' (Ministry of Education, British Columbia 1994: 3). How important are assessment tasks? Give details about how you might incorporate them into your program.

3. If teachers are to recognise the diverse nature of the student population and the importance of developmental learning they must choose appropriate assessment techniques. Select four or five techniques which you consider are suitable and give reasons for your choice.

4. Develop a checklist or a rating scale to assess whether students have acquired particular process skills. How would you use it? Indicate some possible advantages and disadvantages in using a checklist.

5. Good record keeping is essential if maximum benefit is to be derived from a variety of assessment techniques. What are some important practical considerations that must be followed? What involvement should students have in record keeping? Give examples.

6. The best reporting is where parents and teachers have ongoing communication and face-to-face discussion. Is this achievable in practice? Is there a danger of quick and easy reporting formats being implemented which are mechanistic and lacking in real information? Discuss.

7. 'The process of selecting samples of work and assembling them into a portfolio is profoundly important to children' (Hebert, 1998: 583). Discuss some of the advantages and disadvantages of using portfolios in studies of society and environment.

10

Inquiry Approaches and Student Projects

Introduction

In the typical classroom it is highly likely that the teacher is doing most of the talking. The opportunities for a student to initiate a discussion, or even to respond to a question, are usually very limited. Teacher-centred modes have traditionally been accepted over the decades, especially in studies of society and environment where large amounts of factual information are typically presented to students.

However, there are other modes of teaching, such as inquiry, problem-based learning and issues-centred instruction, that enable far greater opportunity for students to develop higher-order thinking skills.

In this chapter, these approaches are examined in some detail. The nature of 'inquiry' is highlighted by comparing it with other terms. Following this, a conceptual model depicting various components of inquiry is presented. The various steps of inquiry are examined in the latter sections of this chapter, using illustrations from primary and secondary schools.

■ Some Definitions

If we inquire into something, we are directing our thoughts and actions towards developing a better understanding of it. If the 'something' is a specific problem, then we may be sufficiently motivated to work at the problem until it is solved.

Students have a range of natural curiosities, and in a given school day they might inquire into a vast array of topics, many of which may have little to do with the formal curriculum! It is the task of the teacher, therefore, to harness these natural curiosities into ways of thinking which are logical, rational and sustainable.

Therein lies a major problem. Teachers have to be comfortable with using an approach that is dynamic and interactive (Leppard, 1993b). Rossi (1995) contends that such an approach produces dilemmas for the teacher, such as:

- What knowledge should guide the inquiry?
- How do you integrate student knowledge and experience with subject matter knowledge?
- What type of classroom environment is needed for students to discuss issues in a thoughtful and productive way?

Hawley and Duffy (1998) argue that for many teachers it is difficult to make the transition from didactic teacher to probing facilitator. It is equally difficult for students to make the transition from traditional forms of classroom instruction. As noted by Leppard (1993b), students have to become comfortable with the insecurity of flexibility. Notwithstanding, there are enormous opportunities for students if they get involved in an inquiry approach (Strasser *et al.*, 1971) such as:

- they will learn more about themselves, their environment and others in it;
- they will expand their repertoire of productive ways of working on problems they encounter;
- they will develop their ability to deal productively with frustrations that arise as they inquire.

Inquiry has been defined in many different ways by various authors, and other terms such as problem-based learning, critical thinking and issues-centred instruction have been used as synonyms. Inquiry, put most simply, is the sustained examination of a few topics, where students ask challenging questions and where they generate original and unconventional ideas and explanations (Newmann, 1990). However, it may be more fruitful to demonstrate how it differs from other terms often used synonymously.

Problem-based learning (PBL) uses a real-world problem as the context for an in-depth investigation. The key element is that the problems the students tackle are ill-structured—they include just enough information to suggest how they might proceed but never enough information to enable them to solve the problem without further inquiry (Checkley, 1997). Teachers who use a problem-based learning approach become tutors or coaches, helping students understand their own thinking (Savoie and Hughes, 1994). Inquiry is very similar to problem solving except that on occasions, relatively open ended issues may be the topics of attention and may have no immediate solution.

Critical thinking is a term commonly used to describe a student's ability to use convergent thinking processes, such as being able to examine the logical aspects of a problem and being able to make pragmatic judgments. Beyer (1985) emphasises the reasoned judgment aspect of critical thinking. Leming (1998) supports a developmental approach and notes that truly reflective judgment only occurs for students at the higher stages. Inquiry can contain many divergent thinking elements, such as creative thinking, in addition to convergent thinking elements and is practised at primary and secondary levels of schooling.

Issues-centred instruction is a more recent term (Chilcoat and Ligon, 1998). Although it has many inquiry characteristics such as encouraging students to solve contemporary problems and is based upon reflective thinking, the focus is on team approaches and collaborative learning. Students work in a mini-community and make collective decisions (Parker, 1996). Students pool their energies and ideas, drawing on the actual experiences and knowledge of each group member. According to Chilcoat and Ligon (1998), students gain communal strength— they learn to work together, to share ideas, to seek and build consensus and to make and honour collective decisions.

Recently, writers have extolled the virtues of constructivist pedagogy where students construct meaning from their activities (Rainer, Guyton and Bowen, 2000; Olsen, 2000).

It can be seen from the above examples that a generic inquiry process is inherent in all the other terms and so this will be used throughout the chapter.

Several advantages in using an inquiry approach have been presented by various writers, including the following:

- It is economical in its use of knowledge— only knowledge relevant to an issue is examined rather than a mass of facts being learnt as an end in itself.
- It enables students to view content in a more realistic and positive way as they analyse and apply data to the resolution of problems.
- It is intrinsically very motivating for students. It encourages students to reflect on certain issues, to search out relevant data and to come to decisions that are meaningful to them personally. In doing so they develop important metacognitive skills.
- It highlights the various agendas and biases of traditional custodians of knowledge and points students to the very real ambiguities of a post-modern world.
- It enables teacher–student relations to assume a healthier tone as the teacher becomes more a facilitator of learning and less a director of teacher-dominated activities.
- It provides superior transfer value when compared with other teaching methods. (It is difficult to find unequivocal evidence on this assertion, although it does appear to be likely.)

By contrast, there are many critics of an inquiry approach. The most common arguments include the following:

- It takes an inordinate amount of class time and out-of-school time compared with other teaching methods used in the typical school program, with its rigid scheduling of classes.
- It requires different mental processes such as analytic and whole-field cognitive sets—it may not be useful for all areas of teaching.
- It can be professionally hazardous to deal with some inquiry problems, especially controversial issues.
- Students prefer the traditional chapter-chapter approach—they don't want to be involved in thinking.
- Involving students in inquiry deludes them into thinking that they can solve all or most social problems.
- It is difficult to evaluate with traditional achievement tests—for example, how do you evaluate the thought processes used by a student engaged in an inquiry program?

■ A Conceptual Model

Sometimes a model can clarify how a concept is commonly used. It can be argued that as far as inquiry is concerned, there are really three dimensions that are critical: the inquiry atmosphere, the procedural continuum and the content continuum.

The inquiry atmosphere is an overarching dimension and consists of the socio-psychological background of the class, including in particular the quality of interactions between the teacher and the students. The model is illustrated in Figure 10.1 and described in more detail below. The procedural dimension refers to the set of procedures or steps required for an inquiry activity. The content dimension refers to the concepts and understandings that a student brings to bear on an inquiry situation.

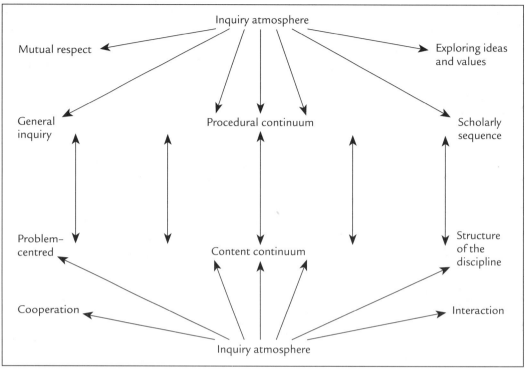

Figure 10.1 *Model of inquiry*

The inquiry atmosphere dimension

A desired inquiry atmosphere occurs in a classroom where there is a continuous re-examination of assumptions and accepted inquiry procedures and values. The degree to which this goal is reached depends upon the attitudes and responsibilities of both the teacher and the students. Leppard (1993b) suggests that the preferred teaching–learning relationship must be transactional rather than transmissive.

The teacher must challenge and continuously prod students to explore and test new alternatives, to ask students to defend their views publicly and to legitimise creative expression and perform diverse managerial tasks. Another important task for the teacher is to provide springboards for inquiry. Maxim (1983) points out that the teacher must give students last-resort assistance so that inquiry won't bog down, and to avert premature closure.

The students, for their part, are encouraged to become personally involved in problems, and to develop a self-directed quality of inquiry. To do this may entail acquiring procedural skills of inquiry as well as skills in creative, critical, open-minded and intuitive thinking.

Although some students will develop these skills without any difficulty, others will need assistance. Haycock (1991: 19) suggests that students will acquire these skills if the teacher interacts constantly with them

- by asking questions such as: *What does that information mean to you?*
- by prompting their basic understanding by asking questions such as: *Do you think it means X? Why?*
- by assisting them in their efforts by reading, listening or reviewing resources with them;

- by tracking each student with simple record-keeping devices such as checklists or rating scales.

When students and teachers alike are involved in these responsibilities, an educational environment conducive to active inquiry teaching is achieved.

The procedural continuum

Along the procedural continuum, a variety of positions can be noted. At one end is the extreme case where literally no procedural activities are required or suggested by the teacher. The guiding motivation for the students is their own levels of curiosity, inquisitiveness and tenacity to seek out answers. Some argue that this is the natural way of learning—that it is not subject matter that makes some learning more valuable than other learning, but the spirit in which it is done. Nelson (1992) points out the value of having at least some educational experiences that are not goal oriented, in which students inquire merely because they have an impulse to do so.

Nevertheless, such an interpretation of inquiry teaching can lead to difficulties in terms of curriculum planning and school organisation. It would appear that a more common position on the procedural continuum is where some standardisation of inquiry processes is set down. Academics have coined their own idiosyncratic phrases to describe the processes of inquiry teaching, but most include such steps as: becoming aware; identifying issues/hypotheses; searching out information; testing hypotheses; and reaching conclusions.

The content continuum

Two major positions can be noted at the extremities of the content continuum—the problems approach and the structure of the discipline approach. The problems approach

places the onus on the students to select and become involved in personally meaningful topics and to construct novel solutions (Byrnes and Torney-Purta, 1995). Hunt and Metcalf (1968) suggest that the problems selected should include topics from the 'closed areas' such as race or minority group relations, social class, sex, religion and morality. Oliver, Newman and Singleton (1992) use the term 'public issues' to highlight problems or value dilemmas which persist throughout history and across cultures. The important consideration is that the topics satisfy felt student needs. It seems highly probable that several, if not all, of the disciplines from the studies of society and environment might be utilised in the analysis of a particular topic. Perhaps this is exactly what inquiry teaching should be about. Kaplan (1964) maintains that inquiry teaching is autonomous insofar as the domain of truth has no boundaries, and that techniques, concepts and laws should be taken from any discipline when and if they can be used to clarify a topic. Undoubtedly the problems approach offers a genuine, comprehensive inquiry orientation. However, a relatively structureless Socratic style of discussion provides tremendous difficulties for curriculum development and administration.

The structure of the discipline approach has been the model adopted by many curriculum developers as noted in Mehlinger and Davis (1981) and Barth (1991). It can be accommodated with a scholarly inquiry procedural form, and to this end has been used by academics to further the development of their own particular discipline. The predominant emphasis is on cognitive skills, although some minor representation of the affective domain is usually included. The primary goal of proponents of this type of inquiry teaching is to provide disciplined rigorous investigation of specific concepts and generalisations considered central to a particular discipline. The selection of the concepts is considered to be more valid than the personal autonomy of the students. These academics are quick to point out the benefits of studying major concepts rather than wads of outdated facts, of being able to transfer learned concepts to new situations, and of being able to use the same conceptual tools and understandings (at a lower level) as the professional social scientist.

Despite their popularity, much has been written about the undesirability of the 'rediscovery' courses. Students undertaking these courses are encouraged to become sleuths confined to a carefully preplanned set of circumstances, such as the 'salted mine' atmosphere of many teaching units.

■ The Inquiry Process

Various writers have developed their preferred steps in undertaking inquiry. One of the earliest advocates of inquiry was John Dewey (1933: 9) who detailed five stages as follows:

1. suggestions, in which the mind leaps forward to a possible solution;
2. an intellectualisation of the difficulty or perplexity that has been felt (directly experienced) into a problem to be solved, a question for which the answer must be sought;
3. the use of one suggestion after another as a leading idea, or hypothesis, to initiate and guide observation and other operations when collecting factual material;
4. the mental elaboration of the idea or supposition (reasoning, in the sense in which reasoning is a part, not the whole, of inference); and
5. testing the hypothesis by overt or imaginative action.

An inquiry process which was published in Victoria in the *Social Education*

Framework P–10 (Ministry of Education Victoria, 1987) is worth special attention. This inquiry suggests that there are eight important steps:

1. tuning in;
2. deciding directions;
3. organising ourselves;
4. finding out;
5. sorting out;
6. drawing conclusions;
7. considering social action; and
8. reflection and evaluation.

Linked to each of these eight steps is a series of questions and a number of related activities which can be used by a teacher (see Figure 10.2). Of course, in practice, the actual steps used by a teacher and his or her students will vary greatly and seldom will the process occur as neatly and precisely as shown in Figure 10.2. However, these eight steps are a useful framework for an analysis of the inquiry process. Each is discussed more fully in the next section.

Tuning in

One of the most difficult aspects of the inquiry process is 'turning the students on'. It is all very well saying that students have to experience a felt need, but how does this come about?

A teacher can certainly stimulate students by asking a variety of probing questions such as some of those listed in Figure 10.2.

- What do we already know about . . .?
- How does this affect us?
- What do we want to find out about . . .?

Another technique that can be extremely effective is to develop particular inquiry springboards to stimulate students. Students' curiosity can be aroused on a largely cognitive level by simply producing unfamiliar examples for them to study. For example, Beyer (1971) used the following list of Hausa words and their English equivalents to introduce a topic on an African tribe.

Hausa	English
auduga	cotton
akiviya	goat
albasa	onion
aljumma'a	sabbath, Friday
Allah	God
alwashi	agreement
araha	cheap
bara	servant
bashi	to owe
bauta	slavery
birni	walled town, city
bukka	tent
cukumara	cheese
da	son

Beyer then asked them to infer characteristics about the Hausa people from an examination of the words listed.

A second example of an inquiry springboard is where students are presented with an apparent contradiction to their biases and values, either visually (photographs, cartoons), on audiotape, videotape, CD-ROM or computer program (Interactive Multimedia, 1993) or by the use of drama (Goalen and Hendy, 1993). Topics might include the Eskimos' treatment of their elderly relatives or even the lifestyles of people living in slum quarters of Australian cities.

A third example of initiating student interest is by the use of case studies. Each of the three short excerpts in the following examples provides an historical interpretation of Edward Hargraves and his efforts to find gold in Australia. The first example, written for primary school children, differs on several points of fact from the second example, written for secondary school students. The third example, written by an academic, shows Hargraves in a completely different light. Which historian are we to believe? Do historians deliberately alter facts

as they write up their accounts? How can we find out about the 'real' Hargraves? Consider this first account for primary school children:

The first discovery of payable gold in Australia was by a man named Edward Hargraves. As a boy of 16 he had come to this country, but dissatisfied with farm life he had left New South Wales to try his luck on the goldfields of California. There he was struck by the resemblance of the country to that which he knew back home. 'If there is gold in California' he said to himself, 'then there is surely gold in New South Wales'.

With a certain valley near Bathurst in mind, Hargraves returned to Australia in January, 1851. A month later he was at Summerhill Creek, near the Macquarie River, ready to begin his search. Stooping over the creek, he shovelled a spadeful of wet earth into a tin dish. Then he rocked the dish to and fro just under the surface of the water, to wash away the dirt. He knew that if there was gold in the soil it would work to the bottom as the soil was washed away. We can imagine his delight when he saw at the bottom of the dish several tiny specks of glittering metal. Again and again he filled the dish with soil, always with the same result. Greatly excited, Hargraves hurried back to Sydney to report his find. The Government was delighted with Hargraves' news and rewarded him with a grant of the equivalent of $20 000. (Williams and Eakins, 1970: 128; primary school text)

Here is another version, this time written for secondary school students:

In January 1851, E. H. Hargraves returned to Sydney from the California goldfields with an anxious heart. Without any real knowledge of geology he had compared the geological formations in California with what he had seen in New South Wales eighteen years before, and concluded that gold must exist in Australia. On arrival in Sydney he told friends and acquaintances of his expectations, and one and all derided him as mad. Undaunted by their ridicule

Questions	Steps of inquiry	Activities
· Why should we investigate this? · What do we already know? · How does this affect us? · What do we want to find out? · What feelings or opinions do you have? · What is the issue?	**Tuning in** Identifying and defining the issue This involves activities designed to: · generate interest; · establish current knowledge; · draw on past experiences; · identify possible aspects for investigating.	· examining an artefact or document · a field trip · discussing a value dilemma · having a visitor to the class · predicting a given situation · considering a challenging question · considering a case study · studying maps, photos, posters, cartoons · performing a task, game or role play · word associations
· What would happen if . . . ? · What guess could we make about . . . ? · What are we likely to see when . . . ? · How can we explain . . . ? · What do we want to focus on? · What questions do we need to ask? · Why is this happening?	**Deciding directions** Formulation of hypotheses Involving: · choosing a focus; · extending the scope; · identifying and refining questions.	· brainstorming for suggestions · posing solutions to problems · predicting outcomes or consequences · formulating propositions · hypothesising · identifying questions to guide investigation · developing tentative explanations
· How are we going to conduct our inquiry? · How can we plan to do it? · What type of information do we need and how do we find and collect it? · What is the best way of allocating tasks?	**Organising ourselves** Organising an approach to the inquiry is crucial and relates closely to the *Deciding directions* stage.	· setting contracts · drawing up a plan · forming small groups · setting appropriate tasks · creating an individual project · locating resources · drawing a timeline
· How are we going to find out about this? · Who, what, where has/is information we can use? · How relevant or useful is this information? · Whose views are reflected in this information?	**Finding out** The collection of data is not an end in itself, but a means towards developing understandings.	· excursions and field trips · guest speakers · surveys and interviews · film, literature, music · magazines, newspapers, books, articles · conducting experiments · collecting and analysing statistics, maps and charts · evaluating primary sources, case studies, etc · seeking opinions

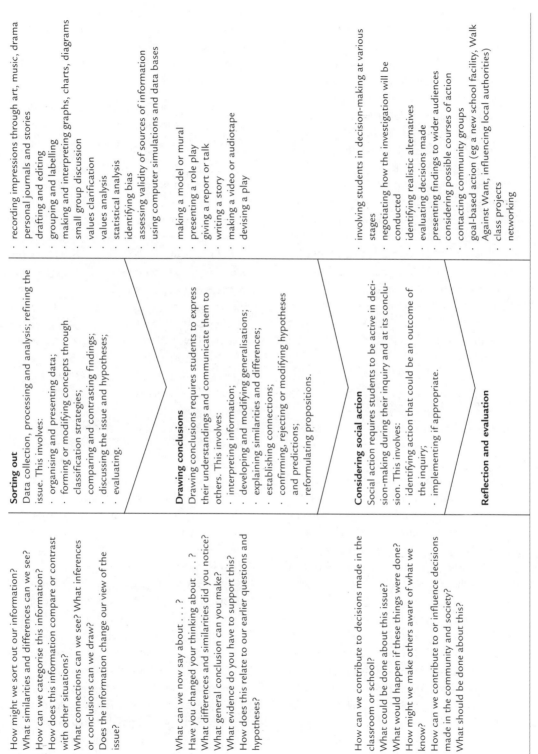

Sorting out

Data collection, processing and analysis; refining the issue. This involves:

· organising and presenting data;
· forming or modifying concepts through classification strategies;
· comparing and contrasting findings;
· discussing the issue and hypotheses;
· evaluating.

· recording impressions through art, music, drama
· personal journals and stories
· drafting and editing
· grouping and labelling
· making and interpreting graphs, charts, diagrams
· small group discussion
· values clarification
· values analysis
· statistical analysis
· identifying bias
· assessing validity of sources of information
· using computer simulations and data bases

· How might we sort out our information?
· What similarities and differences can we see?
· How can we categorise this information?
· How does this information compare or contrast with other situations?
· What connections can we see? What inferences or conclusions can we draw?
· Does the information change our view of the issue?

Drawing conclusions

Drawing conclusions requires students to express their understandings and communicate them to others. This involves:

· interpreting information;
· developing and modifying generalisations;
· explaining similarities and differences;
· establishing connections;
· confirming, rejecting or modifying hypotheses and predictions;
· reformulating propositions.

· making a model or mural
· presenting a role play
· giving a report or talk
· writing a story
· making a video or audiotape
· devising a play

· What can we now say about . . . ?
· Have you changed your thinking about . . . ?
· What differences and similarities did you notice?
· What general conclusion can you make?
· What evidence do you have to support this?
· How does this relate to our earlier questions and hypotheses?

Considering social action

Social action requires students to be active in decision-making during their inquiry and at its conclusion. This involves:

· identifying action that could be an outcome of the inquiry;
· implementing if appropriate.

· involving students in decision-making at various stages
· negotiating how the investigation will be conducted
· identifying realistic alternatives
· evaluating decisions made
· presenting findings to wider audiences
· considering possible courses of action
· contacting community groups
· goal-based action (eg a new school facility, Walk Against Want, influencing local authorities)
· class projects
· networking

· How can we contribute to decisions made in the classroom or school?
· What could be done about this issue?
· What would happen if these things were done?
· How might we make others aware of what we know?
· How can we contribute to or influence decisions made in the community and society?
· What should be done about this?

Reflection and evaluation

Figure 10.2 *Model of inquiry learning (Source: Ministry of Education Victoria, 1987)*

he set out from Sydney for Bathurst, from where, in the company of a bushman named Lister, he set out down the Macquarie River, followed one of its tributaries, then went along a creek that flowed into that tributary, and finally found himself in the country he was so anxious to see. In his excitement he told Lister that gold lay under their very feet. But the bushman was just as incredulous as the mockers in Sydney. So Hargraves dug a panful of earth, washed it in a water-hole, and exclaimed 'Here it is. This is a memorable day in the history of New South Wales. I shall be a baronet, you will be knighted, and my old horse will be stuffed, put into a glass case, and sent to the British Museum!' On his return to the inn at Guylong that night Hargraves wrote a memorandum on the discovery which he sent to the colonial secretary, Deas Tomson, who announced the discovery in the *Sydney Morning Herald* on 15 May, 1851. (Clark, 1963: 113; secondary school text)

The following account diverges considerably from the other two.

One man whose activities should have been watched in May 1851 was Edward Hammond Hargraves, a professional persuader, aged 34, of huge physique and slim principles. His success as a gold finder and his influence on decisions that month came not from a knowledge of geology but a rare gift for public relations. His skill in publicity has gone unseen but it coloured the respect he got from later generations, raised him to a fame that Marshall the Californian gold-finder never attained, and even obscured his skill as a publicist. Hargraves is usually described—for so he described himself—as a New South Wales squatter who knew intimately the Bathurst country. In fact his career covered many trades and much territory. He was a sailor, an overseer on a station, ran a property at Illawarra on the south coast, and was agent for a shipping company by the timber-stacked wharf at East Gosford where he built a hotel aptly named 'The Fox under the Hill'. Losing his hotel in

the depression of 1843, he ran a few cattle on the northern rivers while his wife kept a store. Lazy and amiable, he failed in these ventures and was easily swept into the avalanche that fell on California in 1849.

Hargraves was in California for just over a year (he said he spent two) and he may not have dug for gold for half a year.

'Of all the classes of men', observed Bayard Taylor in 1819, 'those who pave streets and quarry limestone are best adapted for gold-diggers.' Hargraves was no street-paver, if we believe his companions. He preferred to pave with his imagination, and he cleverly created the idea that he was not only an experienced digger but also a geologist and seer. He claimed supernatural powers throughout his mining career. 'I myself, sir', he told the editor of the *Sydney Empire*, 'have never yet been deceived by nature.' He claimed the unique power of being able to look at a quartz and determine whether it contained gold. One impudent South Australian tested him by producing two pieces of quartz rich in gold, and was told that both pieces were barren. Another gift was the ability to predict from ten miles away whether the country was auriferous. He could have discovered Ballarat and Bendigo by the shape of the hills, he said. He had travelled more than Keats in the realms of gold, but in his long searches he denounced many goldfields that were to prove rich, and extolled many that were to prove poor. In geology he was a genial charlatan. Hargraves claimed that his knowledge of geology made him the great Australian benefactor, and his claim is still current. He observed, he said, that the geology and landscape of California resembled country he had once visited near Bathurst and therefore he hurried back to Australia to find payable gold. This claim seems to err in at least four ways. First, he did not find payable gold. Second, he knew that gold had been found across the Blue Mountains before he left California. Third, he did not have Bathurst in mind, for in March

1850 he wrote from San Francisco to a Sydney friend that he knew of a gold region 'within three hundred miles of Sydney', and as his conduct shows that region was Wellington and not Bathurst. Finally, Hargraves did not return primarily to find gold. His close Californian friends say he returned mainly at the request of his wife who was in debt, and in order to escape a second winter on the slopes of the Sierras. Why then did he plant the seeds of myth? From 1852 he spent much time agitating for larger government rewards for his discovery, and he sensibly realised that his reward might be larger if he stressed the indispensable nature of his services. (Blainey, 1962: 129–130)

An examination of these three accounts raises all sorts of issues about the 'real' Hargraves. Students might be sufficiently motivated by these case studies to want to explore this episode of Australian history in more detail themselves. It gives them the same control over definition and interpretation that professional historians have always claimed for themselves (Kobrin *et al.*, 1993; Romanowski, 1996).

The inquiry springboards that you may use as a teacher will obviously vary with the interest of your class, their levels of attainment and the resources available. In most instances it is assumed that students themselves will initiate topics, under inquiry learning situations. However, it would seem wise for the teacher to have ready source inquiry springboards to cater for various contingencies.

Deciding directions

This inquiry step is vital for students and teachers. It requires a closer analysis of what appears to be a problem/issue and then trying to find some focus or hypothesis to guide subsequent actions. Students and their teacher need to ask and respond to some basic questions such as:

- What do I/we want to focus on?
- Why is it important to me/us?
- What questions do I/we need to ask about . . .?
- Which questions do I/we most want to answer? Why?
- Do I/we understand the questions?
- How can I/we explain . . .?

The talking over of the issue between a student and the teacher or between small groups of students and the teacher is vital. In so doing, they are making the issue a 'legitimate class inquiry'. The reactions and suggestions made to a student or a small group will make it possible for the inquirers to fine-tune what they want to do. Thus, although an inquiry issue may be initiated as a problem for one individual, the talking through occurs in a social context, and so most inquiry projects become group activities. Levstik and Smith (1996) argue that if insufficient time is given to this phase, only low-level questions will be generated.

Some writers argue that this step involves formulating specific hypotheses. For example, Banks and Clegg (1990) suggest that students must be able to state precise and researchable questions and that these must be able to be tested. These authors support a scientific version of inquiry that would be on the far right of the procedural and content continua as depicted in Figure 10.1. Yet all students should be able to develop a focus that is clear and practical. In so doing, they should be able to distinguish between hypotheses that are researchable and those that are problems of value and decision making. Many questions about dogma and belief cannot be answered by the inquiry process.

The teacher has a pivotal role in helping students clarify what they want to do. It is a delicate, guiding role for the teacher because he or she must be supportive about students' ideas, no matter how trivial and inconsequential they seem, while at the same time asking students to clarify and justify their choices.

By the end of this step students should be able to come up with a specific focus for their study, which in the process has been discussed and legitimised by the group. It might be expressed as a specific hypothesis or it might be listed as an explicit issue, combined with two or three key questions.

Organising ourselves

Organising the inquiry is closely related to setting the direction, and the two steps could occur concomitantly. Some typical questions that students need to consider include:

- How am/are I/we going to conduct the inquiry?
- What type of information do I/we need?
- Will most of the information be available in the school library or will it be necessary to go to community sources?

- Who will do the various tasks in our group?
- How will the project be written up and/or presented to the rest of the class?

A major concern for both students and the teacher is to establish what it is reasonable to do within a specific length of time. That is, specific 'contracts' may be established for individual students or small groups, indicating the amount of work to be done, how it is to be presented and how it will be assessed. Alternatively, the teacher might establish general procedures for all students. Obviously, the more elaborate the inquiry, the more time will be required. Perhaps larger groups may be needed, with team members having specific tasks allocated to them.

Finding out

An enormous amount of data is available for inquiry activities. The main task here is deciding which data will be most useful for

Students observing the behaviour of creatures in an aquarium

the time available for studying it. It is therefore critical for the students and the teacher to resolve some of the following questions:

- How are we going to find out about . . .?
- Where do we go for this information?
- How reliable is this information compared with that from other sources?
- How else might we find out about . . .?
- Is the source of information the best one to use in the time available?

Sources of data include those immediately available in the school environment, as well as those that may require contacting outside individuals and groups (Haas and Laughlin, 2000). As indicated in Table 10.1 (Maxim, 1983: 177), many sources are available to primary school children, so long as they are encouraged to develop some basic research methods. A similar listing of sources and research skills for secondary school students is depicted in Table 10.2.

Books, journals and magazines are a major source of information for many inquiry projects. Visual sources, such as photographs, illustrations and old advertisements, are often a rewarding source, especially for primary school students. They are often more willing to engage in an interpretation of visual than of written sources (Levstik and Smith 1996). Training in library skills should start in the very early primary school grades if students are going to cope with searching out and extracting relevant library data. More specialised scanning and summarising skills are appropriate for senior grades. Searching through primary data records, such as registers of births and deaths and historical diaries and official photographs, can be an exhilarating experience for senior secondary students (Kirman, 1995). However, they need to have a clear purpose and to be systematic in the way in which they search out and record information.

Observing specific activities and events can

Table 10.1 *Research methods appropriate for primary school children*

Research method	Sample situation
Observation	· how letters go through the post office · methods of using a butter churn · old catalogues or picture collections
Interview	· people's feelings about a topic · resource people to gain information · individuals with interesting experiences
Survey	· traffic flow at an intersection · children's food preferences
Collections	· textiles from countries around the world · children's food preferences · need for a school newspaper
Measurements	· amount of rainfall during a specified period · distance from home to school · weight and height of kindergarten children compared with Year 6 children
Experiments	· effects of various soils on plant growth · how advertising influences buying habits · different sounds made by musical instruments from other countries

Table 10.2 *Sources for inquiry projects with secondary school students*

Sources	Examples	Skills needed
Materials	· reference books · newspapers · magazines	· special reading and writing skills (critical analysis, synthesising, summarising)
Specific activities	· sporting event · dramatic performance · processing in a factory	· observation skills
Individuals and groups	· specialist · local identity	· interviewing skills · observation skills · survey skills

also be an important activity for an inquiry project. Within the school environment there are numerous opportunities for observation that may be relevant to a particular project, for example standing in a queue at the student cafeteria and observing the behaviour of those people waiting to be served, or observing shoppers' activities at the local supermarket.

At the secondary school level, it is possible to use participant observation and non-participant observation activities. Both forms have their strengths and weaknesses. Participant observation enables a person to witness events at first hand, but interpret them according to a personal set of values; you are on the spot and so can follow up any unexplained behaviour by questioning other members of the group. Non-participant observation involves being more selective about what is observed, but it has the disadvantage that the event is not experienced at first hand.

Individuals, including leading figures in the local community, sporting celebrities and retired local identities, can be important sources for inquiry projects. Although observation skills will undoubtedly be used, additional skills, such as interviewing and survey skills, are often needed.

Interviews can be undertaken by students

of all ages and some valuable data can be obtained this way (Downs, 1993). At the primary school level, short and simple interviews can be used. Before doing them children should practise their interview techniques in class and prepare their method of recording answers to their questions. Laughlin, Hartoonian and Sanders (1989) note that collecting oral histories is an excellent way to introduce young children to the bonds between generations. Interviewing senior citizens about what primary school was like when they attended school can be fascinating for young children. They can ask questions about what subjects were taught, what games were played, how they travelled to school and what forms of discipline the teacher used.

At the secondary school level, unstructured or structured interviews can be used. With unstructured interviews it is more difficult to maintain the original focus and keep to time limitations, but students can uncover additional valuable information. Deer, Jarvis and White (1987) provide some useful reminders for students who intend to interview persons for an inquiry project:

1. Determine who is to be interviewed:
   (a) Do they have the authority to give me the information?

(b) Will they be willing to give me the information?

2. Prepare an interview schedule.
3. Decide on how the interview is to be recorded:
   (a) written down;
   (b) recorded on a tape recorder.
4. Conduct a preliminary trial of the interview:
   (a) to refine the techniques to be used;
   (b) using a few friends not to be included in the sample.
5. Carry out a preliminary trial of the analysis and tabulation. Analyse the data obtained and try to set it out in a table.
6. Make arrangements for the interview. Ensure that a convenient time is arranged.
7. Analyse the information obtained.
   (a) Develop appropriate tables.
   (b) Write up a report based on key ideas.

Survey skills can also be used to find out how particular individuals and groups respond to a specific inquiry issue (Alleman and Brophy, 1994). A sample survey, as its name implies, involves selecting a sample of individuals and asking (surveying) them to give their responses to a set of questions. Even primary school students can appreciate the need to be very careful about selecting a representative sample for their survey and become aware of what can happen if they don't do this carefully. Even very brief surveys with only three or four questions can still be extremely effective, such as the one in Figure 10.3.

Students can also use questionnaires to elicit the information they need. If there are no local people suitable to respond to a particular inquiry issue, the questions may have to be mailed to respondents. It is important that a representative sample is chosen for a questionnaire and that enough people are included in the sample. It has to be assumed that there will be a wastage in the return rate, often as high as 50–60 per cent of the total mailed out.

Care has to be taken to ensure that the questionnaire layout is attractive and easy to follow. The types of items it usually includes are:

- open-ended questions;
- single-choice questions;
- multiple-choice questions.

Open-ended questions typically ask a respondent to give a written response to a brief statement. An example at primary school level is shown in Box 10.1. Note, however, that although this type of item

---

Box 10.1 *Example of an open-ended question*

Question 1: What do you think about traffic in our town?_____

_____

_____

Family survey

1. How do you travel to work? _____

2. Do other people travel with you?_____

3. How long does it take you? _____

4. If your wish could be granted, how would you like to travel to work? _____

_____

Figure 10.3 *Example of a survey used by primary school children*

allows respondents a range of different answers and opinions, it is very difficult to score and tabulate.

Single-choice questions typically require a yes/no or a true/false response. They are very easy and quick for a respondent to complete and they are also simple to score. However, some respondents may feel that the restricted response category is unsuitable to answer some items and, as a consequence, they may omit these items or refuse to complete the questionnaire altogether. An example of a single-choice question that might be used at the secondary school level is shown in Box 10.2.

Multiple-choice questions are frequently used because they tend to incorporate the advantages of the other two forms of question with few of the disadvantages. That is, they enable respondents to select from a range of items, yet they are still relatively easy to score and to tabulate. An example of this type of question at the secondary school level is shown in Box 10.3.

Questionnaires can provide a valuable source of data for an inquiry activity, but can involve considerable expenses (typing costs, stationery, postage) and sufficient time has to be allowed for distribution and return of the questionnaires. Deer *et al.* (1987: 195) provide some very useful reminders to students involved in constructing questionnaire items and some helpful hints of ways that can be used to increase the rate of return from respondents (see Table 10.3.)

Case studies can also be developed by students if they want to study a particular individual or group intensively. For example, at the primary school level a student might do a case study of a well-known local identity. This could involve the student going to the identity's home a number of times over several weeks to discuss a particular topic, eventually collecting much valuable information from which key points and examples could be selected to portray the person. The completed case study report might be several pages or more in length, depending on the age level of the student involved. Case study approaches are especially useful at the secondary school level with subjects such as:

- the needs of the elderly;
- discrimination against minority groups;
- housing conditions and urban living.

All of the above methods for finding out information are based on the assumption that students will collect the data systematically and that they will be sensitive to the feelings of the people they contact. Deer *et al.* (1987) suggest that student inquirers should be sensitive about the welfare of their subjects and should not persist with questions that invade their privacy. They also advise students to be objective in drawing conclusions from their research, and to be scrupulous about acknowledging sources of data and in using direct quotes.

Box 10.2 *Example of a single-choice question*

Question 1: Noise pollution is a major problem in our town.   Agree/Disagree

---

Box 10.3 *Example of a multiple-choice question*

Question 1: Noise pollution in our town is mainly due to:

(place an X in the most appropriate box)

☐ radios

☐ street repair equipment

☐ fire engines

☐ discos

Table 10.3 *Guide to questionnaire construction*

The following list of questions should lead to the construction of a good questionnaire:

1. Have I given the respondent a good reason for answering the questionnaire?
2. Does the respondent have the information to answer the questions?
3. Have I asked the questions in such a way that there can be no other interpretation than what was intended?
4. Is the questionnaire long and tedious to answer?
5. Have I made sure that each question refers only to a single issue?
6. Have I included trivial questions which are not worth asking?
7. Have I asked for information that is readily available elsewhere?
8. Are the questions likely to embarrass people?
9. Is the questionnaire neatly presented?

To increase the rate of return, the following steps can be taken:

1. Include a covering letter explaining the nature and importance of the research. Include also an official statement from your school or college indicating the school's permission and endorsement of the procedure.
2. Assure the respondents that their information will be confidential.
3. If you can raise sufficient funds, include stamped return address envelopes or, if the area is not large, return to the people concerned and collect the questionnaires personally.
4. Follow up people who do not respond with a courteous reminder.
5. Choose the best time to send out the questionnaire. Avoid times such as holidays when people are away and the end of the financial year when business firms are usually very busy with stocktaking.

Developing interviewing skills

Sorting out

The next step, sorting out the information, is a very demanding one. Matters which have to be resolved include:

- How should the data be sorted out and classified?
- What patterns, similarities and differences seem to be emerging?
- Should we use these patterns as a basis for classifying?
- What connections can we see?
- What inferences or conclusions can we draw?
- How do these conclusions relate to our original issue/hypothesis?

The type of sorting out will depend greatly on the range and nature of the data collected. Statistics on people's actions/behaviours can be presented in tables as frequencies or percentages or as bar graphs (see Figures 10.4 and 10.5). Various computer programs are available to produce spreadsheets. At senior school level more sophisticated statistical procedures can be used including measures of central tendency (mean, median and mode).

Sometimes the statistical data doesn't become meaningful until it is transformed into graphs or diagrams. There are various ways of providing these visual displays. Some common examples include:

- pie graphs—for showing relationships/proportions between two or more factors;
- histograms—for showing frequencies (see Figure 10.6);
- line graphs—for showing frequencies;
- contingency tables—usually for showing the concurrence of two variables (see Figure 10.7).

The analysis of materials such as diaries, newspaper clippings and articles is far more

Traffic Survey	
Time: 11:00–11:30 Day: September 28	
Surveyors: Roger, Debbie, Susan	
Number of	
Cars	*32*
Trucks	*14*
Station Wagons	*12*
Vans	*9*
People who waved	*39*

Figure 10.4 *Traffic survey conducted by Year 4 students*

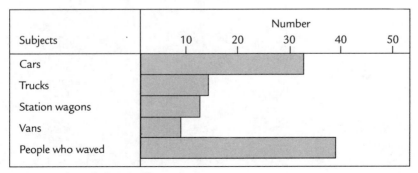

Figure 10.5 *Bar graph made from traffic survey data*

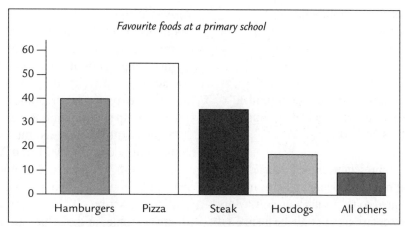

Figure 10.6 *An example of a histogram*

Association between a student's religion and school attended			
	Protestant	Catholic	
Government schools	650	40	690
Non-government schools	50	300	350
	700	340	

Figure 10.7 *An example of a contingency table*

difficult to undertake objectively. Summaries should be made with major points highlighted. Any incidences of bias and repetition must be noted. The amount of detail and level of sophistication will, of course, depend on the ages of the students.

A preliminary analysis of data can often cause some concern about deficiencies in the process used. In certain circumstances, time permitting, it may be possible to collect some additional information. Some useful questions to ask include:

- Does the data collected answer the original questions/hypotheses?
- Are there any other ways we might have gone about solving the problem?
- Do we need to gather new data to confirm the answers?
- Would recording and organising the data in new ways change the answers?

- Are our answers clearly supported by our data?
- Are we surprised by any answers?
- Which answers interest us the most?
- How did we decide which data to use and which to reject?
- Would I/we plan things differently if the project was done again on another occasion?

Drawing conclusions

This inquiry step involves a student in making concluding statements about his or her inquiry project; they have to be directly related to the original questions/hypotheses. Depending on the nature of the inquiry, various modes may be used to communicate the findings. Some examples include:

- written accounts, essays, statements;
- visual presentations (overhead transparencies, slides);

- videotapes and audiotapes;
- oral presentations;
- role play, dramatisation;
- debate;
- creation of a mural;
- creation of a three-dimensional model;
- broadsheets, charts and diagrams (see Figures 10.8 and 10.9).

The form of presentation will depend upon the age level of the students and the amount of time allocated to the inquiry project. More elaborate presentations can only be justified if the project is a very detailed one, involving several months of effort.

Considering social action

As indicated earlier, in the conceptual model there are many different approaches to inquiry, and many of them assume that it is an academic activity that involves finding answers to particular hypotheses, and that no follow-up social action is warranted.

Some writers, such as the Ministry of Education Victoria (1987) and Welton and Mallan (1987), argue that student inquiry can and should lead to personal reflection and social action. If, for example, students discover some undesirable social practices then they may become committed to alleviating the situation.

REASONS FOR BRITISH SETTLEMENT IN NEW SOUTH WALES

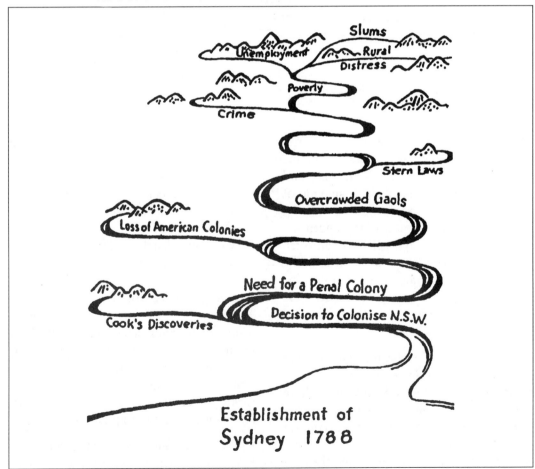

Figure 10.8 *An example of a river diagram to show historical developments*

   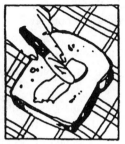

Figure 10.9 *An example of a linear chart depicting the production of bread*

Few would protest about students petitioning the local police force for an additional pedestrian crossing near their school or writing letters to the local newspaper. Yet more militant actions might be chosen by some students, including street marches, gang initiatives or reprisals and activities bordering upon the anti-social and unlawful. Although unlikely, it is still possible for inquiry projects to stimulate such activities. Others argue that authoritarian, traditional methods of teaching are just as likely to cause some students to embark upon anti-social activities.

More recently, writers such as Cumbo and Vadeboncoeur (1998) contend that 'service' learning, where students learn experientially and actively through participation in meaningful service that meets actual community needs, can provide an important focus for student action. An example might include students working to reclaim the wetland behind their school.

Reflection and evaluation

Clearly, it is important for students to reflect upon what they did and did not accomplish in their inquiry project. Small-group discussions can give them a useful opportunity to reflect upon each other's accomplishments.

The teacher has the difficult task of trying to evaluate the quality of inquiry projects. A variety of evaluative techniques can be used, including objective tests, rating scales and checklists. Deer *et al.* (1987) provide useful checklists for use at both primary and secondary school levels (Table 10.4).

Self-evaluation is of special importance to inquiry if students are going to develop as self-directed learners. A related term that now occurs frequently in the literature is meta-cognition, which refers to what individuals know about their own cognitive processes and the outcomes of those processes (Woolever and Scott, 1988). Students need to be able to monitor their own performance, especially in terms of how they approach problems and how they implement strategies (Wilen and Phillips, 1995).

At the primary school level students can be asked to think about such matters as:

• What things did I do well in this project?
• What things will I do better next time?
• What parts of the project did I find interesting?
• What was the most difficult thing about the project? Why?
• If I was starting over again, what things would I do differently?

At the secondary school level students can reflect upon a range of issues related to their inquiry project. For example, they might want to question personally, and in small groups, such matters as:

Table 10.4 *Criteria for assessing inquiry projects*

Primary school level

1. Does the project communicate information clearly?
2. Is the project problem defined?
3. Does the project show evidence of:
   (a) data collection?
   (b) analyses of information?
   (c) organisation of information?
   (d) evaluation of information?

Secondary school level

1. Clarity	·	Is the topic clearly stated and are all the purposes and procedures used clear?
2. Methodology	·	Are the methodologies chosen appropriate to the topic?
	·	Is there evidence of a systematic approach to the study of the topic?
	·	Is there an awareness of both the limitations and the values of the methodologies used?
3. Subject matter	·	Is the subject matter accurate, relevant to the topic and adequately explained?
4. Integrative skills	·	Does the project hold together?
	·	Do the conclusions follow from what precedes?
	·	Is personal experience related to the public traditions of knowledge?
5. Presentation skills	·	Are the ideas effectively communicated?
6. Originality	·	Does the project have evidence of some originality in design, execution and presentation?

- How appropriate was the topic studied?
- Were the issues/hypotheses manageable and realistic?
- What skills did I use well in collecting information?
- What skills do I need to improve upon?
- Could I have improved my data analysis and my presentation of the project?
- What have I learnt from doing this project?
- How can this new knowledge be applied to any social action?

Laughlin *et al.* (1989) suggest that a pie diagram such as Figure 10.10 is useful for students to reflect upon the amount of time they spent on the different processes. It is also a helpful diagnostic tool for teachers to use to demonstrate specific student achievements or weaknesses.

As noted by Deer *et al.* (1987), self-directed learning should be a central goal in inquiry approaches. Providing opportunities for students to undertake their own self-evaluations can help them realise that other self-directed learning activities are worthwhile. For students with limited experience in self-directed learning, the transition from teacher-dominated activities can be quite protracted and even traumatic.

■ **Personal Interest Project—
A Successful Inquiry Case Study**

At the secondary school level the emphasis upon organising teaching subjects in terms of the subject disciplines limits the opportunity for inquiry approaches. One notable

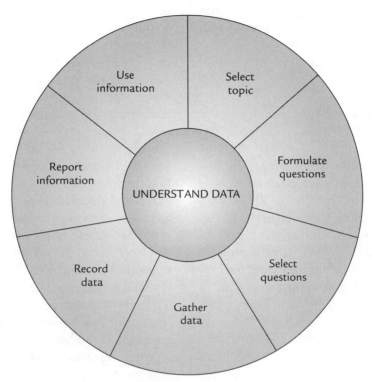

Figure 10.10 *Diagrammatic representation of processes*

exception has been the development of a personal interest project (PIP) which is a requirement for all Year 12 students studying the Society and Culture syllabus as part of the Higher School Certificate examination in New South Wales. A PIP provides excellent opportunities for students to pursue an inquiry topic and the guidelines associated with this innovation are very supportive for students and teachers. Feedback from schools has been very encouraging since it was first introduced in 1985. The example cited by Dufty (1999) is graphic. A female student was committed to doing her PIP on Vietnam veterans, after suffering the trauma of witnessing her father commit suicide following his wartime experience.

Each PIP consists of a 4000-word project and comprises 30 per cent of the total course. PIPs must be based on a personal interest topic related to the fundamental concepts of the course. Students are encouraged to select topics which are cross-cultural in emphasis—they must gather their own primary and secondary source data and demonstrate that they have systematically investigated their chosen topic.

The topics have been far-ranging in scope since PIPs were first introduced in 1985. Some of the formats have included written, diagrammatic, statistical and visual records or combinations of these. Students are encouraged to draw upon public knowledge but especially their personal experience, observations, feelings and ideas. Some examples of topics include:

- 'Us and Them'—the relationship between ethnic students and Australian students in the school community;
- 'To Coffee and Conversation'—communication and group dynamics;

- 'Continuity and Change through Three Generations'—using letters, photographs and family correspondence;
- 'Being Different in Society'—a study of cerebral palsy.

Each PIP must consist of four elements as listed in Table 10.5.

For many students, a PIP can be stimulating but also intimidating, especially if it is not planned over a period of time beginning early in Year 12. The PIP requires students to become active learners and this involves a change in role for many students and their teachers. Deer (1991) provides some strategies to help students and teachers make the transition from teacher-directed to student-directed learning (see Table 10.6). The impact of PIPs in New South Wales has been very positive. Smith (1991) concludes that PIPs have been a major success since their assessment has increased from 20 per cent to 30 per cent of the total course. Various support structures have been developed to ensure their success, such as certificates for the best 100 PIPs each year, and establishing a Society and Culture Association which runs workshops and conferences for teachers and students and produces a regular journal. As noted by Morrison (1992: 45) in *The Society and Culture Association Journal*, students doing PIPs begin to see the course concepts in action and discover more about themselves and their own values and beliefs.

Similar research projects can also be developed successfully with primary school students. Hartman, De Cicco and Griffin (1994) describe how intermediate teachers in a primary school dispense with their normal routine for one week each month and lead groups of 10 students into in-depth projects on topics such as recycling, electricity and astronomy.

Table 10.5 *Preparing and presenting your personal interest project*

Each personal interest project is to

- be a topic of the student's own choice
- be related to the course
- develop appropriate methodologies
- include a cross-cultural perspective

The presented project must include the following components:

1. *Introduction*
   A brief description (no more than 500 words) on what the topic is about, why this topic was chosen and in what ways it contributes to a better understanding of society and culture.

2. *Log* – based on the student's personal interest project diary.

3. *Central material of the Personal Interest Project*
   In written form and may be accompanied by photographs, tables, graphs and/or diagrams (between 2 500 and 5 000 words).

4. *Conclusion*
   A statement (no more than 500 words) of what the student learned from the personal interest project.

Table 10.6 *Some strategies for the transition from teacher-directed to student-directed learning*

Stages	Some teaching activities	Some learning activities
1. Announcing the project	· Discuss interest areas with students. · Explain what is required.	· Students list goals they would like to reach by the end of stated periods
2. Initial enthusiasm	· Set expectations and limits. · Help students explore alternatives. · Establish one-to-one conferences to discuss learning.	· Student self-diagnosis of skills each needs. · Students role play activities they are about to experience in reality, e.g. interviewing.
3. Shock of recognition	· Clarify new teacher and student roles: 'this you can expect from me; this I expect from you.' · Discuss purpose and direction, examine optional routes to goals. Help but do not rescue: 'I refuse to do for you what you can do for yourself.' Re-negotiate topics, setting more reasonable goals.	· Small groups form to discuss PIP progress. · Students overcome apathy by completing a task successfully. (Teachers help them to finish any task by any means.)
4. Crisis	· Permit time for reflection on personal difficulties with tasks and acceptance of personal responsibilities for them. · Help students identify their best ideas. · Prepare students to get started in their best ideas.	· Students break their activities into a series of sub-tasks with a time sequence: 'The first step is . . ., which I will finish by . . .'. · Students identify pay-offs and constraints involved in each sub-task.
5. Realism	· Make opportunities for students to report to the class on their PIP. · Reward them for their efforts. · Reaffirm the value of challenge, struggle and personal work.	· Students rate themselves on time management, organisation, accomplishment and resource identification
6. Commitment	· Conduct individual conferences to establish pattern of self-evaluation (e.g. 'Give your own grade and defend it') and to intensify internal rewards (e.g. 'what values are you experiencing from your accomplishment?').	· Groups discuss behavioural changes and successes achieved by each individual.

continues . . .

Table 10.6 *Some strategies for the transition from teacher-directed to student-directed learning (continued)*

Stages	Some teaching activities	Some learning activities
7. Achievement	· Increase freedom and responsibility of students. · Implement self-evaluation and reporting. · Set the date by which all will share their accomplishment.	· Students demonstrate their accomplishments to peers, teachers and parents. · Students are introduced to the pursuit and in-depth mastery in one area.

■ Concluding Comments

Inquiry approaches are very challenging for students and teachers. Because students inquire about many aspects daily (albeit informally), it is difficult to guide them into using a more formal process of problem awareness, hypothesising, finding information and drawing conclusions. Even very young children are aware of discrepancies in events, but they may have little motivation to explain them. Older students may react hastily to unexplained events and may not be prepared to examine discrepancies in any systematic way. It is therefore important to note that inquiry approaches should be introduced early in the primary grades and used regularly (but not exclusively) so that students gradually acquire the necessary information-processing skills (Welton and Mallan, 1987). By the time students enter secondary school, they should have some of the skills required to embark upon various inquiry projects.

It is essential that teachers receive training for inquiry approaches and that support materials are readily available. The availability of alternative syllabuses which highlight skills learning is an important incentive for secondary school students and teachers (McKeown and Beck, 1999). The personal interest project, available to senior school students in New South Wales, and described in this chapter, has proved to be a very important inquiry-oriented component of the Society and Culture Syllabus.

QUESTIONS AND ACTIVITIES

1. 'Inquiry approaches can be very demanding and rewarding for students and teachers but initial forays should be limited and exploratory.' Discuss this statement and argue for or against it. Describe a topic/activity you might use to develop an inquiry approach.
2. How important is self-evaluation by the teacher and students to the inquiry approach? Is this simply an end-of-unit activity or should it occur throughout the unit? What organisational procedures might you use for self-evaluation?
3. Inquiry approaches can cause severe demands on external resources such as community libraries and personnel in local agencies. Sometimes student inquirers may inadvertently persist with lines of inquiry that invade people's privacy. What steps would you take to ensure that students are sensitive to these concerns and that goodwill with external agencies is maintained?
4. Metacognitive skills involve students in monitoring their degrees of understanding, being conscious of tasks to be undertaken and knowing the strategies that facilitate thinking. How can teachers support the development of these skills?
5. Gold mining, gold miners and their way of life has a fascination for many Australians. Investigating a gold-mining ghost town provides enormous opportunities to develop inquiry skills at all levels of schooling. Select a ghost town(s) in your state and plan an appropriate inquiry activity.
6. 'The inquiry process, supported by recent advances in computer technology, enables even greater opportunities for students.' Discuss.

11

Simulation Games

Introduction

Simulation games can be a powerful tool for teachers to explore values, issues and problems in studies of society and environment. They have steadily gained ground as a viable teaching technique over recent years.

This chapter focuses on a teaching technique with tremendous potential for teachers. Simulation games have been widely used since the 1950s. They continue to be used extensively in the studies of society and environment field, especially in cross-cultural/multicultural studies. Their use has increased rapidly in business courses and in international relations.

After a preliminary discussion of terms, the major emphasis in this chapter is on detailed, practical suggestions about how teachers can create, implement and evaluate their own simulation games. Details are also provided about the criteria that may be used for selecting from the range of commercially developed simulation games.

It is crucial to be aware of the value of simulation games—after all, every teacher is concerned about effectiveness in the classroom. No one would be so rash as to suggest that simulation games can solve all classroom problems and that they should be the teaching technique. However, there is a need to consider simulation games as another medium of instruction, another technique to add to the repertoire.

The decision to use a particular teaching technique, such as simulation games, should not be made until the teacher is certain that it will suit the particular goals of the selected unit of study and the class of students. Fowler (1994) and Di Nicola (1997) suggest that the simulation games technique is a very powerful tool for developing interpersonal communication, interpupil cooperation and social exchange behaviour, group process, personalised inquiry and open-ended decision making. Seidner (1995) asserts that simulation games can trigger changes in attitudes, behaviour and creativity. Diehl (1991) and Ellington (1995) note that many recent simulation games stimulate higher cognitive processes to generate problem solving without producing gender differences.

■ Major Terms

The term 'simulation' really refers to some model of reality. It may be a simplified model or a highly complex one (Peters, Vissers and Heijne, 1998). Social simulations tend to mirror the process that goes on in society, such as patterns and problems concerned with race, prejudice and discrimination. Physical simulations are often more complex because they recreate the physical attributes of such phenomena as stream erosion or space flight.

When participants are being trained to learn specific skills, game fidelity—the extent of correspondence between the simulation/game and the setting being simulated—is of major importance (Druckman, 1995).

Teachers use physical simulations, such as globes or sand-tray models, every day. 'Computer simulations' can recreate all kinds of processes, both physical and social. Examples include weather patterns, bushfires, global air pollution, transport systems and power stations (Crookall and Arai, 1995; Risinger, 1996). Computer simulations can be far more realistic (see also Chapter 12) but they can only provide limited peer interaction and discussion (Walford, 1995).

Games are not strange to us. The name 'game' applies to any activity in which participants cooperate or compete to achieve the game objectives according to prescribed rules of play. Games can vary from noughts and crosses to Monopoly, British Bulldog and hopscotch.

When simulations are merged with games, the result is simulation games. According to Van Sickle (1986), a simulation game is a setting in which participants make choices, implement those choices, and receive consequences for those choices in an effort to achieve given objectives all according to explicitly stated rules which refer to a model of an empirical system in the real world. Simulation games might involve cooperation or competition among the players. Sometimes there is more than one winner. A simulation game usually involves a number of actors who are required to act out roles according to certain guidelines. The interaction between these role players is not only crucial to the realism of the simulation, but also to the success of the game in achieving its goals. In some simulation games, the role interactions may involve movement in the room, for example bartering for goods, making speeches and other forms of interaction. In other simulation games, these activities are already built in by using a board format. Participants in these board games still take on certain roles but their activities are more circumscribed. All simulation games require decisions to be made by role players. In many, feedback is received at regular intervals so that role players can gauge the relative success of their decisions.

This classification of simulation games into board games and role-playing games is a common one. To illustrate the above, Environmental Gaming Simulation (Midden, 1990) is a board game for upper primary and lower secondary students. Between 10 and 40 players can be involved in designing a housing

MR SPEAKER, PLEASE TELL MS PRIME MINISTER THAT WHILST SUCH LANGUAGE *MAY* BE IN HANSARD, ... WE WON'T HAVE IT IN THIS CLASSROOM...

development using wooden blocks for houses, green sponges for trees and vegetation, yarn for streets, thread for bike trails and small rocks for historical sites, on a game board representing a 60 hectare (150 acre) site.

Players are assigned various roles that help make explicit the interlocking and often conflicting interests represented in community development such as real estate developer, contractor, banker, lawyer, merchant, neighbour, landscape architect, city planner, National Trust and environmentalists. Role cards provide details of the basic concerns and priorities of each player. Project cards are selected by players during the simulation game and these provide specific cost–benefit and environmental impact arguments that can be used to support or oppose a particular building project.

Survival and Hope (Global Education Centre, 1996) is a board simulation game which enables players to gain an understanding of some of the frustrations and privations of being a refugee. According to Wildy (1997) players move around the board experiencing situations of chance and hope. Two playing boards are supplied so that a whole class can play at the one time.

The Parliament Pack Guide (Departments of the Senate and the House of Representatives, 1987) is a role-playing simulation game. Role profiles are provided about such key roles as Speaker, Chairman of Committees and Prime Minister. Other students become engaged in supporting roles in activities such as question time in Parliament. Role cards such as that shown in Figure 11.1 provide basic information that students can use in their respective roles.

No Friends but the Mountains (Major, 1996) is a role-playing simulation game that focuses on Kurdish nationalism and the Kurdish struggle for autonomy. Students are assigned to play the roles of politically active individuals from Kurdistan, Turkey and Iraq in the first phase; delegates are then selected to represent each community and they have to argue their case before a panel of five students representing the United Nations.

Speaker
of the House of Representatives

- is the head of the House of Representatives
- is elected by secret ballot
- sits in the Speaker's Chair
- usually does not take part in debates
- calls Members who wish to speak or ask questions
- puts the questions on which Members vote, and announces the result of each vote
- is a member of the government party, but is expected to be fair to both sides
- understands the rules (Standing Orders) and makes sure they are followed
- keeps order in the House of Representatives

Figure 11.1 *Example of a role card in* The Parliament Pack Guide *(Departments of the Senate and the House of Representatives, 1987)*

The scoring system is based upon Quality of Life Points. Initial allocations are made to each community and then scores are adjusted after each round, based upon successful or unsuccessful negotiations. In the debriefing session, participants explore causes of conflict and analyse different diplomacy strategies.

■ Advantages and Disadvantages of Simulation Games

Although there has been increasingly strong support for simulation games over recent years (Crookall and Arai, 1995; Walford, 1995) the evidence is still confusing and there are many unanswered questions (Druckman, 1995; Cherrington and Van Ments, 1996), such as:

- How does involvement in the simulation game affect learning?
- What is the relationship between motivational and learning variables?
- Does what one learns in a particular simulation game transfer to other situations?

There are considerable problems in measuring the effects of simulation games as an instructional technique. With other forms of instruction it is possible to test learning outcomes because it is reasonably assured that all students will learn the same thing. As noted by Bredemeier, Bernstein and Oxman (1982: 416): 'A simulation game inevitably provides for more diversity of experience for players than a traditional lesson; indeed it may not be the same experience for anyone'. Even so, the evidence suggests that simulation games are at least as effective as other teaching techniques (Table 11.1).

Bredemeier and Greenblat (1981) divided learning into three parts: subject matter, attitudes and learning about oneself. With reference to subject matter, they concluded that the research evidence suggests that simulation games are at least as effective as other methods and are more effective aids to retention. With reference to attitudes, the evidence suggests that simulation games can be more effective than traditional teaching techniques in bringing about positive attitude change. With reference to learning about oneself the evidence indicates that self-awareness is enhanced.

A review by Randel *et al.* (1992) examined 69 research studies reported in a 28-year period. They concluded that 39 per cent of the studies found differences favouring simulation games, 56 per cent of the

Table 11.1 *Twelve good reasons for using simulation games*

1. Allows students to get fully involved in learning.
2. Encourages self-development in students.
3. Students can communicate more confidently.
4. Allows students to see events occur over accelerated time.
5. Allows concepts to be more easily understood.
6. Provides students with immediate reinforcement.
7. Discipline is less of a problem.
8. Students work together toward common goals.
9. Students take initiatives to seek information.
10. Students become more aware of their own values and learn about themselves.
11. Students can greatly increase their intercultural understandings.
12. Students develop increased problem-solving skills.

comparisons between simulation games and conventional instruction showed no difference, 5 per cent found differences favouring conventional instruction.

Van Sickle's (1986) meta-analysis of 42 studies revealed that simulation games provided modest positive effects over other instructional methods for attitude change, but no differences were noted for knowledge acquisition.

It is clear that there are methodological problems in demonstrating the superiority of simulation games. Morgan (1991) notes some of the difficulties in using pre-test/post-test designs and developing appropriate measurement instruments. Randel *et al.* (1992) note the possible confusion between preferences expressed by players and what it is they actually learnt from games.

Morgan's (1991) study of 'Econ and Me' with 300 students in 11 primary schools indicated that students' success in problem solving increased markedly during the playing of this simulation game. Diehl's (1991) study of 'Crisis' also indicates that participants commented on the problem-solving/decision-making skills which they developed, and the pleasure of working together in groups.

There is little doubt that simulation games have a high popularity rating with students and teachers alike (Williams and Williams, 1987; Barak, 1987; McKenna, 1991; White, 1992; Tamura, 1992). The enthusiasm of teachers and students is evident in accounts of specific simulation games, as revealed by the use of such terms as 'fun', 'excitement', 'challenging', 'addictive'. Learning happens because participants are active and not passive in the process—the excitement and electricity in the air is all-consuming (Petranek, Corey and Black, 1992).

The first quake has struck, and my chair is rocking. No, it's not the chair, just the screen

moving back and forth with a screeching sound—very convincing. Fires are breaking out everywhere, and there is flooding in the streets. Are there enough fire stations in the city? As mayor, I can place more out there if I need them. A second jolt hits. I decide to start bulldozing streets to stop the fire from spreading. Water mains are bursting, and flooding streets complicate matters. A third jolt hits and the fires are spreading fast. Everything I do does not seem to be done fast enough. I cannot put enough fire fighters into the city. I cannot bulldoze enough ways through the city to slowdown the spreading fires (p. 165).

Disadvantages

Just as it is difficult to provide evidence of the advantages, it is extremely hard to find evidence of the shortcomings of simulation games. Perhaps simulation games are time consuming, but this depends on what they are being compared with, the nature of the activity and many other factors. It could also be said that laboratory experiments are time consuming! The introduction of simulation games into a classroom can be easy or difficult depending on previous classroom practices and students' expectations.

In some cases the playing rules for simulation games are very complex and are difficult for students to learn. Further, management problems can arise when playing simulation games. Classrooms can become very noisy and students sometimes become overly hostile in playing their respective roles.

In some circumstances, teachers may feel their roles are being threatened in simulation game situations, especially if they are accustomed to a traditional expository role (Schug and Beery, 1987). Teachers do get concerned about simulation games which oversimplify real-world actors and actions and thereby misinform students (Chapin and Messick, 1999).

■ Designing and Developing a Simulation Game

We often stand back and look in awe at the massive array of commercially produced materials available for use in classrooms. Glistening packages, complete with CD-ROMs, computer disks, cassette tapes, glossy charts, cards and instruction manuals may give the impression of quality, perfection and suitability. Yet these very sophisticated packages lack some basic essentials. For example, they are not normally intended for a specific class of students, as they have to be marketed for a wide range of student interests and abilities.

A strong case can be made for classroom teachers developing simulations specifically tailored for their own unique situations. This requires only a few materials and a little creativity (Welton and Mallan, 1987; Seidner, 1995). There may be a particular ethnic composition in the school's community that affects the lifestyles of the students and could never be captured in the spirit of a universally available commercial simulation game. The teacher may have qualities which make certain kinds of simulation games easy to use but other kinds difficult.

Ellington (1995) contends that most primary school teachers have all the intrinsic skills needed to design perfectly workable simulation games provided they are given a little basic guidance. He notes, with regret, that the rigid, subject-based and content-centred structure of the secondary school curriculum lessens the motivation for secondary school teachers to develop their own simulation games.

It is argued by some writers, for example Gustafson (1993) and Ellington (1995), that when students are involved in the construction of simulation games they can gain valuable insights into value issues and real-life dilemmas. They argue that these planning experiences are far more rewarding than just playing the simulation game.

Simulation games can vary from relatively unstructured role-playing activities to tightly controlled activities, including board games and computer-assisted games (see Chapter 12 for a discussion of computer-assisted simulation games). The planning components do not alter very much and they take little effort to master. They include the following:

- *Objectives*—what is to be achieved by the simulation game?
- *Scenario*—what is the setting to be? What is the time period?
- *Roles*—who or what are the chief persons or organisations to be portrayed?
- *Role profiles*—what are to be the objectives of each of these role players or role groups? How are they to behave? What resources (money, power) are available to them?
- *Role interaction*—what kinds of activities are desired between these role players?
- *Procedures and win criteria*—what sequence of activities must occur? What activities are permitted/not permitted? What actions need to be taken for a person to win (if this is a desired objective)?
- *Presentation format*—will the simulation occur as role playing or a board game or a combination of the two? How will groups be arranged? What resources will be needed?
- *Debriefing*—after the simulation game has been completed, what follow-up activities will take place?

How to start

Education experts seem to have a habit of recommending logical ways of planning teaching activities. For developing simulation games, they would no doubt insist that the game is a linear exercise in which teachers should start off with specific objectives and then work toward devising roles, role profiles, scenario, operations and finally the debriefing (Figure 11.2).

This may be the way that many teachers develop teaching units, but such creative thinking can take many forms. Creativity can come from sudden flashes of intuition while taking a shower or cursing a fellow driver at a traffic light. There therefore seems to be no harm at all in commencing a simulation game design at any point in the sequence and then working either forwards or backwards (Figure 11.3).

The order in which the elements are discussed below is just one possible sequence:

1. scenario;
2. objectives;
3. roles and role profiles; and
4. role interaction.

Scenario

The scenario can follow logically from the objectives but it may have been thought about much earlier. It seems that a lot can be gained from considering a number of scenarios before settling down to the task of a final selection. Certainly the general scenario has to be relevant to the simulation game objectives, which will preclude some geographical areas and time periods. The scenario also has to be sufficiently elaborate to be a realistic portrayal for the participants. They will require sufficient detail in the specific scenario to enable them to play their roles. Above all, the scenario has to be interesting and enjoyable. A consideration of these criteria will eliminate a number of earlier bright ideas, but hopefully enough will remain to ensure an appropriate selection.

The scenario can be presented in a number of stimulating ways. A single paragraph may be sufficient to provide the information required. For example, in the SEMP simulation game *Community Disaster* (Curriculum Development Centre, 1978), the following scenario is provided:

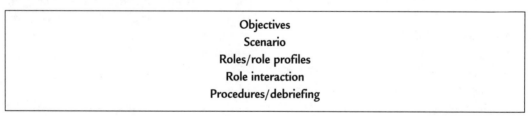

Objectives
Scenario
Roles/role profiles
Role interaction
Procedures/debriefing

Figure 11.2 *Steps in creating a simulation game*

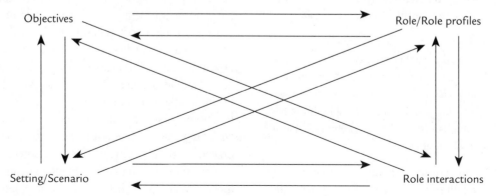

Figure 11.3 *Alternative routes in creating a simulation game*

Scenario

The action takes place between two groups—the larger group representing particular elements of society, the other representing the remnants of society in the aftermath of a natural disaster.

The larger group is subdivided into three smaller groups to represent the State Emergency Service or disaster organisation (A), volunteer organisations (B) and the third group represents government departments such as Health, Transport, Public Works, Social Security, etc (C).

Synopsis of events

Urbana is a coastal resort town with a population of approximately 10 000. The town grew and developed around a ria (a drowned river valley) and unfortunately, due to lack of control over zoning ordinances, has many areas which are liable to flooding.

The residents are painfully aware of this weakness in their town, since there is now a strong likelihood of severe flooding due to the threat of a tidal wave caused by recent earth tremors off the coast. Warnings are broadcast to the residents to move to higher ground.

Meanwhile, the Disaster Organisation at Sydbourne, 800 kilometres away, has been alerted to the threat and is making plans to deal with the situation. Eventually, the tidal wave arrives with disastrous results. Communications with the town are cut, and the small group of survivors now have to fend for themselves as best they can, since they are isolated from outside help.

After some time, a tentative radio link is established and a message is passed to the Disaster Organisation outlining the predicament of the victims. The resources of society are mobilised to cope with the situation, and while this is being organised an advance party is sent to Urbana to carry out relief work.

Due to further complications arising from the aftermath of the disaster, the remaining population of the town must be evacuated. This requires close cooperation between relief workers on the spot and elements of society at large. The effort is coordinated and directed by the Disaster Organisation at Sydbourne.

Finally, a welfare program is launched to cope with the newly located population of Urbana.

A transparency of the locality is sometimes provided in the form of a simplified street map or diagram. Of course, some simulation games have very elaborate scenarios and can consist of plastic relief map models and plastic building pieces to represent land-use patterns.

Other simulation games include miscellaneous pieces to add to the scenario details. The list is endless, but includes such items as posters, airline tickets, petition forms, bills of sale, title deeds, affidavits and drivers' licences. Sometimes more sophisticated multimedia presentations are included by using combinations of CD-ROMs, video and cassette tapes. All these extras are useful if they are readily available and if they add meaning to the simulation game. The main problem, of course, is living with the inventories and the counting required for a large number of small items.

Objectives

The desired objectives of a particular simulation game may surface immediately, beyond the awareness that there is a certain curriculum problem to be solved. It is likely that a number of general goals will be formulated in the first instance, but chances are that these will be vastly changed once the game has been played for the first time. For example, there might be a general goal to heighten respect and concern for the environment which in turn leads to specific objectives about ecology or land management.

We tend to be unaware of hidden intentions that only emerge when playing a simulation game. Debriefing and evaluation exercises often reveal all kinds of instructional objectives which were not explicit or intended in the original design.

Roles and role profiles

The establishing of roles for a simulation game is rather time consuming, even after decisions have been made about a particular theme with one or more key role players. When it comes to the actual planning operation, deciding how many key role players are required is critical. There is always an optimal number that ensures plenty of role interaction without making it too complicated for the participants. Nevertheless, it is important to ensure maximum participation from all students and not just a select few.

Of course, the number of key role players can be kept to a minimum by several techniques. Chance cards, special dice and formulae can be used to enforce additional decisions apart from those made by the role players. In this sense, these resources are covert role players.

The age and experience of players determine the amount of information included in the role profiles

By assigning one role to more than one person, it is possible to reduce the complexity of a simulation game. For example, in a simulation game with only 10 roles, a number of these might be played by three or more persons per role to represent a society, organisation, club or institution. If there are only a small number of roles available in a simulation game, it may be necessary to have two sessions operating concurrently in the same or adjoining rooms so that all students can participate. The mind boggles at the organisational and supervisory difficulties that can occur in these situations, and this should only be attempted by an experienced teacher.

The Rules of the Game (Lederman and Stewart, 1991) provides seven group roles but it is possible to have 1–6 players for each group role. Each group has to communicate messages effectively through the organisational hierarchy. Details of group roles are communicated to participants via coloured card decks.

If a game provides too few roles, one solution is to assign additional organisational roles to individuals not involved as key role players. Most simulation games require a number of tasks to be undertaken, such as reading out important announcements, timing the action sequences, collecting result slips, decision slips and other written messages, compiling running totals and monitoring the general progress of each group. This technique enables the simulation game to run more efficiently and also provides the teacher with an opportunity to participate as a role player. Nothing earns a teacher more respect from students than taking on a role that is the object of considerable scorn and criticism!

Having made decisions about the number of individual and group role players required, it is then necessary to devise suitable role profiles. The kinds of role profiles produced vary from brief descriptions of a general role, which enable the players to exhibit a wide range of behaviours, to those in which the range of behaviours is strictly limited.

Obviously the degree of detail included in role profiles will vary to suit the purpose of each simulation game and the age and experience of the players. If the role activities are to be limited by the materials supplied, then there is little need to provide complicated role profiles that will only confuse the participants. However, it is important that role players know the type of behaviour expected of them, the goals to which they should be aspiring, the procedures or rules of play and, if relevant, the particular win criteria which affect them. Certainly, explicit information like this enables role players to learn their task quickly, as indicated in the following role profile taken from *Board of Education v. Bridget C. Mergens* (Levitz, 1990).

Role 1—Members of Conflict Resolution Council

1. You hear disputes that arise in the school setting.

2. You do not have the authority to impose a decision on the disputing parties.

3. You are to assist the parties move from their initial positions to other possible options that might satisfactorily resolve the dispute.

The Process

Council members will insist on the following ground rules:

1. No interruptions while one party is speaking.

2. All parties must have an opportunity to speak.

3. All must be as open and honest as possible.

4. All must be willing to try to resolve this matter between themselves.

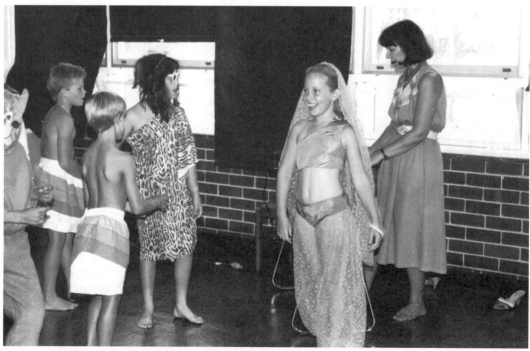

By using a few props, role players can identify more readily with their role

Role interaction

The specifying of role interactions within a diagrammatic model is a useful first step. However, the relative weightings of the interactions in terms of those that are rewarded and those that are not is very much a question of speculation at this stage. As a result of trial and error, some interaction patterns will be found to be spurious or insufficiently rewarded. This trial and error period of sorting out the role interactions is part of the tuning up that is needed in the creation of all simulation games.

■ Some Examples of Creating Simulation Games

Having provided some basic information about the major components used in a simulation game, it now seems appropriate to create some examples to indicate how simulation games can be used in teaching studies of society and environment.

Example 1: Brainstorming

Perhaps the teacher of a Year 9 class is unhappy about the way in which a topic on Aborigines is presented; for instance, perhaps the materials used to present the problems of Aborigines living in urban centres are not realistic. The teacher can visualise the kinds of interaction which might take place if this problem were presented in a simulation game.

Perhaps a board game could be devised with specific rules as to where players can live, what items of food and clothing they can buy, what kinds of jobs they can get and so on. The board game is thus replicating a number of the deprivations and frustrations that Aborigines suffer in the real situation. A spinner could be used as the basic means of controlling moves. From these general thoughts it is useful to proceed to a consideration of some of the role interaction details of this game.

As a guide, it is important to consider the following questions:

1. How many players are needed to produce the interactions wanted?
2. What rules are needed so that if Player A does X then Player B cannot do Y?
3. How complicated are the sequences? Can they be simplified at all without losing any of the interactions?
4. What actions must not occur? What steps are needed to prevent them?

The initial idea might be to have six players in the ratio of four non-Aboriginal to two Aboriginal. To insert some 'real-life' inequalities into the simulation game, it would be necessary to limit the opportunities for the two Aboriginal players compared with non-Aboriginal players. This could be achieved in several ways. One method would be to arrange the numbering on the spinner dial so that the numbers the two Aboriginal players need to get past certain points on the board are very difficult to obtain. Alternatively, if it was desired to prevent the two Aboriginal players from buying property in the European-dominated area X, this could be achieved by providing a lesser number of tokens, or paper money, to these players at the commencement of the game.

A matrix is a useful planning device to ensure that the desired activities are in fact possible. In a board game, this might be a two-dimensional diagram to check that the limitations on being accepted into certain occupations are carefully enforced. In a role-playing simulation game, it is equally important to ensure that specified interactions do occur and that others do not. Taking the example of Aborigines in an urban area and using it in a role-playing simulation game, it might be considered necessary for such actors as the police officer, magistrate, shopkeeper and hotel keeper to interact with the Aborigines, but not the lawyer, dress designer or wealthy residents. These interactions could be summarised on a chart to check that all essential interactions are included or excluded as necessary (Figure 11.4).

By starting off with a very vague idea about a topic on Aborigines and race relations, it is possible to build up a simulation model to include roles and role interactions. A lot of thinking is required about the essential roles in terms of the game's objectives. It is also important that the role interactions injected into the simulation game mirror the actual life situations. Once these details have been finalised, the scenario, operating instructions and debriefing can be completed relatively easily.

Example 2: Brainstorming

In primary school, despite good intentions, we tend to inflict an enormous amount of factual detail on our students in an endeavour to teach them about famous explorers and public figures. It is relatively easy to enlist their attention and keep them interested, but far more difficult to engage their feelings about a particular historical

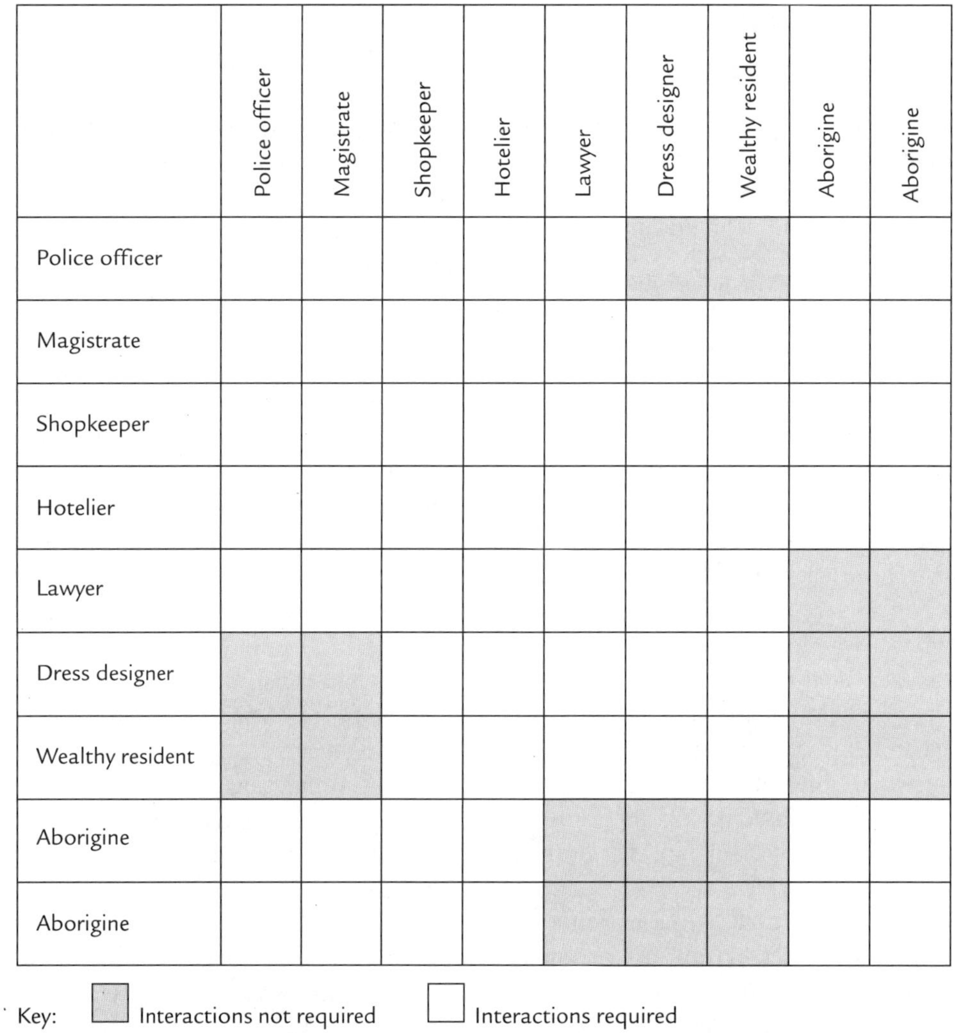

	Police officer	Magistrate	Shopkeeper	Hotelier	Lawyer	Dress designer	Wealthy resident	Aborigine	Aborigine
Police officer						▓	▓		
Magistrate									
Shopkeeper									
Hotelier									
Lawyer								▓	▓
Dress designer	▓	▓						▓	▓
Wealthy resident	▓	▓						▓	
Aborigine						▓	▓		
Aborigine						▓	▓		

Key: ▓ Interactions not required　☐ Interactions required

Figure 11.4 Interactions required between participants in an urban Aborigines game

figure. How do we get them to think about the constant dangers these people faced? What was it really like to explore completely unknown territory?

Let us consider the example of Ferdinand Magellan. Is it possible to go beyond the dates and figures related to the life of Ferdinand Magellan and relive some of the frustations, dangers and satisfactions that this great explorer experienced? How could we share these experiences with primary school children? Perhaps a simple board game could

be developed to enable children to empathise with this early explorer and some of the difficulties he encountered (Figure 11.5). There were certainly a number of problems that Magellan had to solve, for example:

1. Wind systems:
   • What winds could he rely upon?
   • How regular were they?
2. Food:
   • What types of food could he take aboard his ships?

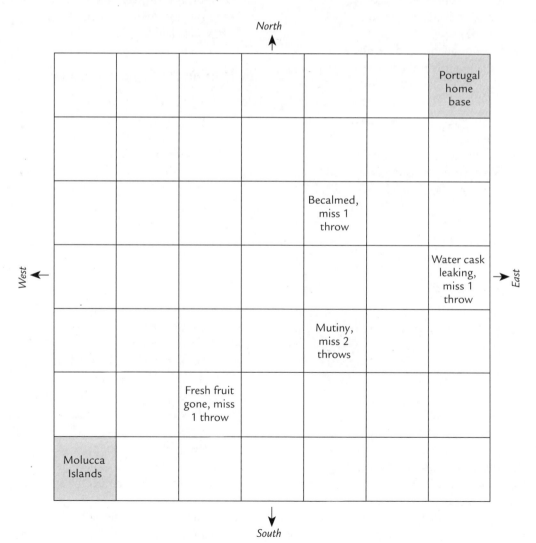

Figure 11.5 *Navigation chart for board game about Ferdinand Magellan*

- Where were known sources of food en route?
- What foods could be preserved in some way?
- What fresh fruit could be obtained?

3. Water:
   - What was the minimum amount needed by his men each day?
   - What was the maximum amount that could be stored on each ship?
   - What kinds of water container were used?
   - What were known sources of fresh water en route?

4. Calamities:
   - How frequently did storms occur?
   - How great was the risk of shipwreck?
   - How difficult was it to navigate a ship in those days?
   - What sorts of errors in navigation were made?
   - Did mutinies occur often?
   - What types of sickness were common on board these ships?
   - How common were attacks from enemy ships?

5. Uncertainties:
   - How concerned were the explorers about their ignorance of the country they were trying to find?
   - Were they uneasy about not knowing when they could next obtain fresh food?
   - Were they confident that the rewards they hoped to find were worth the risks?

These problems could be incorporated into the board game either as obstacles on the game route or as wild cards to be introduced during the game. A navigation chart similar to the one displayed in Figure 11.5 could be used by two players, one for the navigation and decision making, and the other for recording the decisions and consequences.

The dice or spinner used to select moves should be marked so that the most frequent numbers occur for southwesterly and westerly movements on the navigation chart.

At the end of each game, each pair of players could reflect on the successes and failures they had during their voyage. Further attempts could be made to see whether they could get from Portugal to the Molucca Islands in a reduced number of moves. This could then become the basis for a class discussion of the probabilities of success involved in the voyage and lead to some realisation of the tremendous risks that these early explorers had to take.

■ Running a Simulation Game

Developing the appropriate skills for creating a simulation game is certainly of paramount importance to the teacher. It is, however, also most important that teachers give sufficient time and thought to polishing their creations and to setting up appropriate procedures for putting these creations into operation as part of their curriculum (Di Nicola, 1997).

'Polishing' the product

For many, the meticulous checking and rechecking of details is time consuming and for some it may be plain boring. However, it is extremely unlikely that the first draft of a newly created simulation game is in a flawless format ready to be used. Parts will need to be revised, sections deleted and additions made. Nevertheless, it is better that time be allowed for these modifications so that monumental flops in the classroom can be avoided. The following headings are included as a guide for checking, but they are certainly not intended to be a complete listing.

Student learning opportunities

It is important to reconsider the intended activities of the simulation game. Unless students are involved in making decisions and reflecting on the consequences, little is gained from simulation games other than the mechanical activities of throwing dice and moving tokens on a board. Although the role interactions were carefully designed with student learning in mind, it is necessary to reassess the simulation, now that the product has been completed. As in all design activities, the learning activities must be appropriate to the declared objectives.

Game rules

The rules for any simulation game are usually included in order to optimise certain desired role interactions. If the intention is that only certain role actors are to interact, then appropriate rules must be included to achieve this. However, if the rules become complicated to the point of sustained confusion (a certain amount of confusion is normal when embarking upon a simulation game), then the position must be reviewed. The optimal situation appears to be when players have a range of decision options open to them, are knowledgeable about them and feel free to exercise choices.

The details of any game rules, both behavioural and administrative, are normally included in an instructor's or game director's manual. The behavioural rules might refer to whether written or spoken contacts are permissible or whether talking to delegates about their voting preferences is permitted. Administrative rules normally refer to such items as the sequence in which operations are to occur or the procedures for reporting information.

Playing materials

Playing materials come in all shapes, sizes and colours and their diversity gives some indication of the creativity of their designers. It needs to be remembered that the playing materials included in any given simulation

game need to satisfy some basic criteria. The materials must be:

- essential and appropriate to the game and convey meaning to it, rather than distract the concentration of participants;
- durable and reusable by players on a number of occasions;
- contained in sturdy containers which allow maximum access, yet enable individual items to be separately stored;
- easily recognised and retrievable by participants through a comprehensive marking and inventory system.

Tokens

Tokens are common to many simulation games and are used for various purposes, including the marking of player movements on a board, providing resources (money, status) for a certain role and identifying individual participants.

Spinners, dice or chance cards

These are included in many board games and, to a lesser extent, in role-playing games. The degree to which they are used depends on how many interactions are already inherent in the game design. In a role-playing game, the roles might be designed so that a few additional chance factors are required. Alternatively, a board game that has no specific role actors might require spinners and chance cards to create some real-life situations.

Chance cards are certainly easier to use to plan probability percentages than spinners or dice, although the excitement generated by turning up a card is likely to be less than that created by watching the oscillations of a spinner. The proportion of cards in each of the desired categories will be determined by the game design.

Display materials

Display materials are sometimes included in simulation games to build up the general atmosphere. In some simulation games, CD-ROMS, videotapes, audiotapes or overhead projector transparencies can be used as an initial impetus, especially when it is felt that participants need certain background information prior to their involvement in a game. Charts, posters and other visual materials can be shown to children during a game.

Recording of participants' activities

The recording of players' interactions is a vital activity in most simulation games. Feedback is occurring, and is required, throughout a game and so an accurate listing of transactions is needed, together with a suitable method of displaying this information. Also, data about participant activities is of great value as a basis for follow-up discussion during the debriefing sessions. Students may be unaware of the reasons for their actions until they are jolted by a specific question such as why they exchanged goods X for goods Y.

Packaging

The packaging of a simulation game needs more than cursory thought. Once a number of different cards, sheets, spinners and charts have been collected, it is important to obtain containers that will store the materials safely. Simple book jackets, folders and cardboard cylinders are generally not strong enough, so more durable flip-top cardboard boxes are often needed. Tiny markers and other smaller items need to be separately housed in tins and jars. The materials are made more accessible if they are colour coded and clearly labelled. A full inventory of materials needs to be included and prominently displayed on the container.

Ready to run
Personal preparedness

Whether the simulation game is one which has been personally developed or a commercial game to be modified, a number of final preparations are needed before it is ready to be used with a class.

The basic task is to become aware of all the actions that the students might make during the simulation game. This is not as easy as it might sound. It is necessary to read through a simulation game and try to anticipate all the interactions which might occur.

If a commercial simulation game is being used, it is likely that a comprehensive game director's manual which lists a number of the actions available to participants has been included. At best, it is only possible to become aware of some of the interactions in advance. In the relatively open situations which occur in simulation games, unanticipated interactions will frequently occur. As a preparation for these 'awkward' moments it is helpful to actually play the game with some friends prior to using it with a class. It will not be possible to learn all the moves, but it will give a sound background and perhaps increase confidence prior to the first class session. A full-scale playing of the simulation game before using it with the class is ideal, but not always possible.

School staff preparedness

Using simulation games in a classroom requires different teacher strategies and these in turn may affect other members of a school's staff, in some cases adversely. The differences are partly administrative (double periods and large rooms may be needed), but also pedagogical (students are encouraged to be self-directed and active).

Most problems can be overcome by careful development of strategies, both short term and long term. If the principal at a school is firmly convinced of the value of simulation games, it is likely that there will be little resistance from other staff members. However, as a more practical suggestion, it is valuable to find a fellow staff member with a strong interest in simulations or in team teaching. The rest of the staff should be kept informed of the benefits of including simulations in their teaching repertoire.

Class preparedness

Assuming that the idea of simulation games has been broached with administrative staff and has received their support, it is now necessary to ensure that the class makes the maximum use of the experience. A first step is to determine the number of students who can be involved in the activity. The majority of simulation games allow for 30 participants, although there are a number which have an upper limit of 15 and, in some instances, a maximum of up to 45. It is very likely that it will be necessary to make some changes because of the size of a class.

Apart from the numbers problem, it is necessary to work out a plan for casting the role players. Students who are skilful in a certain role will certainly help your simulation game to proceed smoothly, but beware of always using the obvious student for a role, as this will tend to stereotype these persons (Chapin and Messick, 1999). Academically slower students should have opportunities of taking on difficult roles, but there must be some balance in the selection. If more than one person is assigned to a role, it is very helpful to include students of widely differing academic ability, thereby allowing one to learn from the other. Other ways of selecting role players are by asking for volunteers or some form of random selection. Board games seem to be best suited to the latter, but some judicious combination of selection and using volunteers may be necessary for role-playing simulations.

Having decided on the number of role players and the total number of students to be involved, the next major decision is where to stage the simulation game. If a lot of space is needed for a role-playing activity, it may be very difficult to provide the necessary space in a classroom. If no gymnasium or school hall is available, the other alternative is to use buildings away from the main classrooms, such as lunchrooms or even school ovals. School verandahs can be very suitable for small groups involved in board games so long as the noise level can be restrained. Some school principals are receptive to the idea of using nearby church and municipal halls for these purposes. In Australia, the climate may often allow this sort of activity to be conducted outdoors.

In some situations, there are advantages to be gained by encouraging students to dress up for their respective roles. As indicated previously, simulation game kits usually include badges, arm bands and other distinguishing marks for role participants. It is conceivable that simulation games about pirates, the Eureka Stockade or a famous court case might be enhanced if participants don scarfs, waistcoats or wigs. It really depends on the way a class reacts to dressing up. If they see it as an opportunity for acting out their roles more fully it will certainly be worth including.

Once all these organisational problems have been sorted out, everything is in order to commence the simulation game. Of course, a class needs to be given some advance notice of what they will be doing. Ideally, a class period should be used the day before for an explanation of necessary points. It is not realistic to expect that students will be able to grasp the basic elements of a simulation game on the day they are required to play it. On the other hand, too much detail about the operation of the game may kill its appeal and spontaneity. The ways in which it is introduced to them will vary with the subject matter and the ages of the students, but the following are some possibilities:

• Provide a summary sheet for each student. This sheet sets out the aims of the simulation game, the role players, scenario and a brief description of the sequence of events. This method is particularly useful with senior secondary school classes. Some students may have difficulty in visualising the simulation game by this method alone.

- Provide all the paraphernalia of the simulation game for students to handle and read. This will involve circulating the role cards, scenario sheets, role badges, tokens and scoring sheets. This method is a good 'hands-on' experience for students, especially if there are opportunities for students to discuss aspects of the game with each other and with the teacher.

- Provide all the paraphernalia as above and then play some sections of the simulation game on a trial basis. You will need a period of at least 80 minutes to do this. Some simulation games are hard to play in discrete sections or are difficult for students to follow unless the full scale operation is commenced.

It's running

Before students come into the room, it helps to have all materials set out on the desks or tables. Some of the items needed include:

- blank paper—sets available for each group or individual;
- marker pens, pencils—sufficient for each group or the individual role players;
- role cards—for individuals or groups;
- resource materials—for example, paper money or tickets; and
- recording sheets—sufficient for each group per round.

In addition to these materials, it is necessary to provide whiteboard space or extra portable whiteboards to record progress results, and to have a time device and bell.

Once the students have arrived in the room and are ready to start the simulation game, it is usually necessary to give a brief résumé of the points discussed in the introductory session. They need to know:

- the purpose of the simulation game;
- the goals of each player;
- the sequence of events; and
- the first move and the sequence of interactions during the first round.

As soon as play has commenced, it is important for the teacher to fade into the background. While the simulation game is in progress, the teacher can make a number of unobtrusive observations about student behaviour. The actions of role players should be noted so that these can be referred to during the debriefing phase. In board games, the teacher can move from group to group, watching students' moves and, on occasions, counselling students. In role-playing games, the teacher will probably not need to move about the room, but should be in a position from which to observe and note specific actions of participants.

During the simulation game, the teacher's main task is to see that the rules and time limits are observed and that differences of opinion do not hold up the sequence of events (Di Nicola, 1997). In deciding whether to stop or play one more round, it is best to err on the side of stopping if excitement is high. More impact is gained by a few action-packed rounds than by extending the activities because they seem to be going well.

■ Debriefing Activities

Many people have the misconception that once a simulation game has been played the activity has been completed. In some ways, the most important activity of all, debriefing, is still to come (Seidner, 1995).

Debriefing is a process in which participants of a simulation game are led through a purposeful discussion of that experience with the objective of transforming the experience into positive and lasting learning (Crookall, 1995). As noted by Lederman (1992), the debriefing process assumes that:

- the experience of participating in a simulation game has affected the participants in a meaningful way;
- a processing of that experience is necessary to provide insight into that experience and its impact.

Debriefing is not asking who won when the time is up; neither is it raising such platitudes as 'Did you like the game?' or 'Is it better than doing normal school work?'. Debriefing is searching for the why, as well as the what and the how, of the simulation game.

Participants actively involved in a simulation game only have the time and motivation to see that their individual or group's interests are maximised. They do not see what other groups are doing or thinking, except as it relates to them. Consequently, they do not obtain the total picture of the simulation game without some form of post-game discussion.

As in other forms of teaching, we cannot assume that students know why they do certain things. With regard to simulation games, we cannot assume that they know why they made certain moves and counter-moves or behaved in a certain way in acting out a role. They need time to ponder over what they did and so discover why.

For the teacher, the debriefing period is the first occasion to really find out what students have learnt from their simulation experience. Admittedly, the teacher may have noted students' intensity and their verbal exchanges during the game, but this provides little feedback about the levels of student under-standing. Probing questions, discussions and follow-up activities are needed to ascertain just what the students have gleaned from their activity.

The debriefing session can take many forms ranging from teacher directed, to learner based with the teacher as facilitator, to an autonomous group with no teacher direction. Lederman (1992) and Thiagarajan (1992) contend that the learner-based approach is by far the most productive in getting participants to examine and analyse their inner thoughts and reflections. It depends on the age range of the students, the type of simulation game, the classroom atmosphere and teaching style used by the classroom teacher.

Post-experience debriefing can also involve emotional recovery from critical incidents (Lederman and Kato, 1995: 236). Teachers should facilitate this emotional recovery but need to take care that students don't engage in communication which is too self-disclosing. There are ethical issues here and the teacher may need to protect potentially naive participants from disclosure which might be costly emotionally (Richetti and Sheerin, 1999).

There can also be cultural issues. Not all students will support similar cultural norms—there may be various cultural interpretations, and in some instances embarrassing situations can occur if there are breaches of cultural norms (Hofstede, 1986).

Of course, a comprehensive debriefing session can only be achieved if accurate records of student behaviour are available. This data may have already been collated by special role players (group leaders, coordinators), by the observational records kept by the teacher or by audio-visual records (Table 11.2). Written documents kept by each group are useful sources of information. They can be used to question students about decisions they made during the game. Anecdotal records and observation schedule data are also of considerable value, as they provide impressionistic accounts of the interactions which occurred. However, the really telling sources of data are audio-visual

Table 11.2 *Data available for debriefing sessions*

Types of summary data	Types of audio-visual data
Inventory sheets	Audiotape recordings
Petition forms	Video recordings
Daily record sheets	35-mm slides and prints
Whiteboard summaries of sales, outputs	Camera prints
Transaction sheets	
Diary entries	
Scoring sheets	
Tally sheets	

records, especially videotape recordings. Students are often amazed to see how they behaved during the game and really enjoy the opportunity of reliving the experience.

Debriefing sequences

As noted above, debriefing processes can vary from highly structured dialogues to non-directive discussions. Yet most follow a sequence which starts with factual questions before moving to more personal, value-laden questions. Petranek *et al.* (1992) refer to the four Es sequence, namely events, emotions, empathy and explanations. Lederman (1992) has a similar approach but uses the terms systematic reflection, intensification and personalisation, and generalisation and application of the experience. Although different terms are used by different authors, there appears to be consensus among specialists that there is a general progression, or sequence, from factual summarising to wider-ranging applications of the issues, to studies of individual value stances.

There is also the matter of timing of the debriefing session. Steinwachs (1992a) argues convincingly that debriefing should occur immediately after the simulation game ends. Participants need assistance withdrawing from the experience. Steinwachs advises against giving students a break period—rather they should move to an area of the room (preferably a circle of chairs) where they can be seated and where they can examine the experience together. As detailed in Table 11.3, there are some preparatory tasks that a teacher should do before the debriefing period. The role of facilitator of a debriefing session is also a difficult one, and some of the tips included in Table 11.3 may be of some assistance.

Summarisation phase

Students are normally quite eager and willing to talk about the game in which they have just been involved. It is important to talk about major events/happenings before the more controversial issues are raised. As indicated in Table 11.3, questions should be asked by the teacher which encourage students to reflect upon their experiences (Hawley and Duffy, 1998). These preliminary oral discussions might be undertaken with the full class or in some instances with small groups of students.

Some useful questions for this phase might include:

- What happened in this simulation game?
- What transactions did you make?
- What were your greatest frustrations and/or successes?
- What decisions did you (or your group) make and why?

Once the more factual details have been aired, it is then possible for probing to occur

Table 11.3 *Hints to facilitate the debriefing process*

Prepare for the debriefing by:

· setting aside adequate time;
· identifying some analogies you might want to draw upon;
· preparing a set of questions to facilitate movement through the debriefing phases.

Facilitator hints:

· keep out of the substantive 'give and take' for the most part. Avoid telling players what you think they should have learned;
· affirm everyone who contributes by paraphrasing or repeating some key words;
· if a question is working well, keep asking it over and over again, although rephrasing it slightly each time;
· respect and use silences as spaces for thinking, absorbing;
· help those who tend to dominate to be more sensitive to others' needs.

into the reasons behind students' actions. This may involve a second, separate debriefing period. Sometimes these sessions can be quite protracted as some students will want to discuss a topic or problem in detail.

Application phase

Here the emphasis is on extending the students' newly found insights. Given that they have developed certain attitudes or skills from playing the simulation game, it is now necessary to see whether they can apply these to related situations.

Case study examples are a useful method for both primary and secondary school students. A variation of this approach is to provide a situation related to that used in the game in which students are required to build on skills and attitudes they developed from playing the simulation game.

Another approach for post-game follow-up is to ask students to evaluate critically or revise a simulation game using their own set of priorities and values. At the secondary school level especially, it can be most revealing to discover the degree to which a simulation game appears to the students to be valid. This will involve discussing the specific objectives of the game and its built-in assumptions and restrictions.

Petranek *et al.* (1992) suggest journal writing as a valuable extension of the application phase. These authors argue that assumptions made during the oral debriefing can be verified in each student's journal. They consider that journal writing enables a student to shape his or her ideas and to become involved in speculative questioning.

Integration phase

Students are quick to sense class activities which are worthwhile compared with those which are included as stop-gap measures. The teacher should select a timeslot in the teaching program for the simulation game so that it follows directly from previous class work or serves as a stimulus for subsequent class activities. It is necessary, both during the debriefing periods and subsequently, to link activities which happened during the simulation game with other subjects, or aspects of subjects, being studied in the course. Some students will see the connection automatically, but the astute teacher will be on the lookout for examples to provide contrasts and comparisons.

Because the topics of simulation games tend to span several subjects, it is relatively easy to integrate them across the curriculum; for example, primary school students can follow up a simulation game with art and craft lessons, literature study and science lessons related to the subject of the game. At the secondary school level it is more difficult to find opportunities for cooperative planning between a number of specialist teachers. Nonetheless, there are opportunities for students to compare characters from simulation games with real-life people and famous characters from the past. Tape recordings of famous leaders and guest speaker visits could be a useful follow-up to some simulation games. Many local, national and international activities in the political arena could be compared with those encountered in simulation games.

■ Selecting Commercial Simulation Games

Although the focus of this chapter has been on the activities involved in creating simulation games, it is also possible to get some very good ideas from commercial versions. This is especially the case over recent years with the spate of high-quality computer simulation games now on the market (Nelson, 1992). The playing of commercial products alerts a teacher to some of the processes and principles involved in creating his or her own simulation game.

Making an initial choice

One of the difficulties in choosing a simulation game is obtaining sufficient information about the game to make an informed choice regarding its suitability. A typical summary for a simulation game includes information on the style of simulation, number of participants needed, recommended minimum length of playing time, age level, price and the address from which it can be obtained. A small number of bibliographies on simulation games exist, including Crookall and Oxford (1990),

Dukes and Matthews (1993), Steinwachs (1992b) and Muir (1996). From time to time, specific bibliographies on the studies of society and environment area are published, such as Muir (1996). (Listings are also available for computer-assisted simulation games; see Chapter 12.) According to Schug and Beery (1987), the number of simulation games available at primary school level has not been as great as the number and variety available for secondary school students.

Unless a teacher can visit a bookshop and examine the materials, this summary information will probably be insufficient to make an informed decision. However, some booksellers will forward simulation games to prospective buyers on a trial basis, which should largely overcome this problem of lack of information.

There are other important considerations too, such as the actual cost of commercial simulation games. Although the typical cost per game is between $30 and $100, prices do go up to $300 and higher. For many teachers, obtaining $30 or more for a simulation game from school funds can be difficult. From the publishers' point of view, the limited sales volume for simulation games and the myriad of non-standard items (dice, blocks, stickers) have the effect of making them high-cost products. There seems little way around this problem except for teachers in neighbouring schools coming to some mutual arrangements for sharing commercial games.

The length of time required for running a simulation game is always stated in a standard bibliography; however, the time period suggested may be far in excess of the amount of time provisionally allocated. It is often extremely difficult to vary the number of participants or modify the simulation game without greatly affecting its impact. These are all extra problems and may make the task of selecting a simulation game just too difficult to carry out.

On the positive side, commercially produced simulation games have been produced by specialists, are thoroughly field tested and are presented as extremely attractive and durable packages.

Firming up on a selection

If it is possible to narrow the choice of commercial simulation games down to three or four, it is a good idea to search out specific evaluative data about them. A number of simulation games such as *SimCity* (Wright, 1989) or *Barnga* (Thiagarajan and Stein-wachs, 1990) are well known and are presently being used in several countries. It is relatively easy to find additional descriptions of these games by reading relevant sections from some of the standard simulation references.

If critical reviews of well-known simulation games are required, these are generally found in journals such as *Simulation and Gaming* (Sage Publications). These follow-up references and articles, however, are only available for well-known simulation games and it is far more likely that cheaper and relatively unknown products will be selected by the teacher. In these circumstances, it is helpful to develop a checklist for appraising a simulation game.

Based upon the components described earlier it is possible to develop criteria for evaluating a simulation game (Table 11.4). Taken together, the information provided from these six questions gives an accurate picture of the game. The most fundamental question is, of course, the first one. If the simulation game is based on a clearly conceived, well-developed problem, and on one which is relevant to the real world, then it will probably be successful.

It may be possible to collect data on these

Table 11.4 *Evaluation elements and criteria*

Elements	Parts of a game	Criteria
1. What is the central problem presented in the game?	Problem	Clarity Conceptual content Utility Relationship to real world
2. What choices are available to players?	Choices	Soundness
3. What are the different moves/ activities provided for players?	Moves	Consistency
4. What are the rules for the game?	Rules	Lack of distortion Relationship to problem
5. How is the game organised?	Organisation	Inclusiveness Sequencing Relationship to choices, moves, rules
6. What summary activities conclude the game?	Conclusion	Adequacy Applicability Relationship to problem Relationship to activities

six questions by simply reading the items included in the simulation package. If the kit can be obtained on a trial basis, it can actually be played with a class. Of course, these categories can also be used to appraise personally created simulation games as well as the commercial versions.

■ Concluding Comments

Simulation games can provide the teacher with a powerful tool for exploring values, issues and societal problems. Furthermore, students tend to derive considerable enjoyment from playing simulation games.

Although a variety of commercial products are available, it is quite an easy matter, and educationally profitable, for teachers to develop their own simulation games. So long as a few basic guidelines are followed, as explained in this chapter, there is no reason why viable simulation games cannot be produced by individual teachers.

Simulation games are here to stay. In educational circles over the last 30 or so years, simulation games have steadily gained ground as a viable teaching technique. According to Walford (1995) and Wolfe and Crookall (1998) new uses and variations continue to be developed, but the *raison d'être* of a simulation game continues to be that it raises our imagination and counteracts much of what we lose from traditional methods of teaching and learning.

Pederson (1995) sums it up when he states that simulation games provide a safe place to ask dangerous questions.

QUESTIONS AND ACTIVITIES

1. With reference to a class you have taught or are teaching, reflect upon a values issue which you typically teach didactically but which could be presented as a simulation game.
    * What would be the major objectives of such a simulation game?
    * How would you optimise specific interactions?
    * Which roles would you develop and why?
    * Have you ideas about an effective scenario?
    * What specific debriefing techniques would you use?

2. It is sometimes argued that simulation games are too time consuming to be considered seriously as part of a teacher's repertoire. Present an argument to demonstrate that the time needed for simulation games can be justified because of the superiority in achieving effective outcomes.

3. Explain why the debriefing element of a simulation game is an important aspect for both the teacher and his or her students.

4. To what extent is role taking through dramatic representation an important element of the studies of society and environment field? Consider a topic(s) you might develop into a simulation game that could enable participants to become involved in dramatic representations.

12

Personal Computers

Introduction

Personal computers have had a significant impact on teaching and learning activities in schools in recent years. There are several reasons for this. The number of personal computers in schools have increased, improving students' access to this new technology. At some schools, students own laptop computers which they can use at school, and at home, for personal needs. Computers have become more powerful, providing access to more sophisticated software which operates quickly and efficiently. The range of useful, dependable and reasonably priced software has continued to grow. Peripheral devices have become more affordable, presenting new opportunities for students to access information (from CD-ROM, for instance) or to present work requirements (using laser printers and scanners). Communication using computers has become simple and cheap, opening up new sources of information on the Internet and World Wide Web and new opportunities for national and international collaboration with other students on research projects. In many schools, computers are now integral resources in classroom learning activities.

This chapter describes computer applications that are particularly relevant to study of society and environment teachers and makes suggestions about incorporating computers into classroom learning activities. Attention is given to databases, spreadsheets, simulations, information retrieval, presentation and communications software, and to possible uses for these types of software in social inquiries.

These applications (described in the first part of this chapter) involve teaching and learning with new technology in the classroom. In the studies of society and environment field, however, we are also concerned with teaching about computers and investigating how new technology has shaped our society and how it will continue to do so. The nature of the changes, the effects on individuals and the responses they evoke should be topics of investigation and discussion. Therefore, the latter part of this chapter addresses the issues involved in helping students to develop an understanding of the impact of computers on society and the concerns that have been raised about this new technology.

A practical approach is taken throughout the chapter. Basic terms and applications are explained, some examples of software that can be used in the classroom are described and suggestions are provided about teaching with and about computers in studies of society and environment. The final section of this chapter identifies electronic resources (online journals and discussion groups, units of work and lesson plans, software reviews, curriculum documents), and other useful sites for teachers on the World Wide Web.

■ The Benefits of Personal Computers in the Classroom

Although the price of computers has dropped markedly, they are still a major financial outlay for schools and individuals. Teachers must be able to justify how computers can contribute to the achievement of learning outcomes, and how they can be integrated into classroom learning activities. Some of the important reasons for using computers are outlined here.

Motivation

Many teachers have found that computers can improve students' motivation in learning activities. The computer is not a gimmick; its capability to do things that could not previously be done in the classroom makes it a valuable resource. For instance, in a collaborative environmental project on the Kids Network (KIDNET), students in Grades 4, 5 and 6 in metropolitan and rural schools in the USA pooled data collected locally,

analysed trends and discussed issues about acid rain by using this electronic network. The impact of investigating this issue in this way is evident in a comment by one student: 'Before, I knew a little about acid rain, but I didn't care. Now I do. I want to do something about it. I will always remember' (Upitis, 1990: 242). In this project, computers enabled students to investigate and discuss an important issue which would not have been possible without access to rapid electronic communication.

Decision making and problem solving

Teachers have also found that computer software helps students to develop decision-making and problem-solving skills such as posing solutions, considering alternative courses of action, sharing and challenging ideas and evaluating evidence. These skills are often involved when students work on simulation software in small groups (see Chapter 11). For instance, after using a simulation of community development (*SimCity*), teachers reported that:

> Students seem to be motivated by 'gaming'. The problem-solving orientation challenges their creativity and allows for multiple solutions. The active, non threatening environment of simulations offers participation without risk-taking. Computer technology enhances simulations in a number of ways. Immediate feedback and record keeping streamlines decision making. The situation can be controlled and manipulated easily to provide various levels of difficulty and complexity. (Teague and Teague, 1995: 22)

Decision making and problem solving skills can, of course, be developed in a variety of ways but good software can provide a challenging environment for them.

Group work

In a well-organised classroom, where students are working on a variety of

The personal computer can provide a focus for group-based student activities

activities, the computer can provide a focus for group activities. While small groups complete various activities 'off' the computer, other groups take their turn at working with a particular piece of software. Good software encourages students to discuss the procedures to follow to reach desired outcomes, and to consider other points of view as well as their own when working towards the solution of problems. An example of this form of classroom organisation is the integrated, or thematic, approach often used with adventure and simulation software (see the section on simulations later in the chapter) but it can also be used successfully when children work with databases, spreadsheets, communications and other types of software (see under 'Databases', 'Spreadsheets' and 'the Internet and World Wide Web' below).

Inquiry learning

Most curriculum guidelines promote inquiry learning—that is, collecting and analysing data and forming tentative generalisations from the analysis—as students investigate and explain aspects of the social world (see Chapter 10). Computers and appropriate software such as open databases (discussed more fully in 'Databases' below) provide a useful resource for teachers to implement inquiry strategies with students in the classroom (Sage, 2000).

The reasons for this relate to the software being used and to the power of the computer to store and process information quickly and accurately. Unlike some other software, which requires students to select the correct answer from various options (such as choosing the 'right' answer from among the alternatives presented in a tutorial program), open databases and similar software provide a framework, or structure, to guide students in their inquiries.

For instance, an open database requires information to be entered in a particular way, thereby encouraging accurate and systematic data collection and recording. Questions about this data also have to be framed in a certain way if the software is to be operated successfully, encouraging students to think carefully about questions they want to investigate. This requirement is, in itself, a resource teachers can use to develop inquiry strategies for students. The computer is totally responsive to their needs and interests—they have control over the questions that can be asked and are not limited to the alternatives anticipated by the developer of the software. Therefore, the computer encourages interaction between the user and the data being analysed as ideas are tested and tentative generalisations reached. Because it handles information quickly and accurately, the computer (and the software) enables students to focus on the questions that are most relevant to their inquiries and to search for trends and relationships in the data (see also Chapter 10).

Access to resources

So much information is now available in digital (computer readable) formats such as CD-ROM (see 'Information retrieval' below) and from sites on the World Wide Web (see the section entitled 'the Internet and World Wide Web') that it is often impossible to rely only on traditional print materials (such as books and newspapers) as sources in student inquiries in studies of society and environment. CD-ROM based encyclopedias, for instance, are cheaper to purchase than printed volumes so these can be updated more frequently (an important consideration with tight school budgets), providing students with access to more recent information on topics they are investigating. CD-ROMs often make use of various media (sound, video clips, photographs) providing richer sources of information than that found in print materials. This is an appealing feature of multimedia software for many students. Importantly, the ease with which relevant information can be located using keyword searches or hypertext links enables students to broaden their search for relevant information—such as using a CD-ROM containing articles from a major metropolitan newspaper—in ways which would not be possible even if they had access to the original printed sources.

Presentation of work

Information available in digital formats can also be incorporated in printed or computer-based presentations (see 'Presentation software' below) of student work (Ryan, 2000). Some CD-ROMs contain files of images (sometimes called 'clip-art') which are not subject to copyright restrictions and these can be copied and included in printed reports. When students have access to a digital camera, images can be captured and used in printed documents or imported into other software and used to create a computer presentation of the outcomes of an inquiry. These resources help students preparing reports because the text and images can be easily manipulated until they are satisfied with the final presentation. Students also avoid the tedious tasks of copying and redrafting work often associated with pen and paper techniques. Many students find the techniques involved in preparing reports using computer software engaging, and take considerable pride in the quality of their final presentation.

These are some of the important reasons for using computers in studies of society and environment. Computers are an essential resource in enhancing students' learning experiences and helping them to achieve curriculum outcomes. In the following sections of this chapter, some of the ways computers can be used in the studies of society and environment curriculum are outlined.

■ Hardware

Only a basic knowledge of the physical components ('hardware'), in a technical sense, is necessary before the computer, and other peripherals such as printers and modems, are set up in the classroom. The major hardware components are either already physically part of the computer (such as CD-ROM drives) or they can be easily connected (see Figure 12.1).

The **hard disk drive** is a permanent storage medium for the most frequently used software (see the section on software below). The capacity of the hard drive is usually specified in gigabytes, or 'G'. Computers typically used in schools have storage capacities in the range of 4–6 G.

The **floppy disk drive** is used to install new software (supplied on disk) on the hard drive, to 'back up' (duplicate) files in case the hard disk fails or to transfer these files to another computer.

The **CD-ROM drive** is used to access software supplied on CD-ROMs. Multimedia software containing text, graphics, animations, sound and video clips is usually supplied in this format since the large storage requirements for several examples of this type of software would quickly exceed the permanent storage available on the hard disk.

The **modem**, connected to both the computer and a telephone line, is used to access remote databases and networks (see the section entitled 'The Internet and World Wide Web').

Other peripherals which can be connected to the computer include scanners, video cameras and microphones.

When computers have been **networked** (that is, linked together by cable) in one

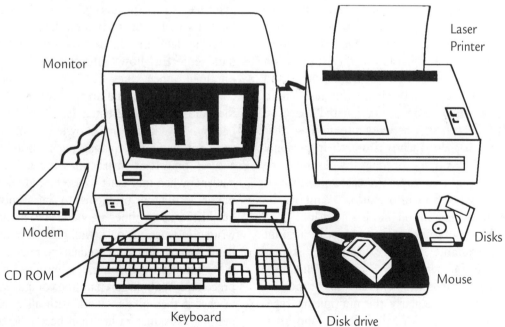

Figure 12.1 *The basic components for setting up the personal computer for the classroom*

room, or at different locations around a school, software installed on one computer (sometimes called a fileserver) can be accessed by users with other computers.

■ Software

Although there may be different arrangements at particular schools, software can usually be accessed in a number of ways. Some applications, such as wordprocessing, database and spreadsheet software, are usually available on the hard disk when the computer is initially purchased. Other software is supplied on floppy disk or CD-ROM and then installed on the hard disk, a simple procedure which involves following the instructions presented on the screen. Alternatively, software supplied on CD-ROM is accessed directly when the CD-ROM disk is inserted in the drive. When computers are networked, frequently-used software is available from a central location (fileserver).

Some software is **read only** in nature; for instance, the information available on a CD-ROM encyclopedia can be read but not altered. Other software, such as open database software (see under 'Databases' below), only consists of the **application** which students need to create, sort and present their data. Hence, students need blank floppy disks (or designated space on the fileserver in a network situation) so that they can permanently store their personal database. Copies of data files should be stored on two disks in case one disk is damaged and information cannot be recovered from it on another occasion.

An important consideration is the amount of available RAM ('Random Access Memory'), temporary (internal) memory needed to operate software. A lot of modern software, particularly the multimedia type, requires at least 16 Mb of RAM (and often more) to run efficiently. Student frustration with software that runs slowly, or classroom management problems when students can't utilise the software because it has 'crashed', can be avoided by reading the software documentation and checking this basic requirement.

Software is easy to run (by double-clicking on the icon on the screen) and use (by clicking on the command buttons on the screen palettes or menus). However, knowing what happens when these command buttons are chosen, and the various ways in which the software can be utilised, often takes some time to learn. Documentation accompanying the software usually outlines simple step-by-step procedures to follow and other aids (such as a 'Help' folder and introductory tutorial) can often be of assistance.

However, it is best to find some time to become thoroughly familiar with the software before using it in classroom activities. Taking a laptop computer, with a copy of the software loaded on the hard disk, home for the weekend is sometimes the best way to do this. For example, if a database is to be used, it is a good idea to complete a 'pilot study', with a limited set of data, to become familiar with how the database can be structured and the data entered, how information can be obtained once the database has been completed, and the different ways in which the data can be presented (see 'Databases' below). A thorough knowledge of the software minimises management problems, ensures that clear instructions are given to students when they start to use it, and allows minor settling-in problems to be resolved quickly. It is sometimes a good idea to prepare written instructions on a wall chart mounted beside the computer for students to refer to as they familiarise themselves with a new procedure. With this preparation completed, a teacher is then able to work with all groups needing assistance rather than becoming tied up with the group using the computer.

Teaching strategies

It is also important that teachers give careful attention to the teaching strategies that will be used to incorporate the computer into classroom learning activities (see also Chapter 4). Computers are used more successfully in classrooms where the chief mode of organisation is small-group work. While one group is working on the computer, using a database, simulation or some other piece of software, other groups can be involved in activities related to the topic under investigation. These activities might include research from relevant books (library skills), report writing (language), mapping (studies of society and environment) and modelling (art/craft). This integrated or thematic approach to learning activities (Dawes and Robertson, 1991; Stewart, 1990) can be used with many different types of software. Here the role of the teacher is to manage the resources that students need and guide each group as it works on a project.

When students have finished using the computer they can continue with other activities, and another group of students can take over the computer to examine the questions they have formulated. If a printed copy of some of the information required to use the software (such as the information contained in a database, or the map needed in a simulation game) is also available, students can use it to think about the questions that might be asked about a database, or the strategies that might be used in a simulation, before they begin using the software. This printed material might also help students to confirm information previously located in a database or the effects of actions taken in a simulation after they have used the computer. This helps to reduce the need for students to gain access to the computer.

■ Databases

A database is a collection of data that can be compared with a drawer (file) containing many information cards (see Figure 12.2).

Each card in the file is called a record, in the same way as people talk about student records, cemetery records or census records.

Each record contains a number of fields (or categories). For example, each card (record) in a student records file (database)

File of data

Student Records

Figure 12.2 *A database can be compared with a card filing system*

might contain the fields 'surname', 'other-names', 'address', 'telephone' and 'age' (see Figure 12.3).

There are basically two types of database that might be used:

1. those that contain pre-stored data (sometimes called 'closed', 'fixed' or 'structured' databases); and
2. those that contain file management routines only (sometimes called 'open', 'flexible' or 'unstructured' databases).

The differences between each of these are described in the following sections.

Databases containing pre-stored data

'Closed' databases are available on many topics—such as natural disasters, bush-rangers, Olympic Games results, census data, countries of the world, prime ministers of Australia—which students in studies of society and environment might investigate. These are useful resources since, in many cases, the information they contain is never out of date (such as a database on bush-rangers or early explorers in Australia) and they can be used whenever these topics are investigated. With other databases (countries or prime ministers), 'updates' of the software can be purchased (usually at a discount on the normal price) so that students have current information to work with.

For King and Country (Queensland Department of Education, 1989), a kit which examines Australia's involvement in World War I, contains an interesting example of a closed database. Each record in the database contains personal and military service details about 307 Queenslanders who died during that war. The information for each enlistment is organised into a number of fields including 'place of birth', 'school', 'address on enlistment', 'rank' and 'unit'. Information from the database is accessed by selecting the relevant field and typing a specific request. For instance, the 'address on enlistment' field would be selected and the name of a town entered if students were attempting to locate enlistments from a particular area. Like other closed databases, this one enables students to ask historical data questions and to test the adequacy of their hypotheses quickly and easily. The speed with which the database can provide answers enables a wide range of different questions and hypotheses to be explored.

Databases with file management routines

These programs allow students to create their own databases with their own information in the fields they select. Records can be added, removed or changed. These databases can usually perform other functions: information

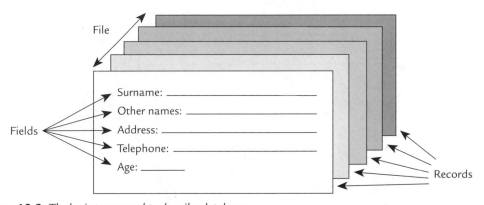

Figure 12.3 *The basic terms used to describe databases*

can be sorted into alphabetical or numerical order, and reports can be based on the requests formulated. Often these reports can be presented in graphical (e.g. bar graphs and pie diagrams) and/or statistical form (e.g. the minimum and maximum values in the selected field).

Cemetery records database

The process involved in preparing a database can be illustrated with a specific example based on cemetery records. To prepare the database, fields like those shown in Box 12.1 could be selected.

Fields like 'SEX' and 'GRAVE_EXISTS', which might not be part of cemetery records, can be added to the database to assist with the analysis of data.

Once information has been entered in these fields for each record, the completed database can be used to analyse trends and relationships. For example, students could investigate:

1. whether the cause of death was related to age, the month of year, or sex;
2. how closely the expression 'three score years and ten' fits the data;
3. differences between the ages at which males and females died.

Three further suggestions for databases illustrate how a range of different activities in different areas of the curriculum can be integrated when planning classroom learning activities.

Personal features database

In studying individual physical character-istics, primary school children could record information about members of their own class. Depending on how the inquiry developed, fields like those in the following list might be relevant: height, weight, hair colour, eye colour, shoe size, clothing size, eye shape, face shape, reach, age and gender.

To record the necessary information, children would have to note their personal characteristics on a survey sheet. The children would also need to discuss how to record 'eye shape' and 'face shape', using common descriptors or numbers for the various types. They would also need to measure and record such variables as 'height' and 'weight' accurately. Once the database had been compiled, they could use the

---

Box 12.1 *Fields for a database of cemetery records*

Field name	Information in this field
DATE	Date of interment
MONTH	Month of interment
YEAR	Year of interment
SURNAME	Surname of person
FIRSTNAME	First name(s)
AGE	Age at death
SEX	Sex
DENOM	Religious affiliation
CAUSE	Cause of death
LASTRES	Last residence
GRAVE_NO	Grave number
GRAVE_EXISTS	Whether grave can be located

graphical and statistical facilities to summarise the information, and write their own requests to examine relationships in the data (e.g. between 'height' and 'shoe size', or between 'reach' and 'age').

Awards database

As part of a unit of work on awards, students could compile a database about recipients of the Order of Australia, using lists published in newspapers on Australia Day. Selected fields might be 'surname', 'other names', 'title', 'sex', 'service' being recognised, 'place' and 'state'. Various analyses could be completed with this database. For example, male and female recipients of awards could be totalled and the reasons for differences could be discussed. The number of awards from each state could be determined, and an analysis of their distribution completed. The categories of service (e.g. 'community',

'sport', 'farming') for which awards are made could also be identified and the reasons why there are many recipients in some categories (e.g. sporting awards) could also be discussed.

Local environmental study database

When students are studying the local environment (e.g. the school grounds) information collected could be entered into a database for later analysis. The fields chosen to compile the database would depend on the particular purposes of the study; however, the fields for a database on trees growing locally may include: 'name', 'location', 'height', 'girth', 'origin' (native or exotic), as well as details on bark, leaves and flowers. This data could then be analysed to develop profiles of the vegetation in the vicinity, so that generalisations about desirable changes (e.g. new plantings) could be made.

Databases can be valuable sources of information for student projects

■ Spreadsheets

The survey is one of the most widely used techniques for obtaining information about the social and physical environment. Organisations or groups that have to make decisions often use some form of survey to gather information. A local government authority, for example, might survey ratepayers to determine their preferences regarding the location of a kindergarten or health centre. Or a group of residents, upset about a decision to rezone parkland for car parking, might support their case with the results of a survey.

Similarly, students often need to make surveys as part of the studies of society and environment topics they are investigating. For example, these surveys may gather data on:

- attitudes towards environmental and social issues;
- impressions and knowledge of the local area;
- personal preferences and behaviour.

This data enables students to make decisions or reach conclusions about the topic. When surveys are used as part of classroom learning activities, difficulties sometimes occur with the analysis of data and the presentation of results. The calculations involved in the analysis of data and the presentation of results in the form of charts can be tedious and time consuming. These problems can reduce student interest and involvement. To overcome them, the computer can be used to do the 'hack work' while students focus on refining their questions or interpreting the results once the data has been summarised.

Spreadsheet software can be particularly useful when data has to be analysed and results presented in charts. A spreadsheet provides a framework, presented as columns and rows, and information can be entered in the cells in the matrix. Three types of information can be placed in cells: labels, numbers and formulae. In the example shown in Box 12.2, labels are displayed in column A (rows 3–7). The percentages of responses on the first question are displayed in column B. These percentages were obtained by entering the appropriate formula in cell B3; then, using a special feature of the software (a 'Fill Down' command), automatically changed and entered into cells B4 to B7 without

Box 12.2 *Spreadsheets can be used to analyse and display questionnaire responses*

	A	B	C	D	E	F
1						
2	QUESTION 1					
3	Strongly Disagree (9)	43%				
4	Disagree (5)	24%				
5	Neutral (2)	10%				
6	Agree (3)	14%				
7	Q.1 Strongly Agree (2)	10%				
8						

having to amend and enter the formula for each cell. The chart was prepared by simply highlighting data in columns A and B and selecting the 'Make Chart' command. The chart was then rotated horizontally and scaled to fit the page.

Spreadsheets can be used to analyse and display results quickly (Box 12.3), saving students the lengthy and laborious tasks of numerous calculations and redrafting charts. Students can then focus on interpreting the data and searching for trends and relationships. When the analysis is completed the charts can be included in the final report.

■ Simulations

A simulation is a model, or representation, of something real. Simulations are used when there are dangers or difficulties (such as organisational demands) involved in providing real first-hand experiences for students. They may take many forms. They might be simplified models or more complex representations of some aspects of something (see Chapter 11).

Computer simulations offer several advantages over other forms of simulation (such as board games). For example, students can gain greater experience with important factors because the computer can handle more variables and more complex calculations than an individual player can in a board game. High-quality simulation software makes use of colour, graphics, sound and action, which is highly motivating for students. The computer can respond quickly when different options are entered, and a simulation usually only takes a short time. Good software also contains facilities to 'save' completed work so that students can resume a simulation later on. They can also usually obtain a printed copy of the results of their efforts.

Simulations can be used in studies of society and environment for a wide variety of topics: for example, climatic conditions, exploration, archaeology, survival on a desert island, life on the goldfields, the clean-up of oil spills and voting patterns.

An interesting program is *Investigating Lake Iluka* (Interactive Multimedia, 1993), a simulation based on Lake Illawarra (NSW). The software, available on CD-ROM, provides opportunities for secondary school students to investigate the ecosystems—urban, mangroves, estuaries and open waters—of the lake and the impact of urban development on the environment. Information about the lake is available from multimedia sources—newspaper clippings, radio discussions, videos and reference works. Features of the ecosystems can be sampled with physical, chemical and biological 'tools' such as a thermometer for measuring air, water and soil temperatures and water quality tests for pesticides and nutrients. The software has a built-in 'notebook' so that students can save text from the program or make individual notes which can be edited later and included in reports.

This software could be used in various ways. The multimedia resources can help students identify the plants and animals which live in different ecosystems. The measuring tools allow students to 'use' testing devices appropriately, perhaps as preparation for a future field trip to a local lake. Or the software can be used to investigate challenging environmental problems, such as resort developments or nutrient pollution, and assessments made of the impact these changes might have on the lake ecosystems. Work in other curriculum areas might also be incorporated—students could debate the impact of development on the lake ecosystem and research the effects of similar developments in other places. When used in this way, the software can become a central resource in an integrated unit of work covering several curriculum areas.

Box 12.3 *Spreadsheets can be used to display data in different ways*

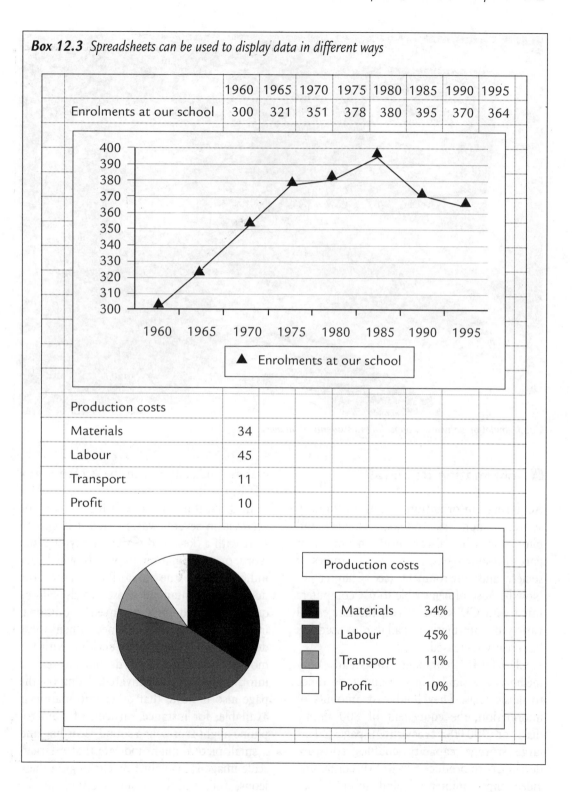

	1960	1965	1970	1975	1980	1985	1990	1995
Enrolments at our school	300	321	351	378	380	395	370	364

▲ Enrolments at our school

Production costs								
Materials	34							
Labour	45							
Transport	11							
Profit	10							

Production costs

■	Materials	34%
■	Labour	45%
■	Transport	11%
□	Profit	10%

Good simulation software is appealing to students of all ages

■ Information Retrieval

Acquiring information from secondary sources such as books, videos and photographs has always been an important part of resource-based learning in studies of society and environment (see Chapter 3). Now because of being able to use computers fitted with CD-ROM drives, the range and variety of information available to students has greatly increased.

CD-ROMs (compact disk-read only memory) are similar in size and appearance to music CDs. They hold vast amounts of information, the equivalent of 800 floppy disks or 300 000 typewritten pages! This large storage capacity enables software developers to produce CD-ROMs containing video clips, animations and sound. Text, graphics, voice recordings, maps, photo-

graphs and music can be stored on a CD-ROM.

Information on a CD-ROM can be accessed in several ways. Often it is best to start with a 'keyword search'; by typing in a word or combination of words which are indicative of the material sought, the documents containing those words can be quickly located and displayed. Additional information can be obtained when these documents are viewed. By clicking with the mouse on highlighted words, links to related information can be activated. Icons on the page also indicate that other information is available; for instance, an icon of a microphone might represent a sound recording and a small picture might indicate that a larger-scale image is available. By clicking on these icons, this additional information can be quickly obtained.

CD-ROMs are a standard student resource for research-based activities in studies of society and environment. The audio and video components of CD-ROMs are appealing to students, and the search and retrieval facilities of these huge databases are powerful and easy to use. While schools may find it difficult to budget for hardware and software purchases, consideration should be given to making several suitably equipped computers available for student use in the library.

CD-ROMs are available on many topics in the studies of society and environment curriculum. Two such examples are briefly reviewed here.

Making Multicultural Australia (Board of Studies, New South Wales, 1999a) was prepared as support material for the New South Wales Australian History Years 7–10 syllabus. The three CD-ROMs explore the roles of different cultural groups in Australian society. They contain graphical images (photographs, cartoons, posters and video clips) and sound recordings (music, audio segments) about people, events and issues, as well as extensive documentary sources (reports, legislation, media reports) about the cultural diversity of Australian society. These images and recordings can be easily located by clicking on command buttons displaying pictures and/or labels of the type of available material. Other icons, such as direction arrows and labelled buttons, enable users to 'navigate' easily through the material on this CD-ROM. The advantages of having historical sources like this available on CD-ROM are that (1) students can review material which they cannot usually access, and (2) the images and sounds 'bring to life' the explanations in textbooks, encouraging empathy with the people and events portrayed.

Another example which effectively utilises the huge storage capabilities of CD-ROMs is *Elemental* (Board of Studies, New South Wales, 1999d). This multimedia package presents a wide range of resources about the exploration, mining and processing of minerals and the environmental management of mining activities. The three CD-ROMs in the package present hundreds of full-colour photographs, charts and diagrams, numerous video and audio clips and extensive text-based resources. These information sources can be used by students investigating the minerals industry, and support other topics in science, geography, business studies, economics and environmental studies.

■ The Internet and World Wide Web

The facilities available on the Internet, and the development of easy to use software to access them, have encouraged many schools to subscribe to this electronic network. The opportunities for students to communicate with other students, locate relevant resources and publish information for others to read (functions outlined in the following sections) have created some exciting new opportunities for teachers to enhance learning activities in the studies of society and environment curriculum.

What is the Internet?

Physically, the Internet is the world's largest internetwork, connecting (using fibre optic cable and telephone lines) a vast number of networks around the world. A communications protocol called TCP/IP (Transmission Control Protocol/Internet Protocol) enables computers connected to a network to communicate so that information can be passed across networks. Functionally, the Internet is used to communicate (e.g. electronic mail), transfer files (e.g. documents and software) or publish (e.g. on a World Wide Web site).

How do you connect to the Internet?

The Internet is accessed by using a computer, modem and a telephone line. Communications software, installed on the hard disk fitted to the computer, connects the user's computer with another maintained by an Internet Service Provider (ISP).

To use the Internet it is necessary to obtain an account through an ISP. The provider may be a commercial network, an employing authority, a local university or a computer users' group. When an application for an account is accepted, a personal address is issued. This address is used to connect, through the ISP, to the Internet. It is also the unique location where a user's electronic mail is stored.

The costs of obtaining and using an account vary greatly and it is worthwhile 'shopping around' for the best value. Some ISPs charge a joining fee, monthly subscription and connection fee (each time the service is accessed), while others provide a minimum allocation of hours connection time each month for a fixed fee. It is useful to have a local telephone number to access the account to minimise call charges.

When the account has been established, it is possible to use the Internet in many different ways. Two of the features—electronic mail and the World Wide Web—most commonly used by schools are outlined here.

Electronic mail

Text messages exchanged on a computer network are known as electronic mail or email. Electronic mail is most commonly used to exchange private messages with another user with a known address. However, group-based communication is also possible in cases where a message addressed to a 'group mailbox', such as a 'listserv' or 'mailing list', is distributed to multiple recipients linked to this mailbox. In this way, email can be used to discuss topics among

users who have subscribed to the listserv, as well as for one-to-one messaging. It is probably a good idea to subscribe only to moderated listservs, where messages are scrutinised for inappropriate language and content before they are made available for all subscribers to read.

Information about schools in Australia and other countries with electronic mail addresses (and World Wide Web sites) can be found in Box 12.4.

Information about electronic mailing lists (listservs) for students can be found at the World Wide Web sites displayed in Box 12.5.

World Wide Web

The most popular part of the Internet for many teachers and students is the World Wide Web (WWW or Web). There are several reasons for this. The software used to access the Web is freely available from ISPs or locations ('sites') on the Web itself. This software has a graphical interface and most of the procedures needed to operate it can be activated by simple 'point and click' techniques using the mouse. The WWW is a huge resource of freely available material; thousands of sites developed by universities, government departments, research centres, community organisations, businesses and individuals contain potentially useful information for schools. Information is presented in different formats—text, video, audio and graphics—and this can be appealing to peruse. A keyword search can be completed

---

Box 12.4 *World Wide Web sites with information about electronic mail addresses of schools*

Education Network Australia (EdNA)
  www.edna.edu.au
International WWW Schools Registry
  web66.coled.umn.edu/schools.html

Box 12.5 *World Wide Web sites with information about listservs*

Listserv	URL
KIDLINK	www.kidlink.org/english/society/nations.html
Intercultural E-mail Classroom Connections (IECC)	www.stolaf.edu/network/iecc
Global SchoolNet	www.gsn.org

The following sites contain the names of listservs which may be of interest to teachers and students.

The Global Schoolhouse	www.gsn.org/teach/index.html
Australian Curriculum Studies Association	www.acsa.edu.au

---

to locate possible sites; then, only a simple click with the mouse on the title of a site is needed to move directly to it. Another popular feature is the way in which information at one site is often linked to related information on the same site or a different site at another location. By following these links ('surfing'), information at various sites can be quickly reviewed.

Finding sites on the World Wide Web
Sites on the WWW are identified by a unique address called a Uniform Resource Locator (see Box 12.6). These can be accessed in several ways:

- when the URL is known, the address can be entered and the site opened (see Box 12.7);
- when searching for sites, keywords about the information sought can be entered and a search completed (see Box 12.8). A list (sometimes a very long one!) of potentially useful sites is displayed when the search is completed;
- when reading information at one site, a

Box 12.6 *Components of a URL*

http://www.theage.com.au/

HyperText Transfer Protocol—the method used to transfer data.	World Wide Web.	Domain Name—here, *The Age* newspaper in Melbourne.	This is a Commercial site. Others could be network, government and organisation.	Country—ie Australia. Nothing here may indicate site is in USA.

Each site on the WWW has a unique Uniform Resource Locator. Some sites may have longer URLs. These contain the directory path to specific pages at the same site.

Box 12.7 *Entering the URL is a convenient way to access a site on the World Wide Web*

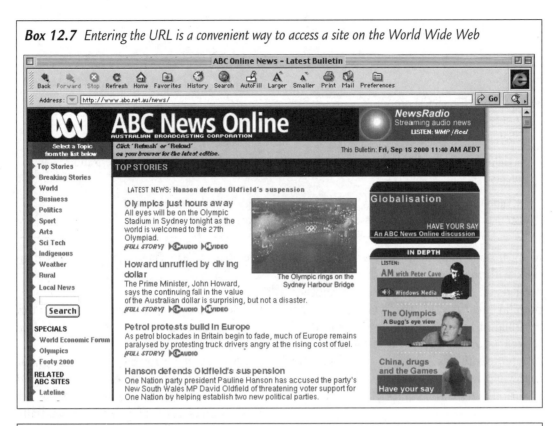

Box 12.8 *Using keywords to search for sites on the World Wide Web*

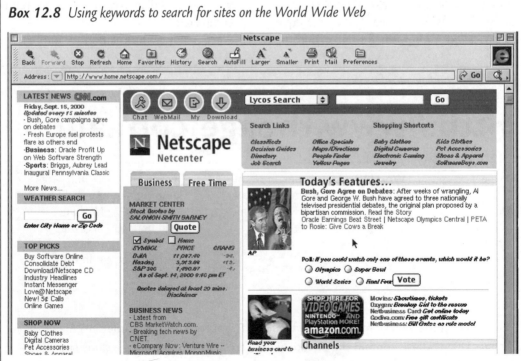

click on highlighted text or designated symbols will activate a link to another site with other information.

Using the World Wide Web

The WWW can be used to obtain information or to publish information.

The WWW is a huge resource of freely available, interesting and up to date information on topics often investigated by students. When information is located it can be downloaded to the hard disk on the computer. When the connection to the WWW has been closed this information can be printed, or edited and copied into printed reports.

The WWW is also a place where student work can be published. Well-presented reports can be added to the school's WWW site and made available to students in other schools.

The World Wide Web—issues for schools

The WWW is a vast electronic network with exciting resources for teachers and students in studies of society and environment. However, providing and maintaining student access to the WWW raises issues which teachers need to address if this global network is to be used effectively in curriculum activities.

Efficiency   Access to the WWW, in a technical sense, is dependent on the computer hardware used, especially the modem, and the quality of the network connection. If lengthy delays in accessing sites and downloading information are to be minimised (but not always avoided), it is necessary to use a 'high-speed' 56.6 kbs ('kilobytes per second') modem. This is a technical issue which can be addressed by schools. However, many connections, especially for schools in rural areas, have to be made on telephone lines—rather than fibre optic cable networks now available in

metropolitan areas—and these can be the source of delays in accessing the WWW and transmitting data.

Delays in data transmission may impose limits on the use made of the WWW in schools. Students may need to be advised only to access specific sites where URLs are known (to minimise searching time). Or, useful sites may be identified and saved to the hard disk on the computer so that they can be retrieved rapidly for students to use at specific times. Another approach, in schools with a local area network (LAN), is to archive frequently required WWW sites on the fileserver. When this is done, relevant material can be accessed quickly and in a way which emulates the WWW experience for students (Massie, 1997).

Organisation   Difficulties locating relevant information arise because: (1) the WWW is not divided into sections where homogenous sites are located (unlike a library where books with similar content are classified together); and (2) there is no control over the quality of sites (unlike a book which is subject to editorial scrutiny before publication).

It is possible to search the WWW and obtain a list of sites which match the criteria (keywords) specified. However, the list of sites obtained using this search facility may be very long, and a considerable amount of time may still be needed to peruse each site. It is often frustrating to find that many of the sites identified in the search contain only trivial information. Hence, when students use the WWW to locate information about specific research interests, the time needed to do so may be difficult to schedule.

Sometimes a better way to locate information is to use an index maintained by another party (e.g. professional association, commercial organisation). An example is the *Index of Australian Sites* (www.sofcom.com. au). This site also has a search facility to locate email addresses and newsgroups. Another example is *Virtual Tourist* (www.vtourist.com) which has a map guide to regional information on the WWW in many countries.

The National Council for the Social Studies WWW site (www.ncss.org/online) is another good place to start looking for information. At this site, resources and links are categorised under 10 themes (many familiar to Australian teachers of studies of society and environment).

The home page of a government WWW site is also a good starting point. For instance, the Australian Government site (www.nla.gov.au) provides access to reports, media releases and publications, as well as links to other government departments.

Quality There are many educationally valuable sites on the WWW. When planning units of work, it is a good idea to identify these sites and make them accessible via the school LAN. In this way, the suitability of the content on particular sites can be checked before students commence work on a topic. If assistance is needed, checklists can be used to evaluate the quality of WWW sites (Leeman, 1999; Risinger, 1998; Wilkinson, Bennett and Oliver, 1997). However, sites on the WWW cannot always be examined before students are given full access to them and this presents particular problems for schools. Since some sites contain material potentially offensive to many people, the terms and conditions of student access to the WWW needs consideration. In cases where students will be given full access to the WWW, three approaches to managing student access can be considered (Futoran, Schofield and Eurich-Fulcer, 1995):

1. Restrict access to scheduled classes. This ensures that what students see and do on the WWW is supervised by teachers and more likely to be directed towards specified curriculum activities than the exploration of other sites. However, this approach curtails independent research activities and restricts access to those times during the day when connections to the WWW can be slow and inefficient.

2. Limit access to particular sites. This is often done with the cooperation of an ISP. This makes supervision easier; however, it also limits student access to potentially useful resources.

3. Provide open access, and counsel students about appropriate behaviours. These behaviours are sometimes outlined in 'acceptable use policies' (AUPs) which require the signature of student, parent/guardian and teacher before access is granted to the WWW. An AUP outlines appropriate online behaviours ('netiquette') and the consequences of transgressions (inflammmatory email, distributing obscene images) of codes of conduct. This may be the best way for senior students completing projects on individual topics to have access to the unique resources for research available on the WWW.

The WWW presents new opportunities to enhance curriculum experiences. However, specifying the terms and conditions under which students can access the WWW is an issue for schools to address before these opportunities can be fully realised.

Planning learning activities on the World Wide Web

The WWW is a recent innovation and the ways in which it might be used in schools have yet to be fully explored. At present, the WWW is often viewed as just another source of information, along with books, audio-visual resources and other materials for students investigating topics in the school curriculum. This view of the WWW may remain for some time because of restrictions on student access, technical limitations of networks and inexperience about the educational potential of this new medium.

However, it is possible that the WWW (or other electronic networks like it) may play a more central role in educational activities in the future. As the efficiency of networks to transmit data improves, and student access becomes more widely available, the ways in which the WWW can be used for educational activities will be explored more fully. In the future, the WWW may not only supply *content* to supplement existing resources; it may also be the *medium* by which investigations are conducted. The potential of the WWW as a medium to conduct investigations, as well as a source of content, is illustrated in the following example.

A visit to Canberra

Many primary and secondary school students visit the national capital each year to experience 'first-hand' national collections (National Library, Australian War Memorial), institutions (High Court, Australian Institute of Sport) and exhibitions (National Gallery, Old Parliament House). This field trip provides opportunities for students to gather additional information about topics studied in the curriculum, enhance understandings about the role of national institutions in decision making, administration and management, and to empathise with cultural and historical events depicted in national collections.

As well as using a field trip like this to introduce topics, or to reinforce them (see Chapter 4), a wide range of curriculum outcomes can also be achieved when students are involved in planning and organising a field trip. To do this, the WWW becomes a valuable resource to identify sites to visit, plan activities which might be completed at each site, and arrange transport (to the national capital and between various venues).

A good place for students to start is the tourist site (www.canberratourism.com.au). Here, information about major government sites, art galleries, historical collections and science and technology exhibitions can be viewed. Essential information about opening hours, admissions charges and contact details and maps displaying the location of venues can be printed and used for initial planning of the field trip. A calendar of events in the national capital can also be printed so that these events can be considered for inclusion on the itinerary.

Once a tentative schedule of visits has been prepared, students could take 'virtual tours' of specific sites to identify the particular exhibits they wanted to view. For instance, on the National Library site (www.nla.gov.au) they could take an 'online tour' of the reading rooms and collections; at the Parliament House WWW site (www.aph.gov.au) they could check the dates the House of Representatives and Senate is sitting; and, by accessing the WebCam at the Space Station (www.cdscc.nasa.gov), they could get a 'real-time' view of one of the tracking telescopes. Other sites in the national capital could also be visited in this way, and decisions made about their inclusion on the itinerary.

Once a tentative itinerary has been prepared, students could return to the tourism site. Contact details for tour operators and accommodation venues could be accessed at a special section of this site for school groups. The links at this site save students valuable time; they can quickly get started on detailed planning without having initially to locate and review sites which may be relevant for their purposes. Electronic mail messages could then be sent to confirm costs and the availability of accommodation. Students travelling to Canberra could use the WWW to plan other travel arrangements. For instance, students from Victoria could plan train travel to Canberra by accessing the

V/LINE site (www.vline.vic.gov.au) to obtain timetables, network maps, interstate connections and fares. Students from schools further afield could use the online schedule information from Qantas (www.qantas.com.au) to submit queries regarding flights on the particular dates they wished to travel so that travel plans could be finalised.

Involving students in planning a field trip increases interest in the venues to be visited. At the same time, students gain valuable skills—locating and using electronic sources of information, decision making and cooperative learning. Hence, the WWW is used to investigate topics and develop relevant skills, not just as the source of printed reference material which supports other classroom activities. *A visit to Canberra* indicates some of the ways in which a 'virtual' unit of work can be developed. Other innovative examples are sure to appear as teachers think about the WWW as the medium, as well as the source of content, for activities in the studies of society and environment curriculum.

■ Presentation Software

Presenting the findings of an investigation is an important part of student inquiry projects in studies of society and environment (see Chapter 10). Visual material prepared using presentation software—such as PowerPoint and Persuasion—can enhance many oral reports.

Some of the features of this type of software help students develop skills to communicate information effectively. Text and graphic images can be displayed. For instance, images captured from a CD-ROM of clip-art and charts prepared using spreadsheet software (see Box 12.9) can be included on each slide. These enhancements maintain interest and highlight key findings for members of the audience. The order in which slides are presented can be easily changed, so attention can be given to the best sequence to present material. And, since only a limited amount of information can be presented on each slide, the key points which will be presented need to be carefully identified (note-taking skills).

Many students find the processes involved in creating a slide show absorbing and put a great deal of thought into the best ways to enhance their presentations using this type of software.

■ Why Teach about Computers?

The widespread adoption and use of computers has brought many advantages. In industry, for instance, computers have saved considerable expense in the design and manufacture of goods and in the control of routine operations and processes. In business, word processors have eliminated tedious copy typing, and spreadsheet software has enabled quick and accurate financial accounting and forecasting. Other areas to benefit are publishing, banking and tourism.

Despite these advantages, there are widespread concerns about computers. In the main, these relate to:

- changes in employment that this new technology has brought about;
- using computers to store information; and
- computer crime.

These are important concerns and they are matters of public debate that should be investigated and discussed.

Employment

Computers have created new jobs, made other jobs redundant and raised the level of skill required of those seeking employment in a wide range of occupations, with implications for education and training. Some

Box 12.9 *A slide from a computer-based presentation*

Family History Project

Grade 6 - Toorak Central School - 1932

significant questions for investigation about these changes include:

- What changes in work patterns and practices will the new technology incur? What impact will these changes have on the way we view 'employment', 'un-employment' and 'leisure'?
- Who is responsible for the development and implementation of policies and practices related to new technology?
- Who will be advantaged and dis-advantaged? What assistance should be provided to those forced to adjust to changing employment patterns?
- Will computers encourage creativity, self-fulfilment and participation, and develop positive attitudes to work?

Such questions are important because many people feel threatened by computers, and think they contribute to redundancy and limited job opportunities, especially for school leavers. When employment is available, computers are often blamed for excessively high levels of education and training. Therefore, giving students oppor-tunities to appraise these changes, and the demands they make on them personally, are important components of any studies of society and environment program.

Information storage

Computers have vastly increased the amount of information that can be stored, and many people have expressed concern about the collection, recording and distribution of this information. Not only has the quantity of information increased enormously, but the range of possible uses of such information has widened immensely in recent times. The capacity of computers to locate quickly the information held in documents and databases, and to present it in a variety of ways to suit particular purposes, raises questions about privacy, access and power. Some of these concerns are:

- What information should be stored?
- Who will have access to this information?
- How will the information be used?
- Who will own the information? Will it be passed on to others?
- Will access to the information decrease or increase the disadvantage of some groups in society?

These fundamental questions of human rights, power and social justice should be dealt with explicitly in studies of society and environment programs (see Chapter 14).

Computer crime

As society relies more on computers to handle banking and other financial matters through automatic teller machines and credit card transactions, new opportunities have become available for criminal activity.

Losses are also reported, from time to time, by large organisations that use computers to handle financial transactions. This 'white collar' crime, which is often difficult to detect, can lead to financial hardship for individuals and substantial losses for large organisations.

Some of the issues of concern in this area are:

- What is the nature and extent of computer crime? Are adequate safeguards in place to protect computer systems?
- What legal sanctions are in place to deal with computer crime? Is this type of crime viewed in the same way as other criminal activity?
- Who is responsible when a crime is committed—the organisations that control the computer system or the individuals who use it?
- What consumer legislation is in place to protect users? Is it adequate? Can it be improved?

Studies of society and environment teachers have a role in assisting students to examine such issues involved in the impact of computers in society. Students need to be in a position to make appropriate personal responses as well as an informed contribution to discussing these issues.

■ Teaching about Computers— Some Suggested Program Outlines

Developments in technology and the effects these can have on individuals and groups in society have been, and will continue to be, an important part of the content which is studied in the studies of society and environment curriculum (De Coker, 2000). This is evident in the outcomes identified in curriculum guidelines. For instance, in the Human Society and Environment K–6

Syllabus (Board of Studies, New South Wales, 1998a: 21) students are expected to:

- explain how people and technologies in systems link to provide goods and services to satisfy needs and wants (SSS1.7);
- describe how and why people and technologies interact to meet needs and explain the effects of these interactions on people and the environment (SSS2.7).

In the *Curriculum and Standards Framework II* (Board of Studies, Victoria, 1999: 431) the expected outcome that students will 'compare different types of work' (SE3.3) is considered to be evident when students can 'identify the impact of technological changes in different types of work'. Statements like these can be the basis for units of work, or parts of units, that examine the social implications of computer-related technology.

Example 1

Primary school students could examine 'the development, application and use [of technology] in different times and places' by focusing on families in the past, present and future. Students might start by: listing the ways they travel to school and the ways their parents travel to work; appliances and tools used in the home and the workshop; and the activities they engage in during leisure time. Data might be collected via surveys and interviews, and tentative generalisations made about the technologies, including computer technology, that they presently use.

A second component of this topic might relate to the use of technology in the past, and students might visit a local historical park to collect information on the contents of rooms in authentically furnished period houses. Students might also interview grandparents and take notes from reference sources in the library. Generalisations about the past use of tools and appliances might be compared with those based on their earlier study of their present situation.

A third component of the study might involve speculation about how technology might develop in the future, with a particular emphasis on how computers might influence everyday activities completed by the family.

Another approach is to examine the impact of technology on a particular industry. A case study of the newspaper industry, for example, could document the specific changes wrought by computer-related technology, and examine the assumptions prompted by such changes. By visiting the local newspaper office, and researching other books and audio-visual materials, students could investigate who instigated the technological changes and examine the nature of their authority or power. They could examine why different individuals and groups (e.g. management and unions) might have supported or opposed these changes, and find out what actions these groups took to make or restrict change. The effects of these changes on those involved—who benefited and who was disadvantaged by the changes—might also be investigated.

Other case studies could also be completed. Relevant excursions and other fieldwork to view examples of computer-related technology, and to talk to those most directly involved with this new technology, would help students evaluate the nature and scope of computer technology and its impact on individuals and groups in society. Similarly, case studies of office work, agriculture, heavy industry, communications and the fast-food industry provide considerable scope to investigate the impact of computers. The nature of work patterns and practices, the availability of employment and the level of training required, for instance, might be investigated.

Example 2

Another approach is to consider relevant issues about computers while students are actually involved in computer activities.

For example, if students were involved in compiling a database of households as part of a local area survey they could examine some important questions about access, privacy and crime along with the original research questions. They could conduct a survey and ask respondents if their father and mother worked full-time and part-time (to collect information on 'employment'), and if they owned a videocassette recorder, computer, colour television and CD player (to estimate 'socioeconomic status'), and then discuss the implications of unauthorised access to this data. Since the computer can locate quickly the households owning one or more of the items mentioned and in which both parents work full-time, a database of this kind could help criminals seeking the best targets for burglary. This example illustrates some of the potential dangers of unauthorised access to information, and shows how social issues may be considered on two levels simultaneously.

Another method is to include investigations of new technology in existing units of work. For instance, investigations of print-based and television advertising could be extended to include advertising on the WWW. Both the content of advertisements, including the continuation of gender stereotyping (Knupfer, 1998), and the techniques (such as animation) used to attract attention to products and services could be compared with print and television advertising. The placement of advertisements might also be investigated— are advertisements displayed at random or targeted towards particular users? How is advertising regulated on the WWW? What legislation has been enacted, and how can this be implemented on a network which crosses national boundaries? What policies are followed by the major providers of WWW services? As new technology is increasingly incorporated into learning activities, new questions related to usage can and should be addressed.

■ Electronic Resources for Teachers

There are now many sites on the WWW with resources for study of society and environment teachers. These resources take many forms. The *CSS Journal* (www.cssjournal.com/journal/) can be accessed electronically on the WWW. This journal publishes articles about computers and related technology in social studies classrooms at all levels.

The WWW sites maintained by state education departments, national organisations (such as the Curriculum Corporation and Education Network Australia) and subject associations (see Box 12.10), provide many valuable resources. These include units of work, lesson plans and software reviews. Curriculum guidelines can also be downloaded as pdf (portable document format) files, then searched electronically or printed for reference purposes. Online discussion groups are also operating at many of these sites. In these forums, teachers can discuss current issues and request assistance from others about teaching and learning in the studies in society and environment (and other) curriculum. Many of these sites also provide links to other professional associations, as well as links to organisations which provide information and resources about curriculum topics. The WWW is now a valuable source of ideas for teaching purposes, as well as a means to keep up to date with professional publications and to initiate and maintain contacts with other teachers.

Box 12.10 *Australian WWW sites for teachers*

Victoria
Board of Studies (www.bos.vic.edu.au)
Education Department (www.softweb.vic.edu.au)

New South Wales
Board of Studies (www.boardofstudies.nsw.edu.au)
Department of Education (www.dse.nsw.edu.au)

Queensland
Board of Senior Secondary School Studies (www.qbssss.edu.au)
Queensland School Curriculum Council (www.qscc.qld.edu.au)
Education Department (www.qed.qld.gov.au)

Northern Territory
Board of Studies (www.nted.nt.gov.au/ntbos)

South Australia
Department of Education, Training and Employment (www.sacsa.nexus.edu.au)
Senior Secondary Assessment Board (www.ssabsa.nexus.edu.au)

Western Australia
Education Department (www.eddept.wa.edu.au)
Curriculum Council (www.curriculum.wa.edu.au)

Tasmania
Education Department (www.doe.tased.edu.au)

Other organisations
Australian Federation of Societies for Studies of Society and Environment (www.pa.ash.org.au)
Curriculum Corporation (www.curriculum.edu.au)
Education Network Australia (EdNA) (www.edna.edu.au)

■ Concluding Comments

This chapter has dealt with two major aspects which teachers need to consider in relation to computers and studies of society and environment. The first section on learning *with* computers described database, spreadsheet, simulation, information retrieval, presentation and communications software, and gave examples of the teaching strategies teachers could use with computers in the classroom. The second section focused on what students might learn *about* computers—the purposes computers serve and the impact they have had on individuals and groups in society. It was suggested that since computers raise concerns related to work, information technology and crime, these should be investigated as part of the studies of society and environment curriculum. This section outlined some examples of units of work dealing with these concerns.

The number of computers in schools and the quality of available software present many opportunities for studies of society and environment teachers to enhance learning activities for students. At the same time as the impact of new technology creates new opportunities and benefits, however, problems and concerns also arise. Therefore, teaching with and about computers are important components of both the content and implementation of the studies of society and environment curriculum.

QUESTIONS AND ACTIVITIES

1. Plan a unit of work in which various resources are used, including computer software. Assume that you have one computer permanently available in your classroom for students to use. Outline some activities that students could carry out as part of this unit of work. How would you organise classroom activities to ensure that all students gained access to the computer?
2. Review an example of computer software that could be used as part of a unit of work in studies of society and environment. Briefly describe the objectives of the software, any knowledge and skills that students should have to use it successfully, and the curriculum topics for which it might be used.
3. This chapter mentions several examples of databases that students might compile. Can you think of other studies in which information collected by students could be analysed by using open database software?
4. Search the World Wide Web for resources on a selected topic. Record the URL, and briefly describe the contents, of three useful sites.
5. Collect newspaper articles that examine the impact of computers on society. Identify any concerns expressed about the use of new technology. Do you think these concerns are justified?

13

Aboriginal Studies and Torres Strait Islander Studies

Introduction

The inclusion of Aboriginal studies and Torres Strait Islander studies within schools is increasing dramatically and is especially relevant to studies of society and environment. At federal, state and territory levels, important curriculum development activities are occurring.

We must have a national approach that ensures that every child going to school in this country has the opportunity to have a proper basis of understanding of Aboriginal and Torres Strait Islander history and cultures. And . . . we need to teach the teachers, because a great many teachers are like me, at school they didn't have the opportunity to develop any proper basis of understanding of the very things they have to teach now and in the years ahead.

(Robert Tickner, former Federal Minister for Aboriginal and Torres Strait Islander Affairs, in Board of Teacher Registration Queensland, 1993: 14)

This statement has recently been echoed by the state, Commonwealth and territory Ministers for Education in announcing the national goals for schooling in the twenty-first century. They state that schooling should be socially just, so that:

- students' outcomes from schooling are free from the effects of negative forms of discrimination based on sex, language, culture and ethnicity, religion or disability; and of differences arising from students' socioeconomic background or geographic location;
- the learning outcomes of educationally

disadvantaged students improve and, over time, match those of other students;

• Aboriginal and Torres Strait Islander students have equitable access to, and opportunities in, schooling so that their learning outcomes improve and, over time, match those of other students;

• all students understand and acknowledge the value of Aboriginal and Torres Strait Islander cultures to Australian society and possess the knowledge, skills and understanding to contribute to, and benefit from, reconciliation between indigenous and non-indigenous Australians;

• all students understand and acknowledge the value of cultural and linguistic diversity, and possess the knowledge, skills and understanding to contribute to, and benefit from, such diversity in the Australian community and internationally.

The inclusion of Aboriginal studies and Torres Strait Islander studies within education systems can assist in addressing each of the above points.

Studies of society and environment, by its very nature, permeates the school curriculum in everything we do. If we are teaching about Roman numerals in maths, for example, we are learning something about that particular society. From experience, and observations of many classrooms, teaching and learning in all areas draws on the principles used and knowledge gained across the curriculum. For example, English is used to present maths problems; areas of maths are used in technology; science is applied to health and physical education and so on. Studies of society and environment can be seen as encompassing all areas of the curriculum.

So, too, should Aboriginal studies and Torres Strait Islander studies be an everyday part of the teaching and learning that happens in schools. With the development of the statements and profiles in eight learning areas and subsequent adaptations in the states and territories came the opportunity to 'secure' Aboriginal Studies and Torres Strait Islander studies within studies of society and environment and to 'inform' other learning areas. This served to draw teachers' attention to the culture strand of studies of society and environment and its strand organiser Aboriginal and Torres Strait Islander Cultures (see also Chapter 8).

Aboriginal studies and Torres Strait Islander studies are beginning to be seen as increasingly important areas of the studies of society and environment curriculum. The review and subsequent strategies of the National Aboriginal and Torres Strait Islander Education Policy (NATSIEP), NATSIEP recommendations from the Royal Commission into Aboriginal Deaths in Custody and the report of the Inquiry into the Separation of Aboriginal and Torres Strait Islander Children from their Families have highlighted the importance of the need for Aboriginal studies courses in the education of all Australians.

Many teachers and curriculum writers refer to Goal 21 of the NATSIEP, which has as its aim 'To provide all Australian students with an understanding of and respect for Aboriginal and Torres Strait Islander traditional and contemporary cultures'. Further, the NATSIEP review expanded this goal with a priority being 'to promote, maintain and support the teaching of Aboriginal and Torres Strait Islander studies, cultures and languages to all Indigenous and non-Indigenous students' (National Aboriginal Education Committee, 1985: 61). All education systems have provided funds so that teachers will have access to endorsed publications and professional development in order that this priority can be addressed.

This chapter begins by outlining the scope of Aboriginal studies and Torres Strait Islander studies and then details the outcomes which it is hoped will be achieved. Some general approaches to the teaching of Aboriginal studies and Torres Strait Islander studies are discussed, followed by views of future directions.

Aboriginal societies and Torres Strait Islander societies are studied in a variety of schools throughout the country, from those having no or few Aboriginal or Torres Strait Islander students through to those in areas made up almost entirely of indigenous people. This chapter describes for the benefit of teachers some of the particular issues, and techniques that may help to address these issues, in teaching Aboriginal studies and Torres Strait Islander studies in different schools. Finally, developments in the field are outlined and some resources in Aboriginal studies and Torres Strait Islander studies are listed.

■ The Scope of Aboriginal Studies and Torres Strait Islander Studies

Aboriginal studies and Torres Strait Islander studies have not always been seen as important areas of study and have usually been placed within the area of 'history'. It is only recently that these studies have been seen as contemporary and studied within the area of social education. In some schools Aboriginal studies and Torres Strait Islander studies have been treated in a limited and superficial way, usually during National Aboriginal and Torres Strait Islander Week (NAIDOC). This has now been vigorously countered across the country. For example in South Australia and Tasmania, where *Aboriginal Perspectives Across the Curriculum* (*APAC* and *TasAPAC*) have been published and are used extensively, in Western Australia with the release of *Aboriginal Studies K–10*, in Queensland with *A Framework and Guidelines for Aboriginal*

Studies and Torres Strait Islander Studies P–12 and the development of the *Pilot Senior Syllabus in Aboriginal and Torres Strait Islander Studies*. Much of the work in recent years has been based on the *National Principles and Guidelines for Aboriginal Studies and Torres Strait Islander Studies K–12* (Curriculum Corporation, 1995a). In addition, the Catholic Education Office at Cairns has produced a very usable Torres Strait Islander kit, while the Regional Equity and Development (READ) School Support Centre has the *Torres Strait Islander Cultural Resource Kit* which includes booklets, videos, maps and stimulus pictures of past and contemporary Torres Strait Islander life. All states and territories have produced resources specific to language group and site, including materials for use with Aboriginal students and Torres Strait Islander students.

The inclusion of Aboriginal studies and Torres Strait Islander studies within schools is increasing and in 1995 it became mandatory within Tasmania to include Aboriginal studies within the school curriculum. Aboriginal studies and Torres Strait Islander studies can now be seen in the curriculum of tertiary education students, and is often found in university social science subjects. An Aboriginal Studies Association has operated from New South Wales since 1990, convening national conferences where practical issues for teachers are highlighted. Other associations such as the Australian Curriculum Studies Association and the Australian College of Education include Aboriginal and Torres Strait Islander education on the agenda.

It is necessary to clarify the scope of Aboriginal studies and Torres Strait Islander studies. 'Aboriginal studies and Torres Strait Islander studies' mean what the titles imply: studies about Aboriginal societies and Torres Strait Islander societies. As Aboriginal cultures and Torres Strait Islander cultures are based on quite different customs, beliefs and values, these societies must be studied separately.

The *National Principles and Guidelines for Aboriginal Studies and Torres Strait Islander Studies K–12* recommend three approaches for Aboriginal studies and Torres Strait Islander studies that can be implemented separately or in combination: as a discrete course/subject; as units within other subjects; and across the curriculum in each of the eight learning areas. The inclusion of Aboriginal studies and Torres Strait Islander studies has an enormous, exciting, scope. These studies take in an historical perspective of more than 50 000 years, a perspective that overshadows the non-indigenous Australian in terms of the diversity of cultures, complexity and longevity. As more Aboriginal people and Torres Strait Islander people have become involved in education at all levels, an emphasis has been placed on Australian indigenous cultures as living cultures, and, as expressed in the Queensland Board of Senior Secondary School Studies (BSSSS) Pilot Syllabus, 'Such a focus will enable students to analyse their own and other cultures and to develop the skills to recognise the part they play in creating culture, as well as the ability to understand how their cultural identity is constructed'.[1]

It is important to emphasise that the scope of Aboriginal studies and Torres Strait Islander studies is not limited to presenting indigenous material to non-indigenous students. In schools with mixed populations (both indigenous and non-indigenous), and particularly in community schools catering for students who speak their own languages and follow customary ways, studies endorsed by the community would assume an integral and natural place as a focus for the curriculum.

As the *National Aboriginal and Torres Strait Islander Education Policy* (Commonwealth of Australia, 1989) states, there is a need for all Australian students to gain '. . . an understanding of and respect for Aboriginal [and Torres Strait Islander] traditional and contemporary cultures'. Aboriginal studies and Torres Strait Islander studies can become an everyday part of the learning of all students, and does not have to be relegated to a unit within a subject, a discrete course or perspectives across the curriculum. For example, Kerry Hampton, a teacher from Myrtle Park Primary School in Tasmania, can see that the book *Moonglue* by Daisy Utemorrah can be read aloud, with students being asked to write about ways that the children can be unglued. There is no mention of 'today we are going to do Aboriginal studies', but through reading an Aboriginal story by an Aboriginal author, this book becomes a natural part of the curriculum.

Other current titles which could be used in similar ways include:

Bip, the Snapping Bungaroo by Narelle McRobbie. Bungaroo is 'turtle' in the language of the Yidin people of Far North Queensland. The illustrations by Grace Fielding are exceptional, and can be used effectively to fire students' imagination.

Caden Walaa was written and illustrated by Karin Calley, with a translation into Guugu Yimithirr by Noel Pearson. The title literally means 'Caden, watch out'. It is written in two languages, Guugu Yimithin and English, and readers are shown how to pronounce Guugu Yimithin words in the back of the book. Young children (and some adults) enjoy the story and have great fun with the illustrations.

Betty and Bala and the Proper Big Pumpkin by Lorraine Berolah, Lilyjane Collins and Noel Cristaudo is an entertaining picture book about Betty and Bala's adventures.

There is a glossary at the beginning, which explains some of the Torres Strait terms used, and is a great introduction to today's Thursday Island.

Dan's Grandpa by Sally Morgan and illustrated by Bronwyn Bancroft tells about a boy's respect for and feelings for his grandpa. Colour and design throughout would provide a basis for discussion.

Me and Mary Kangaroo is a true story of Kevin Gilbert's childhood memories. It is mostly about Gilbert's adventures with Mary Kangaroo, but there is a surprise on almost every page. He cleverly introduces rhyming prose throughout and the story appeals to a wide age range.

A Boy's Life is a book about the trials and tribulations of the late Jack Davis's early life. It is full of humorous incidents and others which are tinged with sadness.

Broken Dreams is the winner of the 1991 David Unaipon Award for first-time Aboriginal and Torres Strait Islander authors. Bill Dodd's story was written with the aid of a specially designed finger splint and a typewriter donated by the people of Mitchell, his home town.

Caprice—A Stockman's Daughter by Doris Pilkington. This fictional account of one woman's journey to recover her family and heritage won the 1990 David Unaipon Award. Set in the towns, pastoral stations and repressive institutions of Western Australia, it is a moving story of three generations of Yamatji women, encompassing many contemporary issues.

Writers of curriculum documents are becoming increasingly aware of how little time teachers have for actually developing units of work to be used in the classroom. To this end, writers have begun to heed the request from teachers for sample units of work. Examples of these are *Signposts . . . to Country, Kin and Cultures* (secondary) and *Footprints . . . to country, kin and cultures*, both published by Curriculum Corporation in 1997. These set out the desired outcomes, the most appropriate resources for the task and a procedure to be followed. While this procedure can be followed in detail, it is hoped that in the areas of Aboriginal studies and Torres Strait Islander studies, teachers will adapt the unit to the local area. Karen Martin, an Aboriginal teacher from Stradbroke Island, has written a unit for lower primary, with the main objective being for students to 'recognise that Aboriginal children are Australian children'. Martin suggests a range of recommended resources and guides teachers through a process wherein students look at Aboriginal children of today and the past, and the ways in which their education is achieved. She follows this through the study of families and excursions (real or imaginary) to significant sites and Aboriginal organisations. Similarly, Judith Ketchell, a Torres Strait Islander teacher, presents teachers with ways of learning about Torres Strait Islander families, their cultures, languages and environment. Ketchell includes information about available resources that will support the study of Torres Strait Islander societies.

■ Objectives of Aboriginal Studies and Torres Strait Islander Studies

In order for students to gain from learning about Aboriginal societies and Torres Strait Islander societies, it is essential to understand their importance and the educational outcomes these programs seek to attain. One of the most important goals is for all students to learn about the people and history of the country in which they live. This knowledge can only give students a perspective on *their* history and their place within it.

Aboriginal studies or Torres Strait Islander studies as a generic study can assist students to develop an understanding and respect for indigenous traditional and contemporary cultures as part of their own heritage and provide insights into the diversity, complexity and distinctiveness of Aboriginal cultures and Torres Strait Islander cultures.

Teachers can assist students to explore values appropriate to living within a culturally diverse society, while promoting the rights of people to hold different values, attitudes and beliefs (see also Chapter 7). Learning in this area allows students to develop a knowledge and understanding of the effects of invasion, intrusion,[2] settlement and colonisation on Aboriginal societies and Torres Strait Islander societies and to recognise how indigenous people and their cultures influence contemporary Australian society. It provides students with opportunities to appreciate the interrelatedness of languages and cultures and to learn from the experiences, knowledge and achievements of indigenous people while developing the ability to recognise prejudice, stereotyping and racism. The study of Aboriginal societies and Torres Strait Islander societies develops and enhances students' skills relating to social and environmental investigation.

It is also important for individuals from all cultural groups to learn about themselves. This is best achieved not merely by studying one's own society and culture directly, but by examining other societies and cultures which in some respects are quite different. By this means, students are able to reflect on their cultural characteristics relative to those of others. For non-indigenous Australians, a study of traditionally orientated and contemporary Aboriginal lifestyles or Torres

Strait Islander lifestyles is likely to facilitate this.

A further benefit of Aboriginal studies and Torres Strait Islander studies for non-indigenous people is that it can offer advantages for skills development. By describing rival interpretations of history from indigenous and non-indigenous perspectives, students will begin to acquire an idea of history, seeing it as person made, constructed rather than unalterable. Further, Aboriginal studies and Torres Strait Islander studies can offer teachers and students a far less ethnocentric view of Australian history and societies than that previously presented.

The possibility of introducing a less ethnocentric approach into the classroom has been facilitated by the publication, in recent years, of a number of books, videos and compact disks suitable for schools. These publications, such as *Frontier* (ABC TV, 5, 12, 19 March 1997), challenge the previously accepted view of Australian history and specifically deal with resistance to invasion, contact and white administration.

There are other benefits for all Australians. Aboriginal studies and Torres Strait Islander studies are increasingly assisting non-indigenous people to become aware of the natural environment of Australia while studies of indigenous forms of land and sea management can provide mechanisms for more sustainable use of that environment. See, for example, *Our Heart is the Land* (Shaw, 1995), where aspects of the environment are described in Aboriginal reminiscences from the Western Lake Eyre Basin.

The potential benefits of Aboriginal studies and Torres Strait Islander studies for indigenous students are also considerable. It is important for any people to know their own history. The history of a people is bound up with pride in their origins. It facilitates an understanding of how society came to be as it now is and the ways in which it might change for the better. These are things which most Australians can take for granted, but as can be seen historical and other books have only recently begun to tell accurate stories of Aboriginal people and Torres Strait Islander people.

Aboriginal studies and Torres Strait Islander studies may, or may not, play a part in creating a school environment which is more conducive to the success of indigenous learners. It is believed that if Aboriginal studies and Torres Strait Islander studies are a natural part of the school's curriculum, then indigenous students can see that their cultures are valued, especially if these studies are a part of everyday learning and teaching.

Research conducted by Groome and Edwardson (1996b) among 42 Aboriginal students shows that the students saw a need for '. . . their schools to explicitly recognise their Aboriginality and provide them with resources for personal and cultural identity development'. This should not be difficult for schools to achieve, yet one common concern voiced by these students was that there should be more Aboriginal studies. Few of the schools visited by the researchers taught Aboriginal studies as a separate subject and where it was taught not all students agreed about the appropriateness of the delivery. Research evidence in other countries shows that schools that provide (1) support to students from different cultural backgrounds and (2) studies of those cultures are more successful than those that focus solely on the dominant culture. Successful schools are those that draw on and integrate the students' own cultural backgrounds and involve members of those cultural groups in the delivery of programs. As noted in Craven (1999):

> Most teachers have never even met or spoken to an Aboriginal person, and that has its own effect, but when an Aboriginal person speaks to them about their history, it ceases to be just a history lesson. People are confronted with a new way of looking at the world, and must decide what they are going to do about that. (Craven, 1999: 183)

Students are more comfortable where their languages and the familiar concepts of their cultural background are valued and the use of them is encouraged. This is supported by such statements as:

> School plays an important part in shaping and affirming the learner's developing sense of identity. Recognising and valuing individual identity has important educational implications for all children, but particularly for those whose cultural, religious and linguistic background may be largely unfamiliar to the teacher. (Education Department of Western Australia, 1994b: 3)

It can be seen that to 'put down' another language such as Aboriginal English or a Torres Strait creole makes a student feel like a second-class citizen, and doesn't allow other students to appreciate diversity. If a teacher is racist in this manner, it legitimises similar racist behaviour in students. Similarly, teachers have tended to see the use of a first language like Aboriginal English or Torres Strait creole as a sign of low ability and/or low attainment and are only now beginning to recognise that English is a second, third or even a fourth language for many indigenous students. A successful school is one where the aim is to graduate students from different cultural backgrounds who have competencies in and the ability to cope in two or more different cultures. This is an area where Australia at large does not give the credit due to indigenous students, as a great percentage of Aboriginal people and Torres Strait Islander people must carry around the knowledge of two cultures and socialisation patterns in their heads. They must operate within two cultures all the time. How much easier it must be for a monocultural student to cope.

A major difficulty for many Aboriginal students and Torres Strait Islander students is the way in which they are identified by school staff members. According to Groome and Edwardson (1996a), a student may be quite comfortable with their identity, but become confused by teachers' unwillingness to accept this identity, and students' comments revealed a strong sense of resistance springing from the failure of schools to recognise their Aboriginality. This is due more often than not to teachers' commonly held stereotypes of indigenous people. If students do not fit the stereotype, their identity is denied. In discussing this issue, Craven (1999: 52) points out that:

> Much anguish is caused to Indigenous Australians when other Australians fail to comprehend or accept the indigenous identity of fair-skinned Indigenous people. Such misconceptions ignore the reality of Australia's history. Many Indigenous people are not dark-skinned and are, just as the rest of the nation, diverse in physical appearance. We have heard many anguished parents describe how school staff have refused to appropriately acknowledge fair-skinned Indigenous children's identity and culture. We have also comforted young children who have been told by their teachers that they are not Indigenous because they are not dark-skinned.

The NSW Aboriginal Education Policy stresses how important it is that schools should assist indigenous children to be secure in their own identity in stating that students '. . . have the right to be Aboriginal and to express their own unique cultural identity'. It is widely recognised that a secure identity is a likely prerequisite for the success of indigenous students in the school setting. Marsh (1994: 23) emphasises the priority given to the special needs of Aboriginal students and Torres Strait Islander students, highlighting the fact that

they are '. . . enshrined in the national goals and strongly supported in ongoing Commonwealth programs'. That the Commonwealth is concerned about the positive self-identity of indigenous students and its relationship to school outcomes is evidenced by the 1999 research funded by the Department of Education, Training and Youth Affairs (DETYA) into this aspect of students' lives.

Aboriginal studies and Torres Strait Islander studies can work towards this goal both directly and through indirect influence on home and school relationships. Effective Aboriginal studies and Torres Strait Islander programs, particularly those that involve members of the local indigenous community, raise awareness of school staff members to indigenous issues and clearly signal that the school respects and is actively supporting indigenous people and their cultures (Craven, 1999; Curriculum Corporation, 1995a, 1997b; Groome, 1994.) *The National Principles and Guidelines for Aboriginal Studies and Torres Strait Islander Studies K–12* provides principles for curriculum development, while *Signposts . . . to Country, Kin and Cultures* (Curriculum Corporation, 1997b: 5) addresses protocols and conventions that should be observed when involving Aboriginal people and Torres Strait Islander people in a school program.

■ Teaching Approaches

There are several approaches to teaching Aboriginal studies and Torres Strait Islander studies.

The museum, or tea towel, approach

Of all the ways that Aboriginal studies and Torres Strait Islander studies are introduced to the classroom, this approach is probably the least valuable. Groome (1994: 3), in reflecting on Aboriginal studies, says:

The museum or 'tea towel' approach

For many years teachers regarded teaching about Aboriginals as an uncomplicated and non-threatening area of the curriculum. All that they needed were some pictures of Aboriginal people living in remote areas, some stencils of boomerangs and spears, a 'Dreamtime' story or two. Yet much of what happened was myth making. The 'Aboriginal people' that were taught about in these lessons were fabrications in the minds of the educators.

The approach outlined by Groome does not allow Australian students to recognise current issues in Aboriginal societies and Torres Strait Islander societies, and does nothing that leads to the attainment of realistic educational outcomes. The museum or tea towel approach is, unfortunately, still alive and well in some Australian classrooms. Indeed, it remains attractive to some teachers for a number of reasons and thus represents a particular hazard to sound teaching practice. This unwelcome approach is often supported by a host of commercially available blackline masters that do little to raise students' (or teachers') awareness of indigenous cultures. One distinctive example is a stereotypical drawing of a chubby, almost naked, child, all parts of which are numbered, that students are required to

colour according to the numbers. Many Aboriginal families are offended when their children are required to carry out this procedure and question the relevance and validity of the exercise, especially in relation to the impression gained by all students of the image presented. It does little for Aboriginal students' and Torres Strait Islander students' positive self-identity.

The museum approach deals mainly with pre-contact, and not at all with contemporary Aboriginal studies and Torres Strait Islander studies. Hence its name. It not only isolates one unrepresentative lifestyle, but also does so in a superficial manner. In particular, it deals with content in a way that tends to focus on such phenomena as the mechanics of hunting and gathering activities and related tools, or perhaps deals in a cursory way with the Aboriginal Dreaming or Legends of the Torres Strait. It rarely explores the interrelationship of traditional Aboriginal societies and Torres Strait Islander societies with the environment, let alone the social and cultural practices of which food collection is a part.

The rationale for the museum approach appears to be that students can at least come to value pre-contact Aboriginal societies or Torres Strait Islander societies, and this is accomplished by furnishing some information about them. A cynical observation would be that such an approach takes little preparation, implementation and evaluation. There are grave risks and limitations in this approach, of which teachers need to be aware. It is implicit in the museum approach that past indigenous societies are the most valuable or at least the only indigenous societal form worthy of mention. Even so, the content gives few insights into traditional Aboriginal societies in particular. The complexity and diversity of these societies are subsumed in the stereotyping of Aborigines as 'the noble savage'. Thus a major exception to the museum approach is

Using a kit to explore Aboriginal and Torres Strait Islander cultural factors

that it fails to develop knowledge of and respect for indigenous societies and cultures.

A further problem is that there is no serious attempt to come to terms with issues of culture contact, that is, social and economic change through interaction with non-indigenous people and the broader issues of race relations. In particular, the way in which these have shaped the contemporary lifestyles of the majority of Aboriginal Australians and the history of our society is sadly neglected. Since the position of indigenous people in present-day society can only be understood in terms of continuous and discontinuous cultural elements in indigenous cultures and societies, it is clear that the objectives of the museum approach do not include such an understanding. As was pointed out in the previous section, Aboriginal studies and Torres Strait Islander studies must lead towards an understanding of contemporary issues which affect indigenous people.

Not surprisingly, some of the strongest criticisms of this approach have been levelled by indigenous people themselves. 'It is unfortunate that much of the information which exists about Aborigines in Australian schools is often stereotyped, inadequate, anachronistic and even racist' (National Aboriginal Education Committee, 1985: 172).

On the other hand, a course such as the pilot Queensland *Senior Secondary School Syllabus in Aboriginal and Torres Strait Islander Studies* (1998) takes in not one limited dimension but many dimensions. There is an interrelationship of ecological, economic, social and cultural dimensions that avoids stereotyping and provides a foundation for an understanding of both the effects of European invasion, intrusion and occupation and contemporary Aboriginal lifestyles.

The museum approach is not flawed merely in its lack of depth and scope. It teaches just another series of facts that is likely to be compartmentalised and will do nothing to change attitudes. It makes no attempt to enable students to begin to see through the eyes of others. To 'get inside' indigenous cultures in some sense is probably a prerequisite to any significant and durable understanding of them. This is a difficult task for non-indigenous teachers to achieve, and is compounded by the fact that the majority of school material is written by non-indigenous people. As Tripcony (1998) notes, 'If resource materials are to be developed locally, Aboriginal and/or Torres Strait Islander parents and community members must be consulted'. This indicates that indigenous involvement in the planning, production and delivery of Aboriginal studies and Torres Strait Islander studies is very important. However, in the context of the museum approach, there is little scope for indigenous involvement and it usually becomes a kind of entertainment activity, with no sound pedagogical basis.

The museum approach fails to teach the skills that could underpin an appreciation of indigenous societies and cultures. Positive attitudes are most likely to be sustained where students have tools that will enable them to analyse social phenomena. These 'tools' include cognitive skills, taking in analysis, hypothesis-making, problem-solving, inquiry and research skills. Also, most importantly, there is a social skills dimension enabling indigenous and non-indigenous Australians to communicate with each other on a personal level. It is important to see not only what is wrong with the museum approach and what should happen to change it, but also why it survives. This begins to open up the area of practical problems in teaching Aboriginal studies and Torres Strait Islander studies. One reason the

museum approach is employed is simply because it can seem unproblematic. In particular, it relies on the popular dissemination of myths from teacher to student.

Teacher expertise in the selection of content is often deficient (Catchpole, 1981), tending to focus on the superficial. One reason for this is the traditional perception of Aboriginal studies and Torres Strait Islander studies as low-status, non-academic knowledge, as reflected in the scanty resources put into it until recently. Moreover, many teachers are not only faced with a shortage of materials, but they also lack the detailed knowledge that would allow them to make appropriate choices. The museum approach tends to be non-valuative and as such plays down the controversial. Sometimes this is viewed as desirable. Teachers are not always encouraged to deal with controversial or potentially divisive issues, and pressures on schools to avoid these have sometimes been considerable. It is therefore not altogether surprising that teachers tend to omit sections of Aboriginal studies and Torres Strait Islander studies that deal with controversial content.

The case studies approach

It is difficult to conceive of a successful Aboriginal studies or Torres Strait Islander studies program that ignores case studies. A case study is a piece of research that investigates and records the lifestyle of a group of people in a particular location (see also Chapter 4). The main strength of this approach is that it enables teachers to avoid generalisations about Aboriginal cultures or Torres Strait Islander cultures. Moreover, it has the potential to incorporate the four essential aspects of any Aboriginal studies or Torres Strait Islander studies course. These are:

1. traditional—the pre-European situation;
2. transitional—invasion and/or intrusion to present;

3. contemporary—the present situation; and
4. issues—for example health, deaths in custody, the Stolen Generations and land rights.

There are both local and regional case studies available which can be used as a model for schools to develop their own. For example, a local case study could be an examination of the language or cultural groups which live(d) in the area of the present school community.

The Cairns Catholic Education Office Torres Strait Islander material is invaluable as is *Voices on the Wind*, a Victorian kit containing videos and teachers' notes. Both of these publications were developed in response to a perceived need.

A *regional* study has wider scope and may deal with more than one group. For example, *Living with the Land: Aborigines in Tasmania* provides an introduction to the lives, aspirations and history of Aboriginal people in Tasmania. Although this material is intended for upper primary and secondary students rather than the earlier grades, a framework has been developed for K–4 where information from the publication could be used. The Tasmanian Education Department has also published *Taraba, Tasmanian Aboriginal stories*, retold by Rosemary Ransom and illustrated by students, that can be used extensively with all age groups.

A *local* case study often begins with a study of the environment in which local Aboriginal people or Torres Strait Islander people live or lived, and is developed by researching the names of specific groups and their languages and the impact of non-indigenous colonisation of the area. Two models for local case studies that teachers will find invaluable are the Education Department of South Australia's (1992c) case studies *The Adnyamathanha people*, and *The Kaurna people: Aboriginal people of the Adelaide*

Plains, which are Aboriginal studies courses explaining the histories, cultures and lifeways of the Aboriginal people of the Flinders Ranges and the Kaurna Plains. These are part of the 8–12 Aboriginal studies program that has been developed to meet the needs of students, teachers and Aboriginal people.

The case studies approach not only enables students to explore the relationship between indigenous people and their environment, but also explores the diversity of indigenous societies through concrete examples. This is accomplished by starting with a local case study that has immediate relevance (although it is quite possible to begin with a study of the nearest traditionally oriented people) and moving on to a regional study. Here it is often quite possible to use a regional case study that has already been developed. Indeed, teachers new to Aboriginal studies and Torres Strait Islander studies may initially prefer to work entirely through developed case studies and teachers can obtain such a study to use as a model for developing a case study of their local area. A case study is, however, ideally a piece of research and when treated as such it can teach the cognitive and social skills that should underpin an appreciation of indigenous societies and cultures. These can include research, hypothesis-making, inquiry and problem-solving skills. As stated above, the case studies approach can cover a wide range of content. A further dimension of the case studies approach is that it can facilitate the process whereby non-indigenous students learn about their own cultures. Students undertaking a course in adult basic education find this particularly valuable.

Comparative studies are also useful. These can occur through comparison between an indigenous society and an Anglo-European society, an area often fraught with difficulties as differences between the two may be viewed in a biased way as indigenous deficits. Price and Smith (1997) explore a writer's bias in several ways, and ask teachers to work with students towards achieving a positive image. It is possible to approach comparative studies through a study of environmental issues. For example, the sustainability of indigenous and non-indigenous cultures can be compared. Indigenous technology can be seen in terms of long-term sustainability and positive impacts, with the notion of 'primitive technology' questioned. The role of indigenous knowledge in conservation and land management has grown in recent years, while European methods of land use are posing an increasing threat to the natural environment. Duncan and Greymorning (1999: 163–172) have prepared a chapter about the Ainu of Japan, the Sami of Northern Europe and indigenous North Americans that is a useful basis for comparative studies. Teachers sometimes find that teaching about an issue relating to indigenous people in another country is a useful lead-in to Australian indigenous studies, as it assists in making students more receptive.

Education departments are, in general, developing case studies to provide a core in Aboriginal studies and Torres Strait Islander studies that can be used for comparative studies and also to serve as models for local studies. In South Australia, for example, Aboriginal study units for Years R–7 include a study of the lifestyles of four South Australian Aboriginal groups. Similarly, in all states and territories, teachers have access to developed case studies and expertise in creating their own. Students and their schools are often proud of their case studies and these can be extremely valuable in that they can make a contribution to recording information about Aboriginal cultures and Torres Strait Islander cultures.

Aboriginal studies and Torres Strait Islander studies can also be given great impetus by exchange of case studies between schools along song-lines and trade routes. This is a trend that is certain to gather momentum, making comparison progressively easier as more territory is mapped. After all, with respect to case studies, state boundaries are artificial.

Information imparted through teachers, videos, books and other resource materials takes on greater significance when, for example, an Aboriginal person who is a member of one of the Stolen Generations is actually in the classroom describing her or his experiences or feelings. The video, *You Can Do It Too: Aboriginal Studies and Torres Strait Islander Studies Across the Curriculum*, shows the moving reaction and growing understanding of students to the words of an Aboriginal speaker describing his family's ordeal.

Indigenous parents and caregivers, members of local, regional and state Aboriginal and/or Torres Strait Islander Education Consultative Groups (AECGs)[3], indigenous education consultants, Aboriginal and Torres Strait Islander Education Workers (AIEWs), hourly-paid instructors (or Aboriginal school visitors), land councils and indigenous culture teachers are possible resources here. Many Aboriginal people and Torres Strait Islander people may also agree to being interviewed away from the school, especially those who are in paid employment and find it difficult to visit a school.

Possible indigenous and non-indigenous sources used in developing case studies include websites, local and state libraries, museums, state archives and heritage units, local collectors of artifacts, local councils, churches, missions and newspapers. The library of the Australian Institute of Aboriginal and Torres Strait Islander Studies (AIATSIS) in Canberra can provide information on request about many Aboriginal groups and Torres Strait Islander groups, as can the Aboriginal and Torres Strait Islander

Commission (ATSIC) Office of Public Affairs. Information is also available from the Office of Torres Strait Islander Affairs. The Council for Aboriginal [and Torres Strait Islander] Reconciliation has been a source of information and materials.[4]

The social concepts approach

As conceived in Aboriginal studies and Torres Strait Islander studies, this approach aims not so much at teaching the facts about one or more indigenous groups as at presenting concepts that will allow students to understand general relationships such as those between indigenous people and their environment. An understanding of certain key concepts like cultures and values is gradually built up through various kinds of generalisations, particularly from case studies (see also Chapter 4).

In the units offered in South Australian primary schools, units begin with the study of 'me' and continue with family, children of different backgrounds and Aboriginal people in Australia. This is followed by an investigation of 'home' after which children begin to look at the Dreaming and the purposes of Dreaming Stories. Through Dreaming Stories, concepts of Aboriginal spirit ancestors, rules for living, and caring for the environment are explored. Students thereby begin to acquire the concept of the Dreaming and, in turn, Aboriginal lifestyles before European settlement, Dreaming trails and culture contact, family relationships and Aboriginal people and their communities today. These concepts are developed through storytelling, excursions, language, art and music. In a similar fashion, higher level concepts such as culture are generated. This approach also lends itself to the use of some of the methods employed in the disciplines from which the target concepts are drawn. These might include inquiry methods, testing of hypotheses and ways of organising data.

Apart from cognitive and social skill development, students gain valuable insights into the disciplinary viewpoints themselves.

It is clear that this approach offers quite a sophisticated way of building a knowledge of concepts needed to understand not only Aboriginal cultures but also other cultures. As such, it has attracted the interest of curriculum developers in Aboriginal studies and Torres Strait Islander studies fields. It is significant that Aboriginal studies and Torres Strait Islander studies programs that employ this approach show a good deal of variety in the choice and ordering of target concepts. Teachers in other locations should be aware, if they wish to use this as a model, that considerable curriculum development would be required. Dedication and commitment to the task, as well as the means to employ Aboriginal people and Torres Strait Islander people and the assistance of curriculum specialists, would need to be clear at the outset.

The social issues approach

This approach uses factual information to focus on a series of complex social issues or problems. These might include problems of social change and 'people in transition', taking in a culture clash between indigenous and non-indigenous people in colonial and contemporary periods. Other issues might include indigenous health, housing, Aboriginal deaths in custody, the Stolen Generations, education, employment, over-representation within the criminal justice system and those other issues which are of major concern to Aboriginal people such as the High Court Decision on Native Title, land rights, self-determination and self-management. For example, the *Aboriginal Land Rights (What Does Everyone Else Think? What Do I Think?)* topic for secondary schools in South Australia takes in a cultural analysis of current affairs and social and political issues. In another area, and in order to assist teachers to introduce studies about the Stolen Generations, a topic that is extremely sensitive, a unit called 'The longest journey' was written for inclusion in *Different Dreams* (Curriculum Corporation, 1998). This book is the fourth (and last) in the Integrated Units series.

The rationale for the social issues approach is that, through exposure to factual information, students will be able to begin to talk about and evaluate, in an informed way, the main social issues affecting Australian indigenous people. In turn, this will provide a way for students' attitudes to be tested against the facts.

A major benefit of this approach is that it has the potential to bring Aboriginal studies and Torres Strait Islander studies into the contemporary world. Many contemporary Aboriginal studies and Torres Strait Islander studies courses are rightly concerned with developing a cognitive appreciation of indigenous societies and cultures, but fail to deal adequately with the contemporary world of most indigenous people. If they do, they tend to paint a picture of indigenous people enjoying many of the benefits of both worlds but suffering few social and economic disadvantages. The starting place for teachers is data on indigenous people, and this can be obtained through Australian Bureau of Statistics publications, such as *Working it Out: Core material for Australian Studies* (Australian Bureau of Statistics, 1995). ABS publications give statistical information, usefully displayed in graphical form, on a number of social indicators.

Before teachers begin to use this data, however, it is essential to be aware of some possible pitfalls associated with the social issues approach. First, it may not deal sufficiently with the complexities of issues and risks, and may present an account that tends to belittle indigenous societies. While it

may be necessary to explore negative aspects of many contemporary indigenous lifestyles such as high unemployment, poor housing, over-representation within the criminal justice system, unsatisfactory health status and low life expectancy, it is possible to focus quite unconsciously on the negative in a way that is counterproductive to the objectives of Aboriginal studies and Torres Strait Islander studies. Of particular importance is the need to avoid stigmatising indigenous people as negative statistics or 'problems'. A related hazard is to generate 'blame-the-victim' attitudes, to the disadvantage of Aboriginal people and Torres Strait Islander people.

This approach at times also tends to imply the existence of a glorified, problem-free pre-contact lifestyle, and in doing so perpetrates the myth that Aboriginal people and Torres Strait Islander people, other than those maintaining a tradition-oriented lifestyle, have somehow 'fallen from grace'. This is particularly offensive to urban indigenous people whose lifestyles are at least partly shaped by their own culture and resistance to assimilatory pressures.

One useful strategy that will assist teachers in avoiding the above problems is to use comparative data to explore causes. For example, data on indigenous and non-indigenous health could be presented and then discussed with reference to a number of related themes. This might include traditional and contemporary lifestyles, historical factors such as the assimilation policies and the effects of dispossession and disenfranchisement.

In the lower secondary unit 'I Spik Prapa' developed by Price and Smith for *Signposts* (Curriculum Corporation, 1997b), students examine information about Torres Strait Islander issues and then focus on a particular issue of their choice in social survey and research components of the unit. However, these are preceded by a study that ensures in-depth understanding and appreciation of

Maganiu Malu Kes (Torres Strait Islander) societies and cultures. The study includes: Maganiu Malu Kes Buai Time and History; Cultural Identity: Torres Strait Islander Flag; The Maritime Strike of 1936; Langus Blo Maganiu Malu Kes Buai Giz (languages belonging to Torres Strait Islander people); the Mer High Court decision on Native Title and Investigating the Concept of Bias.

In sum, the social issues approach remains an important way of moving Aboriginal studies into the contemporary world. It comprises an important segment of various programs which are usually aimed at upper primary and secondary school students.

The perspectives approach

This approach aims to include Aboriginal or Torres Strait Islander viewpoints or 'perspectives' in the context of various subject areas. The rationale is that Aboriginal studies and Torres Strait Islander studies should be taught 'across the curriculum' and that if indigenous perspectives are included in the curriculum then Aboriginal studies and Torres Strait Islander studies will assume a natural place and, in time, become fully integrated. The perspectives approach lends itself to utilisation in a great many subject and topic areas. Local area studies can begin with a study of indigenous people and trace their movements until the present day. In New South Wales, an Aboriginal perspective on geography includes a study of the difficulties faced by Aboriginal and non-Aboriginal communities and their responses to changing Australian environments (Board of Studies, New South Wales, 1992a). 'Aboriginal Land Rights', the South Australian topic for secondary schools, provides support materials, including copies of European and church viewpoints as well as those from a variety of Aboriginal language groups.

Many schools approach Aboriginal studies and Torres Strait Islander studies through the Arts, while English and drama have great potential, with the possible inclusion of stories, novels, poetry and plays by Aboriginal authors and Torres Strait Islander authors. In environmental studies, students can compare the effects of indigenous and Anglo-European relationships with the environment, for example by looking at effects on particular land areas and ecological systems.

While the perspectives approach has potential in a range of subject areas and is widely used, it is controversial. By offering a more discreet way of introducing the study of indigenous people, it has been argued that it avoids the possibility of becoming counter-productive through inciting racist sentiments. When used exclusively, perspectives tend to lead to a shallow treatment of Aboriginal cultures and Torres Strait Islander cultures. However, there is no doubt that it has a useful place as a supplement to other approaches, such as case studies.

■ Teaching in Different Types of Schools

It is not possible to develop a single Aboriginal studies and Torres Strait Islander studies program that will be suitable for all schools. Differences in school populations have implications for teaching Aboriginal studies and Torres Strait Islander studies.

Aboriginal studies and Torres Strait Islander studies for non-indigenous students

Aboriginal studies and Torres Strait Islander studies can be of great interest to non-indigenous students. However, one obstacle to meeting the objectives of Aboriginal studies and Torres Strait Islander studies is the ethnocentricity of children who may have minimal knowledge of other cultures. In practice, the objectives that are most problematic are:

- facilitating an understanding and appreciation of Aboriginal cultures; and
- encouraging students to review their own culture, relative to others, that is, to reflect on their own culture.

There are techniques that teachers will find useful in meeting these learning goals and that can complement a range of approaches. Role play is one of these (see also Chapter 11). Primary students can, for example, act out indigenous social relations by taking the roles of Aboriginal people, in particular 'skin groups', as described by Aboriginal culture teachers or outlined in various publications including *The Dreaming and the Environment* unit for years R–3 children (Education Department of South Australia, 1988). This unit offers further examples of techniques that facilitate an understanding of Aboriginal societies and cultures 'from the inside'. The structure of this unit focuses on elements of Ngarrindjeri culture, beginning with 'The Dreaming Story' that employs role play in the context of a social concepts approach. There are also teaching techniques that enable students to reflect on themselves and their own culture.

A issue that will inevitably confront all Aboriginal studies and Torres Strait Islander studies teachers in non-indigenous (and also mixed) schools is that of racism (see also Chapter 15). It is particularly important in terms of teacher confidence to think about racism and have particular strategies at hand to deal with it. Most Australian states and territories (and their education systems) now have an anti-racism legislation with strategies for implementation.[5]

In terms of approaches, it is through case studies that racism is best addressed, since this employs concrete examples. The best teacher

techniques handle racism in an open and objective fashion rather than a repressive one that does nothing to change attitudes (see Chapter 15). Moreover, repression tends to make racism a covert or subculture activity where racist sentiments will find expression in school graffiti. One useful way of dealing with racism is to take racist comments that are voiced in school as examples of the phenomenon and then outline the negative effects of racism. Literature that expresses racist sentiments is still held in many school libraries and this can be treated in the same fashion to illustrate racist beliefs. One class or group exercise is to have students identify racist passages in books and rewrite them from an Aboriginal or Torres Strait Islander point of view. The Education Department of South Australia has developed a useful document for teachers, entitled *Developing Positive Attitudes to Diversity and Difference in a Culturally Inclusive Society*; and as well as providing written material, the New South Wales Department of Education and Training has produced *Is different, is interesting: Anti-racism discussion video for secondary schools*. Teachers may also find sections of *Footsteps . . . to Country, Kin and Cultures* and *Signposts . . . to Country, Kin and Cultures* useful in guiding role play and discussion.

Aboriginal studies and Torres Strait Islander studies for rural, remote and urban indigenous students

Indigenous people from these groups generally make up a significant proportion of mixed school populations. They are often a heterogeneous group and are influenced to different extents by the language and traditions that have been maintained. Many have been subjected to the forced loss of language; and in some areas Aboriginal English or a creole is their first language. Conversely, indigenous people living in remote areas in particular have often

Cultural studies are best taught by a family or other member of the children's indigenous group

retained their own language and other traditional cultural characteristics. Most indigenous people have strong family and kinship relationships. This group is catered for by many different kinds of schools, most of which pay an increasing regard to indigenous cultures and languages. For example, Yeperenye school, which teaches Arrernte (and other) children in the Alice Springs area, gives first priority to confirmation of their identity. Aboriginal studies· is, therefore, integral to the curriculum rather than peripheral. The Yeperenye curriculum teaches traditional values, including knowledge of the land based on the creation, bushcraft and contemporary Aboriginal values. It also has a positive self-identity focus, where students are involved in a reaffirmation of continuing cultural knowledge and traditions.

Because of the heterogeneity of indigenous students in mixed ·schools, it is essential for teachers to ascertain the cultural backgrounds of their students, as indicated by, for example,

use of customs and involvement in traditional activities. There must be no inference that any particular indigenous lifestyle is superior or more natural than any other or that there is a natural 'progression' to Anglo-European lifestyles. Nor should it be assumed that all children come from the same group, as this is often not the case. For students pursuing urban indigenous lifestyles, the focus on case studies is particularly important, and this approach represents nothing short of a breakthrough in Aboriginal studies and Torres Strait Islander studies. However, much will depend on the degree of sensitivity shown by non-indigenous teachers. As indigenous children may belong to different language and cultural groups, teachers will need to have, and demonstrate, respect for this. A useful technique is to spend some time in class finding out where each child comes from in terms of country and locating these areas on a map or model. Having acknowledged these different backgrounds, students may be much more likely to accept a case study that does

Exploring social and cultural issues through technology

not deal with their own group, as long as it does not transcend the law. Non-indigenous teachers may find that indigenous students are understandably sensitive to the teaching of their cultures by someone outside it, and in these situations cultural studies, which are taught by a family or other member of their immediate group, should replace the Aboriginal studies and Torres Strait Islander studies case study. This is also relevant in urban situations, where parents may not wish to have their children learning about their culture from someone outside (Riddiford, 1992).

In some areas the curriculum is decided by an all-indigenous body; however, in all situations it is vitally important to seek advice from parents, caregivers and other members of the indigenous community about the kinds of study in which they want to see their children engaged. Aboriginal people and Torres Strait Islander people are the custodians of indigenous cultures, and every effort must be made to ascertain the kinds of programs indigenous community members wish to see operating in the school. It is not enough to develop a unit of work and then ask for it to be 'rubber-stamped'. There should be genuine consultation where teachers appreciate that indigenous adults can be involved in various capacities, with roles being negotiated. Sometimes Aboriginal people and Torres Strait Islander people are quite confident about planning the program, making sure material is accurate and ensuring that acceptable viewpoints are expressed. Others may also want to be more involved in the teaching programs. Sensitivity on the part of a non-indigenous teacher means asking the right people, which involves making contacts—through students, indigenous people employed in the school or the department, Aboriginal Student Support and Parent Awareness (ASSPA) program committees, or local Aboriginal and/or Torres Strait Islander Education Consultative Groups—and then giving those in the community time to respond rather than announcing a short time line. The important thing to keep in mind is that indigenous people must be consulted before planning begins. Indigenous people, like anyone else, do not wish to be consulted merely to obtain their imprimatur after the event.

Many indigenous people report that contacts by teachers that are only made for school purposes are not likely to be successful. It is important to get to know Aboriginal people and Torres Strait Islander people in the community on an informal, out-of-school basis. Sensitivity can also involve flexibility in moving into an environment where those involved feel comfortable. This sometimes means conducting Aboriginal studies and Torres Strait Islander studies classes away from the classroom and the school building. Tripcony (1990) suggests that teachers working in these areas should ensure that:

- projects address basic education needs inclusive of indigenous culture and language concerns as supported by local communities;
- the continuous involvement of indigenous educators and communities occurs;
- membership of all management committees comprise a majority of indigenous people;
- indigenous parents, carers and (other) community members participate in decisions regarding the planning, delivery and educational services for indigenous students;
- distance and bicultural educators are involved in the development, delivery and evaluation of educational services for indigenous students;

- social justice principles are adhered to, and outcomes met;
- nationally agreed curriculum endpoints are used as a basis of planning, without modification of mainstream objectives; and
- as an integral part of all projects, evaluation and review processes, indigenous students, parents, carers, (other) community members, tutors and consultative/advisory groups should be involved, as well as teachers, distance educators and appropriate system's representatives.

The above can be used as guiding principles in achieving equitable outcomes.

■ A Personal Reflection

We should really look at how we teach and try to be inclusive of Aboriginal cultures and Torres Strait Islander cultures without marginalising or trivialising.

The days are past when teachers say 'We're going to do Aborigines this week'. Things Aboriginal or Torres Strait Islander should enter in *all* we teach. Perhaps it is easier for some teachers than others, but it is important to look at the outcomes we want our students to achieve and work towards these.

Whether or not an education system uses the national statements and profiles, it is worth remembering that a great deal of work and consultation took place in their development. Therefore, the outcomes at all levels can be used as a guide by a teacher who wishes to venture into the area of Aboriginal studies and/or Torres Strait Islander studies.

Within the national statement and profile for studies of society and environment, outcomes within the culture strand and the particularly the strand organiser, Aboriginal and Torres Strait Islander Cultures, are very clear, as are the pointers that can assist teachers to decide the level of students.

For example, consider Place and Space, level 4, People and Places: 'At level 4, a student: Describes how people's beliefs and practices influence the way they interact with places'. There is nothing in the outcome or pointers that mentions Aboriginal places or Torres Strait Islander places, yet in identifying 'significant places of importance to various cultural groups . . .' it is possible that students and teachers could suggest perhaps Uluru, or if in Tasmania, Risdon Cove.

As another example, consider level 7, Time, Continuity and Change, Understanding the Past, where the outcome is that a student 'analyses some effects of major ideologies on world affairs'. One of the pointers here would have the student identifying 'changes in the application of ideologies' (. . . the Roman Empire after the adoption of Christianity). What could be more natural than to look at indigenous Australia after the introduction of Christianity? This would open up opportunities for students to study the ways in which Aboriginal people and Torres Strait Islander people have combined older beliefs and practices with the newer concepts.

A third example pertains to People and Places at level 2, where the outcome is to 'describe choices people make in their use of places'. The following is recommended.

First of all, the teacher should look at the resources available to assist in achieving the outcome. There may be some teaching units already available in the school.

Next, the teacher should think about other areas of the curriculum. Perhaps in technology classes, students could be designing houses and allocating particular areas for particular uses. In English, students may be enjoying a book such as *A House for Wombats* (Jane Burrell and Michael Dugan). In learning about other languages, students could be learning about place names in other languages.

The teacher needs to find as many books as possible about places and have them available for students' use. Some titles would be:

A Home Among the Gum Trees by John Nicholson; *Mrs Frisby and the Rats of NIMH* by Robert C O'Brien; *The Fat and Juicy Place* by Diana Kidd; *My Place* by Nadia Wheatley and Donna Rawlins; *Acacia Terrace* by Barbara Ker Wilson; *Digging to China* by Nadia Wheatley.

Then the teacher needs to look at the available data about his or her students. It is possible that a class comprising, say, 28 students would have a variety of cultural backgrounds. The teacher should discuss the topic with their parents or carers, and invite them not only to talk about using areas in and around the home, but to talk about styles of housing they have seen and experienced in different areas of the world. Students could prepare questions prior to the visit.

The following activities would be appropriate:

- Read a section of the story of *Stig of the Dump* (or another story you find appropriate) to the whole class. Discuss why Stig may have chosen to live here. Have students talk about the ways in which people use different areas within the home. These could include indoor and outdoor areas. If possible, have guest speakers talk about how they use areas within the home for specific purposes.
- Invite discussion from students about the different climates within Australia and whether or not all homes should be built alike. Students could be prompted to think about homes in the Torres Strait where it is quite hot all year around and homes in colder areas like Canberra or Tasmania. Would people in the Torres Strait have the need for a fireplace?

	Family reasons	Cultural	Employment
Sydney			✔
Macquarie Harbour	✔		
Wallace Rock Hole		✔	

- From books and magazines supplied for students' use, have students find information about different styles of housing. They could then illustrate, group and label different styles of housing, either individually or in a small group.
- Ask students to think about moving to another location, and to list what they would see as being important in selecting a home. Students could work in small groups and be allocated a specific location, such as Yuendumu (desert), Geraldton (seaside), Thredbo (snow country), Norfolk Island, Sydney (busy metropolitan), Broome (hot seaside), Strahan (cool seaside) and so on.
- Discuss what is available in the local community in terms of what students have nominated as being important. Of these, ask students to talk about what facilities they and their family members currently use. These could include the sports ground, cinema, McDonald's (and other fast-food outlets), shopping centre, video store, service station, clubs, newsagent, library, swimming pool, places of worship.
- Students could then graph which of these are used more frequently by adults and more frequently by younger people. Can students think of any facilities that would be used mostly by females and mostly by males?
- Ask students to think about why people may choose to live in what may appear to be inhospitable places.

It's all about making the curriculum relevant to and inclusive of the students, and making things Aboriginal and Torres Strait Islander an everyday occurrence rather than an artificial, isolated experience. Any Aboriginal students or Torres Strait Islander students should then be able to see that things related to them and their cultures are just as important as those of the wider Australian society and just as highly valued. Although celebrations such as NAIDOC (National Aboriginal and Torres Strait Islander Day Observance Committee) Week or Culture Week can be enjoyed by everyone in the school, activities can be quickly forgotten or lead students and teachers to feel that this is the only time things Aboriginal and Torres Strait Islander need to be addressed.

■ Resources in Aboriginal Studies and Torres Strait Islander Studies

Two of the most useful resources that guide teachers in the selection of resources that will support Aboriginal studies and Torres Strait Islander studies are the *Recommended Books for Aboriginal Studies* (Education Department of South Australia, 1992), which also lists 'not recommended' publications, and the *Aboriginal Studies and Torres Strait Islander Studies: A Resource Guide for Schools* (Nean *et al.,* 1995). The latter was formulated through extensive consultation between indigenous and non-indigenous people across the country and contains a set of criteria for the evaluation and selection of materials. The video and teachers' notes *You Can Do It Too: Aboriginal Studies and Torres Strait Islander Studies* (Curriculum Corporation, 1996) depicting school-based programs across the country is a useful tool for teachers and parents.

Another is the oral histories kit *Telling It Like It Is* (1992), the publication of which was organised by Margaret Cranney of the Australian Institute of Aboriginal and Torres Strait Islander Studies. This kit comprises two books and a video: *Telling It Like It Is: A Guide to Making Aboriginal and Torres Strait Islander History*, by Penny Taylor; *Lookin' for your Mob: A Guide to Tracing Aboriginal and Torres Strait Islander Family Trees*, by Diane Smith and Boronia Halstead; and the video *Back trackers*.

Of great value to teachers and senior secondary school students is the *Journal of the Australian Institute of Aboriginal and Torres Strait Islander Studies*. It provides insights into traditional and contemporary Aboriginal cultures and Torres Strait Islander cultures and covers a variety of topics.

Over the past few years there has been a growth in the output of kits, some of which are most useful resources. For example, *Koori Images and Discussion Starters* and *Aboriginal Visions* are both projects sponsored by the New South Wales Department of School Education's Aboriginal Education Unit. *The Bush Food Poster Kit* and the *Art Poster Kit* are produced by the Western Australian Aboriginal Education Resource Unit. It is worthwhile pointing out that materials intended for use in the classroom that do not acknowledge appropriate consultation with Aboriginal people and/or Torres Strait Islander people should be checked out with the state education systems' Indigenous Education Units, since

what is acceptable in one part of Australia may not be in another. Of course, such difficulties should not arise when teachers are using their local publications such as *Aboriginal Studies R–12* (Education Department of South Australia, 1988), *Australian History: an Aboriginal Perspective* (Education Department of Western Australia, 1996a), *The Torres Strait Islander Cultural Resource Kit* (READ Centre, Cairns) which acknowledge full participation of indigenous people.

Other useful materials include: the ACT Department of Education and Training's *From Ochres to Eel Traps, a Resource Guide for Teachers about Aboriginal Science and Technology*; a series of photographs of Aboriginal children commissioned by Swan Hill North Primary School's ASSPA program committee for use as a stimulus response resource in the classroom; *Unity: 'Linking Together Faith and the Community'*, a preschool and primary school resource kit folder, Catholic Education Office (n.d.). The kit is composed of curriculum development guidelines, posters and items of Aboriginal material culture and Torres Strait Islander material culture. The curriculum development guidelines are modelled on *Aboriginal Perspectives Across the Curriculum* (APAC), which was developed by the Department of Education and Children's Services in South Australia. The guidelines have been developed in light of the *National Principles and Guidelines for Aboriginal Studies and Torres Strait Islander Studies* and the *Resource Guide for Aboriginal Studies and Torres Strait Islander Studies*. These curriculum development guidelines use the National Statements and Profiles for curriculum development in the key learning areas as a framework for implementation. They also utilise the Religious Education Statement and Profile for curriculum development in Catholic schools. The sections on terminology and resource evaluation are especially useful. The Aboriginal and Torres Strait Islander Commission (1999), *As a Matter of Fact*, answers the myths and misconceptions about indigenous Australians and can also be found on the ATSIC web page at http://www.atsic. gov.au.

■ Concluding Comments

The integration of Aboriginal studies across the entire curriculum is the common goal of many educators. There are also some highly controversial issues within the field that will have to be resolved in the near future. One is the place of Australian languages in Aboriginal studies and Torres Strait Islander studies. Language can be the vehicle of culture but there is no clear consensus among educators and Aboriginal communities on the issue of teaching Australian languages in schools.

QUESTIONS AND ACTIVITIES

1. Examine how Aboriginal studies and Torres Strait Islander studies are presented at a school at which you are teaching or have taught at recently. If there are alternatives or refinements you would suggest, why would you do so?
2. Select a recently produced Aboriginal studies and Torres Strait Islander studies unit and comment on:
    (a) the teaching approach used (explicit or implicit);
    (b) its likely impact upon teachers.
3. Examine the National Statement for studies of society and environment and critically analyse how Aboriginal studies and Torres Strait Islander studies are incorporated.

■ Endnotes

1. This syllabus was developed in consultation with Aboriginal people and Torres Strait Islander people, with the BSSSS committee chaired by a Niugi woman and educator, Ms Penny Tripcony. The syllabus had a three-year trial period in approved schools followed by a pilot period and evaluation.
2. Some Torres Strait Islander people prefer to use the term 'intrusion' in relation to contact and hostility that occurred between 1606 and 1871, with ownership of the land being claimed by government post-1871 as 'invasion'.
3. Some AECGs continue to have elected members, while others, such as advisory boards, are composed of members selected by the relevant education authorities.
4. At the time of writing, the Council for Aboriginal Reconciliation has 1 January 2001 as an end date.
5. The New South Wales Department of School Education Whole School Anti-racism Project is an example, and is composed of four booklets: *School Communities Investigating Racism*; *Understanding the Issues*; *Strategies for Change*; and *Anti-racism Planning Guide*.

14

Civics and Citizenship Education

Introduction

Civics and citizenship education, as an explicit part of the school curriculum, has had a fluctuating history in Australia. In the early part of this century and up until the 1960s there were many textbooks that set out programs of civics education for primary and secondary students. There was Charles Long's The Citizen Reader, *published in 1906, Walter Murdoch's* Australian Citizen, *published in 1916, and Alice Hoy's* Civics for Australian Schools, *published successively between 1925 and 1945. Yet by the 1960s, programs of civics and citizenship education seem to have disappeared from Australian schools, except in Queensland where there remained the Citizenship Education syllabus.*

It was against this background that successive Commonwealth governments have supported initiatives to ensure that civics and citizenship education gains a place in the school curriculum. Yet these initiatives have been relatively recent. In June 1994 the then Prime Minister, Paul Keating, announced the establishment of a Civics Expert Group 'to provide the Government with a strategic plan for a non-partisan program of public education and information on the Australian system of government, the Australian constitution, Australian citizenship and other civic issues' (Civics Expert Group, 1994: 1). Work started in June 1994, the Prime Minister had his report by December, three months were allowed for public responses and the Prime Minister announced the government's response in June 1995, although financial provision for the program had already been made in the May budget. (The government announced in the 1995/1996 budget that $25 million was to be allocated 'towards a comprehensive civics and citizenship education program. The centrepiece [being] a $20.6 million contribution to a program of civics and citizenship education in schools and other education sectors' (Office of the Prime Minister, 1995: 3).)

Both the public and government response to the report were overwhelmingly positive:

> The Commonwealth's proposed civics and citizenship education program will ensure that Australians have the opportunity to become informed about our system of government, our Constitution, and other civics and citizenship issues . . . (Office of the Prime Minister, 1995: iii)

The government allocated more than $25 million dollars to a new program of civics and citizenship education. Planning commenced but an election intervened and by March 1996 a new government was in office with a new social and political agenda. It was not clear for some time whether civics and citizenship education would be part of this agenda but in May 1997 the new government's plans were revealed:

> The Government is committed to ensuring that all students have opportunities to learn about the system of government in Australia . . . The Discovering Democracy program will help students gain knowledge of Australia's achievement as one of the world's pioneering democracies. (Kemp, 1997: 2)

From the level of government, at least, there has been agreement on the importance of civics and citizenship education. Given this renewed emphasis, it is important for

Fighting for one's country (World War I)

teachers of studies of society and environment to understand how this new curriculum priority can be incorporated into existing curriculum and teaching practice. In this chapter, five broad issues will be addressed:

1. Why civics education at this particular time?
2. What are the main concepts and learn associated with civics and citizenship education?
3. What lessons are there to learn from previous attempts to incorporate civic education into the school curriculum?
4. What might a coherent program of civics and citizenship education look like?
5. What resources are available for civics and citizenship education?

■ Why Civics Education at this Particular Time?

There are at least three possible answers to this question and the one a teacher will choose will affect the kind of program he or she develops. Each of the possible answers will be explored in turn. A summary of the issues raised in this section has been included in Table 14.1.

1. A deficit in civic knowledge

As part of the process of the Civic Expert Group's work, Australian National Opinion Polls (ANOP) Research Services was asked to conduct 'a benchmark study . . . into the Australian community's knowledge about governmental, constitutional, citizenship and civic issues' (Civics Expert Group, 1994: 130). The outcomes of this study revealed a 'a high level of community ignorance about Australia's system of government and its origins' (Civics Expert Group, 1994: 132), with people in the 15–19 years age group described as having a 'level of ignorance [that] is striking' (p. 134). Stuart Macintyre

(1996: 4), Chair of the Civics Expert, group has raised the spectre of a 'a civic deficit' by which is meant a deficit in civic knowledge. The ANOP polling indicated that there were important facts that Australian citizens, young and old, did not know. For example, '87% of Australians have only the sketchiest knowledge of the Constitution, . . . 78% lack knowledge of the functions of the High Court . . . 70% do not understand the historical basis of the federal system' (Macintyre, 1996: 7).

> How can these citizens, whether as republicans or monarchists, follow the current constitutional debate? How many of those who, in various public opinion polls, say they would prefer a directly elected head of state to one appointed by parliament appreciate that the present arrangements for appointing the head of state are even less participatory than either of these alternatives? (Macintyre, 1996: 7)

Thus correcting this *civic deficit* became a rationale for civics education: ensuring that the community has an adequate knowledge base on which to make important decisions that will affect it.

2. Civic megatrends

Paralleling a deficit in civic knowledge, there are civic issues the understanding of which demand much more than simple recitation of a predigested body of knowledge. Macintyre (1996: 1) identified three such issues: 'multiculturalism, the recognition of ethnic and cultural diversity; reconciliation, the recognition of the special status of the indigenous peoples of this country; and republicanism, the recognition of constitutional self-sufficiency'. Writing prior to the report of the Civics Expert Group, Kennedy (1995a) also identified these issues but included the recognition of the changing status of women in society as a significant reformational process. In addition, he

Table 14.1 *Rationales for civics and citizenship education*

Reason	Explanation
There is a *deficit* in *civic knowledge*.	The community in general, but young people in particular, appear to know little about the formal structures of government and the constitutional arrangements that govern Australia as a democratic society.
Civic megatrends have fundamentally changed the social and economic landscape for all Australians.	Within Australia issues such as multiculturalism, reconciliation with indigenous Australians, the role of women in Australian society and constitutional debate concerning an Australian republic have had serious social and political implications for all Australians. Externally, the process of globalisation, the role of new international cooperatives such as the Asia Pacific Economic Community, the new peace-keeping role of the United Nations, the propensity for international intervention to safeguard human rights and the pervasiveness of communications and information technology all highlight the increasing interdependence of the global community. This points to the necessity for Australia to look outwards and to appreciate its role in the global community.
Civic realities for young people are often far removed from the 'public knowledges' that adults often believe are important for young people to know.	The prevalence of youth cultures has been well documented. These might be represented by rave parties, moshing, the availability of hard drugs and alcohol, homelessness, alienation, lack of employment opportunities or a general feeling of being 'different'. The fact is that young people inhabit a world that is as much structured by their own values and mores as those of their parents or the community.

pointed to a range of international events and activities that had the potential to shape the future: APEC, the globalisation of the economy, the impact of communications technology and the changing role of the United Nations.

These very broad influences and issues might best be understood as 'civic megatrends'—complex issues demanding a response that is at once knowledge based and values based. The kind of knowledge required is interdisciplinary and integrated while the values must be firmly embedded in a vision that focuses on the good of all rather than the selfish demands of individuals. These megatrends were seen to have the potential to define who Australians are at the end of the twentieth century and shape whom they will become in the current millennium. They will involve all Australians and, of course, they must inform any civics education program.

3. *Civic realities*

It would be easy to draw links between the so-called civic deficit and civic megatrends to show how the two might be related. What kind of knowledge is needed if the community is to understand and actively contribute to shaping its own future? Yet it is not as simple as that. There are also what are best described as the civic realities of everyday life—living and working in a democratic society. Civic realities do not always show Australian towns and cities at their best. Drug taking is on the increase, violence is becoming an increasingly common feature of urban life, homelessness is not uncommon, alcohol consumption and gambling among young people is a fact of life and youth unemployment continues to soar. Given this context, an emphasis in civics education on the recitation of facts, such as the name of the Speaker of the House of Representatives or the name of the tribunal that handed down the *Mabo* decision, seems to miss the point. This is not the world of young people—it is a construction of the world that adults believe is important. Yet if civics education is to speak to young people, then part of it at least must address *civic realities*—the things that matter to young people, the things that can help them understand the world in which they live and give them a stake in the future that rightly belongs to them.

Programs of civics and citizenship education could be developed from any one of these rationales. Yet any approach based on a single rationale would somehow be deficient. The richness of civics and citizenship education derives from its reliance on multiple approaches that recognise the complexities of the world in which young Australians now live and the peculiar needs of young people in fast-changing local and global environments. The challenge for civics and citizenship education is to meld together civic knowledge, civic megatrends and civic realities in a way that will meet the multiple needs of young people. Disembodied facts, unrelated to everyday life and real needs, will not solve any of the current problems and will not connect young people to a future that should be full of hope and promise. To be successful, civics education must speak to young people—to use Stuart Macintyre's (1995: 16) sentence, 'we must connect young Australians with the substance of their citizenship'. This is a significant task for teachers of studies of society and environment.

■ Main Concepts and Learnings

In this section, literature on civics and citizenship education will be reviewed with an emphasis on recent Australian literature. Reference will also be made to international literature where this provides some insights into current initiatives in Australia.

Despite the lack of emphasis on the explicit teaching of civics and citizenship education in the school curriculum, there has been a growing literature and interest in Australia on the topic and this has increased since the release of *Whereas the people . . .* (Civics Expert Group, 1994). Australia is now participating in a major international comparative study of student understanding of civic education. As a part of this study, a review of the current status of civics was conducted (Print, Kennedy and Hughes, 1999) and both the trial and final versions of the questionnaire have been administered to samples of students (Kennedy and Mellor, 1999). Researchers have focused on areas such as teacher understanding of civics (Dunkin *et al.*, 1998; Jimonez, 1999), pedagogical practices (Treadgold, 1999; Jimonez and Hunter, 1999) and policy-focused studies (Kennedy and Connor, 1999; Kennedy, 1997b). In addition, there has been a significant range of literature seeking to come to grips with the broad conceptual and theoretical issues in the area. Much of this will be reviewed below in order to outline what the main concepts and learnings are in civics and citizenship education. Table 14.2 highlights how the main issues addressed in this section are related to program planning and course development.

There has been a range of views expressed on the nature and purpose of citizenship

(Hamot, 2000). One set of differences centres on the relative emphasis to be placed on the public or common interest as distinct from private interests. The question is raised as to whether civics education should promote one at the expense of the other. Macintyre (1996), Kennedy (1995a), Crittenden (1995), Saunders (1996), Hill (1996) and Thompson (1996) support the notion of a common citizenship underpinned by a set of common values. It follows from this position that one task of civics education is to engender support for what all citizens share in common, including values, political structures and a willingness to participate actively in democratic processes. Equally strong arguments are made to highlight the importance of individual interests and the need to safeguard these in a democratic society (Hogan, 1996; Gilbert, 1993; Singh, 1993; Wyn, 1995; Watts, 1995). Diamond (1994) has pointed out that the tension between these two positions might be resolved if it is kept in mind that individual interests can only be safeguarded by a political and legal system that guarantees freedom of thought and action. Thus civics education can highlight the importance of individual interests while seeking support for those institutions and the values that allow individual interests to flourish.

The tension between public and private interests is nowhere better demonstrated than in the way different groups prefer to see themselves depicted as citizens. Foster (1996) has pointed to the inadequacies of *Whereas the people* . . . (Civics Expert Group, 1994) in relation to women. Foster argues that the role of women as citizens has not been adequately conceptualised or understood. In the same way, Woods (1996) points to the complexities of citizenship for Aboriginal and Torres Strait Islander people. Woods does not want to be subsumed into a common citizenship but rather seeks to maintain an identity that has the potential to contribute to new understandings about modern citizenship. Civics education, therefore, must recognise the contribution of difference and diversity in modern society and not seek to submerge them.

Support for private interests has been criticised for overemphasising the rights of citizens at the expense of their responsibilities. Rights have been described broadly to mean social, political and economic rights (Gilbert, 1992; Watts, 1995; Pixley, 1993). Musgrave (1994) regards this as a consumer approach to citizenship by which rights and entitlements are amassed in the interest of individuals. He argues strongly that young people ought to be made aware of their duties and responsibilities as citizens. For civics education it is not one or the other: rights and responsibilities are both important parts of learning about citizenship. The issue is establishing the relationship between rights and responsibilities so that they are seen as complementary rather than mutually exclusive.

The issue of rights and responsibilities as aspects of civics and citizenship education raises more direct questions about the knowledge base of civics education. There are strong advocates for history as providing the knowledge base for civics education (Civics Expert Group, 1994; Young, 1996), while others point to the strengths of the principles and concepts underlying studies of society and environment (Hogan, Fearnley-Sander and Lamb, 1996). Woods (1996) argues strongly for grounding civics in Aboriginal and Torres Strait Islander studies. Saunders (1996) sees the need for citizens to have an understanding of the system of government if they are to participate effectively in democratic decision making. Lepani (1996) focuses on the needs of the knowledge economy and highlights the importance of developing systems thinking and information literacy as necessities for effective citizenship.

Other writers come at the issue from a different perspective. Brennan (1996) talks in terms of pedagogies (group work and group-based assessment), school governance and the meaningful involvement of students and community-based research projects involving students. Wyn (1995) agrees with the experiential approach advocated by Brennan (1996) and argues that young people need to be equipped with the means to overcome the unequal power relationships that characterise modern society and that impact on youth in particular. Watts (1995) echoes a similar view by calling for civics and citizenship education to be an empowering process that will result in young people having a real sense of social agency.

For civics and citizenship education the positions outlined in the above paragraphs cannot be seen as competing. Valued knowledge must be defined irrespective of the discipline base from which it is to come. Clearly history and political science will have a strong claim on curriculum developers. Yet it will need to be remembered that history and politics are embedded in social contexts and these will have to be recognised and articulated in a formal learning program. At the same time, the experience of participation and democratic decision making will be important ways for students to learn about citizenship. Knowledge and experience will need to be welded together in any civics education curriculum.

All of the above suggests what many writers have also argued, that values will play a key role in civics and citizenship (Kennedy, 1995b; Hill, 1996; Clark, 1996; Thompson, 1996). Yet values education is one of the most contested areas of the school curriculum. Nevertheless, the Civics Expert Group (1994) went so far as to articulate a set of shared values that might form the basis of civics and citizenship education. Gaining commitment to these raises significant issues

for teachers but assuming that there are no common values will raise issues of a different kind. Values do underpin democratic decision making and young people will need to be made aware that their own values will determine particular courses of political and social action (Kaplan, 2000). For teachers the values question may well be resolved by pedagogical considerations and these have been discussed in the literature.

All writers on the question of pedagogy have called for an active and engaging approach to the teaching of civics and citizenship education (Berrell, 1993; Wyn, 1995; Mellor, 1996; Brennan, 1996; Kennedy, 1996). Such a call is perhaps easier to make in rhetorical form than to translate into practice. Nevertheless, it is a reminder that transmission approaches to teaching and learning have little role to play. This is a particularly important point to make in relation to the role of disciplines such as history and political science in any program of civics education. Advocates for history such as Young (1996) and Mellor (1996) go to great lengths to point out that approaches to teaching in that area should be based on inquiry and understanding, not simple transmission. This is an important barrier to break down, since so often discipline-based teaching is associated with transmission strategies. Disciplines can be taught in that way, but they need not be.

There is clearly much to consider in designing new programs in civics. Table 14.2 summarises the elements in program design that are important.

The rationale for this decision-making framework can be easily articulated:

- Early civics texts, for example, were not inclusive of all Australians—they very often neglected Aboriginal people, women and non-Anglo-Celtic people (Murdoch, 1916; Thorn and Rigg, 1923; Hoy,

Table 14.2 *Making decisions about civics education programs*

Aspect	Dimensions	Explanation
1. Content	1.1 Is citizenship defined inclusively?	An inclusive citizenship is one that does not exclude any individual or group.
	1.2 Are difference and diversity recognised as positive aspects of citizenship?	
	1.3 Are the common values underpinning citizenship articulated?	
	1.4 Will students learn about both formal and informal political structures and processes?	Formal structures of government as well as the processes associated with civil society
	1.5 Are citizens portrayed as active and involved in democratic decision making?	
2. Teaching/ Learning	2.1 Is an approach to teaching used that actively involves students?	This does not necessarily refer to a single teaching strategy or methodology.
	2.2 Is there a strategy for teaching about values?	
	2.3 Does learning involve students in activities outside of the classroom?	
3. Outcomes	3.1 Will the outcomes assist students to become active citizens?	
	3.2 Will the outcomes assist students to understand essential features of the democratic system?	
	3.3 Will the outcomes assist students locate themselves as part of an historical and political process?	

1925)—hence the call for the new civics to be inclusive of difference.

- Early versions of civics were often dominated by a concentration on the structures of government, neglecting the role of more informal and grassroot influences on the democratic process—hence the emphasis on civil society.
- Citizenship was often seen as a list of facts to be learnt rather than as an active process in which all citizens could be involved—hence the emphasis on active involvement.
- Thomas (1994) has pointed to poor

pedagogy as one reason for the failure of the early civics—hence the emphasis on active learning and engagement.

Another way of looking at the characteristics of good civics education programs is to be aware of how they are constructed in other countries. In the USA, for example, attention has been paid to the explicit statement of basic values, opportunities for students to debate and discuss civic issues, links with civic organisations, involvement of students in monitoring public policy and ensuring that students have the opportunity to meet with exemplary citizens (Center for Civic Education, 1995: 6). Each of these has been used as a criterion for good civics education programs.

While these points reflect a particular cultural perspective they are in general consistent with a number of emphases also identified in the Australian literature: civics and citizenship education should be active rather than passive, concerned with the community as a whole rather than just the structures of government and seek to promote a critical rather than an unthinking citizenry.

■ Lessons to Learn from Previous Attempts

Civics education played an important role in the school curriculum up to the 1950s. There were advocates in universities and in education departments. This point can be illustrated by referring to some popular civics texts of the time. It is important, however, to look at what can be learned from past experiences with civics education. As schools embark on civics education in the new millennium, what are some of the issues they will need to consider?

One popular text for upper secondary students was that of Alice Hoy, a lecturer in history method at Melbourne Teachers' College. She published successive editions of *Civics for Australian Schools* from 1925 to 1945, with the latter edition still containing the *Introduction* that had been written in 1917 by Frank Tate, Director of Education in Victoria. Hoy was a proponent of using history to teach civics:

> Many of our civic institutions cannot be properly understood without reference to history, and for that reason the study of civics and history will always to some extent go together. (Hoy, 1925: Preface)

Yet Hoy's civics text was not overly academic. While Hoy recognised the need for young people to understand the machinery of government it was not as an end in itself:

> the machinery of government is therefore studied only in order that we might understand the greatest of the agencies on which the public welfare is promoted . . . civics deals with the affairs of every day life. (Hoy, 1925: Preface)

It was the 'affairs of every day life' that dominated Hoy's text. For her:

> The study of Civics should direct our attention to these matters of common interest and it should show us just how as citizens, we are concerned in them . . . Ask yourself: How can I make my country a finer country? (Hoy, 1925: 2)

Teachers and students using Hoy's text were, in fact, being conscripted into a 'civic ideal' in which all citizens were assumed to benefit from the State and hence were exhorted to become involved in and understand the institutions of the State. Early citizenship training in Australia focused on both rights and responsibilities, but more particularly the latter.

A contemporary text with that of Hoy's first edition was Thorn and Rigg's *Handbook of Civics* published in 1923. Its contents were not dissimilar inasmuch as it covered the machinery of government and the work of government and there was a similar commitment to exhorting students to promote the common good. Yet it differed philosophically in the relationship it saw between civics and more traditional school subjects:

> though much can be learnt through story and song, the deeds and thoughts of great men, the elements of Geography and History, it is good for the child that he [sic] should be brought from time to time sharply up against the material and social problems of the world in which we live. (Thorn and Rigg, 1923: 2)

This problem orientation is in contrast to the discipline orientation adopted by Hoy and herein lies a problem for civics education today. Is civics education today to be embedded in a single discipline or should it be issues based? The Civics Expert Group made its view very clear:

> We believe that a knowledge and understanding of the history of Australians is an essential foundation for Australian citizenship. It should be a core element of the curriculum for all students up to school leaving age. (Civics Expert Group, 1994: 52)

History clearly has an important role to play in promoting civic understanding but is it robust enough to link with the needs and concerns of young people? This is an issue that current efforts at civics education will need to address. There are excellent examples of history curriculum design that have been problem based, for example the New South Wales *History Stages 4–5 Syllabus* (Board of Studies, New South Wales, 1999b). It should not be impossible to link that kind of history with the Change and Continuity strand of the nationally developed *Curriculum Statement on Studies of Society and the Environment* or its local variation. This leads to another issue.

The Studies of Society and Environment Curriculum and Profiles, or a local variant, will provide the broad parameters for civics education in some although not all states and territories. A good deal of work will need to be done to construct from the framework an articulated K–10 civics education program. The process elements are certainly there, but content will need to be specified and integrated. This issue will be addressed directly in a later section of this chapter.

Julian Thomas (1994) has argued that civics education has been missing from Australian schools for the past 40 or so years. When history and geography were melded into social studies, civics somehow disappeared. It also suffered a bad press, often being associated with poor teaching practices and an inability to attract the interest of students. These problems might also be seen as applying to other elements in the school curriculum, but the real problem for civics was that it never succeeded in becoming a subject (Thomas, 1994). It was always a part of other subjects and therefore dispensable. The status of civics and citizenship education will continue to be in issue for nowhere is it being proposed that there be a new subject. Will it avoid the same fate this time round?

The next section of this chapter will outline how different states and territories have decided to handle the civics and citizenship components of their studies of the society and environment curriculum.

■ A Program of Civics and Citizenship Education

While civics and citizenship education was an initiative of successive Commonwealth governments, there is considerable evidence that it has been taken up at the state and territory level with a good deal of seriousness. When the Minister for Education and Training in New South Wales was introducing the second reading of the *Education Reform Further Amendment Bill 1997*, he referred to a program of state-wide testing in, among other things, Australian history, geography and civics. The purpose of this testing program was 'to ensure that the study of Australian social and political institutions forms part of the experience of every school student' (Aquilina, 1997: 4). The minister went on to say that:

> The government sees much of this knowledge and understanding being achieved in the context of learning about Australian Geography and History. We do not envisage Civics as an additional subject within the curriculum. Placing the external examinations at the end of Year 10

will help to ensure these subjects are treated more seriously (Aquilina, 1997: 4).

In Victoria, the review of the *Curriculum Standards Framework* (*CSF*) has also singled out the importance of civics. In seeking to determine curriculum priorities, civics has been singled out as one of six priority areas in addition to literacy and numeracy. The rationale for choosing civics was:

> Through a study of civics and citizenship, students not only gain knowledge of the institutions of our democratic society, but also come to an understanding of the shared values which underpin Australian society, including tolerance, mutual respect and commitment to common ideals. (Board of Studies, Victoria, 1999: 7)

The review also saw studies of society and environment as the natural home for civics and citizenship since it 'will support students in becoming active and informed citizens with the ability to exercise judgement and responsibility in matters of morality, ethics, the law and social justice' (Board of Studies, Victoria, 1999: 3)

This general support for civics and citizenship education has been translated into syllabus design in most states and territories. As the following examples show, while there is agreement in principle on the importance of civics and citizenship, there are also different ways of approaching its incorporation into the school curriculum.

The Queensland School Curriculum Council trialled a draft studies of society and environment syllabus throughout 1999 (Queensland School Curriculum Council, 1999). It has approached civics and citizenship in two different ways, one of which might be seen as implicit and the other explicit.

The design of the 1–10 syllabus document itself offers implicit support for civics and citizenship. The key values on which the entire syllabus are based are democratic

process, social justice, ecological and economic sustainabilty and peace. These values inform the main concepts that drive the curriculum. These concepts are grouped under processes (investigate, create, participate, communicate, reflect) and strands (Time, Continuity and Change, Place and Space, Culture and Identity, Systems, Resources and Power). This framework provides the opportunity for many issues associated with civics and citizenship to be investigated. The expected key learning area outcomes also highlight what could be seen as significant civics and citizenship learnings:

* understand past ideas, events and actions;
* understand social, natural and built environments;
* understand the ways people form groups and develop material and non-material aspects of cultures;
* understand human experiences in various economic, business, ecological, legal, political and government systems;
* investigate events concerning societies and environments by applying socio-cultural and socio-critical inquiries;
* understand and value the diverse and dynamic nature of societies and environments by creating and communicating enterprising responses in a range of genres;
* participate cooperatively to reflect and act upon ethical and informed visions of possible and preferred futures (Queensland Curriculum Council, 1999: 14).

Yet the syllabus goes further than these outcomes, highlighting the relationship between the syllabus strands and expected civic learnings as shown in Table 14.3.

To give added emphasis, an optional subject syllabus in civics for Years 9 and 10 is provided. It lists expected civics learning outcomes for levels 5 and 6. It does this by drawing on the core learning outcomes for the *1–10 studies of society and environment*

Table 14.3 *Relationship between studies of society and environment strands and civics*

Strand	Civics emphasis
Culture and Identity	The primacy of culture in the construction of identities and ways of understanding these
Systems, Resources and Power	Public institutions, economic, legal and government systems. Uses of public power. Values of justice, sustainability and social cohesion
Time, Continuity and Change	The origins of many contemporary civic practices
Place and space	Location and spatial relationships in the structure and function of society, including public policy, environmental issues, and the processes of the social, natural and built environments

Source: Based on Queensland School Curriculum, 1999: 48.

syllabus (Queensland School Curriculum Council, 1999) and including additional civics learning outcomes as well as learning outcomes that go beyond level 6. Schools can use this framework to develop their own civics courses. The following advice is provided about the teaching and curriculum contexts for civics education so that the expected learning outcomes are highly contextualised:

Civics learning:
- is active and participatory;
- focuses on the contemporary and is relevant to student lives;
- promotes a sense of belonging and is placed within the context of social life;
- develops a sense of confidence in one's identity;
- promotes living together with a strong sense of community;
- holds as central understandings of legal, economic, social and environmental processes;
- encompasses a view of global to local without a stated hierarchy;
- focuses on understandings of the nature and structure of social systems and institutions and their impact on citizens;
- promotes the study of how key values have been and can be used, defined and debated,

both in abstract terms and in real contexts in a range of places, past and present;
- develops appreciation of the different perspectives people have on values and value issues, and how cultural and other differences can influence these perspectives;
- encourages critical and creative thinking and developing socially critical participation;
- involves making decisions and choices and taking responsibility for these choices; and
- promotes understanding. (Queensland School Curriculum Council, 1999: 47–48)

It should be noted, however, that even with this very strong emphasis, civics education is not compulsory for all students. Nevertheless, the structure of the syllabus and the focus on particular learning outcomes should ensure that Queensland students will have an exposure to important civic learnings.

In Western Australia the *Society and Environment Learning Area Statement* (Western Australia Curriculum Council, 1998) has taken a somewhat different approach to civic education, although there are similarities. As in Queensland, there is implicit support for civic education in both the rationale and structure of the syllabus.

The rationale outlines the broad directions

of the syllabus but there is specific support for developing and encouraging civic responsibility:

> The Society and Environment learning area, with its focus on civic responsibility and social competence, has a unique place in the Curriculum Framework. Its basic aim is to give individual students the ability to make reasoned and informed decisions as citizens of a culturally-diverse, democratic society in an interdependent world. (Western Australian Curriculum Council, 1998: 3)

This broad support is translated operationally through the structure of the syllabus in which seven key learning outcomes are defined, with the seventh being 'Active Citizenship':

> Students demonstrate active citizenship through their behaviour and practices in the school environment, in accordance with the principles and values associated with democratic processes, social justice and ecological sustainability. (Western Australian Curriculum Council, 1998: 4)

Essential knowledge and skills are then mapped against this outcome across four broad areas of young people's development: early childhood, middle schooling, early adolescence and late adolescence. In this way, students throughout the full range of their years of schooling will have the opportunity to experience activities that will assist them to become active citizens. Yet these are not the only experiences that students will have in the area of civics and citizenship.

Other key learning outcomes driven by concepts such as natural and social systems, culture, time, continuity and change, place and space and resources will also contain material and activities that will contribute to civics and citizenship. For example, during the years of early adolescence students seeking to achieve the learning outcome for natural and social systems will undertake work concerned with the political, legal and economic structures of Australian society.

This will contribute specifically to civics understandings and will complement participatory citizenship activities that were carried out under active citizenship.

A final contribution to civics and citizenship will be made by the expected learning outcome related to Investigation, Communication and Participation. This outcome points to the kind of teaching and learning strategies that are expected to be used in the learning area. Students should be involved in active inquiry so as to develop skills that will enable them to collect, analyse, synthesise and evaluate information. In turn this should assist them to be able to make judgments about complex social, political and environmental issues. This kind of decision making is seen to be essential for citizens in a democratic society.

Thus in Western Australia there is considerable implicit support for civics and citizenship without any explicit examples of what a civics course might resemble or any compulsion to include civics and citizenship in school courses. There is little doubt, however, that a coherent approach to civics and citizenship could be developed from the Western Australian syllabus.

■ Resources For Civics and Citizenship Education

The most significant resource that has been produced for civics and citizenship education in Australia is the *Discovering Democracy* curriculum materials that have been made available to all Australian schools. These have been developed over the past three years and have been distributed to every school in Australia. They have been trialled in selected schools (McCrae, 1999) and extensively reviewed by academics (Hogan and Fearnley-Sander, 1999; Gill and Reid, 1999) and teachers (Wise, 1999; Lamerton, 1999; Clayton, 1999; Cross, 1999). They now sit in their green (Secondary) and blue (Primary) boxes, probably in the library, in schools across the country. The green and blue boxes have been supplemented by a set of Readers providing original source material for the primary and secondary years. The scope of these materials has been summarised in Table 14.4.

Despite the comprehensive nature of the *Discovering Democracy* materials and the attempt to provide a scope and sequence across primary and secondary schools, they are more likely to be 'dipped into' and used selectively rather than as a complete curriculum. For this reason, the materials make an excellent starting point for any teacher or school considering the development of a civics and citizenship education program. Hirst's *A Guide to Law and Government in Australia* (1998) is ideal for teachers wanting to refresh their subject matter knowledge. They will soon see that it presents a particular view of Australian history that can be easily balanced by reading Stuart Macintyre's recently released *Concise History of Australia* (Macintyre, 1999).

The *Discovering Democracy* materials are well supported by a website maintained by the Curriculum Corporation: http://www. curriculum.edu.au/democracy/index.htm. Of particular interest on this site is a Resource Database (http://www.curriculum.edu.au/ democracy/resource/resource.htm) that allows active searching for materials suitable for both primary and secondary students. This site also provides discussion groups, a facility that allows for email information to be sought from the Curriculum Corporation, an up to date newsletter and materials on teaching strategies.

There is a considerable range of web-based materials that can support teachers in this area. Table 14.5 lists a selection of these with a brief description of each site.

Table 14.5 is by no means an exhaustive list, but it does highlight the Internet as a significant source of information about civics and citizenship education.

Other resources are also available and accessible. There is nothing like a newspaper to raise current issues about civics and citizenship. Indeed it can be argued that highlighting issues that are current and relevant to young people is the best way to promote good civics teaching. The community itself is a resource. There are people from the community who can come into the classroom (MPs, local councillors, community leaders) and there are places in the community that students can visit (parliaments, town halls, electoral offices, trade union offices, etc.). Civic life takes place in the community, so it makes sense to utilise community resources as much as possible.

Of course, the classroom itself can be a resource for helping students understand democracy. Brennan (1996) has argued this case well. Clayton (1999) provides an excellent example of how democratic classroom practices that provide for student participation and involvement in decision making can lead students to be engaged with the more formal aspects of civics education. The practice of democracy can come together with the theory when students become part of a democratic process.

■ Concluding Comments

Clearly, the design of new programs of civics and citizenship education will provide a challenge for teachers already concerned with an overcrowded curriculum. Yet unlike many other demands being made, it can probably be argued that the concern of civics and citizenship education is a central concern for young people themselves and for society as a whole. A critical and intelligent citizenry is not an optional extra for a democratic society: it is the means by which such a society ensures its survival. Civics and citizenship education, however, will only regain its place in the

Table 14.4 Discovering Democracy *curriculum materials at a glance*

Themes	Primary		Secondary	
	Middle	Upper	Lower	Middle
Units				
1. Who rules?	· Stories of the People and Rulers	· Parliament versus Monarch	· Should the People Rule?	· Parties Control Parliament
2. Laws and Rights	· Rules and Laws	· The Law Rules	· Law	· Human Rights · Democracy Destroyed (+ Theme 1)
3. The Australian Nation	· We Remember	· The People Make a Nation	· Democratic Struggles	· Making a Nation · What Sort of Nation
4. Citizens and Public Life · Each theme is linked to state and territory curriculum requirements · Teachers' Guides for Units and Readers	· Joining In	· People Power	· Men and Women in Public Life	· Getting Things Done
Australian Readers*				
· Videos and CD-ROMS for selected units · Posters · *A Guide to Law and Government in Australia* for teachers	· Good Rulers and Bad Rulers · Living with Rules and Laws · We Are Australian · Lest We Forget · Good Neighbours	· Liberty, Equality, Fraternity · This is My Country · True Patriots · From Little Things Big Things Grow · Juice	· Who Should Rule · When Law Breaks Down · Stories We Tell About Ourselves	· Political People · Law and Justice · Equality and Difference

* '*The Australian Readers* are collections of factual and fictional, historical and contemporary texts that deal with civic and citizenship themes' (Curriculum Corporation, 1999: 3).

Table 14.5 *Web-based resources for civics and citizenship education*

http://www.centenary.org.au/	The Constitutional Centenary Foundation provides details about the forthcoming Centenary of Federation as well as support materials dealing specifically with the Australian Constitution.
http://www.abc.net.au/ola/citizen/default.htm	Open Learning Australia in conjunction with the ABC have developed a site that outlines the history of democracy in Australia. Extensive use is made of primary source material.
http://www.peo.gov.au/	The Parliamentary Education Office is located in Parliament House, Canberra. It has an extensive range of materials related to the Commonwealth Parliament as well as a visitors program for schools.
http://www.opennet.net.au/2000hbook/postgrad/x5100.html and http://www.opennet.net.au/2000hbook/ugrad/dem11.html	Open Learning Australia has developed two subjects that can be studied online: 1. Civics and Citizenship Education; and 2. Citizenship and Australian Democracy. Details about these units can be found on the Griffith University website (http://www.gu.edu.au).
http://www.civiced.org/	The Center for Civic Education has spearheaded much of the recent work in the USA around the development of standards for civics education. While it is specific to the USA, it is also instructive for Australian educators to be aware of developments elsewhere.

school curriculum if the content is relevant and the pedagogy is engaging. Without such approaches, history may well repeat itself and civics will once again disappear.

QUESTIONS AND ACTIVITIES

1. How would you explain at a parent–teacher night why civics education is now part of the school curriculum? How would you explain it to students?
2. Should civics education be confined to the studies of society and environment key learning area? How might it be incorporated into other parts of the curriculum?
3. Why do you think that civics education was such an important part of the school curriculum at the beginning of the twentieth century? Why is it important at the beginning of the twenty-first century?
4. Why are values such an important part of civics education? What do you think are the common and agreed values in Australian society?
5. What are the common features of civics and citizenship education in the different states and territories? What do you think are the essential features of any civics and citizenship education curriculum?

15

Multicultural Studies

Introduction

Multicultural education assumes that the future of our society is pluralistic.
It assumes that teachers want all their students to succeed at school.
This is indeed a tall order. Substantial reforms are needed if students from
diverse backgrounds will all have the opportunity to succeed.
There are numerous social and political issues involved. However, at the school level,
teachers can draw on inclusive strategies that will help students develop their self-respect
and provide for equal opportunity.

■ Multicultural Education

In every Australian classroom there are
students from diverse backgrounds. As educators it is our task to respond to their diversity.

Within a country there can be various
minority groups. In the case of Australia this
includes Aboriginal and Torres Strait
Islanders and various immigrant groups.

Multicultural education is a relatively
recent term which only appeared in the
literature in the 1970s. There are other terms
which have been used such as 'multiethnic',
'cultural diversity', 'cultural pluralism' and
'global interculturalism'.

According to Banks (1997) multicultural
education has three major components:

1. an idea or concept;
2. an educational reform movement; and
3. a process.

Many writers espouse *ideas* or *concepts*
about multicultural education. Smolicz
(1997) describes it as an overarching
framework of shared values. For example, all
students should have equal opportunities to
learn regardless of the racial, ethnic, social
class or gender group.

Educational reform movements try to
bring about school reform. For example, the

Commonwealth Multicultural Education Program in 1979 was provided with $5 million to implement general programs highlighting the historical, social, aesthetic and cultural backgrounds of particular ethnic groups; to implement community language programs; to establish English as a second language programs; and to operate bilingual education programs (Cahill, 1996).

Since the 1980s, multicultural education has broadened its focus. According to Garcia and Briggs (1998) it is now a movement concerned for marginalised groups (females, recent immigrants, poor students, students with physical and mental disabilities, gays and lesbians) and their voices in the curriculum. Dolby (2000) and May (2000) contend that multicultural education is now well positioned to address these issues as well as general issues of class and culture.

Above all, multicultural education is a continuing *process*. Schools are an ideal vehicle to promote the process but the rate of progress can be exceedingly slow and various obstacles can occur. Chapin and Messick (1999) contend that the organisation and management of many classrooms often denies the process.

Yet it can also be argued that studies of society and environment offers tremendous opportunities for multicultural content and perspectives. Children's literature provides stimulating accounts about children from different ethnic groups. Multicultural activities such as ethnic meals and celebrating special events can assist students' appreciation of different cultures.

More important, thought-provoking discussions can develop over particular value issues. Ideological stances about discrimination and race can lead to a variety of reactions. This teaching field lends itself to interactive learning techniques such as inquiry learning, cooperative learning and social issues approaches.

■ Multiculturalism in Australia

It can be argued that Australia has always valued diversity within a context of unity. The original Aboriginal population consisted of diverse linguistic and cultural groups. The first British settlement was largely monolingual but by the 1860s the discovery of gold caused many overseas groups to enter Australia and there emerged a number of languages other than English, such as Chinese, German and Italian.

By the 1870s the multilingual/multicultural phase had started to subside as Education Acts were passed in all states and these decreed secular instruction and minimal requirements in English.

The Boer War and then World War I saw a need for Australia to identify with the British Empire. According to Clyne (1997) this was often expressed by xenophobia and intolerance towards languages other than English. 'Anti-foreigners' and 'Anti-German' measures were demanded by pressure groups such as the Returned Sailors and Soldiers Imperial League of Australia.

This negative and assimilationist stance continued into the 1950s even though World War II ceased in 1945. The refugee immigrants who arrived in Australia in the late 1940s and 1950s under large-scale immigration schemes were given limited facilities. Interpreting and translating facilities were inadequate and few of the employment officers had any knowledge of the European languages.

Recognition of Aboriginal and Torres Strait Islander people over the centuries is indeed damning. There was no recognition of these peoples in the Australian Constitution of 1901. Until the White Australia Policy was abolished in 1972, Australia was officially defined as white. Social Services were largely unavailable to Aboriginal and Torres Strait Islander people until the 1950s. It was only

School communities include families from diverse ethnic groups

in 1967 that they were awarded full citizen-ship rights as a result of a national referendum. According to Burridge (1999) there have been many examples of institutionalised racism, discrimination and neglect, which have perpetuated the cycle of poverty and disadvantage.

For all minority groups living in Australia, both Aboriginal and Torres Strait Islander people and immigrants, it was the 1970s which provided major initiatives. Clyne (1997) argues that this was due to two major, interrelated factors:

1. A recognition of the rights, cultures and languages of ethnic groups that was developing worldwide.
2. An acknowledgment that the shared experience of many Australians was largely multicultural.

The recognition of the rights of ethnic groups was tackled at local and national levels but especially by the Labor government in its 1972 election campaign. The new Labor government produced a number of policy changes, championed by the flamboyant and trilingual Immigration Minister, Al Grassby.

External events also played their part. The British had withdrawn their bases east of the Suez Canal. The importance of the monarchy was greatly reduced. There were many examples of second-generation Australians of non-British descent who had risen to positions of authority in society. A common perception emerged which seemed to celebrate the distinctiveness of Australia and Australians—it truly had a cultural diversity.

The 1970s and 1980s were boom times for proponents of multiculturalism. The *Review of Post-Arrival Programs and Services for Migrants*, known as the Galbally Report (1978), led to multiculturalism becoming official government policy. The Commonwealth Multicultural Education Program was established and funded projects on languages other than English (LOTE), and developed strategies to combat prejudice, racism and stereotyping.

Matriculation examinations were widened to include a range of languages used in the Australian community. Multilingual channels were introduced on radio and television. The SBS television channel, in particular, has been very successful in attracting viewers, including many monolingual English-speaking viewers.

Yet there were attacks on multiculturalism in the 1980s (for example, Blainey, 1980) and especially as a result of increased trade with Asia. According to Singh (1995) Australia's cultural mixing with Asia has accelerated over the last two decades and this has caused problems. Asian cultures are now firmly established within Australia and this has produced positive and negative effects. The contributions of Asian Australians in terms of cuisine, music, the visual arts and drama have been enormous. Yet conflicts have arisen from anti-Asian racist attacks and in some cases the media has sensationalised these acts of violence and vandalism.

Singh (1995) contends that Australia is being constructed from within and without, locally and globally. The Australian culture is a hybrid, and it has been affected by and continues to be influenced by Asian cultures. Fitzgerald (1990) contends that the Asian influence on the national vision in Australia is considerable. He concludes that Australia needs to become more Asianised in order to remain a prosperous and influential nation within the Asia-Pacific region (Parry, 1998).

The fragility of multiculturalism was highlighted in the late 1990s. A new political party, the One Nation party, led by a federal government independent, Pauline Hanson, was conceived in Queensland. The party espoused strong anti-Asian and anti-Aboriginal views (Parry, 1998). In her Maiden Speech to Parliament in December 1996, Hanson claimed that Australia is 'in danger of being swamped by Asians' and 'headed for civil war . . . Between 1984 and 1995, 40% of all migrants coming into this country were of Asian origin. They have their own culture and religion, from ghettos and do not assimilate.'

One Nation party meetings across Australia attracted large followings, especially from rural dwellers. The state elections in Queensland in 1998 provided a landslide victory for One Nation when 11 of the 79 One Nation candidates were elected to Parliament.

The Prime Minister, John Howard, may have unwillingly supported the One Nation party by his government's announcement of changes to the multicultural policy and by public statements made by his ministers that appeared to question the contribution of diverse cultural values (Parry, 1998).

The dissent and demonstrations that occurred across the country prior to the federal elections in 1998 had the potential to divide Australian society. The Liberal and National parties belatedly entered the fray in 1997 and denounced the racist policies of One Nation. The National Party, which had the most to lose in its rural electorates, vigorously criticised Pauline Hanson and her party. At the federal election in October 1998, One Nation fared very poorly and Pauline Hanson was not re-elected.

The One Nation party is still represented at state and federal levels and it may be that its agenda is still influencing government attitudes towards Asian migration although at a greatly reduced level. The authors of the One Nation Web page may have been overly optimistic in October 1998 when they concluded: 'Pauline Hanson will forever remain the spark that allowed Australians to question what they had not dared to before and for that we thank her and the enormous role that she played in this country's history' (p. 7). The Asian press have been alarmed by One Nation activities. Kell and Singh (1999) contend that Australia's image has been tarnished and that many Asians fear what is perceived to be racial vilification.

■ Major Terms in Multicultural Studies

There are a number of concepts which are central to understanding multicultural studies, such as culture, ethnicity, race, ethnocentrism, prejudice and pluralism. The first three are described in more detail in the subsequent sections.

Culture

The concept of culture is hard to define. Nelson (1992) defines culture as the pattern of life or system of beliefs characterised by unique artifacts and behaviours—including food, clothing, customs, housing, laws, crafts, tools, myths, language and religion. Two important elements about culture are that it is a very broad concept and that culture is learned. The culture of any country is constantly changing.

It is often argued that being part of a culture enables a person to be guided by a set of principles or rules of action on how to act in commonly recurring situations. Yet the principles or rules can be vague and even contradictory.

A one-culture outlook assumes that the principles and rules of action pertaining to that culture are all-embracing for everyone. This assimilationist stance does not consider the cultural heritage of others and is not generally accepted in contemporary Western societies.

A multicultural society supports and encourages the existence of a diversity of cultures. In practice, this is the major challenge for schools. As noted by Banks (1994), how do you create a cohesive and democratic society while at the same time allowing students to maintain their ethnic, cultural, socioeconomic and primordial identities? Put simply, how do you create equal educational opportunities for all students?

It is an extremely difficult task because all students learn differently, whether they are from the one culture or different cultures. Further, attitudes toward schools and teachers vary between cultures.

Ethnicity

Ethnic groups are characterised by specific values, perspectives and ideologies even though they can be all citizens within a mainstream society.

The concept of ethnicity refers to a feeling of identification or belonging to a particular culture. Persons can vary in their amount of intensity about an ethnic belonging. It can be reinforced and strengthened by associating with others sharing the same background.

In Australia the number of ethnic groups have risen considerably over recent decades. As depicted in Table 15.1, ethnic groups that have increased greatly in numbers include persons born in Hong Kong, Vietnam, Malaysia and South Africa. The Asian influence has been particularly marked. For example, perspectives from Australian Vietnamese (Wapner, 1995) and Australian Chinese (She, Colleen, 1995) provide fascinating insights.

Racism

According to Partington and McCudden (1992: 188) 'racism is a belief that one's perceived superiority is a consequence of genetic superiority. One is believed to be born superior.'

Racism is:

- intolerance or prejudice against particular groups or persons;
- often discriminatory;
- when minority viewpoints are excluded.·

Examples of racism include:

- name-calling;
- racial jokes;
- deliberate exclusion of someone because of race or culture.

Table 15.1 *Birthplace of settler arrivals*

| Birthplace | Percentage of total arrivals | | | | |
	1971–75	1976–80	1981–85	1986–90	1991–95
UK and Ireland	41.2	25.7	25.2	19.5	14.7
New Zealand	3.2	12.6	10.6	12.7	12.6
Italy	3.4	1.8	0.9	0.4	1.5
Yugoslavia	7.3	2.2	1.6	2.0	3.8
Greece	3.8	1.5	0.8	0.6	0.4
Vietnam	(b)	9.8	10.3	6.8	5.9
Germany	1.9	1.4	2.5	1.0	3.9
USA	3.6	1.7	1.8	1.5	2.3
Lebanon	2.3	4.9	1.5	2.4	1.5
Netherlands	1.0	1.3	1.4	0.4	1.3
India	2.2	1.2	1.8	2.4	5.5
South Africa	1.1	3.0	2.7	2.7	4.1
Poland	0.4	1.0	3.2	1.3	0.8
Turkey	2.2	1.4	0.8	0.9	0.6
Philippines	0.6	2.3	3.4	5.9	4.8
Malaysia	0.9	2.4	2.3	4.5	3.8
Hong Kong	(b)	1.5	2.2	5.1	5.7
Kampuchea	(b)	0.7	2.2	0.8	0.6
Other	24.9	23.6	24.8	29.1	26.2
Total	**100.0**	**100.0**	**100.0**	**100.0**	**100.0**

(a) Permanent arrivals only.

(b) The statistics for this country are not available but are included in 'Other'.

Source: Australian Bureau of Statistics (1996 Year Book: 173).

Yet the overwhelming evidence is that notions of race are socially constructed (Epstein, 1993). The biological variations between people of the same 'race' are even greater. However, it is still very common to use the term 'race' to categorise persons having certain essential characteristics.

'Racism' feeds on the concept of race. According to Epstein (1993) racism can best be understood in terms of a process which results in disadvantage for particular groups. Australians are often accused of being racist towards Aboriginals (Craven, 1999). A number of countries demonstrate racist (anti-semitic) behaviour against the Jews.

Racism is a process which changes over time and place. It can occur at macro levels (national and state) and also at micro (community) levels. Inevitably, prejudice and power play a part in the construction of racism, as do anxiety and fear.

In schools, trying to achieve access and equity for all students is complicated by racist attitudes and practices. Unfortunately personal and institutional racism is present in numerous schools. Many of the problems in schools, such as gang behaviour and team violence, can be attributable to racist roots (Parks, 1999). Racist beliefs and attitudes may have been socialised over a number of generations. Preventive measures to reduce racism such as conflict resolution and peer mediation can sometimes be effective. But it is also the case that students develop racist attitudes at a very young age—'they form their own impressions early on, and they sense the dissonance between the reality of life and the pretty pictures offered in school' (Elrich, 1994: 13).

■ National Goals, Concepts and Values and Multicultural Studies

In 1989, 10 national learning goals were publicly announced by state, territory and Commonwealth ministers at the Hobart Declaration on Schooling (Australian Education Council, 1989b). A number of these referred to multicultural priorities, namely:

To develop in students:

- a knowledge and appreciation of Australia's historical and geographic context;
- a knowledge of languages other than English;
- an understanding of, and concern for, balanced development and the global environment; and
- to provide students with an understanding and respect for our cultural heritage including the particular cultural background of Aboriginal and ethnic groups.

Subsequently the Australian Education Council's (AEC) Curriculum and Assessment Committee (CURASS) strove diligently to operationalise the goals into national statements and profiles for eight learning areas. The learning area most applicable to multicultural education was clearly studies of society and environment. The 1993 AEC meeting failed to get national agreement on the statements and profiles and, as a consequence, states and territories have developed their own variations.

The Victorian Board of Studies produced a Curriculum and Standards Framework for

Global perspective   Futures perspective

all schools in Victoria in 1996. A second document, entitled *Curriculum and Standards Framework II*, was trialled in 1999. A final edition is being distributed this year (2000).

In the Victorian learning area studies of society and environment, although the emphasis has changed to a marked concentration upon history, geography and economy and society, there is evidence of multicultural considerations. For example, the rationale refers to:

- the need to study communities and nation states at local, national and international levels;
- the need to develop students' knowledge and understanding of Australian society, within the Asia-Pacific region and as part of the wider global community.

A specific goal (one of five), states that 'students undertaking study in SOSE learn about cultures other than their own, and the contribution that these make to a unified and diverse society' (Board of Studies, Victoria, 1999: 418).

The Queensland School Curriculum Council produced a draft entitled *Studies of Society and Environment Key Learning Areas* in 1998. In it, four key values are emphasised, namely:

1. democratic process;
2. social justice;
3. ecological and economic sustainability;
4. peace.

Of these, 'social justice' is particularly relevant to multicultural education because it involves students understanding, reflecting on and applying such concepts as:

- equity and equality
- respect for diversity
- social well being
- human rights
- discrimination
- fairness
- anti-racism
- human welfare
- cultural sustainability
- disadvantage
- anti-sexism
- social sustainability

(Queensland School Curriculum Council, 1998: 3)

The human society and its environment K–6 syllabus, distributed by the Board of Studies in New South Wales in 1998, also emphasises multicultural education. In the introduction it is stated that:

> The content presented in this syllabus is inclusive of all learners. It incorporates gender, Aboriginal, citizenship, multicultural, environmental, work and global perspectives, and encourages the inclusion of studies of Asia where appropriate. It also recognises the importance of concepts that will support reconciliation between Aboriginal and non-Aboriginal Australians, such as the recognition of spirituality and shared heritage. (Board of Studies, New South Wales, 1998a: 5)

The four interrelated strands within the syllabus include:

- Change and Continuity
- Cultures
- Environments
- Social Systems and Structures.

The Cultures strand is particularly relevant:

In learning about cultures, students develop understanding about themselves, both as individuals and as members of groups. They identify and appreciate human similarities and differences. Understanding cultures helps students to relate to others in appropriate and socially just ways and to recognise the fact that, in democratic and culturally diverse societies, there are a variety of viewpoints that different people hold, and that these can influence behaviours.

Students learn that culture is transmitted by the shared understandings and practices of various groups based on inherent birthright, language, religion and belief systems, education, moral and ethical codes, the arts, symbolism, customs, rituals and practices such as rites of passage. Students need to understand the diverse cultures of Australia and their origins, including Aboriginal and Torres Straits Islander cultures and the shared Australian culture. They need to appreciate that cultures are dynamic and evolve over time. (Board of Studies, New South Wales, 1998: 10)

■ Teaching Approaches

It is one thing to espouse goals and concepts for multicultural education but a very different matter to develop appropriate teaching and learning activities in the classroom.

Banks (1997) contends that it is easier to describe the challenges than to conceptualise, develop and implement creative ways to deal with the challenges. He urges that the purpose of multicultural education is to help transform and reconstruct society. Yet it is evident that there are few schools that have been successful in developing a transformative role (Allen, 2000). There are many cases of 'soft' variations of multicultural education.

Sleeter (1991) identifies five different approaches, namely:

1. a human relations approach geared to increasing student sensitivity toward others;

2. an approach which caters for minority groups and focuses upon such aspects as self-esteem;
3. separate multicultural subjects or units;
4. mainstream teaching units which have been broadened to include various multicultural orientations;
5. mainstream teaching units which include a major transformative orientation and focus especially upon social justice.

Singer (1997) notes that approaches can vary from tokenism and little more than studies of heroes and holidays to in-depth studies. Teachers can organise their approach as a teaching unit of a few weeks within a subject (for example, no. 1 above), as a separate subject for specific students (for example, no. 2 above), as a separate elective subject (for example, no. 3 above) or as an integrated subject which encompasses a number of fields such as music, maths, art, science and literature (for example, nos 4 and 5 above).

There are of course various hazards for teachers involved in any of these approaches and some of these are listed in Table 15.2. Ideally, teachers in multicultural classrooms need a number of special qualities to overcome these hazards. Sklarz (1993) contends that a multicultural classroom needs a teacher who is aware of the cultural differences that affect learning styles, behaviour, mannerisms and relationships with school and home (see Table 15.3). According to Guild (1994) our ability to give every student a chance to succeed in school depends upon a full understanding of culture and learning styles.

In practice it is difficult for experienced teachers and newly appointed ones to have these skills (Allen and Labbo, 2000). As the majority of schools in Australia now have multicultural school populations, it is essential that preservice programs prepare student teachers for this actuality. Traditional, monocultural schools are now very rare, if they exist at all.

Larkin (1995) refers to the need for 'culturally responsive' teaching. It is not a particular method but a range of approaches which can foster growth in multicultural classrooms. The following approaches will be described further below:

• Inquiry
• Role playing
• Cooperative learning

Table 15.2 *Some potential difficulties for teachers in teaching multicultural studies*

1. Teachers need to be able to tolerate and mediate personal and group conflicts that naturally arise.
2. It is not helpful to focus on material aspects of a different culture ('museum approach').
3. Teachers must be able to create a classroom climate that encourages trust, respect and support.
4. Teachers need to be self-critical and to be ready to admit that they don't always have the answers.
5. Teachers should not assume that knowledge of a specific culture will necessarily lead to positive activities by the students.
6. Teachers need to be aware that schools are limited in dealing with sweeping social phenomena.
7. Teachers must be willing to see themselves as a resource and guide—they must be willing to experiment with new materials and approaches.

Source: After Dilg (1999) and McLean (1987).

Table 15.3 *Self-rating for teachers of multicultural studies*

Select your preferred response to each of the following questions

A. *What is the most important thing students can gain from interacting with students from other cultures?*
Select one of the following answers:
1. Ability to communicate and work together
2. Understand how we are different
3. Ability to accept people from different cultures

B. *How do students develop a positive cultural identity?*
Select one of the following answers:
1. Provide opportunities for students to learn about different cultural groups
2. Celebrate holidays of different ethnic groups
3. Provide role-playing opportunities for individuals and groups

C. *How do you resolve conflicts of values between students in a class?*
Select one of the following answers:
1. Role play conflict situations
2. Prevent students from discussing issues that could lead to conflicts
3. Read literature accounts of conflict
4. Discuss issues of racism and disadvantage

- Literature-based activities
- Story writing.

Inquiry

An inquiry approach has considerable potential in a multicultural classroom because it enables students to range across a number of learning areas (see also Chapter 10). As noted by Craven (1999) the apparent boundaries between the disciplines disappear when students begin using inquiry tools. There are no single, correct solutions. It encourages students to consider a range of perspectives in keeping with diverse multicultural interests.

Campbell (1996) argues that inquiry approaches are crucial for minority cultures and that 'students of colour and the poor receive least training in this area' (p. 213). The poor and minority students are regularly assigned to basic track classes and don't get the opportunity to develop critical thinking skills.

Singer (1999) recommends combining multicultural education with an inquiry-based approach. He suggests that student-generated questions, especially about social justice, are at the heart of curriculum and can lead to other questions about the past, present and future. However, he warns that opening up classrooms to student voices can lead to unexpected, unpalatable discussions and even heated arguments.

There are a variety of classroom activities that can be used to develop these inquiry approaches (see Tables 15.4 and 15.5). Chartock (1991) advocates a links curriculum whereby students research the links between them and the rest of the world. Additionally, the Board of Studies, New South Wales (1998) has developed a number of learning activities for primary school students under the theme 'This is Me!'.

Cushner (1998) provides a sense of questions that might be used by students for self-reflection and in interviews (Table 15.6). He suggests that it helps students to analyse some cultural differences face to face.

Table 15.4 *Steps in constructing a links curriculum for multicultural studies*

1. In small groups, brainstorm links already known about by class members (e.g. local industry ties with Asian countries).
2. Concentrate upon business, educational and cultural links.
3. Decide which tasks each student member will pursue, for example conduct interviews, check out resources in newspapers and on the World Wide Web, prepare a display.
4. Prepare presentations on countries and the links.
5. Present the project to the class.

Source: After Chartock (1991).

Table 15.5 *Finding out about me*

Some useful learning experiences for young children include:

· Request children to ask parents to explain why their first and middle names were chosen.
· Do any prefer a nickname? What does it mean?
· Ask children to work in pairs so that they are with a child from a different ethnic group. Each partner is to say the other's name and to write it in their language; write out a brief greeting in the other's language.
· Have children trace each other on butcher paper. Outlines are coloured by each child, cut out and displayed in the classroom.

Role playing

Role playing is an important technique for exploring social problems, especially those relating to multicultural issues (see Chapter 11). Apart from giving participants the opportunity to learn new content or skills, role playing gives participants the opportunity to understand the feelings of others. A particular form of role playing, 'socio-drama', can be used to help students and teachers to recognise and solve problems together. However, as noted by Nelson (1992) socio-drama requires:

* considerable practice;
* a positive environment for student discussion;
* exploring through role playing, issues that are of genuine concern to the students;
* a tolerance of no 'right' answers and an acceptance of ambiguity.

It is important to distinguish between the planning and managing of role plays. In *planning* a role play (e.g. community reaction to the location of a new hospital for the mentally disabled), it is necessary to plan the cast of players very carefully, to arrange for any props and to select a suitable location for performing the role play. *Management* of a role play, according to the Board of Studies, New South Wales (1998) consists of briefing the students, stopping the drama after main behaviours have occurred, re-enacting parts of the role play and debriefing participants.

Role plays associated with multicultural topics are included in many simulation games such as 'Survival and Hope' (Global Education Centre, 1996), 'No Friends but the Mountains' (Major, 1996), 'Starpower' (Western Behavioural Sciences Institute, 1969), 'Rafa Rafa' (Shirts, 1976) (see Chapter 11).

Cooperative learning

Cooperative learning provides special opportunities for students to appreciate and

Table 15.6 *Learning about others*

Reflect on and provide answers to the following questions:

a. Whom should you obey? Why?
b. Who makes decisions (at home, school, community)? Why?
c. How should you behave with others (elders, children, neighbours)? Why?
d. Whom should you respect? How do you show respect? Why?
e. How should you act in public so you bring credit or honour to your family? Why?
f. What does it mean to be successful in life? Why?
g. Whom should you trust? Why?
h. What are the signs of success? Why?
i. What provides 'security' in life? Why?
j. Whom should your friends be? Who decides? Why?
k. Where, and with whom, should you live? Why?
l. Whom should you marry? At about what age? Who decides? Why?
m. What is expected of children when they are young? Why?
n. What should you depend on others for? Why?
o. When should you be self-sufficient, if ever? Why?
p. What should you expose to others, and what should be kept private? Why?
q. How should you plan for your future? Why?
r. What should be remembered from your heritage? Why?
s. What was better when you were younger or during your parents' youth? Why?
t. What do you wish for your children that you could not have? Why?

Select another student who is from a different culture and use some of the above questions to interview him/her.

Try to identify areas where there are clear differences between your answers and the person you interviewed.

Were there areas where you were in agreement with each other?

Prepare a short paper that summarises your findings.

Source: Cushner (1998: 133).

learn about multicultural issues (see Chapter 4).

Small groups which adopt cooperative learning principles require students to work together and collectively to achieve certain goals. In this situation, students will often have to work cooperatively with students from other racial, ethnic and religious backgrounds. They will want to stimulate and support each other—to edit each other's work—to listen to and respect other points of view.

According to Singer (1997) cooperative learning groups can only be successful if:

- team members are held collectively and individually accountable for learning by group members;
- team members have the opportunity to play both leadership and supporting roles;
- team members learn how to run meetings, make decisions, divide responsibilities and evaluate progress.

Teachers need to build on the diversity of backgrounds and interests of students

The jigsaw group is a particular type of cooperative learning whereby a topic is analysed and broken down into smaller tasks or activities. Each small group is allocated one of the jigsaw tasks to study. Each group in turn reports back their findings so that eventually a complete picture is built up. This approach can be used very successfully with multicultural topics such as case studies on power, racism and prejudice.

Parent–school evenings provide opportunities for celebrating multiculturalism

Enjoying the spirit of being Australian

Literature-based activities

As noted above, many teachers in Australian schools have homogenous, European backgrounds, even though this is changing. For these teachers to appreciate multicultural perspectives they need to immerse themselves in different cultures, even if this is done vicariously through literature.

Childrens' books based on different cultures are becoming increasingly available from publishers and at relatively low prices. Libraries are also giving much higher priority to multicultural books for students. Even more significant are the rapidly increasing number of materials available on CD-ROM and the World Wide Web (see Chapter 12).

It is vital for students to read about their own culture and to see their lifestyle valued. It can be equally powerful for teachers who have little experience of other cultures.

Klasson-Endrizzi and Ruiz (1995) suggest

that teachers should use 'literature circles', small groups reading from and discussing a specific book. These literature discussions can be a huge awakening and can lead to an explosion of thoughts and ideas. Students will often use these discussions to reveal their own cultural beliefs and understandings to one another.

Van Ausdall (1994) notes that the impetus for literature-based activities rests with the teachers. They have to want to gather literature materials, to want to correspond with teachers worldwide, and to want to develop and grow as multicultural members of a global society.

Story writing

Cushner (1992) argues that one of the major problems for teachers involved in multicultural topics is how to encourage students to reveal aspects of their *subjective* culture. Their *objective* culture is tangible and visible—their dress, mannerisms and food choices. Subjective culture refers to the less tangible aspects such as their values, attitudes and norms.

Storytelling and story writing is a very effective way to explore values and attitudes. Chapin and Messick (1999) suggest using familiar stories such as *The Little Red Hen* to encourage primary school students to develop global versions. As an example, for bread, in *The Little Red Hen*, students might substitute tortillas, pita or fry-bread.

Cushner (1992) cites collaborative story-writing projects he has developed within and between countries. For example, a story was developed up to a point of climax by 4th grade students in Ohio, USA. Then a group of similar-aged students in a school in India completed the story. The endings provided by the Indian students produced surprises for the American students. Quite possibly the Indian students were equally surprised by the initial part of the story developed by the American students. With the use of email facilities it is now far easier for teachers and students to develop partnership story projects between countries.

■ Resources

There is a vast array of materials available within the field of multiculturalism. They include kits and textbooks, trade books (includes fiction, biographies) and various booklets and magazines. In addition, there are now numerous materials available on the World Wide Web and CD-ROMs.

With all these materials, teachers and students need to be aware of bias. Many of the materials have been produced by organisations which are responsible for disseminating specific messages, which, in many cases, can be very limiting.

Some examples of resources available are listed below.

Kits and books

Berger, J. (1996) *The Gaia Atlas of First People*. Sydney: Penguin.

Council for Aboriginal Reconciliation (1997) *The Path to Reconciliation*. Canberra: Council for Aboriginal Reconciliation.

Council for Aboriginal Reconciliation (1997) *Walking Together*. Canberra: Council for Aboriginal Reconciliation.

D'Angelo, P. (1991) *Becoming Australian*. Melbourne: Cambridge University Press.

Department of School Education (1996) *Years 5–6 Global Education Resource Kit*. Sydney: Department of School Education.

Hamston, J. and Murdoch, K. (1996) *Integrating Socially*. Armidale: Eleanor Curtain Publishing.

Nayler, J. (ed.) (1997) *Gender Up Front: Strategies for a Gender Focus Across the Key Learning Areas*. Caloundra: Association of Women Educators.

Newell, S. and Stubbs, B. (1991) *Co-Investigators*. Brisbane: Jacaranda Milton.

Pike, G. and Selby, D. (1988) *Global Teacher, Global Learner*. London: Hodder and Stoughton.

Queensland Department of Education (1994) *Anti-racism Policy*. Brisbane: Queensland Department of Education.

Queensland Government (1998) *Queensland Ethnic and Multicultural Affairs Policy: A Framework for the Management of Cultural Diversity in Queensland*. Brisbane: Queensland Department of Education.

Sidoti, C. (1997) 'Children as citizens,' *Social Educator*, 15, 3.

Suzuki, D. (1993) *Time to Change*. Toronto: Allen & Unwin.

Vasta, E. and Castles, S. (1994) *The Teeth are Smiling: The Persistence of Racism in Multicultural Australia*. Brisbane: Jacaranda.

Trade books

Ashabranner, B. (1986) *Children of the Maya*. New York: Dodd, Mead.

Ashabranner, B. (1984) *To Live in Two Worlds*. New York: Dodd, Mead.

Bode, J. (1989) *Different Worlds*. New York: Franklin Watts.

Coghill, L., Ketchell, J., Martin, K. and Prize, K. (1997) *Aboriginal Studies and Torres Strait Islands Studies: footprints . . . to country, kin and cultures*. Melbourne: Curriculum Corporation.

World Wide Web

Search Engines

http://server1.anzwers.ozemail.net/—Define the ANZWERS you want

http://www.altavista.yellowpages.com.au/—The Alta Vista search

http://www.askjeeves.com/—Ask Jeeves

http://www.hotbot.com—HotBot

http://www.metafind.com/—MetaFind Your Search Spot on the Net

http://www.Yahoo.com.au/—Yahoo! Australia and NZ

Specific references on the Web

http://www.ausaid.gov.au/—AusAid

http://www.austlii.edu.au/links/Australia/Subjects/Aboriginal—includes Torres Strait Islanders

http://www.caa.org.au/—Community Aid Abroad

http://www.hrweb.org/—Human Rights on the Web

United Nations web site

www.un.org/rights/50/kit5.htm

CD-ROMS

Long-time, olden time Aboriginal accounts of Northern Territory, Firmware, Penrith.

Indigenous Australians: an Aboriginal community focus, TAFE Commission, New South Wales.

Chronicle of the 20th Century (1996), DK Multimedia, New South Wales.

Os id—the search for Australian heritage and identity (1994), Board of Studies, New South Wales.

Wayback when: colonial Australian life, Board of Studies, New South Wales.

■ Concluding Comments

Multicultural studies are critical for teachers and students living and working in Australia. Although education administrators appear to be more interested in standards and testing, there is an urgency for schools to have a broad focus whereby diverse student groups can grapple with issues of equity, justice and democracy.

Multiculturalism in Australia developed rapidly during the 1970s and 1980s. During the 1990s there were signs of fragility, if not decline.

Curricula developed nationally, and by individual states, have the potential to promote multicultural goals but this will depend in turn upon the expertise and motivation of teachers and the support provided by education and community agencies.

QUESTIONS AND ACTIVITIES

1. 'The gains of the 1980s in terms of a multicultural perspective in schools have been replaced by a tiredness and smugness and covert hostility which has crept in' (Cahill, 1996: 146).

    Describe some of the developments in the 1980s. What were some significant events in the 1990s? What appears to be the emphasis in the first decade of the twenty-first century?

2. Describe your most vivid memory of an incident involving racial or ethnic differences. Who was targeted and by whom? What events occurred? What was the final outcome? In hindsight, could other strategies have been used to produce a more positive outcome?

3. 'Perceptions that Australian schools are hotbeds of racist, inter-ethnic or sectarian violence or vilification are ill-founded and simply wrong, but racism has a persistent presence in most schools with a probable recent increase' (Cahill, 1996: 121).

    What are some teaching techniques that might be used to reduce racism spreading in a school?

4. 'Multicultural education is a continuing process. One of its major goals in schools is to create justice, equality and freedom' (Banks, 1997: 68).

    Give specific examples of teaching strategies you would use to further these goals.

5. In the early decades of the twentieth century 'whites were held to be superior to Asians, Aborigines and other non-Europeans' (McKay and Pittam, 1993: 17).

    Describe how multicultural policies have reduced, but not entirely eliminated, this stance. Reflect on the mix of ethnic groups at your school. What strategies are used to bring about equity?

16

Gender and Schooling

Introduction

An awareness of gender and its construction, and a resultant commitment to overcome gender inequalities and sexism, should be a core professional responsibility for all Australian teachers.

Teachers are responsible for both monitoring and crafting the messages about gender that schooling delivers to girls and boys. It is now clear that schooling is the medium for a myriad of messages about gender, which are both explicitly and implicitly transmitted to students and teachers. The unspoken messages and ways in which knowledge is constructed in the practices and processes of schooling are referred to as the 'hidden curriculum'. Gender is actively constructed through many aspects of the hidden curriculum (see Box 16.1).

Due to the subject matter, the teacher of studies of society and environment is uniquely placed to assist students in examining social justice issues such as gender, class and race. Because studies of society and environment focuses on people as social beings, as they interact with one another, with the natural and social environment, and in various places through time, it provides an ideal opportunity for teachers and students to examine the construction, constraints and effects of gender. While it appears that boys and girls have largely been offered equal access to subjects found in

351

> **Box 16.1** *Gender and the hidden curriculum*
>
> The unspoken messages and ways in which knowledge is constructed in the practices and processes of schooling are referred to as the 'hidden curriculum'. Gender is actively constructed in the lives of students and teachers through the following aspects of the hidden curriculum:
>
> · school organisation;
> · curriculum offerings;
> · timetabling practices;
> · disciplinary procedures;
> · allocation and use of playground space;
> · post-school expectations;
> · school uniforms;
> · teaching resources; and
> · language used in textbooks.

studies of society and the environment, there is ample evidence that boys and girls have nevertheless had different experiences and have exhibited differing patterns of participation in this key learning area.

While teachers and education systems clearly have a responsibility to actively promote social justice, and to make every effort to achieve equitable outcomes for both girls and boys, it must be noted that education systems are not solely responsible for the inequalities which schooling conveys. This is because schools do not exist in social isolation, but are interconnected with broader societal trends and changes. This two-way process means that societal changes will be reflected in schools, and that changes which are implemented within schools will be reflected in society.

A great deal of research on gender and education has taken place in Australia over the past decade. This research has been located in a variety of disciplines such as education, sociology, philosophy, cultural studies, women's studies and history. Both the research and the gender reform programs which have ensued from the research findings have been the result of collaborations between academics, teachers, bureaucrats, teachers' unions, professional associations, parent bodies and students. This research has concluded that although great gains have been made, true gender equity cannot be said to have been achieved in Australian education. Despite extensive gender reform programs over the past two decades, there is ample evidence that sexism remains widespread and endemic. Kenway *et al.* (1997: 210) revealed in their recent research on gender that progress in the gender debate has stalled and that 'gender reform was on the wane almost everywhere'.

Reform work with girls and boys in Australian schools in the 1970s initially used the term 'sex differences' when referring to males and females. Since the early 1980s, participants in the gender debate have drawn a distinction between notions of sex and gender, and 'gender' has become the preferred term (see Table 16.1). The change from the term 'sex' to 'gender' was informed by a shift away from essentialism, which views the characteristics of males and females as predetermined and biologically given. In contrast to essentialism, a social construction framework rejects the predetermined definitions of masculinity and femininity associated with biological characteristics and instead regards gender as being socially constructed by discourses. A discourse may be described as a set of beliefs, meanings or practices about a given area.

Table 16.1 *Terms and definitions*

Perspective	Term	Definition
Essentialism	Sex	Biologically given characteristics such as reproductive characteristics, X or Y chromosomes, which are predetermined and fixed at birth.
Social construction	Gender	Socially constructed notions of maleness and femaleness, which are constructed through discourses and social practices.

Although gender is constructed differently over time and place, all cultures experience inequality between men and women. The social construction of gender can be used as a mechanism for sustaining male power and dominance (Cockburn, 1985: 168). Gender is constructed by a society in the ways in which it structures families, education and the workforce. Schools are undoubtedly a key site for the social construction of gender. The management, disciplinary procedures and curriculum practices of schools determine the social expressions and construction of gender for both students and teachers.

■ Schools: A Gendered Experience for Students?

Over the past couple of decades, all Australian states and territories have produced various policy statements and directives aimed to reduce sexism and gender bias in schooling. These policies have attempted to bring about equality between the sexes and to examine the effects of gender at the classroom, school and system levels.

These national and state policies evolved as it became apparent that for the greater part of Australia's history the type of schooling offered to boys and girls has been vastly different, in terms of curriculum offerings, subject participation rates, retention rates and post-school destinations. Sadly, despite a great deal of goodwill, research, funding and effort committed to two decades of national and state gender reforms, differential outcomes from schooling still exist for girls in comparison to boys.

The gendered life experience which students bring to the classroom will affect the students' frame of reference in terms of their gender, class and race positionings (Stephens, 1997). In turn, the messages students take from schooling will shape their beliefs about gender, class and race. Lundeberg (1997: 55) believes that subtle gender bias is often present in classrooms, but teachers and preservice teachers may not notice it, at least on a conscious level. Lundeberg (1997: 55) also notes that many studies demonstrate that male students still participate more in class than female students and that male students still receive more attention and more specific feedback from teachers.

When examining the outcomes from schooling for boys and girls, it is unhelpful and rather simplistic merely to ask whether either girls or boys are failing to do well in schools. Rather, Yates (1993: 46) claims that it is more important to explore the messages girls and boys 'are learning from the different experiences

Mothers have to cope with balancing family and work

they have in school, and why they develop the outcomes they do'. Given the pivotal role that schooling clearly plays in the construction of adolescent gender identity, it is essential that as far as possible teachers ensure that schooling ceases to offer negative messages about gender. It is important that all males and all females are offered equitable outcomes from their schooling, regardless of their gender or the types of masculinities or femininities they wish to pursue.

■ Schools: A Gendered Workplace for Teachers?

Not only do schools provide a gendered experience for students, but they also provide a gendered experience for teachers. Although gradual and positive changes have occurred within schools for teachers, schools nevertheless remain a gendered workplace and teaching remains a gendered profession. Teachers, like students, bring gendered experiences from their lives to their teaching. An examination of both teachers' gendered life experiences prior to teaching and their gendered teaching experiences within schools is necessary in order to understand the roles teachers will subsequently play in gender reform work for students in schools. A 1994 report, *Women in the Teaching Profession* (Milligan, 1994: 9), observes that gender is a powerful factor in the daily lives of school teachers, and that 'only an incomplete understanding of schooling is possible if gender dynamics for teachers are ignored'.

The literature on gender and labour reveals that 'occupations, as well as individuals, are gendered' (Williams, 1993: x), and that most jobs in our society are clearly divided into 'men's work' and 'women's work' (Williams, 1993: 1). Further, Cockburn (1985: 169) notes that occupations and jobs are a two-way process: 'people have a gender and their gender rubs off on the jobs they mainly do. The jobs in turn have a gender character, which rubs off on the people who do them'. The sexual division of labour in our society has proved markedly resilient through time and place, and 'there is no evidence at all that the sexual division of labour is breaking down' (Game and Pringle, 1983: 93). Phillips and Taylor (1980: 55) observe that 'even when men and women do work in the same industry, sexual demarcations are still rigidly maintained' and that we see a 'clear distinction between "men's work" and "women's work", with women's work almost invariably characterised by lower pay, lack of craft traditions, weak union organization, and unskilled status'.

Segregation in the teaching workforce

Lee and Taylor (1996: 57) report that 'Australia has the most gender-segregated workforce in the OECD'. It appears that the workforce in schools is also heavily gender segregated. Labour force gender segregation can occur as vertical and/or horizontal segregation. Horizontal segregation is the grouping of men and women in different jobs (see Table 16.2). A second form of horizontal segregation takes place when men and women perform the same job, but perform different tasks and functions as a form of internal stratification or demarcation between the genders within the job. Vertical segregation is the grouping of men in the most senior and highly paid jobs in an occupation, while women occupy jobs with lower status and pay. Teaching has a vertically segregated workforce, with men occupying the majority of executive positions, and a horizontally gender-segregated workforce with women constituting the majority of teachers and internal stratification taking place between men and women who perform the same job.

In 1998, the percentage of male and female teachers in Australia was as shown in Table 16.3.

Table 16.2 *Definitions of horizontal and vertical segregation*

Horizontal segregation	· The grouping of men and women in different jobs; or · Men and women perform the same job, but specialise in different tasks and functions.
Vertical segregation	· The grouping of men in the senior, highly paid jobs, and women in the jobs with lower status and pay.

Table 16.3 *Percentage of male/female teachers in the Australian workforce, 1998*

	% Male	% Female
Primary teachers	23	77
Secondary teachers	46	54
Total teaching force	34	66

Source: Australian Bureau of Statistics (1998).

We are all different shapes ...

... and sizes.

We all have different ideas and personalities, but sometimes people expect us to enjoy certain things ...

... even when we are good at others ...

DON'T be squeezed into a box all your life ... Be free, try hard and you can do *ANYTHING*!!

Clearly, women currently constitute the majority of Australian teachers, forming 66 per cent of the teaching population (see Table 16.3). Throughout most of Australia's history, teaching has been viewed as a largely female occupation, and there is evidence that this trend is increasing. The percentage of female teachers in Australia was 62 per cent in 1992 and 60 per cent in 1984. Jobs which are statistically dominated by women are often linked to stereotypes about 'feminine', nurturing qualities where women are called on to provide services, take care of people and provide emotional labour. *Women in the Teaching Profession* (Milligan, 1994: 1) directly links women's higher numbers in schools with their lower occupational and societal status.

An examination of the internal workings of a primary school reveals significant horizontal segregation, with male and female teachers performing vastly different tasks and functions (see Table 16.4). Male primary teachers are

Table 16.4 *Horizontal and vertical segregation in the teaching force*

	In primary school, are more likely to	In secondary school, are more likely to
Male teachers	Occupy executive positions Teach upper grades Be responsible for Sport Be responsible for IT	Occupy executive positions Teach senior grades Teach science, industrial arts, agriculture
Female teachers	Be classroom teachers Teach lower grades Be responsible for charity organisations, choir	Be classroom teachers Teach junior grades Teach ESL, languages, home economics, library

more likely to occupy executive positions, teach upper grades and take responsibility for sport and information technology. Female primary teachers are less likely to occupy executive positions, and will probably teach lower primary grades and take responsibility for choir, charity work, humanities and literacy. While the percentage of male and female secondary school teachers appears to be more closely balanced than primary teaching, a closer examination of individual teaching disciplines within secondary schools also reveals the presence of horizontal segregation, with male and female teachers performing different tasks. *Women in the Teaching Profession* (Milligan, 1994: 7) reveals that 'men predominate in management roles, in teaching of older students, in teaching of industrial arts, agriculture and science'. In contrast, 'women predominate as classroom teachers, in

teaching of young children, remedial students and students who have English as a second language, in teaching of home economics and languages, in special education and as librarians'. *Women in the Teaching Profession* (Milligan, 1994: 9) also observes that 'schools are places where most of the junior staff are women, most of the senior staff are men, and even when this is not the case, the work is divided into "men's work" and "women's work".'

Schools also exhibit vertical segregation within the teaching force. In 1994 the percentage of male and female school principals in Australia was as shown in Table 16.5.

In secondary teaching, although males occupy 46 per cent of teaching positions, they occupy 83 per cent of principalships (see Table 16.5). In primary teaching, while males occupy only 23 per cent of teaching positions, they

Table 16.5 *Percentage of male/female principals in Australian workforce, 1994*

	% Male	% Female
Primary school principals	70	30
Secondary school principals	83	17
Total school principals	74	26

Source: Grady *et al.* (1994).

occupy 70 per cent of principalships. *Women in the Teaching Profession* (Milligan, 1994) records that although there is a detectable decrease in gender segregation, women remain heavily underrepresented in school leadership and promotions positions, and the improvement in their position is very slow. The recent Senate Inquiry into the Status of Teaching, *A Class Act*, (Senate Employment, Education and Training References Committee, 1998: 120) also concludes that 'given their total numbers in the teaching force, female teachers are grossly under-represented in promotion positions'.

■ Teachers as Gender Reformers

On a daily basis, teachers are faced with innumerable choices between a continuation of the status quo, or the implementation of change and reform. Such daily choices may include the structure of lessons, classroom procedures, evaluation and assessment, classroom management and styles of teaching. Cochran-Smith (1991: 18) claims that 'teaching is fundamentally a political activity in which every teacher plays a part, whether by design or by default'. Teachers therefore make decisions each day as to what stance they will take, whether they will perpetuate injustices such as sexism, or whether they will work to change and reform injustices. Cochran-Smith (1991: 18) believes that teaching is 'part of a larger struggle' and teachers therefore 'have a responsibility to reform, not just replicate, standard school practices'. Teachers who work towards reforming schools have been variously described as reformers, change-agents or as 'teaching against the grain'. Such work always

involves change, as taken for granted assumptions and practices are re-examined and unsettled.

The choice of teachers to work towards reform affords certain satisfactions and rewards, but also introduces other struggles and difficulties. The satisfactions include the sense of professional pride, efficacy and agency which arises from addressing long-standing injustices. Unlike external researchers, teachers are able to work as an insider in schools, implementing and monitoring action research on a daily basis. The difficulties and challenges for teachers involved in gender reform include the following:

- the need to examine the role of gender in their own lives and schooling;
- coming to terms with the contradictory nature of the literature on gender;
- dealing with resistance and other teachers' negative attitudes towards reform; and
- finding ways to work with the various discourses which are found in schools.

Personal reflections

Before participating in reform and examining the role of gender in the lives of students, teachers must first examine the construction of gender in their own lives and reflect upon their own gendered experiences of schooling. Kenway *et al.* (1997: 175) believe that a 'range of conscious and preconscious discourses inform teachers' responses to gender reform, some deeply personal, others deeply professional and political'. Because of individual teachers' different life histories, there are therefore great differences in teachers' enthusiasm for, commitment to and ability to handle reform.

Involvement in gender reform at the classroom, school and system level necessitates personal and institutional change. Kenway *et al.* (1997: 30) argue that gender reform tries to 'unsettle the settled', and that it 'messes with institutional and community traditions and cultures and individual psyches'. Such changes will inevitably be met with some resistance and negative reactions from other teachers, some of whom accept and are supportive of gender reform, and others who are not supportive and view it as a divisive or contentious issue. Even when people are willing to make changes to bring about reform, change can nevertheless be viewed as threatening and difficult. Kenway *et al.* (1997: 89) observe 'how difficult it is to rearrange one's habits, even when willing to do so'. It cannot be assumed that merely pointing out the need for gender reform will automatically lead to commitment and change in teachers and schools. Despite a great deal of knowledge, commitment and goodwill on the part of gender reformers, gender reform has not always been achieved. Kenway *et al.* (1997: 16) conclude that 'goodwill and good intentions are insufficient'.

Even when teachers and preservice teachers are committed to gender reform, the literature, research and populist discourse on gender are frequently contradictory and the issues are increasingly complex. Kenway *et al.* (1997: xv) reveal that 'as the issues have become more subtle, the theories designed to address them have become more complex'. Contradictions about gender abound and it is extremely difficult for the teacher to make sense of the conflicting data. Davies (1994: 264) points out that 'there is no simple recipe

for change in relation to gender inequality'.

Discourses in education

Schools and teaching are influenced and dominated by many different discourses. The success or otherwise of gender reform programs is partially dependent on the current prevailing discourses at the school and system level. For example, in recent years many schools have participated in a discourse of self-governance, which grants greater autonomy to the school and less dependence on central policy initiatives and guidelines. Such a move has implications for gender reform, as these initiatives have traditionally been both centrally initiated and monitored. Under self-governance, gender equity issues may be ignored at the school level, and those who wish to pursue them may find themselves isolated and unsupported. Blackmore (1994: 10) claims that 'research on equity programs with respect to socio-economic disadvantage and gender indicates the need for a combination of central policy guidelines and prescriptions and school based bottom up initiatives, the central policies often merely to legitimate and reinforce existing school-based curriculum and equity programs'.

Curricular discourses

Other discourses found in schools also have a bearing on the implementation of gender reform programs. Kemmis, Cole and Suggett (1994: 129) have identified and analysed three curricular orientations or discourses which may be found in schools, each embodying quite specific beliefs and values about people, power and the role of education in society. These discourses are:

- the vocational/neoclassical;
- the liberal/progressive; and
- the socially critical.

The *vocational/neoclassical* orientation appears to be a particularly dominant discourse in many schools today, and the beliefs inherent in this discourse will impact upon attempts at gender reform. The vocational discourse views education as a preparation for work and the school's role as being one of selecting and preparing students to find their rightful place in society (Kemmis *et al.*, 1994: 129). Grundy *et al.* (1994: 115) note that within this discourse 'it is not the responsibility of the school to try to redress any inequalities that might exist in society, but rather to create products that will fulfil the needs of that particular society'. A school immersed in a vocational discourse will not necessarily see it as the responsibility of the school to unsettle or challenge the status quo. While teachers may choose to pursue gender and other social justice reforms within any discourse operating in schools, it is clear that some discourses make the task easier than others.

Reform and the beginning teacher

Involvement in reform and teaching against the grain can be difficult for experienced teachers, but it is especially difficult for beginning and preservice teachers who may prefer to focus on survival and on learning the craft of teaching and the politics and routines of the school. In addition to competing priorities such as these, beginning teachers may not believe that their teacher training has prepared them for dealing with social justice issues such as gender reform. Trotman (1994: 19)

believes that the preparation of teachers is 'steeped in gendered practice', and does not always adequately prepare preservice and beginning teachers for the important task of gender reform.

Every student in Australian schools has a right to equitable access to positive school experiences and optimal learning outcomes, regardless of their gender, class or race. Irrespective of the approach to curriculum which the individual teacher, and indeed the school, may wish to adopt on the issue of gender in education, there nevertheless remains an onus on all teachers to ensure that the learning opportunities they provide are just and equitable. In order to implement the necessary changes to curriculum and schooling practices and bring about gender reform, teachers need adequate support, encouragement and guidance in their workplaces. The teacher of studies of society and environment has unique opportunities to examine the messages about gender that students receive in the classroom, the school and in the broader society and culture. However, in order for teachers to commit themselves to gender reform, it is important first to understand the history and development of gender debates in Australian schooling, which is outlined in the following section.

■ Changing Notions of Gender through Time and Place

Since the mid-1970s, gender equity has been named by teachers, educators, policy writers, researchers, politicians and the media as an important educational concern in Australia. In the early years this attention was primarily focused on the experience and outcomes of girls in schools, but in more recent

Father hanging out washing

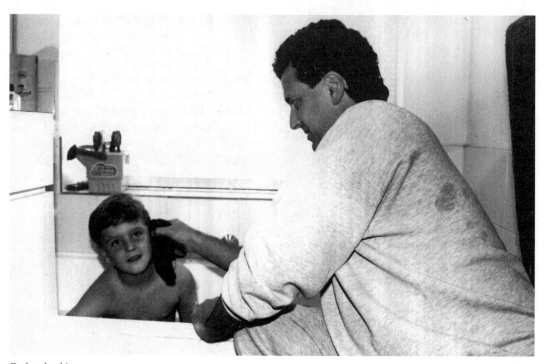

Father bathing son

years attention has increasingly turned to the education of boys. An examination of these gender equity reform programs in Australian schools provides a contradictory picture of great gains achieved on the one hand, and very little progress or change on the other. This contradiction is undoubtedly matched by similar gains and losses within the broader Australian society and workforce.

The changing notions of gender through time and place have come about as a result of shifts in prevailing beliefs, ideologies and theories in society. Different ideologies can be seen to have generated different questions and ways of viewing gender reform. Throughout the past two decades, the focus of gender reform, the questions which are asked, the categories for research, the programs which are implemented and the 'solutions' which are offered have changed according to the beliefs, discourses and hegemonic practices dominant within the education sector and Australian society. In particular, differing perspectives of feminism and masculinity have yielded different constructions of and solutions to the 'problem'. While most gender reform work in schools in the 1980s emanated from the perspective of liberal feminism, the gender reforms of the 1990s have been influenced by disparate and often contradictory discourses or perspectives such as poststructural feminism, pro-feminist masculinity and men's rights masculinity (see Table 16.6).

Although schooling can be seen to have been inequitable for boys and girls throughout most of Australia's history, concerns about gender in schooling are a relatively recent phenomenon. Branson (1991: 96) has pointed out that 'prior to the mid 1970s gender was invisible as a problem for research in education'. Yates (1993: 25) also notes that until 'the 1970s, many reports did not break down statistics by sex', and that those 'which did note different patterns for girls as compared to boys accepted these as reflections of innate differences, or as appropriate given different social roles of men and women'. Yates (1993: 25) believes that the 'particular "facts" researchers choose to gather, and the questions they ask about what they find, are both closely related to more general values about what is important in schooling, and these have changed markedly in relation to gender'. Not only are the curriculum and practices of schools a reflection of a particular time and culture, but even the topics for research and analysis are historical and

Boys cooking

Table 16.6 *Definitions of feminisms and masculinities*

Perspective	Definition
Liberal feminism	Aims to grant women equal access to public life, power and work which has formerly belonged to the male side of the male/female dualism. Is regarded as essentialist, because it accepts the male/female dualism.
Poststructural feminism	Aims to locate and name the discourses through which gender is socially constructed and to deconstruct the male/female dualism.
Pro-feminist masculinity	Is sympathetic to feminism, rejects essentialism and also seeks to deconstruct the male/female dualism.
Men's rights masculinity	Is essentialist and sees men as the victims of all types of feminism. Seeks to maintain the male/female dualism.

cultural constructs which point to the societal concerns of the time.

■ The Education of Girls

Girls, school and society
In early 1974, at the request of the Minister for Education, Mr Kim Beazley (Senior), the Commonwealth Schools Commission set up a Committee on Social Change and the Education of Women. The committee met throughout 1974, investigating the educational needs of women and girls in Australia. In November 1975, the committee presented its report (see Table 16.7), entitled *Girls, School and Society.* This landmark document 'is now seen as a watershed in educational thinking in Australia' (Commonwealth Schools Commission, 1984: 1). The report was radical, far reaching in its claims and bold in naming the causes and consequences of inequitable schooling for girls and boys. In the Preface, the committee unequivocally stated the rationale that 'it is only if we educate women and men equally well that we can achieve a democratic society where women and men regard and act towards each other as equals' (Schools Commission, 1975: vii).

The report received much publicity and generated a great deal of research both in Australia and overseas, which resulted in a greater understanding of girls' disadvantage and the need for intervention to promote equality. The report cited many indicators of inequality between girls and boys in

Table 16.7 *Major Australian policies on girls' education, 1975–2000*

Year	Name of Policy
1975	*Girls, School and Society*
1984	*Girls and Tomorrow: The Challenge for Schools*
1987	*The National Policy for the Education of Girls in Australian Schools*
1991	*Listening to Girls*
1993	*National Action Plan for the Education of Girls, 1993–1997*

schools which included secondary school retention rates; subject participation and university entrance rates. The report focused on the comparative educational qualifications of boys and girls, and the role of the school in maintaining or counteracting influences which encourage sex stereotyping and limiting options available to both sexes. The report explicitly acknowledged that the school was only one of a number of institutions which influenced girls. The commission proposed a number of changes in the education system which would help to counteract the 'limiting messages' girls receive from other social agencies and open up the options available to them. These changes involved both the manifest purposes and organisation of schooling and the perspectives and values that are implicit or 'hidden' in the process. In brief, the changes included:

- the elimination of differences in curriculum offerings;
- the elimination of sex stereotyping in textbooks;
- positive steps to redress the balance of school staffing; and
- recognition of the changing role of parents due to two parents working.

Some of the more radical elements of the report deal with gender formation, paid versus unpaid work, subsistence versus materialism, shared parenting and life choices. One of the most prophetic questions asked in the report was if the objective was 'to make girls more like boys, boys like girls, or to work towards a human variety which transcends sex?' (Schools Commission, 1975: 6). Clearly, this question was not pursued, and much of the energy of gender reforms in the following decade was spent trying to make girls more like boys, instead of working towards this new human variety.

The recommendations found in *Girls, School and Society* prompted each state education department to set up special committees to investigate sexism in schools. The Directors-General in each state and territory subsequently published reports aimed at eliminating sexist practices. Such policies provided the basis for the national policy which followed a decade later. Each state appointed special officers to promote non-sexist education, called Women's Advisers or Equal Opportunity Officers. These advisers organised in-service courses, seminars and conferences for teachers. In addition, most teacher unions appointed committees to investigate the elimination of sexism from classrooms, and employed women's advisers to develop materials for classrooms and to provide support and development for teachers.

Girls and Tomorrow: The Challenge for Schools

In 1981, the Commonwealth Schools Commission established a Working Party on the Education of Girls to determine ways of assisting teachers and parents in the education of girls and meeting the needs of girls through Commonwealth programs for schools. The report, entitled *Girls and Tomorrow: The Challenge for Schools,* was presented in January 1984. It traced the progress and initiatives (or the lack thereof) resulting from *Girls, School and Society.* It argued that 'despite convincing evidence in *Girls, School and Society* of the educational disadvantages suffered by girls, girls continue to be afforded far less opportunity than boys to realise their potential' (Commonwealth Schools Commission, 1984: 2). The major

Publicity showing ways of assisting teachers and parents to meet the educational needs of girls

recommendation of the report was that a national policy was needed which contained 'a strategic commitment to equality of educational outcomes for girls', in order to 'transform rhetoric into reality' (Commonwealth Schools Commission, 1984: 9). In contrast to the egalitarian rationale of *Girls, School and Society*, it can be seen that *Girls and Tomorrow* reflected a utilitarian shift towards economic considerations. The following statement marked this shift from implementing gender reform for the sake of girls and women to doing it for the sake of society, the economy and the children and families of the women.

> A society which wastes a substantial proportion of its human potential limits its own development and creates costs for itself. Women have the potential to contribute significantly to economic recovery. Their earnings are often crucial to the economic security of their families and are essential to

strenghtening consumer demand. (Commonwealth Schools Commission, 1984: 7)

The National Policy for the Education of Girls in Australian Schools

As a result of the recommendations in *Girls and Tomorrow* and the widespread concern for the need for a national policy committed to improving the education of girls, the Commonwealth Schools Commission developed and presented *The National Policy for the Education of Girls in Australian Schools* in May 1987. It received a great deal of support, in particular from the Australian Education Council (made up of federal and state Ministers of Education) and the Commonwealth Government which was developing its *National Agenda for Women* to span the next 15 years. While the substance of *The National Policy* was not new, the explicit articulation of a set of

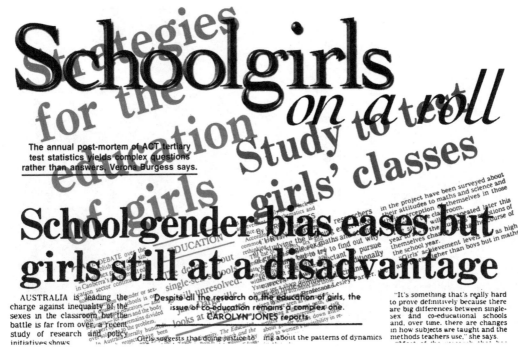

Headlines such as these raise the public's awareness of gender-based issues

commonly accepted understandings and directives based on experience and research was new. *The National Policy* was also a significant document as it was the first national policy in the area of schooling. It was unclear, and has been the subject of much speculation, as to why girls' education was bestowed the honour of the first national policy on schooling. *The National Policy* was unanimously endorsed by all of the state and Commonwealth Ministers for Education (the Queensland Minister for Education abstained from voting) and by the major non-government education bodies in 1987.

The general themes raised in the two earlier reports were reiterated in *The National Policy,* but in a more conservative and less idealistic way. *The National Policy* recommended that each state and territory be required to endorse the policy formally and forward reports on the

development of their own individual strategies for improving the education of girls. For example, the New South Wales Department of Education produced the *Girls' Education Strategy* in 1989, which aimed at focusing more explicitly on actions to improve the educational outcomes from schooling for girls. The Policy Statement set out mandatory principles for schools and systems with guidelines for implementation and accountability.

As a direct result of *The National Policy for the Education of Girls in Australian Schools,* developments and changes took place in areas such as policy development, resource allocation, curriculum offerings and the collation of statistics. Additionally, special projects such as Tradeswomen on the Move and awareness-raising strategies for teachers and students were trialled. Further, *The National Policy* recommended that reviews take place in all school systems to ensure that policies relating to girls' educational needs were incorporated in:

- staff recruitment, selection, promotion;
- inservice and retraining provisions;
- provision of specialist support services;
- system and school evaluation provisions; and
- decision-making structures and processes.

Throughout *The National Policy for the Education of Girls in Australian Schools,* the Commonwealth Schools Commission emphasised the need for the systematic collection, analysis and dissemination of statistical information relating to the issues of education and gender. Consequently, publications such as the *National Data Base on the Education of Girls in Australian Schools* was published in July 1988. Additionally, national reports were published to meet the reporting requirement for each of the states and territories. The last of these reports, *Girls in Schools 4,* was published in November 1991. This publication reported that while a 'considerable amount of work had been done by systems and schools towards making education in Australia more accessible and useful for girls', it could not be said that 'all of the initial objectives had been met on a system wide basis' and that 'further ongoing work needed to be done at all levels to continue striving toward an equitable schooling system' (Department of Employment, Education and Training, 1991: 1).

In order to achieve a more equitable schooling system, a further national document was released in March 1993. This document, the *National Action Plan for the Education of Girls, 1993–97,* identified eight new priorities:

1. Examining the construction of gender
2. Reforming the curriculum
3. Improving the educational outcomes of girls who benefit least from schooling
4. Changing school organisation and management practice
5. Eliminating sex-based harassment
6. Addressing the needs of girls at risk
7. Improving teaching practice
8. Broadening work education.

Although the introduction of the *National Action Plan* into Australian schools during 1993 and 1994 was partially successful, a significant shift was emerging which would replace the emphasis on girls with an emphasis on boys.

■ What about the Boys?

Since the early 1990s the education of boys has emerged as an important and potentially contentious educational issue in Australia and other Western nations such as the USA, Canada and the United Kingdom. Over this decade, concerns about boys have frequently been expressed by the media, politicians, educational policy makers and teachers. Mahoney and Smedley (1998: 42) state that 'it would not be an overstatement to say that much of the world is in a panic about boys'.

The panic and media controversy about boys seems to have arisen as a result of perceptions about boys' academic 'failures' relative to girls' 'successes'. During the early 1990s, the media began to report that girls were outperforming boys in matriculation and university entrance examinations around Australia. In particular, the headlines proclaimed that girls were now coming

The 'what about the boys?' debate is being raised in many quarters

first in traditional male domains such as mathematics, science and technology-related subjects. Yates (1996) and Foster (2000) reveal that the 'debate about boys' results took off not when it was discovered that boys, proportionally to those doing it, failed mathematics in higher numbers than girls', but rather as 'a response to boys beginning to lose out to girls in the very top categories'. The concerns about the achievements of boys in relation to girls began to be expressed with the now-familiar catch-cry of 'what about the boys?'. Further evidence such as boys' low self-esteem, literacy rates and school retention rates and high suicide rates have also been cited to prove concerns about boys.

New South Wales inquiry into boys' education

Growing concerns about boys led to a New South Wales parliamentary inquiry into boys' education, and resulted in a major refocusing of gender reform policies at state and federal levels. In 1994, the New South Wales Government's Advisory Committee released a discussion paper on boys' education, entitled *Inquiry into Boys' Education, 1994*. This report expressed widespread concern about boys' education and demanded system-wide solutions. The report commented that while some people blamed strategies for girls for some of the problems identified for boys, it did not recommend the development of a separate Boys' Education Strategy. Rather, the report recommended an overall strategy of Gender Equity in Education, with programs for boys, programs for girls and programs directed across the system at both boys and girls. Further, the report warned of the dangers of playing off the needs of boys against those of girls.

Despite such warnings given by the advisory committee, the public debate about boys' education developed in an adversarial and potentially harmful way. Mahoney and Smedley (1998: 48) have referred to the 'sex war mentality' which features each year in the media headlines. Blame for the crisis that boys were seen to be facing was often levelled at previous gender-equity policies for girls, and the needs of girls were seen to be mutually exclusive to those of boys. The 'what about the boys?' debate also commonly assumed that the needs of girls had now been fully met and that discrimination against girls had ended. Lingard (1998: 18) observes that the 'contemporary call for a focus on boys' schooling is usually accompanied by the assumption that the feminist reform agenda generally and in schooling specifically has achieved its goals'.

It is important to acknowledge that some of the criticisms that the 'what about the boys?' debate levelled at the previous gender reform programs were valid and needed to be addressed. Yates (1996: 12) notes that 'much of the feminist literature on schools with which we were familiar did treat girls in sensitive detail, while leaving boys as a more shadowy "other"; and treated masculinity as a more crudely sketched out discourse against which femininities were examined'. Kenway *et al.* (1997: 155) suggest that 'many of the boys' claims contain seeds of truth and point to some of the limitations of gender reform programmes'. Yates (1996: 10) concedes that 'gender reform programs cannot just go on improving the competitive outcomes of schooling for some students without, in relative terms, affecting the outcomes of others'.

In an attempt to capture the success of the girls' programs, supporters of boys' programs have often appropriated strategies previously used for girls and unquestioningly applied these to boys. Yates (1996: 7) comments that some of the reform strategies which have been suggested for boys have taken up the issue as if they 'were about abstracted technologies for success, rather than related to historical and social constructions'. Many of the strategies which were previously used for girls, such as the use of role models and single-sex classes, were transplanted directly into boys' programs, despite the fact that many of these strategies were later questioned and viewed as problematic by experienced gender reformers.

Many of the comparisons which were made between 'successful' girls and 'unsuccessful' boys failed to take into account other important variables such as race, class, sexuality and ability (Crocco, 2000). Gender was used as the only lens, and questions were not asked about which boys were being compared to which girls. Lingard (1998: 17) warns of the 'need to consider which boys we are talking about—middle class boys, working class boys, black boys? And which girls?'. Lingard (1998: 17) also draws our attention to the fact that the 'performance of middle class girls in high status subjects is sometimes compared with the poor performance of working class boys on these same subjects and the deduction is made, that all girls are now outperforming all boys'.

Perspectives on masculinity

It is important to note that different participants in the 'what about the boys?' debate have drawn on different theories of masculinities. These differing strands of masculinity have also yielded different constructions of the debate, different initiatives and different solutions to the problem. While there is a myriad of perspectives on masculinity, two perspectives have actively participated in the debate: the men's rights perspective and the pro-feminist perspective. The men's rights perspective sees men as victims of feminism, which has made things worse for men (Clatterbaugh, 1990: 10). This perspective believes that boys in schools are losing out, and are currently suffering in schools because of programs for girls over the past couple of decades. This perspective draws on essentialist beliefs and often advocates the implementation of programs and initiatives previously used for girls, such as programs for improving self-esteem, providing appropriate role models and single-sex classes.

The pro-feminist perspective is sympathetic to feminism and rejects the claim that traditional masculinity is biologically grounded (Clatterbaugh, 1990: 11). Such a perspective has resulted in the problematisation of masculinity. This relatively recent phenomenon in the gender debate has involved naming males as gendered beings, in the same way that females have long been regarded as gendered beings. Kaufman, Westland and Engvall (1997: 119) reveal that in the past men 'have tended to see themselves as free of gender, whereas women have been defined sometimes as though gender is their most significant trait'. This focus has dislodged masculinity from the neutral, normative position which it occupied during the early decades of gender reform, and enabled a simultaneous and more equitable focus on the needs of males and females. Pro-feminists are working together with feminists to achieve a simultaneous focus on the needs

of girls and boys and to evaluate honestly the mistakes and successes of previous gender reform programs for girls.

Regardless of the perspective within which participants in the boys' debate are operating, most agree that the behaviour, attitudes, achievement and aspirations of some boys in schools present problems for themselves, their teachers and other students. Kenway *et al.* (1997: 51) comment that 'boys' low achievement is usually regarded in our schools as more of a problem than that of girls because, on the whole, girls fail quietly, while boys' failure is more noisy and noticeable'. Kenway (1996: 447) notes that feminists have generally supported changes for boys in schools, recognising that 'women and girls have a strong vested interest in an education system that challenges restricted and destructive versions of masculinity—particularly those associated with violence'. However, feminists have rejected attempts within the boys' movement to cast boys as the new victim, and regard this strategy as flawed and divisive.

It can be seen that directions in the gender reform movement have changed considerably over the past couple of decades in Australia as a result of societal, political and educational movements. Debra Hayes (1998: 10–11) has succinctly captured the changes in gender-equity discourses from the early 1970s to the early 1990s as shown in Figure 16.1.

■ Current Understandings on the Construction of Gender

The ways in which understandings and arguments about gender in education have been constructed can therefore be

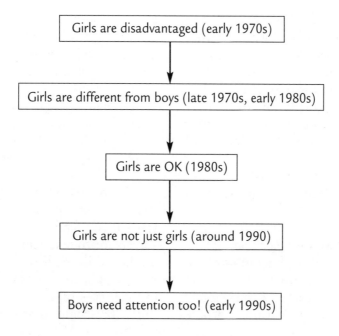

Source: Adapted from Hayes (1998).

Figure 16.1 *Changes in gender equity discourses, 1970s–1990s*

seen to have changed through both time and place. Since the mid-1970s gender reform in Australia has followed many new directions, which have varied from state to state and from rural to urban schools. The various policies that have been written over the past couple of decades provide evidence of society's changing understandings and constructions of gender throughout this time. The changing understandings have largely come about as a result of changes and shifts in the theories and standpoints which have informed the gender debate. For example, as the various feminisms, such as liberal, radical or poststructural, have evolved and changed, the questions that have been asked, the construction and interpretation of the 'problem' and the 'solutions' and strategies posed to overcome gender inequality have constantly changed.

Key elements in the current gender debate

Because current understandings are informed by a variety of strands of feminism and perspectives on masculinity, it is difficult to summarise the current understandings into a single, unitary or coherent summary. Notwithstanding, current understandings in the gender reform debate may be seen to include the following:

- a desire to cease constructing the debate as an either/or situation between boys and girls;
- a rejection of the masculine as normative and a problematisation of masculinity;
- a re-examination of the relationship between sex and gender;
- an appreciation that masculinity and femininity are influenced by multiple and changing discourses;

- a recognition of diversity within categories (which boys? which girls?);
- a desire to open up new discourses and possibilities within femininities, masculinities and sexualities;
- an acknowledgment of the inter-dependence of gender on other variables such as class, race and sexuality; and
- an acceptance of the complexity and the difficulties faced in bringing about gender reform.

The changing focus of the gender debate

It can be seen that throughout most of the past two decades, the needs of boys and girls have been viewed as being largely mutually exclusive. The gender debate within Australian schools has generally been constructed as a war of 'girls' needs' versus 'boys' needs', where the needs of one gender are isolated and pitched against the needs of the other. During the 1980s a reference to gender reform in schools mostly indicated programs and initiatives for girls. Such programs took males and masculinity as the norm, and rendered girls and femininity as the problem or deviance in need of repair. This resulted in male subject choices, characteristics and career choices being viewed as more desirable for girls than traditional female subject choices, characteristics and career choices. Girls were therefore encouraged to elect traditional 'male subjects' such as maths, science and computing, and shun tradi-tional 'female subjects' such as languages, domestic science and humanities. Girls were also encouraged to pursue tradi-tional 'male careers' such as trades, engineering and computing instead of traditional 'female careers' such as nursing, teaching and child care.

The programs which encouraged girls to adopt boys' subject choices and career patterns were largely successful, and ironically this success contributed to a backlash which shifted the focus of gender reform from girls to boys. Consequently, since the mid-1990s a reference to gender generally refers to the needs of boys. Unlike the previous emphasis on girls which encouraged them into male subjects and occupations, the new emphasis on boys did not signal a desire to encourage boys to take up traditional 'female subjects' or 'female careers' or to take females and femininity as the norm. Rather, the new focus on boys sought to cast males as the victims of the successful gender reform programs in the 1980s aimed at making girls more like boys.

Recent years have witnessed such a shift from a focus on disadvantage and victimhood towards finding new ways to cater simultaneously for the needs of boys and girls within an inclusive curriculum. It has been recognised that a boys versus girls construction of the gender debate is adversarial and unhelpful, and that it is time to stop alternating between casting one gender as the 'victim' or the disadvantaged gender who is suffering because of the other gender. Mahoney and Smedley (1998: 49) claim that in order 'for the debate to move forward and begin to address the real problems [of gender] in progressive ways, we need to stop operating between the polarities of the underachievement of boys one decade and girls the next'.

Sex and gender

Throughout the 1980s and most of the 1990s, the insights gained about the social construction of gender have enriched and informed gender debates within schools and the broader society. However, more recently the distinction between sex and gender has become more fuzzy and less straightforward than it first appeared, and questions about where the body stops and gender starts have emerged. These questions are motivated by a desire to search for ways to 'allow sex to inform gender and gender inform sex without again resorting to essentialism' (Williams, 1989: 8). Grosz (1994: 58) argues that 'gender is not an ideological super-structure added to a biological base' and that 'masculine or feminine gender cannot be neutrally attributed to bodies of either sex'. Clearly, the body cannot simply be viewed as a blank slate, which is later inscribed with a socially constructed gender.

More recent understandings on the construction of gender have been largely informed by poststructural work which examines the discourses which construct both gender and the biological body. The multiple, fluid and contesting discourses such as gender, race, class, sexual orientation and age are inscribed in bodies. In the school and in the classroom, multiple and diverse discourses of masculinities and femininities compete and vie for acceptance.

Power

Kenway *et al.* (1997: 100) note that while recent feminist research has drawn on post-structural notions of power, the gender reform policy and advice literature has not really done so yet. Poststructuralist notions of power examine the ways in which discourses compete with each other, and why certain discourses become dominant or powerful within a society. Discourses which are dominant and accepted as 'commonsense' are referred to as hegemonic. For example, while males may choose from a variety of discourses on masculinity, certain discourses will be dominant or hegemonic. This makes it difficult for boys to negotiate the powerful discourse of hegemonic masculinity, and to seek out alternative forms of masculinity. Stephens (1997: 19) alerts us to the fact that 'boys who want to renegotiate the discourses of gender are "policed" by other boys who actively work at upholding a particular hegemonic masculinity'. Kenway *et al.* (1997: 135) observe that the 'literature shows how hegemonic forms of masculinity amongst boys involve derogating the feminine (the soft, the emotional) and purging it from amongst boys' groups and within the self'.

Schools are therefore faced with the challenge of offering students the language and the tools to recognise and negotiate the various discourses which vie for acceptance, and particularly those which have become hegemonic. Boys and girls must be given a language to reflect critically on their own sense of self, in order to change the socially destructive nature of our gendered culture, and to achieve their potential and explore alternative ways of being in the world. In particular, schools urgently need to deal with the forms of harassment experienced by boys and girls who are 'different' and wish to adopt discourses of masculinity or femininity which are not the hegemonic ones (Kenway *et al.*, 1997).

Much of the work and research currently taking place in the area of gender reform is aiming to increase the range of acceptable versions of masculinity, femininity and sexuality which are available to boys and girls in schools. A great deal of this work has been directed towards addressing the issue of homophobia in schools, which Kenway *et al.* (1997: 160) point out is 'a mechanism for policing the masculine self'. The work on homophobia has drawn heavily on recent research into the experience of gay and lesbian students and teachers in Australian schools. Strategies are being developed to address the harassment, bullying and discriminatory behaviour which has often been directed towards gay and lesbian students.

Not only is it important to open up new spaces and alternatives within masculinity, femininity and sexuality for students, but teachers and educators also must recognise and welcome greater diversity within these categories. Over the past decade the dangers of treating 'girls' or 'boys' as an homogeneous group have frequently been acknowledged. Clearly, there is enormous diversity in the label of 'boys' and 'girls', and before it is possible to compare the outcomes of boys to girls, it is important to consider the variables such as class, race and sexuality, which interact with gender. Stephens (1997: 4) notes that 'the links between gender and schooling are not fixed but interact with class relations and change historically'. A recognition of diversity within gender and the impact of class and race inevitably lead to questions about which boys and which girls are disadvantaged.

Social justice

This acknowledgment that gender cannot be regarded as an independent variable, but must be considered in the light of other variables such as class, race and sexuality, has led to a more holistic emphasis on social justice rather than simply gender reform. Such an emphasis not only takes other discourses such as class and race into account, but it removes the emphasis from either girls or boys. Kenway *et al.* (1997: 183) suggest that 'taking the focus off gender and putting it on to social justice appears to present a less threatening and more palatable face to reform'.

Gender reform is now recognised as being more complex and difficult than it was perceived to be several decades ago. Not only has true gender equity proven elusive, but it is difficult to know where to go from here. Lingard (1998: 28) warns that 'gender equity policies and practices in schooling aimed to achieve a more gender-just society' will not be easy. It is clear that much work remains to be done in transforming schools towards more just and equitable environments for both students and teachers. This work must simultaneously take into account the needs of girls and boys, reject competing victims syndromes and work towards integrating understandings of gender with other social justice considerations such as class and race.

■ Gender Reform for the Teacher of Studies of Society and Environment

Gender reform at the personal level

Before embarking on gender reform programs for students, it is helpful for teachers to first address some of these issues at a personal level. Teachers may choose to reflect on and address some of the following issues:

1. examining the construction of gender in their own lives and schooling;
2. forging alliances with other teachers who are committed to equity and

social justice principles and joining equity committees and other support systems;

3. gaining feedback on any gender bias in their teaching strategies; and

4. locating resources and policies at the school and system level.

In addition to implementing gender reform programs for their students, it is often instructive for teachers to examine first the construction of gender in their own lives and schooling. Such a reflection enables teachers to begin to understand the processes which have informed their own gendered identity, beliefs and actions. Because the social construction of gender permeates all areas of our social practices and personal lives, it is often difficult to locate and change these gendered ways of being. However, teachers who are willing to examine and reflect on the construction of their gender in their own lives and schooling are equipped to begin the task of deconstructing gendered social practices. The following

questions may assist teachers in critically reflecting on their own gendered experiences:

In the family

1. What messages were conveyed to me as a child about appropriate 'masculine' or 'feminine' behaviour, clothing, hairstyles, games and presents?

2. Were girls and boys treated equally in my family? Were girls and boys given the same household tasks (e.g. setting the table, washing up, feeding animals)?

3. What were the expectations about tertiary study and careers for males and females?

4. Was gender a factor in my decision to become a teacher?

In the school

5. Was gender used as an organising principle in the school and classroom (e.g. were girls and boys asked to line up separately)?

6. Were teachers' expectations of a 'good girl' different from those of a 'good boy'?

7. Were girls and boys offered the same subjects (e.g. did both boys and girls participate in woodwork, home science, agriculture and textiles)?

8. Were all subjects in the school afforded equal status (e.g. were subjects associated with the feminine, such as history and languages, valued as much as subjects associated with the masculine, such as mathematics and science)?

9. Were girls and boys offered the same sports? Were all sports afforded equal status, rewards and prominence in school assemblies, newsletters and speech nights?

10. Did girls and boys occupy equal spaces in the school and playground? Were some spaces implicitly or explicitly designated as 'boys only' or 'girls only' spaces?
11. How were males and females represented in textbooks? Did males and females receive equal coverage in texts?
12. Were girls and boys disciplined in the same way?
13. Was there evidence of sexual harassment from other students or teachers?
14. Were male and female parents equally involved in schooling (helping with homework, attending parent–teacher nights, assisting in the canteen, classroom help, parents' associations, cooking for fêtes)?

In addition to reflecting on the construction of gender in their own lives, teachers will also benefit from forming strategic alliances with other teachers who are committed to equity and social justice principles (Grumet and Stone, 2000). It is important for beginning teachers 'to work in the company of experienced teachers who are also struggling to be reformers in their own classrooms, schools and communities' (Cochran-Smith, 1991: 17). Most schools will have established committees which implement and monitor equity and social justice initiatives. Such committees provide beginning teachers with strategies, companionship and the necessary support to implement gender reform.

It is also often extremely helpful for beginning and even experienced teachers to call upon other trusted colleagues to provide feedback on their teaching practice and use of inclusive language. This may involve other teachers observing their interactions and questioning techniques in the classroom, in order to detect any gender bias in their teaching. Dawson (1984: 32) reports on how Action Research such as this was implemented at Duffy Primary School in the ACT. The Duffy Primary School staff decided to measure the proportion of classroom verbal interaction that was occupied by teachers and by male and female students, and whether the talk was initiation or response. The research was designed to show whether teachers were giving equal teaching time and attention to boys and girls. Teachers worked in self-chosen pairs to monitor each other and observed teacher–student interactions in the classroom, using a simple monitoring sheet. The results of the Duffy Primary School research showed that boys received 60 per cent of teacher time. Teachers are often surprised by the results of observations in their classrooms. Such evidence provides an opportunity for teachers to reflect critically on their teaching practice, and to 'catch themselves' teaching in gendered ways.

It is essential that teachers acquaint themselves with policies and guidelines on gender equity at the school and system level. Information on departmental policies and resources in each state is provided below. It is important to examine the school policy on gender equity as this will influence your curriculum planning and classroom practice.

Australian Capital Territory

Gender Education is one of nine Across Curriculum Perspectives and is addressed in the *Gender Equity Curriculum Support Paper, 1997*. The paper is available from:

Curriculum Initiatives Section
School Programs Branch
ACT Department of Education and
   Community Services
Manning Clark Offices
186 Reed Street
Tuggeranong ACT 2900
(02) 6207 5111

New South Wales

Materials to address gender education through Personal Development, Health and Physical Education (PDHPE) are available in a kit distributed to NSW government schools—*Girls and Boys at School: Gender Equity Strategy 1996–2000*. Contact:

Specific Focus Programs Directorate
NSW Department of School Education
(02) 9234 4609
www.dse.nsw.edu.au

Northern Territory

The Northern Territory Board of Studies' *Gender Equity in Education Policy, 1999* is available from:

NT Board of Studies
5th Floor, National Mutual Centre
9–11 Cavenagh Street
Darwin NT 0800
(08) 8999 6383
www.ntde.gov.au/ntbos/

This policy is complemented by a Northern Territory Department of Education policy on gender and giftedness—*Gender and Giftedness: Supporting Gifted Boys and Girls in Schools, 1999*. This policy is available at www.ntde.gov.au.

Queensland

The *Gender Equity in Education* policy is supported by procedures and

guidelines in the Department of Education Manual (DOEM) and projects and materials developed by the Equity Programs Unit. Information is available at www.education.qld.gov.au/tal/equity/gcequity/ or contact:

Gender Equity
Equity Programs Unit
Education Services Directorate
Education Queensland
30 Mary Street
Brisbane Qld 4000
(07) 3235 4220

South Australia

Advice and information to support the national policy *Gender Equity: A Framework for Australian Schools, 1997* is available at www.nexus.edu.au/divisions/curriculum/equity or contact:

Gender Equity
Equity Standards
Curriculum Services
Department of Education, Training and
   Employment
(08) 8235 8052

Tasmania

Tasmania's *Equity in Schooling* policy and support materials are available at www.tased.edu.au/eddiv/equity/index.htm or contact:

PEO Equity
Equity Branch
Letitia House, Olinda Grove
Mount Nelson
Department of Education, Tasmania
(03) 6233 7328

Victoria

Information on materials and projects supporting gender education is available at www.sofweb.vic.ed/psupport/ or contact:

Gender Equity Section
Program Support Branch
Department of Education, Employment
  and Training
(03) 9637 2324

Western Australia
As a part of its Social Justice in Education Policy, *Gender Guidelines* are available to support the implementation of gender equity policy. These guidelines are available at www.eddept.wa.edu.au/saer/policy/gender.htm or contact:

Students At Educational Risk
Education Department of Western
  Australia
151 Royal Street
East Perth WA 6001
(08) 9264 4111

Gender reform at the classroom level
The following activities are provided to assist the teacher both in reflecting on their own assumptions about gender, and in designing classroom strategies to implement gender reform in their teaching. The key to gender reform will be an understanding of the assumptions which have formed the gender stereotypes which guide our thinking and actions. However, awareness alone of the social construction of gender is not sufficient—gender reform can only be achieved when these socially constructed gender stereotypes are challenged and deconstructed.

The activity suggestions are provided in outline, in generic form only, and are intended to guide and stimulate teachers in preparing activities relevant to the age and ability level of their students and the area of studies of society and environment into which the activities will be incorporated.

Gender descriptions
Complete Table 16.8 by suggesting adjectives that students believe describe a *typical* male and female (try to group them as opposing pairs).

- Examine each description and try to identify its *source* or basis (why do we think or believe this). Can it be justified?
- Explore why the characteristics of males and females are cast as opposing pairs.
- Show examples of how this description is reproduced or perpetuated in the portrayal of male and female stereotypes (e.g. in fashion, literature, film, advertising).
- Collect examples of magazine/newspaper advertisements that exploit male and female stereotypes.
- How do we react to a person who shows a characteristic that is not stereotypical, for example a gentle man, an aggressive woman? Why do you think we react like this?

Gendered behaviour
Compile a list of behaviours that are not regarded as *typical* of boys and girls in Table 16.9.

- Discuss the possible reasons why we might stereotype each of these behaviours. Can they be justified?
- Can you give examples of rules, structures or institutions that

Table 16.8 *Gender descriptions*

Men are	Women are
strong	weak
tough	gentle
aggressive	timid
etc.	etc.

Table 16.9 *Gendered behaviour*

Boys don't	Girls don't
cook	play football
knit	mow the lawn
cry	punch or fight
etc.	etc.

reinforce these stereotypes (e.g. organised sports)?

- Collect examples of magazine/ newspaper advertisements for children's toys or clothes, or visit a shop, and compile a list of items that are stereotyped as boys' or girls' (especially in the way they are portrayed in the advertising).

Study the range of bicycles available for boys and girls, and compare their characteristics by compiling the information in Table 16.10.

Why do you think boys' and girls' bikes are different? Are there any good reasons for these differences and can they be justified? What would you think if a boy rode a girl's bike and vice versa? Would it matter?

Gender roles

Collect information for Table 16.11 about the duties, tasks, roles, etc. performed in your home, showing who mainly performs each task.

- Categorise each of these roles as either

Table 16.10 *Gendered bicycles*

Feature	Boys' bicycles	Girls' bicycles
Colour		
Name		
Shape/Design		
Accessories		

Table 16.11 *Gender roles*

Job	Male parent	Female parent	Me	Brother or sister
Cooking				
Washing dishes				
Putting out garbage				
Mowing the lawn				
Washing clothes				
Ironing				
Shopping for food				
Making lunches				
Paying bills				
Driving				
Buying gifts				
Child minding/babysitting				
Household repairs/maintenance				
etc.				

a male role, a female role or a role that can be performed by either males or females.

- Justify your categorisation. For example, show that roles categorised as female roles cannot be done, or done as well, by males and vice versa.
- What are the barriers to people performing roles perceived as wrong for one's gender, and how can these be overcome?
- List the benefits to the household of people performing roles outside their gender stereotype.

A similar analysis could be done at school (or any other workplace). In Table 16.12 compile a list of duties performed around the school, including teaching of various year levels, subjects and extracurricula responsibilities. Note whether the job/task is mainly performed by males or females.

- Can you account for the gender dominance of any of these roles? Can any be justified?
- Are there any differences in the way in which males and females perform these roles which might justify this dominance?

Table 16.12 *Duties performed in the school*

Duty	Gender dominance
Executive positions	
Infants teaching	
Primary teaching	
Maths/Science teaching	
Humanities teaching	
Sports coordination	
IT coordination	
etc.	

- Are there any barriers to staff wishing to take on counter-stereotypical roles, and how might these be overcome?

Gendered jobs

Make a list of as many careers as you can think of in Table 16.13. Assign each career to male or female and decide whether the job is perceived to be a 'male' job or a 'female' job. Some examples have been provided.

Gender equity

It is possible to increase awareness of gender equity through activities in which students observe and measure differences in opportunities available to males and females. Some examples are discussed below.

Playground space Draw a map of the school playground, identifying specific areas or facilities such as play equipment, cricket nets and the oval. Make observations about the use of each area of the playground by male and female students and identify any areas where either males or females dominate the use of the space. Is there any justification for this dominance? What strategies can be introduced to overcome this inequitable use of space?

Media analysis Compare the amount of coverage given to males and females in the reporting of sport on television news or in the newspaper. Measure the *quantity* of reports, both in terms of the frequency of reports and the length (minutes or column length). Can you identify any differences in the *quality* of the reports, such as the way the report treats males and females differently, for example by focusing on the physical appearance or features of females. Also

Table 16.13 *Gendered jobs*

Male jobs	Female jobs	Male or female jobs
Carpenter	Nurse	
Firefighter	Child-care worker	
Mechanic	Secretary	
Engineer	Librarian	
etc.	etc.	

compare the messages about men and women which are appearing on the Internet. Determine whether this new technology is merely carrying old messages (Knupfer, 1998: 62).

Text analysis Select a book (e.g. a history text or children's storybook) for students to read and examine for evidence of gendered stereotyping or inequity in the portrayal of males and females. Ask students to rewrite the story or section to address the stereotyping or inequity.

■ Concluding Comments

Over the past two decades, Australian education systems, schools, teachers and students have significantly advanced their understandings of the relationship between gender and schooling. During this period, a host of reports have been written, programs have been designed, and initiatives have been implemented to ensure that both girls and boys are granted equitable access to and participation in education in our society. Despite the significant gains that have

been made as a result of the gender reform process, many challenges lie ahead for Australian teachers and preservice teachers.

In particular, today's teachers are faced with the responsibility of developing inclusive gender programs that will simultaneously cater for the needs of boys and girls, as it is now seen as unhelpful and divisive to view the needs of boys and girls as being mutually exclusive, competing interests. Because teachers of studies of society and environment deal with people as social beings and the social environment, they are uniquely placed to develop programs and classroom activities that deal with social justice issues, such as gender. While the issues currently being addressed in the gender debate are complex and difficult, and the way forward is sometimes unclear, the goal of overcoming inequalities which are attributable to gender, class and race remains one of the most important challenges facing Australian teachers, schools and education systems.

QUESTIONS AND ACTIVITIES

1. Have you examined the construction of gender in your own life and schooling?
2. Have you examined your own teaching to ensure you are giving equitable treatment (time, encouragement, discipline, number of questions) to boys and girls?
3. Have you examined the curriculum offerings in your school? Are all subjects available to both boys and girls? Are the subjects traditionally associated with girls afforded the same status as those traditionally associated with boys?
4. Have you examined the extracurriculum offerings in your school? Are the activities traditionally associated with girls (such as community service and debating) afforded the same status as those traditionally associated with boys (such as sport)? Are the sporting achievements of girls given as much publicity and encouragement of those of boys?
5. Have you located a copy of your school's Gender Equity Policy? Does the policy integrate the needs of girls and boys? Is this policy monitored and evaluated?
6. Have you located state/system-level documents on current gender policies?
7. What resources, such as reports, books, consultants and other teachers who are committed to gender reform, do you have access to at the system and school level?

Glossary

academic rationalism Adherents of this approach argue that the established subject disciplines are the most powerful products to include in the curriculum. These disciplines provide concepts and criteria through which thought acquires precision, generality and power, and exemplify intellectual activity at its best.

anomie lack of the usual social or ethical standards in an individual or group.

artifacts The materials or objects used in a particular culture.

assessment The interpretation of a test score or mastery of specific skills or competencies.

assimilation (policy) The absorbing of minority groups into the majority society.

attitudes Like values, are parts of human feeling. They are related to values but make less use of relevant justifying reasons. They are predispositions leading a person to

respond either favourably or unfavourably to other people, to events and situations, even to objects.

behavioural sciences Psychology, sociology and anthropology, with their shared concerns to describe and explain human behaviour and conduct.

CD-ROM An acronym for Compact Disk-Read Only Memory. This technology uses two basic components—a CD-ROM *player* (similar to a floppy disk drive) and a CD-ROM *disk* (a 12-centimetre rigid plastic disk). CD-ROM disks can hold vast amounts of information which can be stored as text, graphics, sound and video.

centralised planning Curriculum decision making usually undertaken by state or systemic authorities. Curriculum plans under these conditions are often prescribed for local schools to put into operation.

civics education This approach provides students with opportunities to be actively involved in community issues and developments.

clan A group bound by kinship, identified as having a common ancestor.

comparative studies The analysis of similar cultures, groups or countries using a common set of criteria or categories.

computer crime The act of stealing from, embezzling from or defrauding an organisation with the aid of a computer.

computer hardware The physical machinery, including electronic circuitry, which together makes up a computer system.

computer software The programs or instructions that the computer hardware carries out.

concepts The important universal abstractions that are used to label main ideas or generalisations about society.

constitution A written set of principles and statements which provide the basis for a nation's social structures, institutions and laws.

controversial issues Problems and disputes that divide society and for which significant groups within society offer conflicting explanations and solutions based on alternative values.

cultural identity The common beliefs, language, customs, religion, etc. by which individuals are united.

cultural relativism The proposition that cultures cannot be compared with each other.

cultural transmission This approach stresses the importance of disciplinary content, the need to study great lives and to examine the progress of Western civilisation and processes in society.

culture A system of shared meanings and customs that relate to all aspects of a group's 'way of life'. These meanings are learned and are modifiable.

database The collection of information, structured in a particular way, on a computer disk. The two main types contain (1) pre-stored data (sometimes called 'closed', 'fixed' or 'structured' databases), and (2) file management routines only (sometimes called 'open', 'flexible' or 'unstructured' databases). See also *record* and *field*.

deduction The seeking out of specific examples, given a general statement or principle.

devolution of decision making Government policy of shifting curricula decision making to regions and schools.

diorama A three-dimensional display case or box that depicts a specific social scene.

ecological sustainability A set of principles/understandings which highlight the interdependencies between process and products of the environment and the safeguards needed if they are to be maintained for future generations.

electronic mail Text messages exchanged on a computer network are known as electronic mail or email. It can be used to exchange private messages and group messages.

empirical studies Studies of social behaviour, institutions or other phenomena based on observation and experiment.

ethnicity A sense of peoplehood shared by persons who are aware, at least latently, of having common origins, experiences and interests.

ethnocentrism The tendency to see and judge other cultures, cultural and ethnic groups in terms of one's own culture and experience.

evaluation The systematic process of collecting information in order to make judgments or statements of worth.

field A term used to denote the categories into which information is placed in each record in a computer database. See also *record* and *database*.

focus questions The level of questions used to indicate a major line of investigation for an in-depth 'studies of society and environment' unit.

formative evaluation The collection of appropriate information during the planning and implementation stages of curriculum development.

frameworks Guides to assist school communities, teachers, students and parents. They consist of general statements about a rationale for the curriculum area, objectives, learning and teaching, content and evaluation.

gender Socially constructed notions of maleness and femaleness, which are constructed through discourses and social practices.

gender-inclusive education The teaching of units to students whereby there is equality of opportunity for learning for both males and females.

gender segregation This can occur as horizontal segregation, where men and women are grouped into different jobs, and vertical segregation, where men are located in the most senior and highly paid jobs.

generalisations Statements showing the relationship between two or more concepts.

hard disk A rigid plastic or metal magnetic disk fitted to a computer, which provides a permanent storage medium for software. Hard disks can store much greater amounts of software than floppy disks.

humanities A group of disciplines that focuses on the 'life' of humankind and includes language and literature, the fine arts and philosophy. To a less clearly defined extent, history is included.

hypothesis testing A method of scientific investigation in which a provisional statement is put forward, to explain observed facts, and tested using empirical methods.

ideology A set of ideas, which form the basis for a rationale for a course of action, or for explanations of certain occurrences.

inculcation A form of teaching whereby the instructor uses various forms of drill and repetition to ensure that specific facts or principles are learnt.

indigenous The original people of any country.

induction The establishing of a general

statement or principle, given specific examples.

information literacy The skills involved in using information to function in society, to achieve goals and to develop knowledge and potential. They involve the integration of listening, viewing, speaking, reading, writing and thinking.

information retrieval The capacity of individuals to develop the requisite skills to be able to search out, locate and retrieve specific content.

Internet This is the world's largest internetwork, connecting a vast number of networks around the world. The Internet is used to communicate, to transfer files and to publish.

inquiry The seeking out of truth, information or knowledge.

key competencies A term used by the Mayer committee to indicate that some seven generic competencies are required by all students for their participation in the emerging patterns of work and work organisation.

kinship The way people are related to each other.

metacognition Processes undertaken by students whereby they understand how learning occurs and are able to have an executive role in controlling their own learning processes.

modem A device that converts (MOdulates and DEModulates) information so that it can be transferred between computers using telephone lines.

moiety A division of the 'tribe' into two parts, which determines social relationships (in particular, regulates marriage arrangements).

moral education In schools, it involves experiences affecting students' thought and action regarding matters deemed right and wrong.

multicultural education This can be perceived as a concept, as an educational reform movement and as a process. Multicultural education has as its goal providing equal opportunities for students from diverse backgrounds.

multiculturalism An approach to immigration which values the contribution of immigrants with a variety of customs, values and beliefs.

national goals for schooling in Australia The ten common and national goals for schooling in Australia were agreed upon at an Australian Education Council meeting in Hobart in 1989 and have provided the focus for much of the national curriculum endeavours.

national statement A term used by the Australian Education Council (AEC) to describe a set of common terms and agreed definitions, statements about common principles of teaching, learning and assessment, and principles relating to theory-related practice linkage. The AEC has produced a national statement for each of the eight learning areas.

natural environment The total environment, untouched by humans.

outcomes-based education An approach to curriculum planning which emphasises the achievements students have reached at the completion of a subject or unit.

paradigm The particular structures and methods in a given body of knowledge that guide scholars and professionals in the selection and solution of problems, together with their evaluation and analysis.

pedagogy The art and science of teaching children (cf. andragogy: teaching adults).

preliminary evaluation Determining the student's readiness for new instructions.

problem solving Directing an inquiry to solve a particular problem.

profile A framework that can be used by teachers in classrooms to chart the progress of individual learners, by schools to report to their communities, and by systems reporting on student performance, as well as being amenable to reporting student achievement at a national level. The AEC has produced a profile for each of the eight learning areas.

race A term referring to biological/physical distinctions. It is sometimes misused as a synonym for ethnic groups.

racism A set of ideas and behaviour based on a belief in a position of superiority of one cultural group over another, which serves to maintain the superiority of one group over another.

raised relief maps Maps that highlight topography by presenting mountain areas as raised areas and valley lowlands as depressions.

RAM An acronym for *Random Access Memory*. It refers to the internal memory of the computer that provides temporary storage for software or data. Information in RAM is lost when the computer is switched off.

rationale A statement that makes explicit the bases on which a course is developed, which serves to justify the learnings that students acquire and the methods employed in teaching the course.

record A term used to denote each of the items, about which information is stored, on a computer database. For example, in a database containing information about students in a school, each student would comprise one *record* in the database.

reference books Books specially written as an authoritative source on particular topics.

reflective thinking The reconsideration of actions and thoughts to establish future directions.

reliability In measurement, refers to the consistency with which a list or instrument measures any particular phenomenon.

school-based curriculum development (SBCD) Acceptance of responsibility by the schools, from central authorities, for the development of curriculum, appropriate to the needs of the school.

scope The organisation of content material so that one area illuminates another.

self-actualised A person who can be regarded as 'complete', self-directed and accepting responsibility for his or her own personality.

self-directed learning A learning approach which requires students to negotiate the work load in individual subjects and to initiate their own projects and contracts.

sequence The ordering of content material wherein each new component builds on and develops the preceding components.

sex discrimination The individual acts or practices that put people at a disadvantage because of their sex.

sexism The attributes that lead us to expect certain characteristics of behaviour from women and men.

sex stereotyping The linking of certain behavioural characteristics with one sex to the exclusion of another.

skills Associated with knowing, feeling and motor dexterity. Concisely stated, skills are organised and coordinated activities that are built up during repeated experiences.

slide-tape kit Audio-visual materials whereby audio accompaniment is provided with a set of slides. The synchronisation is achieved either manually or by electrical impulses.

social critical theorists These proponents argue that knowledge is tentative and is mediated through individuals and social processes. Students should be empowered to create their own knowledge and question whatever knowledge is presented to them.

social education Refers to the socialising function of the school's whole curriculum, but also includes other institutions such as the family, church and peer group in addition to other social groups and organisations outside the auspices of the school (e.g. the mass media). It includes a

moral dimension and is concerned with students learning how to make choices and effect decisions in accordance with moral and ethical principles.

social élites Groups in society, that have acquired economic, social and/or political power and influence over others, and use this to maintain their position of advantage.

social reality A social situation, or set of social situations, in which the individual is involved.

social sciences A group of disciplines, including the *behavioural sciences*, that applies scientific methods to the study of human relationships and social organisations, by and through which people live together in society.

structure of the disciplines An approach to developing curricula, made popular by Jerome Bruner (1963), in which students, at their level, acquire the major concepts and processes of inquiry which, in total, comprise the unique structure of a discipline.

studies of society and environment This learning area involves the study of people as social beings, as they interact with one another with the natural and social environment in various places throughout time.

summative evaluation The collection of appropriate information following the completion of a program with a view towards determining whether or not the program has achieved its stated objectives.

supra-ethnic values The overarching values that are shared by different ethnic groups.

textbook A book especially written for

students involved in a particular topic or course.

trade books Books that are intended for sale to the general public, including fiction and non-fiction, are considered to be trade books. These forms of literature can greatly enrich teaching in studies of society and environment.

traditional accounts Versions of past events.

traditional culture That which has continuity with the past.

transparency overlays A set of transparencies prepared to the same scale and which can be presented one on top of the other on an overhead projector, to create particular patterns and effects.

validity In measurement, it is the degree to which a test or instrument measures what it is supposed to measure.

values Used as standards of judgment and as criteria of our esteem for people and actions, ideas and objectives. We engage in the process of *valuing* when we make appraisals and when we establish priorities.

values clarification Achieved through participation by students in various activities such as discussion, experience of dilemmas, choosing and ordering items and using artistic expression such as song, painting, simulating or keeping a personal journal.

videotape A cassette tape that records visual and auditory images and which can be replayed on a video recorder.

World Wide Web This is part of the Internet. It is most popular with teachers and students because it is freely available. It is a huge resource of freely available material.

References

Aboriginal and Torres Strait Islander Commission (1999) *As a Matter of Fact*, 2nd edition.

Aboriginal and Torres Strait Islander Studies Unit (periodical) *The Australian Journal of Indigenous Education*. St Lucia: University of Queensland.

Ahier, J. and Ross, A. (eds) (1995) *The Social Subjects within the Curriculum*. London: Falmer.

Aldridge, J. (1986) *The True Story of Spit MacPhee*. Melbourne: Penguin.

Alexander, F. and Crabtree, C. (1988) 'California's new history–social science curriculum promises richness and depth', *Educational Leadership*, 46, 1, 10–3.

Alleman, J. and Brophy, J. (1994) 'Taking advantage of out-of-school opportunities for meaningful social studies learning', *Social Studies*, 85, 6, 262–267.

Allen, J.D. (2000) 'Teaching about multicultural and diversity issues from a humanistic perspective', paper presented at the Annual Conference of the American Educational Research Association, New Orleans.

Allen, J. and Labbo, L. (2000) 'Giving it a second thought: making culturally engaged teaching culturally engaging', paper presented at the Annual Conference of the American Educational Research Association, New Orleans.

Antonacci, P.A. (1991) 'Students' search for meaning in the text through semantic mapping', *Social Education*, 55, 3, 174–194.

Apple, M.W. and Christian-Smith, L.K. (eds) (1991) *The Politics of the Textbook*. New York: Routledge.

Aquilina, J. (1997) Education Reform Further Amendment Bill, 1997. Second Reading Speech in the NSW Legislative Assembly, p. 4 (http://www.boardofstudies.nsw.edu.au/docs_stfreview/aquilina1.html).

Aronson, E., Beaney, N., Stephan, C., Sikes, J. and Snapp, M. (1978) *The Jigsaw Classroom*. Beverley Hills: Sage Publications.

Arrernte Community (1996) *Bush Tucker*. Alice Springs: Department of Education.

Australian Bureau of Statistics (1995) *Australia— Working it out: Core material for Australian Studies*. Canberra: ABS.

Australian Bureau of Statistics (1996a) *1996 Census: School Resource Kit*. Canberra: ABS.

Australian Bureau of Statistics (1996b) *Migration Statistics*. Canberra: AGPS.

Australian Bureau of Statistics (1998) *Schools Australia series*. Canberra: AGPS.

Australian Capital Territory Department of Education and Training (1995) *From Ochres to Eel Traps*. Canberra: DET.

Australian Curriculum Studies Association (1993) *Workshop on Studies of Society and Environment*. Biennial Conference, Brisbane.

Australian Dairy Corporation (1991) *You Are What You Eat*. Sydney: Dairy Foods Advisory Bureau.

Australian Education Council (1989a) *Common Goals for Australian Schooling?* Melbourne: AEC.

Australian Education Council (1989b) *Common and Agreed National Goals for Schooling*. Hobart: AEC.

Australian Education Council (1991a) *Listening to Girls*. Melbourne: Curriculum Corporation.

Australian Education Council (1991b) *Mapping the Environmental Education Curriculum: Report of Project Team*. Melbourne: AEC.

Australian Education Council (1991c) *K–12 Studies of Society Curriculum Map*. Melbourne: AEC.

Australian Education Council (1992a) *Development of the Brief for Studies of Society and Environment*. Melbourne: CURASS.

Australian Education Council (1992b) *Where Do I Go From Here?* Melbourne: Curriculum Corporation.

Australian Education Council (1993) *National Action Plan for the Education of Girls, 1993–97*. Melbourne: Curriculum Corporation.

Australian Education Council (1994) *A Statement on Studies of Society and Environment for Australian Schools*. Melbourne: Curriculum Corporation

Australian Education Council Curriculum and Assessment Committee (1992) *Bulletin No. 1*. Melbourne: CURASS.

Australian Institute of Family Studies (1992) *Family Matters*, 27. Melbourne: AIFS.

Australian Institute of Family Studies (1993) *Families in the 1990s*. Background paper by Dr Don Edgar, Director. Melbourne: AIFS.

Axelson, D. and Nichols, C. (1997) *Multimedia Projects*. Melbourne: Hawker Brownlow Education.

Ball, C. and Ball, M. (1973) *Education for a Change*. Harmondsworth, UK: Penguin.

Bakker, H.E. and Piper, J.B. (1994) 'California provides technology evaluations to teachers', *Educational Leadership*, 51, 7, 67–68.

Banks, J.A. (1994) *An Introduction to Multicultural Education*. Boston: Allyn & Bacon.

Banks, J.A. (1995) 'Transformative challenges to the social science disciplines: implications for social studies teaching and learning', *Theory and Research in Social Education*, 23, 1, 2–20.

Banks, J.A. (1997) *Educating Citizens in a Multicultural Society*. New York: Teachers College Press.

Banks, J.A. and Banks, C.A. (1999) *Teaching Strategies for the Social Studies*, 5th edition. New York: Longman.

Banks, J.A. and Clegg, A.A. (1990) *Teaching Strategies for the Social Studies: Inquiry, Valuing and Decision Making*, 4th edition. New York: Longman.

Barak, A. (1987) 'Increasing the level of empathic understanding by means of a game', *Simulation and Games*, 18, 4.

Barrett, R. (1994) *Australian Environments*. Sydney: Macmillan.

Barron, A.E. and Ivers, K.S. (1998) 'Web pages and K–12 education: a descriptive study', paper presented at the Annual Conference of the American Educational Research Association, San Diego.

Barry, K., King, L., Pitts-Hill, K. and Zehnder, S. (1998) 'An investigation into student use of a heuristic in a series of cooperative learning problem solving lessons', paper presented at the Annual Conference of the American Educational Research Association, San Diego.

Barth, J.L. (1991) *Elementary and Junior High/Middle School Social Studies Curriculum, Activities & Materials*, 3rd edition. Lanham: University Press of America.

Bartlett, V.L. and Cox, B. (1982) *Learning to Teach Geography*. Brisbane: Jacaranda Wiley.

Barton, K.C. (1996) 'Did the devil just run out of juice? Historical perspective-taking among elementary students', paper presented at the Annual Conference of the American Educational Research Association, New York.

Bean, T., Kile, R.S. and Readence, J. (1996) 'Using trade books to encourage critical thinking about citizenship in high school social studies', *Social Education*, 60, 4, 227–230.

Becker, H.J. (1998) 'Running to catch a moving train: schools and information technologies', *Theory into Practice*, 37, 1, 20–30.

Beery, R. and Schug, M.C. (1984) 'Young people and community'. In M.C. Schug and R. Beery (eds) *Community Study: Applications and Opportunities*. Washington DC: NCSS.

Berolah, L., Collins, L. and Cristaudo, N. (1996) *Betty and Bala and the Proper Big Pumpkin*. St Lucia: University of Queensland Press.

Berrell, M. (1993) 'Classrooms as sites for citizenship education'. In K. Kennedy, O. Watts and G. McDonald (eds) *Citizenship Education for a New Age*. Toowoomba: University of Southern Queensland Press.

Berwick, B. (1994) 'Kids behind the camera: Education for the Video Age', *Educational Leadership* 51, 7, 52–54.

Betts, F. (1996) 'Only the best: hot links to good resources', *Educational Leadership*, 53, 8, 38–39.

Bevege, M. (1982) *Worth Her Salt: Woman at Work in Australia*. Sydney: Hale and Iremonger.

Beyer, B.K. (1971) *Inquiry in the Social Studies Classroom: for Teaching*. Columbus: Merrill.

Beyer, B. (1985) 'Critical thinking: what is it?', *Social Education*, 4, 270–276.

Biddulph, S. (1982) *Jobhunt*. Launceston: Biddulph Publishers.

Blackburn, J. (1982) 'Becoming equally human: girls and the secondary curriculum', *VISE News*, July–August, 16–22.

Blackmore, J. (1988) *Assessment and Accountability*. Geelong: Deakin University Press.

Blackmore, J. (1994) 'Devolving equity: megatrend or myopia', *Education Australia*, 28, 8–10.

Blainey, G. (1962) 'The gold rushes: the year of decision', *Historical Studies Australia and New Zealand*, 10, 30, May, 129–130.

Blainey, G. (1980) *A land half one*. Melbourne: Macmillan.

Bloom, A. (1987) *The Closing of the American Mind*. New York: Simon and Schuster.

Board of Senior Secondary School Studies Queensland (1998) [Pilot] *Senior Secondary School Syllabus in Aboriginal and Torres Strait Islander Studies*. Brisbane: Board of Senior Secondary School Studies.

Board of Studies, New South Wales (1985) *Society and Culture*. Sydney: Board of Studies.

Board of Studies, New South Wales (1992a) 'Flashback', *Board Bulletin*, 1, 6, 1.

Board of Studies, New South Wales (1992b) *Geography Syllabus Years 7–10*. Sydney: Board of Studies.

Board of Studies, New South Wales (1992c) *History Syllabus Years 7–10*. Sydney: Board of Studies.

Board of Studies, New South Wales (1994a) *OZ I. D.* Sydney: Board of Studies.

Board of Studies, New South Wales (1994b) *downUNDER*. Sydney: Board of Studies.

Board of Studies, New South Wales (1996a) *Invasion and Resistance: Untold Stories*. Sydney: Board of Studies.

Board of Studies, New South Wales (1996b) *Human Society and its Environment, K–6*. Sydney: Board of Studies.

Board of Studies, New South Wales (1998a) *Human Society and its Environment K–6*. Sydney: Board of Studies NSW.

Board of Studies, New South Wales (1998b) *History Syllabus, Stages 4–5*. Sydney: Board of Studies.

Board of Studies, New South Wales (1998c) *Geography Syllabus, Stages 4–5*. Sydney: Board of Studies.

Board of Studies, New South Wales (1999a) *Geography Stages 4–5 Syllabus*. Sydney: Board of Studies NSW.

Board of Studies, New South Wales (1999b) *History Stages 4–5 Syllabus*. Sydney: Board of Studies NSW.

Board of Studies, New South Wales (1999c)

Making Multicultural Australia. Sydney: Board of Studies NSW.

Board of Studies, New South Wales (1999d) *Elemental. Exploring the Australian Minerals Industry.* Sydney: Board of Studies NSW.

Board of Studies, Victoria (1995a) *Curriculum and Standards Framework: Studies of Society and Environment.* Melbourne: Board of Studies.

Board of Studies, Victoria (1995b) *Studies of Society and Environment, Curriculum and Standards Framework.* Melbourne: Board of Studies.

Board of Studies, Victoria (1999) *The Curriculum and Standards Framework—Towards 2000 and Beyond.* Melbourne: Board of Studies. (http://www.bos.vic.edu.au/csf/csfdiscu.htm)

Board of Studies, Victoria (2000) *Curriculum Standards Framework (CSF II).* Melbourne: Board of Studies.

Board of Teacher Registration Queensland (1993) *Yatha: Aboriginal and Torres Strait Islander Studies in Teacher Education.* Toowong: Board of Teacher Registration.

Boehn, R.G. and Petersen, J.F. (1994) 'An elaboration of the fundamental themes in geography', *Social Education*, 58, 4, 211–218.

Booth, M. (1993) 'Students' historical thinking and the National History Curriculum in England', *Theory and Research in Social Education*, 21, 2, 105–127.

Boston, K. (1992) 'Working for the possible', *Curriculum Perspectives*, 12, 4, 30–31.

Boughton, D. (1993) 'The National Arts Curriculum and Profiles: is uniformity necessary in national curriculum design?', *Curriculum Perspectives*, 13, 1, 64–67.

Bradley, R., Whisson, M. and Murray, L. (1981) 'Simulation as social and cognitive process', paper presented at the annual conference of ANZAAS, Brisbane.

Braithwaite, J., Deer, C., McKinlay, B. and Turner, J. (eds) (1973) 'You, me and us', *Focus: Integrated Social Studies*. Brisbane: Jacaranda Wiley.

Branson, J. (1991) 'Gender, education and work'. In D. Corson (ed.) *Education for Work: Background to Policy and Curriculum.* Philadelphia: Multilingual Matters Ltd.

Bredemeier, M.E., Bernstein, G. and Oxman, W. (1982) 'BA FA, BA FA and dogmatism/ethnocentrism', *Simulation and Games*, 13, 4, 413–436.

Bredemeier, M.E. and Greenblat, C.S. (1981) 'The educational effectiveness of simulation games: a synthesis of findings', *Simulation and Games*, 12, 3, 307–332.

Brennan, M. (1996) 'Sustaining new forms of school life? A response to Stuart Macintyre'. In K. Kennedy (ed.) *New Challenges for Citizenship Education.* Canberra: Australian Curriculum Studies Association.

Brislin, R. and Yoshida, T. (1994) *Improving Intercultural Interactions: Modules for Cross-cultural Training Programs.* Thousand Oaks, CA: Sage Publications.

Broadfoot, P. (1979) *Assessment, Schools and Society.* London: Methuen.

Brookhart, S. and De Voge, J.G. (1998) 'Testing a theory about the role of classroom assessment in student motivation and achievement', paper presented at the Annual Conference of the American Educational Research Association, San Diego.

Brophy, J. and McCalin, M. (1992) 'Teachers' reports of how they perceive and cope with problem students', *Elementary School Journal*, 93, 1, 3–68.

Bruner, J. (1960) *The Process of Education.* New York: Vintage Press.

Bulbeck, C. (1993) *Social Sciences in Australia.* Sydney: Harcourt Brace Jovanovich.

Burrell, J. and Dugan, M. (1985) *A House for Wombats.* Hawthorn, Vic: Hutchinson Publishing Group.

Burridge, N. (1999) 'Reconciliation: bringing the nation together'. In R. Craven (ed.) *Teaching Aboriginal Studies.* Sydney: Allen & Unwin.

Byrnes, J.P. and Torney-Purta J.V. (1995) 'Naive theories and decision-making as part of higher order thinking in social studies', *Theory and Research in Social Education*, 23, 3, 260–277.

Cahill, D. (1996) *Immigration and Schooling in the 1990s.* Canberra: AGPS.

Calfee, R.C. and Chambliss, M.J. (1988) 'The structure of social studies textbooks: where is the design?', paper presented at the Annual Conference of the American Education Research Association, New Orleans.

California State Board of Education (1988) *History and Social Science Framework for California Public Schools*. Sacremento: SBE.

Calley, K. and Pearson, N. (1994) *Caden Walaa*. St Lucia: University of Queensland Press.

Campbell, D.E. (1996) *Choosing Democracy: A Practical Guide to Multicultural Education*. Columbus, Ohio: Merrill.

Campbell, E. (2000) 'Moral lessons: the ethical role of teachers', paper presented at the Annual Conference of the American Educational Research Association, New Orleans.

Cangelosi, J.S. (1992) *Systematic Teaching Strategies*. Melbourne: Longman.

Capel, S., Leask, M. and Turner, T. (1999) *Learning to Teach in the Secondary School*, 2nd edition. London: Routledge.

Carbone, P.F. (1991) 'Perspectives on values education', *The Clearing House*, 64, 5, 290-292.

Carey, P. (1998) 'What does information technology mean for us? Possibilities and problems presented by cyberspace', paper presented at the Annual Conference of the American Educational Research Association, San Diego.

Carter, D., Ditchburn, G. and Bennett, D. (1999) 'Implementing the discovering democracy school materials project in Western Australia: a question of "fit" ', *Curriculum Perspectives*, 19, 3, 53-56.

Catchpole, M. (1981) 'Evaluation guidelines for Aboriginal studies course', *The Aboriginal Child at School*, 9, 3, 23-38.

Catholic Education Office (1996) *The Torres Strait Islander Perspective Kit*. Cairns: Catholic Education Office.

Catholic Education Office (n.d.) *Unity: 'Linking Together Faith and the Community'*, preschool and primary school teacher resource folder kit. (Unpublished). Catholic Education Office, Diocese of Townsville.

Center for Civic Education (1995) 'The role of civic education: a report of the Task Force on Civic Education', paper prepared for the Second Annual White House Conference on Character Building for a Democratic Civil Society, 19-20 May.

Chambliss, M.J., Calfee, R.C. and Wong, I. (1990) 'Structure and content in science textbooks: where is the design?', paper presented at the Annual Conference of the American Education Research Association, Boston.

Chapin, J.R. and Messick, R.G. (1999) *Elementary Social Studies*, 4th edition. New York: Longman.

Chartock, R.K. (1991) 'Identifying local links to the world', *Educational Leadership*, 48, 7, 23-31.

Checkley, K. (1997) 'Problem-based learning', *ASCD Curriculum Update*, Summer, 1-8.

Cherrington, R. and Van Ments, M. (1996) 'Straws in the wind: some perceptions and attitudes toward simulation and gaming in the United Kingdom', *Simulation and Gaming*, 27, 1, 5-22.

Chilcoat, G.W. (1991) 'The illustrated song slide show as a middle school history activity', *The Social Studies*, 82, 5, 188-191.

Chilcoat, G.W. and Ligon, J.A. (1998) 'Issues-centred instruction in the elementary social studies classroom', paper presented at the Annual Conference of the American Educational Research Association, San Diego.

Chilcott, J.H. (1991) 'It is time to change the classroom maps', *The Social Studies*, 82, 2, 44-48.

Children's Book Council (1991) 'Notable 1990 children's trade books in the field of social studies', *Social Education*, 55, 4, 253-260.

Civics Expert Group (1994) *Whereas the people ... Civics and Citizenship Education*. Canberra: AGPS.

Clark, A. (1996) 'Civics and citizenship and the teaching of values', *Unicorn*, 22, 1, 54-58.

Clark, M. (1963) *A Short History of Australia*. Sydney: Mentor.

Clark, M. (1989) *The Great Divide: The Construction of Gender in the Primary School*. Melbourne: Curriculum Corporation.

Clarke, M.M., Madaus, G.F., Horn, C. and Ramos, M.A. (2000) 'Retrospective on educational testing and assessment in the 20th century', *Journal of Curriculum Studies*, 32, 2, 159–182.

Clatterbaugh, K. (1990) *Contemporary Perspectives on Masculinity*. Colorado: Westview Press.

Clayton, G. (1999) 'A long way from the capital', *EQ Australia*, Spring, 1–11.

Clyne, M. (1997) 'Monolingualism, multilingualism and the Australian nation'. In R.J. Watts and J.J. Smolicz (eds) *Cross Cultural Communication*. Frankfurt: Peter Lang.

Cochran-Smith, M. (1991) 'Learning to teach against the grain', *Harvard Educational Review*, 61, 3, 279–310.

Cockburn, C. (1985) *Machinery of Dominance: Women, Men and Technical Know-how*. London: Pluto Press.

Cole, P. (1916) *Civics and Morals*. Sydney: Dymocks Book Arcade.

Collins, C. (1994a) *Curriculum and Pseudo-Science: Is the Australian National Curriculum Project Built on Credible Foundations?* Canberra: ACSA.

Collins, C. (1994b) 'Is the National Curriculum Profiles Brief Valid?', *Curriculum Perspectives*, 14, 1, 45-48.

Collinson, V. (1999) 'Redefining teacher excellence', *Theory into Practice*, 38, 1, 4–11.

Collins Dove (1992) *Social Education*. Melbourne: Collins Dove.

Commonwealth Department of Employment, Education and Training and Australian Institute of Aboriginal and Torres Strait Islander Studies (1992) *Back trackers*. Manuka: Oziris Pty Ltd.

Commonwealth of Australia (1982) *Commonwealth Aboriginal Studies Working Group: Report to the Australian Education Council*. Canberra: AGPS.

Commonwealth of Australia (1985) *Aboriginal Education: Report of the House of Representatives Select Committee on Aboriginal education*. Canberra: AGPS.

Commonwealth of Australia (1989) *National Aboriginal and Torres Strait Islander Education Policy*. Canberra: Department of Employment, Education and Training.

Commonwealth Schools Commission (1984) *Girls and Tomorrow*. Canberra: AGPS.

Considine, D.M. (1989) 'The video boom's impact on social studies', *The Social Studies*, 80, 6, 229–234.

Court, D. (1992) 'Teaching critical thinking: what do we know?', *The Social Studies*, 82, 6, May/June, 115–119.

Couture, J.C. and Dobson, T. (1997) 'Stamping out: student use of e-mail in public school, *Journal of Curriculum Theorizing*, 13, 4, 31–35.

Craven, R. (ed.) (1999) *Teaching Aboriginal Studies*. Sydney: Allen & Unwin.

Crittenden, B. (1995) 'The revival of civics in the school curriculum: comments on the Report of the Civics Expert Group', *Melbourne Studies in Education*, 36, 2, 21–30.

Crocco, M.S. (2000) 'The missing discourse about gender and sexuality in the social studies', paper presented at the Annual Conference of the American Educational Research Association, New Orleans.

Crookall, D. (1995) 'A guide to the literature on simulation/gaming'. In D. Crookall, and K. Arai (eds) *Simulation and Gaming across Disciplines and Cultures*. London: Sage Publications.

Crookall, D. and Arai, K. (eds) (1995) *Simulation and Gaming across Disciplines and Cultures*. London: Sage Publications.

Crookall, D. and Oxford, R. (eds) (1990) *Simulation, Gaming and Language Learning*. Noston: Heink and Heink.

Cross, R. (1999) 'The speaker, the clerk and the hansard reporter', *EQ Australia*, Spring, 13–15.

Cruickshank, D.R., Bainer, D.L. and Metcalf, K.K. (1999) *The Act of Teaching*, 2nd edition. Boston: McGraw-Hill.

Cumbo, K.B. and Vadeboncoeur, J.A. (1998) 'What are students learning? Assessing service learning and the curriculum', paper presented at the Annual Conference of the American Educational Research Association, San Diego.

Cumming, J. (1992) *Resourceful Communities*. Belconnen, ACT: Australian Curriculum Studies Association.

Cumming, J. (ed.) (1998) *Outcome-Based Education: Resources for Implementation*. Canberra: ACSA.

Cunningham, C.J. and Teather, E.K. (1990) 'Black Christmas: a bushfire simulation game', *Simulation/Games for Learning*, 20, 1, 7–17.

Cunningham, G.K. (1998) *Assessment in the Classroom*. London: Falmer.

Curl, D. (1990) 'The changing moods of Kakadu', *Australian Geographic*, 19, July–Sept, 44–71.

Curriculum Corporation (1993) *Statements and Profiles for Australian Schools*. Melbourne: Curriculum Corporation.

Curriculum Corporation (1994a) *Studies of Society and Environment—a Curriculum Profile for Australian Schools*. Melbourne: Curriculum Corporation.

Curriculum Corporation (1994b) *A Statement on Studies of Society and Environment for Australian Schools*. Melbourne: Curriculum Corporation.

Curriculum Corporation (1995a) *National Principles and Guidelines for Aboriginal Studies and Torres Strait Islander Studies K–12*. Melbourne: Curriculum Corporation.

Curriculum Corporation (1995b) *Resource Guide for Aboriginal Studies and Torres Strait Islander Studies*. Melbourne: Curriculum Corporation.

Curriculum Corporation (1996) *You Can Do It Too: Aboriginal Studies and Torres Strait Islander Studies Across the Curriculum*. Melbourne: Curriculum Corporation.

Curriculum Corporation (1997a) *Footsteps ... to Country, Kin and Cultures*. Melbourne: Curriculum Corporation.

Curriculum Corporation (1997b) *Signposts ... to Country, Kin and Cultures*. Melbourne: Curriculum Corporation.

Curriculum Corporation (1998) 'The longest journey'. In *Different Dreams: Integrated Units Collection Years 7 & 8*. Melbourne: Curriculum Corporation.

Curriculum Corporation (1999) *Australian Readers—Discovering Democracy*, Lower Secondary Collection. Melbourne: Curriculum Corporation.

Curriculum Council (1998) *Curriculum Framework*. Perth: Curriculum Council.

Curriculum Development Centre (1977) *Teachers Handbook and Workshop Leader's Handbook*. Canberra: CDC.

Curriculum Development Centre (1978) *Community Disaster*, SEMP Unit on Community Study, Draft edition. Canberra: CDC.

Curriculum Development Centre (1980) *Core Curriculum for Australian Schools*. Canberra: CDC.

Cushner, K. (1989) 'Creating cross-cultural understanding through internationally cooperative story writing', *Social Education*, 56, 1, 43–46.

Cushner, K. (1992) 'Creating cross-cultural understanding through internationally cooperative story writing', *Social Education*, 56, 1, 43–46.

Cushner, K. (1998) *Human Diversity in Action*. Boston: McGraw-Hill.

Cushner, K. and Brislin, R. (1996) *Intercultural Interactions: A Practical Guide*, 2nd edition. Thousand Oaks, CA: Sage Publications.

Cushner, K. and Brislin, R. (1997) *Improving Intercultural Interactions: Modules for Cross-cultural Training Programs*, 2. Thousand Oaks, CA: Sage Publications.

Daniels, K. and Murnane, M. (1980) *Uphill All the Way*. St Lucia: University of Queensland Press.

Darling-Hammond, L. and Ancess, J. (1996) 'Authentic assessment and school development'. In J.B. Baron and D.P. Wolfe (eds) *Performance-based Student Assessment: Challenge and Possibilities*. Chicago: NSSE.

Darling-Hammond, L. and Falk, B. (1997) 'Using standards and assessments to support student learning', *Phi Delta Kappan*, 79, 3, 190–201.

Davidson, A.J., Rowland, M.L. and Sherry, M.F. (1982) *Strategies and Methods: A Guide for Teachers of the Social Sciences*. Melbourne: Victorian Commercial Teachers Association.

Davidson, G. (1987) 'Professional applications of research into metacognition'. In *Professional Psychology Abstracts*, Supplement to APS Bulletin, 4, 2, April. Parkville, Victoria: The Australian Psychological Society.

Davies, B. (1994) 'Gender, policy and teaching'. In E. Hatton (ed.) *Understanding Teaching*. Sydney: Harcourt Brace.

Davis, J. (1991) *A Boy's Life*. Broome, WA: Magabala Books Corporation.

Davis, J.C. and Palmer, J. (1992) 'A strategy for using children's literature to extend the social studies curriculum', *The Social Studies*, 81, 2, 125–128.

Dawes, I. and Robertson, T. (1991) *Hands On. Making Computers Work in the Classroom*. Melbourne: Oxford University Press.

Dawson, L. (1984) 'Towards a non-sexist primary school', *Social Alternatives*, 4, 2, 31–32.

De Coker, G. (2000) 'Heads-up technology', *Educational Leadership*, 57, 8, 61–62.

Dede, C. (2000) 'Emerging influences of information technology on school curriculum', *Journal of Curriculum Studies*, 32, 2, 281–303.

Deer, C. (1991) 'Changing roles for students and teachers in the personal interest project', *Society and Culture Resource Guides*, 3, 2–4.

Deer, C., Jarvis, C. and White, P. (1987) 'Students as Researchers'. In C. Marsh (ed.) *Teaching Social Studies*. Sydney: Prentice Hall.

Department of Education and Children's Services (1995) *An Assessment, Recording and Reporting Resource*. Adelaide: DECS.

Department of Education and Children's Services (1996a) *Aboriginal Land Rights (What Does Everyone Else Think? What Do I Think?)*. Adelaide: DECS.

Department of Education and Children's Services (1996b) *Aboriginal Perspectives Across the Curriculum*. Adelaide: DECS.

Department of Education, Community and Cultural Development, Tasmania (1995) *Studies of Society and Environment in Tasmanian Schools K–8: Guidelines and Support Materials*. Hobart: DECCD.

Department of Education, Community and Cultural Development (1997) *Aboriginal Perspectives Across the Curriculum Tasmanian Edition (TasAPAC)*. Hobart: Department of Education, Community and Cultural Development.

Department of Education and the Arts (1989) *Living with the Land: Aborigines in Tasmania*; (seven titles) 'Invasion', 'Resistance', 'Dispossession', 'From optimism to despair', 'Adapting and resisting', 'Survival', and 'Family and community'. Hobart: Education Department, Tasmania.

Department of Education and the Arts (1995) *Guidelines and Support Materials*. Hobart: Department of Education and the Arts.

Department of Education, Queensland (1992) *Resources in Learning*. Brisbane: Department of Education.

Department of Education, Tasmania (1998) *Taking Action*. Hobart: Department of Education.

Department of Employment, Education and Training (1987) *National Policy for the Education of Girls in Australian Schools*; (1988) *Girls in Schools 1*; (1989)(a) *Girls in Schools 2*; (1989)(b) *What My Mother Told Me*; (1990) *Girls in Schools 3*; (1991) *Girls in Schools 4*. Canberra: AGPS.

Department of Employment, Education, Training and Youth Affairs and South Australian Department for Education and Children's Services (1996) *Aboriginal Perspectives Across the Curriculum*. Campbelltown: Curriculum Resources.

Departments of the Senate and the House of Representatives (1987) *The Parliament Pack Guide*. Canberra: Federal Government.

Dewey, J. (1933) *How We Think*. Boston: D.C. Heath & Co.

Diamond, L. (1994) 'Rethinking civil society: towards democratic consolidation', *Journal of Democracy*, 5, 3, 4–17.

Diehl, B. (1984) 'Evaluations of simulations in a teacher training course', *South Pacific Journal of Teacher Education*, 12, 1, 12–18.

Diehl, B.J. (1991) 'Crisis: a process evaluation', *Simulation and Gaming*, 22, 3, 293–307.

Dilg, M. (1999) *Race and Culture in the Classroom*. New York: Teachers College Press.

Di Nicola, M. (1997) 'Using simulation games', *The Social Educator*, 15, 1, 17–19.

Dinham, S. and Scott, C. (2000) 'Teachers' work and the growing influence of societal expectations and pressures', paper presented at the Annual Conference of the American Educational Research Association, New Orleans.

Dodd, B. (1992) *Broken Dreams*. St Lucia: University of Queensland Press.

Dolby, N (2000) 'Uprooting multicultural education: new identities, new paradigms', paper presented at the Annual Conference of the American Educational Research Association, New Orleans.

Donkin, N. (1979) *Nini*. Adelaide: Rigby.

Downs, J.R. (1993) 'Getting parents and students involved: using survey and interview techniques', *Social Studies*, 84, 3, 104–106.

Doyle, A. (1999) 'A practitioner's guide to snaring the Net', *Educational Leadership*, 56, 5, 12–15.

Driver, R., Asoko, H., Leach, J., Mortimar, E. and Scott, P. (1994) 'Constructing scientific knowledge in the classroom', *Educational Research*, 23, 7, 5–12.

Druckman, D. (1995) 'The educational effectiveness of interactive games'. In D. Crookall and K. Arai (eds) *Simulation and Gaming across Disciplines and Cultures*. London: Sage Publications.

Duck, L. (2000) 'The ongoing professional journey', *Educational Leadership*, 57, 8, 42–45.

Dufty, D. (1999) 'Studies of persons/societies/environments at the turn of the millennium', *The Social Educator*, 17, 1, 24–40.

Dukes, R.L. and Matthews, S. (1993) *Simulation and Gaming and the Teaching of Sociology*, 5th edition. Washington D.C.: American Sociological Association.

Duncan, A. and Greymorning, S. (1999) 'Comparative Studies'. In R. Craven (ed.) *Teaching Aboriginal Studies*. Sydney: Allen & Unwin.

Dunkin, M., Welch, A., Merritt, A., Phillips, R. and Craven, R. (1998) 'Teachers' explanations of classroom events: knowledge and beliefs about teaching civics and citizenship', *Teaching and Teacher Education*, 14, 2, 141–151.

Dunn, R., Beaudry, J.S. and Klavas, A. (1989) 'Survey of research on learning styles', *Educational Leadership*, 46, 6, 50–58.

Du Plass, J.A. (1996) 'Charts, tables, graphs and diagrams: an approach for social studies teachers', *The Social Studies*, 87, 1, 32–38.

Education Department of South Australia (1988) *Aboriginal Studies R–12* (11 titles); *Ourselves and Others*; *Home*; *Winda: A Narrunga Dreaming Story*; *Thukeri: A Ngarrindjeri Dreaming Story*; *Urrakurli, Wakarla and Wildu: An Adnyamathanha Dreaming Story*; *Aboriginal Dreaming Stories*; *The Dreaming and the Environment*; *Aboriginal Lifestyles before European Settlement*; *Dreaming Trails and Culture Contact*; *The Pitjantjatjara People—Lifestyle and Family Relationships*; *Aboriginal People and their Communities Today*.

Adelaide: Education Department of South Australia Publications Branch.

Education Department of South Australia (1991) *Introducing Aboriginal Studies into Schools*. Adelaide: Education Department of South Australia Publications Branch.

Education Department of South Australia (1992) *Recommended Books for Aboriginal Studies*. Adelaide: Darlington Materials Development Centre.

Education Department of South Australia (1992a) *South Australian Recommended Resource Guide*. Adelaide: Darlington Materials Development Centre.

Education Department of South Australia (1992b) *The Kaurna People: Aboriginal People of the Adelaide Plains*. Adelaide: Darlington Materials Development Centre.

Education Department of South Australia (1992c) *The Adnyamathanha people: Aboriginal People of the Flinders Ranges*. Adelaide: Darlington Materials Development Centre.

Education Department of South Australia (1993a) *Developing Positive Attitudes to Diversity and Difference—a Culturally Inclusive Society*. Adelaide: Darlington Materials Development Centre.

Education Department of South Australia (1993b), *Aboriginal Perspectives in Australian Studies*. Adelaide: Darlington Materials Development Centre.

Education Department of Western Australia (1994a) *Student Outcome Statements, Working Edition*. Perth: Education Department of Western Australia.

Education Department of Western Australia (1994b) *Supporting Linguistic and Cultural Diversity Through First Steps: The Highgate Project*. Perth: Education Department of Western Australia.

Education Department of Western Australia (1995) *Studies of Society and Environment: Report of the Student Outcome Statement Trial, 1994–1995*. Perth: Education Department of WA.

Education Department of Western Australia (1996a) *Australian History: An Aboriginal Perspective* (Books 1, 2, 3, and Information Handbook). Perth: Education Department of Western Australia.

Education Department of Western Australia (1996b) *Aboriginal Studies K–10* (Aboriginal Studies, Aboriginal Studies I, Aboriginal Studies II, Aboriginal Studies III and Teachers Information Handbook). Perth: Education Department of Western Australia.

Education Department of Western Australia (1998) *Student Outcome Statements, Society and Environment.* Perth: Education Department of Western Australia.

Education Queensland (1994) *A Framework and Guidelines for Aboriginal Studies and Torres Strait Islander Studies P–12.* Brisbane: Education Queensland.

Education Queensland (2000) *New Basics Project: Technical Paper.* Brisbane: Education Queensland.

Educational Media Australia (1988) *Communities and Ecosystems.* Melbourne: Educational Media.

Educational Media Australia (1991) *National Habitats of Australia.* Melbourne: Educational Media.

Edwards, S.R. (1993) 'Film and television in the classroom', *The New Zealand Journal of Social Studies*, 2, 2, 25–36.

Eggen, P. and Kauchak, D. (1999) *Educational Psychology: Windows on Classrooms.* New Jersey: Merrill.

Eisner, E.W. (1993) 'Reshaping assessment in education: some criteria in search of practice', *Journal of Curriculum Studies*, 25, 3, 219–233.

Eisner, E.W. (2000) 'Those who ignore the past . . .? 12 "easy" lessons, for the next millennium', *Journal of Curriculum Studies*, 32, 2, 343–357.

Eisner, E. and Vallance, E. (1974) *Conflicting Conceptions of Curriculum.* Berkeley, California: McCutchan Publishing Corporation.

Ellerton, N.F. and Clements, M.A. (1994) *The National Curriculum Debacle.* Perth: Meridian.

Ellington, H.I. (1995) 'The future of simulation/gaming in Britain'. In D. Crookall and K. Arai (eds) *Simulation and Gaming across Disciplines and Cultures.* London: Sage Publications.

Elliott, D.L., Nagel, K.C. and Woodward, A. (1985) 'Do textbooks belong in elementary social studies?', *Educational Leadership*, 42, 7, 22–25.

Ellis, A.K. and Fouts, J.T. (1993) *Research on Educational Innovations.* Princeton Junction, NJ: Eye on Education.

Elrich, M. (1994) 'The stereotype within', *Educational Leadership*, 51, 8, 12–15.

Eltis, K. (1993) 'Shaping the curriculum of Australian schools', *Curriculum Perspectives*, 13, 1, 48–52.

Eltis, K.J. (Chair) (1995) *Focusing on Learning: Report of the Review of Outcomes and Profiles in New South Wales Schooling.* Sydney: New South Wales Department of Training and Education Coordination.

Emmer, E.T. and Gerwels, M.C. (1998) 'Teachers' views and uses of cooperative learning', paper presented at the Annual Conference of the American Educational Research Association, San Diego.

Emmer, E., Evertson, C. and Worsham, M.E. (2000) *Classroom Management for Secondary Teachers*, 5th edition. Boston: Allyn & Bacon.

Employment and Skills Formation Council (1992) *The Australian Vocational Certificate Training System.* Canberra: AGPS.

Energy Resources of Australia (mid-1980s) *Ranger Mine and the Environment.* Energy Resources of Australia.

Energy Resources of Australia (mid-1980s) *Safeguarding Ranger Uranium.* Energy Resources of Australia.

Epstein, D. (1993) *Changing Classroom Cultures.* Stoke-on-Trent: Trentham Books.

Eraut, M., Goad, L. and Smith, G. (1975) *The Analysis of Curriculum Materials, Education Occasional Paper No. 2*, University of Sussex, Brighton.

Evans, R.W. (1998) 'Turf wars as a way of life: a framework for understanding the history of social studies', paper presented at the Annual Conference of the American Educational Research Association, San Diego.

Evans, R.W. (2000) 'Defining social studies, again and again, and again', paper presented at the Annual Conference of the American Educational Research Association, New Orleans.

Evers, F.T. (1998) *The Bases of Competence: Skills for*

Lifelong Learning and Employability. San Francisco: Jossey Bass.

Fan, L. and Kaeley, G.S. (1998) 'Textbook use and teaching strategies: an empirical study', paper presented at the Annual Conference of the American Educational Research Association, San Diego.

Fenton, E. (1991) 'Reflections on the "new social studies" ', *The Social Studies*, 82, 3, 84–90.

Ferrett, M. and Traill, R.D. (1994) 'Exploring links between children's fiction and children's understanding of Australian history', *Curriculum Perspectives*, 14, 1, 33–40.

Fetterman, D.M. (1998) 'Webs of meaning: computer and internet resources for educational research and instruction', *Educational Researcher*, 27, 3, 22–31.

Field, S.L., Labbo, L., Wilhelm, R. and Garrett, A. (1996) 'To touch, to feel, to see: artifact inquiry in the social studies classroom', *Social Education*, 60, 3, 141–143.

Fien, J. (1996) *Teaching for a Sustainable World*. Brisbane: Griffith University.

Fien, J. (2000) *Teaching and Learning for a Sustainable Future*, http://www4.gu.edu.au/ext/unesco

Finch, L. (1999) 'Discovering democracy: the last of the Leviathans?', *Curriculum Perspectives*, 19, 3, 63–66.

Filer, A. (ed.) (2000) *Assessment: Social Practice and Social Product*. London: Routledge/Falmer.

Finn, B. (Chair) (1991) *Young People's Participation in Post-Compulsory Education and Training*. Report of the Australian Education Council Review Committee. Canberra: AGPS.

Fitzgerald, T. (1990) *Between Life and Economics*. Sydney: Australian Broadcasting Commission.

Flanagan, R. (1996) 'Unintended results of using instructional media: a study of second and third graders', paper presented at the Annual Conference of the American Educational Research Association, New York.

Flavell, J.A. (1979) 'Metacognition and cognitive monitoring: a new area of cognitive-developmental enquiry', *American Psychologist*, 34, 906–911.

Forman, J.D. (1984) *Doomsday Plus Twelve*. New York: Scribner.

Forrest-Pressley, D.L., MacKinnon, G.E. and Walker, T.G. (eds) (1985) *Metacognition, Cognition and Human Performance*, Vols 1 and 2. New York: Academic Press.

Forster, E.M. (1985) *A Passage to India*. Melbourne: Penguin.

Forster, M. (1994) 'DART: assisting teachers to use the English Profile'. In J. Warhurst (ed.) *Teaching and Learning, Implementing the Profiles*. Canberra: ACSA.

Forster, M. and Masters, G. (1996a) *Portfolios Assessment Resource Kit*. Melbourne: ACER.

Forster, M. and Masters, G. (1996b) *Developmental Assessment*. Melbourne: ACER.

Foster, S., Morris J.W. and Davis, O.L. (1996) 'Prospects for teaching historical analysis and interpretation: national curriculum standards for history meet current history textbooks', *Journal of Curriculum and Supervision*, 11, 4, 367–385.

Foster, V. (1996) 'Whereas the people...and civics education: another case of "add women and stir" ', *Curriculum Perspectives*, 16, 1, 52–55.

Foster, V. (2000) 'Girls; status as learner-citizens: issues for values, education and citizenship education', paper presented at the International Conference on Values, Education and Citizenship Education in the New Century, Chinese University of Hong Kong.

Fowler, S.M. (1994) 'Two decades of using simulation games for cross-cultural training', *Simulation and Gaming*, 25, 1, 18–27.

Fraenkel, J. (1973) 'The importance of learning activities', *Social Education*, 37, 674–678.

Francis, D. and Holt, J. (1997) 'Statements and profiles: where are they now?', *EQ Australia* 3, Spring, 15–18.

Freeland, K. (1991) *Managing the Social Studies Curriculum*. Lancaster: Technomic Publishing Co.

Frymier, J. (1977) *Annehurst Curriculum Classification System: A Practical Way to Individualise Instruction*. Lafayette, Ind: Kappa Delta Pi Press.

Fullan, M. (1999) *Change Forces: The Sequel*. London: Falmer.

Fuller, C. and Stone, M.E. (1998) 'Teaching social

studies to diverse learners', *The Social Studies*, 89, 4, 154–157.

Futoran, G.C., Schofield, J.W. and Eurich-Fulcer, R. (1995) 'The Internet as a K–12 educational resource: emerging issues of information access and freedom', *Computers and Education*, 24, 3, 229–236.

Galbally, J. (Chair Report) (1978) *The Review of Post-Arrival Programs and Services for Migrants*. Canberra: AGPS.

Gall, M.D. (1981) *Handbook for Evaluating and Selecting Curriculum Materials*. Boston: Allyn & Bacon.

Game, R. and Pringle, R. (1983) *Gender at Work*. Sydney: Allen & Unwin.

Garcia, J. and Briggs, G. (1998) 'Promoting the goals of social studies: a historical look (1980–1997) at social studies and multicultural education in the United States and Australia', paper presented at the Annual Conference of the American Educational Research Association, San Diego.

Gardner, P. (1997) *Managing Technology in the Middle School Classroom*. Melbourne: Hawker Brownlow Education.

Gilbert, K. (1994) *Me and Mary Kangaroo*. Melbourne: Penguin Books.

Gilbert, P. (1996) *Talking about Gender*. Canberra: Women's Employment Education and Training Advisory Group, DEET.

Gilbert, R. (1992) 'Citizenship, education and postmodernity', *British Journal of Sociology of Education*, 13, 1, 51–68.

Gilbert, R. (1993) 'Citizenship and the problem of identity'. In K. Kennedy, O.Watts and G. McDonald (eds) *Citizenship Education for a New Age*. Toowoomba: University of Southern Queensland Press.

Gilbert, R. (ed.) (1996) *Studying Society and Environment*. Melbourne: Macmillan.

Gilbert, R., Gordon, K., Hoepper, B. and Land, R. (1992) 'Love's Labours Lost?—writing a national statement', *Curriculum Perspectives*, 12, 4, 25–27.

Gill, J. and Reid, A. (1999) 'Civics education: the state of play or the play of the state?', *Curriculum Perspectives*, 19, 3, 31–40.

Gipps, C. (2000) 'Classroom assessment, learning and teaching: research from elementary schools in the United Kingdom', paper presented at the Annual Conference of the American Educational Research Association, New Orleans.

Gipps, C. and Murphy, P. (1994) *A Fair Test? Assessment, Achievement and Equity*. Buckingham: Open University Press.

Giroux, H. (1980) 'Critical theory and rationality in citizenship education', *Curriculum Inquiry*, 10, 4, 329–366.

Global Education Centre (1996) *Survival and Hope*. Adelaide: Global Education Centre.

Goalen, P. and Hendy, L. (1993) 'It's not just fun, it works!, Developing children's historical thinking through drama', *Curriculum Journal*, 4, 3, 363–383.

Goffman, E. (1976) *Gender Advertisements*. New York: Harper.

Good, T.L. and Brophy, J.E. (1984) *Looking in Classrooms*, 3rd edn. New York: Harper and Row.

Good, T.L. and Brophy, J. (1995) *Contemporary Educational Psychology*. USA: Longman.

Goodrich, H. (1997) 'Understanding rubrics', *Educational Leadership*, 54, 4, 14–17.

Goodson, I.F. and Marsh, C.J. (1996) *Studying School Subjects*. London: Falmer.

Gough, A. (1997) *Education and the Environment: Policy, Trends and Problems of Marginalisation*. Melbourne: ACER.

Grabrucker, M. (1988) *There's a Good Girl: Gender Stereotyping in the First Three Years*. London: Penguin.

Grady, N., Macpherson, R., Mulford, W. and Williamson, J. (1994) *Australian School Principals: Profile 1994*. Adelaide: Australian Principals Professional Development Council.

Graham, R. (1975) 'Youth and experiential learning', *Youth*, Yearbook No. 74, Part 1, Washington, DC: National Society for the Study of Education.

Grahame, K. (1929) *The Wind in the Willows*. London: Methuen.

Griffin, P. and Smith, P. (1998) *Outcome-Based Education: Issues and Strategies for Schools*. Canberra: ACSA.

Groome, H. (1991) 'Getting the pedagogy right: the next phase in Aboriginal studies'. In *Aboriginal Studies in the 90s: Where to Now?* Sydney: Aboriginal Studies Association.

Groome, H. (1994) *Teaching Aboriginal Studies Effectively*. Wentworth Falls: Social Science Press.

Groome, H. and Edwardson, L. (1996a) *Case Study*. Sydney: Aboriginal Studies Association.

Groome, H. and Edwardson, T. (1996b) 'Urban Aboriginal young people and identity'. Unpublished paper.

Gross, R. (1988) 'Forward to the trivia of the 1980s: the impending social studies program', *Phi Delta Kappan*, 70, 1, 47–49.

Grosz, E. (1994) *Volatile Bodies*. Sydney: Allen & Unwin.

Grumet, M. and Stone, L. (2000) 'Feminism and curriculum: getting our act together', *Journal of Curriculum Studies*, 32, 2, 183–198.

Grundy, S., Warhurst, J., Laird, D. and Maxwell, T. (1994) 'Interpreting the curriculum'. In E. Hatton (ed.) *Understanding Teaching*. Sydney: Harcourt Brace.

Guild, P. (1994) 'The culture/learning style connection', *Educational Leadership*, 51, 8, 16–21.

Gundjehmi Aboriginal Corporation (1998) 'The facts of Jabiluka: a guide to understanding the Jabiluka Uranium Proposal', *Issues*, 45, 16–25.

Gustafson, K. (1993) 'Government in Action: a simulation', *Social Education*, 57, 2, 90–94.

Haas, M.E. (1985) 'Evaluating sponsored materials', *How to do it in the Social Studies Classroom*, Series 4, 3. Washington DC: NCSS.

Haas, M. and Laughlin, M. (2000) 'Teaching current events: its status in social studies today', paper presented at the Annual Conference of the American Educational Research Association, New Orleans.

Hachiya, M. (1955) *Hiroshima Diary: The Journal of a Japanese Physician, August 6–September 30, 1945*, translated by W. Wells. Chapel Hill, NC: University of North Carolina Press.

Hackbarth, S. (1997) 'Integrating web-based learning activities into school curriculums', *Educational Technology*, 37, 3, 59–71.

Hahn, C. (1991) 'Controversial issues in social studies'. In James P. Shaver (ed.) *Handbook on Research on Social Studies Teaching and Learning*, 470–480. New York: Macmillan.

Hall, B.W. and Hewitt-Gervais, C.M. (1999) 'The application of student portfolios in primary/intermediate and self-contained/multi-age team classroom environments: implications for instruction, learning and assessment', paper presented at the Annual Conference of the American Educational Research Association, Montreal.

Hallam, J. (1998) 'Jabiluka: what the big fuss Down Under is all about', *Issues*, 45, 4–10.

Hamberger, N. M. (1997) 'From personal to professional values: conversations about conflicts', *Journal of Teacher Education*, 48, 4, 245–254.

Hamblin, D.J. (1973) *The First Cities*. New York: Time-Life.

Hamot, G.E. (2000) 'Democractic citizenship education curriculum reform: a study of three cross-cultural projects', paper presented at the Annual Conference of the American Educational Research Association, New Orleans.

Haney, W. and Madaus, G. (1989) 'Searching for alternatives to standardised tests: why, whats and whethers', *Phi Delta Kappan*, May, 683–687.

Hannan, B. (1992) 'National curriculum: a system perspective', *Unicorn*, 18, 3, 28–31.

Hanvey, R. (1978) *An Attainable Global Perspective*. New York: Center for Global Perspectives.

Harper, J. (1980) *Fathers at Home*. Melbourne: Penguin.

Harris, D. and Bell, C. (1994) *Evaluating and Assessing for Learning*. London: Kogan Page.

Hartman, J.A., De Cicco, E.K. and Griffin, G. (1994) 'Urban students thrive as independent researchers', *Educational Leadership*, 52, 3, 46–47.

Hawley, C.L. and Duffy, T.M. (1998) 'The role of the teacher in simulation learning environments', paper presented at the Annual Conference of the American Educational Research Association, San Diego.

Haycock, C.A. (1991) 'Resource-based Learning: a shift in the roles of teacher, learner', *NASSP Bulletin*, 75, 535, 15–22.

Hayes, D. (1998) 'The displacement of girls as the "educationally disadvantaged" subject: a genealogical tale', *Change: Transformations in Education*, 1, 2, 7–15.

Hebert, E.A. (1998) 'Lessons learned about student portfolios', *Phi Delta Kappan*, 79, 8, 583–585.

Hepburn, M.A. (1993) 'Concepts of pluralism and the implications for citizenship education', *The Social Studies*, 84, 1, 20–26.

Hickey, M.G. (1991) 'And then what happened, Grandpa? Oral history projects in the elementary classroom', *Social Education*, 55, 4, 216–217.

Hildebrand, G. (1989) 'Creating a gender-inclusive science education', *The Australian Science Teachers Journal*, 35, 3, 7–16.

Hill, Anthony (1994) *Burnt Stick*. Melbourne: Penguin Books.

Hill, B.V. (1981) 'Teacher commitment and the ethics of teaching for commitment', *Religious Education*, 76, 322–336.

Hill, B.V. (1988) *Values Education in Australian Schools*. Melbourne: ACER.

Hill, B.V. (1994) *Teaching Secondary Social Studies in a Multicultural Society*. Melbourne: Longman Cheshire.

Hill, B.V. (1996) 'Civics and citizenship and the teaching of values', *Unicorn*, 22, 1, 34–43.

Hirst, J. (1998) *Discovering Democracy: A Guide to Government and Law in Australia*. Melbourne: Curriculum Corporation.

Hirst, P. (1974) *Knowledge and the Curriculum*. London: Routledge and Kegan Paul.

Hofstede, G. (1986) 'Cultural differences in teaching and learning', *International Journal of Intercultural Relations*, 10, 301–320.

Hogan, D. (1996) 'Before virtue: a study in the theory of interests and civics education', *Australian Educational Researcher*, 22, 3, 45–70.

Hogan, D. and Fearnley-Sander, M. (1999) 'An education for heteronomy: a critique of the Discovering Democracy project', *Curriculum Perspectives*, 19, 3, 57–62.

Hogan, D., Fearnley-Sander, M. and Stephen

Lamb, S. (1996) 'From civics to citizenship: *Whereas the people* and civic education'. In K. Kennedy (ed.) *New Challenges for Citizenship Education*. Canberra: Australian Curriculum Studies Association.

Howe, H. (1987), 'Can schools teach values?', *Teachers College Record*, 89, 1, Fall, 55–68.

Hoy. A. (1925) *Civics for Australian Schools*. Melbourne: Lothian Publishing Co.

Hughes, P.W. (1990) *A National Curriculum: Promise or Warning, Occasional Paper No. 14*. Canberra: Australian College of Education.

Hunkins, F. (1980) *Curriculum Development: Program Improvement*. Columbus, Ohio: Merrill.

Hunt, M.P. and Metcalf, L.E. (1968) *Teaching High School Social Studies*. New York: Harper and Row.

Hunt, N.P. (1997) 'Using technology to prepare teachers for the twenty-first century', *Asia-Pacific Journal of Teacher Education*, 25, 3, 345–350.

Hunter, M. (1982) *Mastery Learning*. El Segundo. California: TIP Publication.

Hyerle, D. (1996) *Visual Tools for Constructing Knowledge*. Alexandria, Virginia: ASCD.

Iannaccone, Carmen J. *et al.* (1992) 'Social skills instruction in secondary schools: factors affecting its implementation', *The High School Journal*, 75, 2, December/January, 111–116.

Interactive Multimedia (1993) *Investigating Lake Iluka*. Belconnen: Interactive Multimedia.

Jimonez, S. (1999) 'Conceptions of subject matter: history teachers and civics and citizenship education', paper presented at the Annual Conference of the Australian Association for Research in Education, Melbourne, November.

Jimonez, S. and Hunter, J. (1999) 'Civics and citizenship education: what pedagogy? what possibilities?', *Curriculum Perspectives*, 19, 3, 19–30.

Kagan, S. (1989) 'The structural approach to cooperative learning', *Educational Leadership*, 47, 4, 12–15.

Kain, C.J. (1988) 'Social skills in the school curriculum: a systematic approach', *NASSP Bulletin*, 107–110.

Kanning, R.G. (1994) 'What multimedia can do in our classrooms', *Educational Leadership*, 51, 7, 40–44.

Kaplan, A. (1964) *The Conduct of Inquiry: Methodology for Behavioral Science*. San Francisco: Chandler.

Kaplan, A. (2000) 'Teacher and student: designing a democratic relationship', *Journal of Curriculum Studies*, 32, 3, 377–402.

Kaplan, P.S. (1990) *Educational Psychology for Tomorrow's Teacher*. St Paul: West Publishing Company.

Kaufman, R., Westland, C. and Engvall, R. (1997) 'The dichotomy between the concept of professionalism and the reality of sexism in teaching', *Journal of Teacher Education*, 48, 2, 118–126.

Kearns, J.F., Kleinert, H.L. and Kennedy, S. (1999) 'We need not exclude anyone', *Educational Leadership*, 56, 6, 33–38.

Keating, P.J. (1993) Speech to the Australian Teachers Union National Conference, Melbourne, 15 January.

Kell, P. and Singh, M.G. (1999) 'Australia's image takes a battering in Malaysia', *Campus Review*, 5 August.

Kelly, A. (1988) 'Gender differences in teacher–pupil interactions: A meta-analytic review', *Research in Education*, 39, 1–23.

Kemmis, S. (1986) *Curriculum Theorizing: Beyond Reproduction Theory*. Geelong: Deakin University Press.

Kemmis, S. *et al.* (1983) *Towards the Socially Critical School*. Melbourne: VISE.

Kemmis, S., Cole, P. and Suggett, D. (1994) 'Orientations to curriculum'. In E. Hatton (ed.) *Understanding Teaching*. Sydney: Harcourt Brace.

Kemp, D. (1997) *Discovering Democracy. A Ministerial Statement*. Canberra: AGPS.

Kennedy, K.J. (1992) 'National curriculum: an educational perspective', *Unicorn*, 18, 3, 32–37.

Kennedy, K. (1994) 'Conflicting conceptions of citizenship and their relevance for the school curriculum', paper presented at the Teacher Educators' Conference, Political Education: The role of Political Educators, Parliament House, 7–9 December.

Kennedy, K. (1995a) 'Conflicting conceptions of citizenship'. In M. Print (ed.) *Issues and Practices in Citizenship Education*. Canberra: Australian Curriculum Studies Association.

Kennedy, K. (1995b) 'Civics education in the US is near universal but may be short on values', *ACE News*, 14, 2, 7–8.

Kennedy, K. (1996) 'Civics and citizenship education: a new priority for the school curriculum', a Key Note Address prepared for the Canberra Summer School for Teachers of Studies of Society and the Environment, University of Canberra, 24 January.

Kennedy, K. (ed.) (1997a) *Citizenship Education and the Modern State*. London: Falmer.

Kennedy, K. (1997b) 'Policy contexts for civics education in Australia: can social reconstruction and neo-conservatism co-exist?', paper presented at the Annual Conference of the Australian Association for Research in Education, Brisbane, 1–4 December.

Kennedy, K. and Connor, D. (1999) 'The role of elite policy makers in the construction of civics education in Australia: methodological issues in sampling, identification and selection', paper presented at the Annual Conference of the Australian Association for Research in Education, Melbourne, 29 November.

Kennedy, K. and Mellor, M. (1999) 'Reviving civics education for a new agenda in Australia: the contribution of the IEA study', paper presented at the Annual Meeting of the American Educational Research Association, Montreal, 20–24 April.

Kenway, J. (1992) 'Into the zone of the unknown: profiles, markets and social justice', *Curriculum Perspectives*, 12, 1, 66–72.

Kenway, J. (1996) 'Reasserting masculinity in Australian schools', *Women's Studies International Forum*, 19, 4, 447–466.

Kenway, J., Willis, S., Blackmore, J. and Rennie, L. (1997) *Answering Back: Girls, Boys and Feminism in Schools*. Sydney: Allen & Unwin.

Ker Wilson, B. (1988) *Acacia Terrace*. Gosford, NSW: Ashton Scholastic.

Ketchell, J. (1994) *Torres Strait Islander Families*, Cairns, unpublished paper.

Ketchell, J. (1997) 'Ailan Pasin'. In Curriculum Corporation, *Footprints ... to Country, Kin and Cultures*. Melbourne: Curriculum Corporation.

Kidd, D. (1992) *The Fat and Juicy Place*. Sydney: Angus and Robertson.

Killen, R. (1996) *Effective Teaching Strategies*. Wentworth Falls: Social Science Press.

Killen, R. (1998) *Effective Teaching Strategies*, 2nd edition. Sydney: Social Science Press.

Kirman, J.M. (1991) 'A note on Helga's dilemma: the dark side of Kohlberg', *Social Education*, 55, 1, 33 and 64.

Kirman, J.M. (1995) 'Teaching about local history using customised photographs', *Social Education*, 59, 1, 11–13.

Klassen-Endrizzi, C. and Ruiz, R. (1995) 'Constructing a multicultural orientation through children's literature'. In J.M. Larkin and C.E. Sleeter (eds) *Developing Multicultural Teacher Education Curricula*. New York: SUNY Press.

Kobrin, D., Abbott, E., Ellingwood J. and Horton, D. (1993) 'Learning history by doing history', *Educational Leadership*, 50, 7, 39–41.

Knupfer, N.N. (1998) 'Gender divisions across technology advertisements and the WWW: implications for educational equity', *Theory Into Practice*, 37, 1, 54–63.

Koeller, S. (1996) 'Multicultural understanding through literature', *Social Education*, 60, 2, 99–103.

Kohlberg, L. (ed.) (1975) 'The cognitive-developmental approach to moral education', *Phi Delta Kappan*, LVI, 10, 670–677.

Kohlberg, L. (1966) 'Moral education in schools: a developmental view', *School Review*, 74, 3, 135–143.

Kohlberg, L. and Hewer, A. (1983) *Moral States: A Current Formulation and a Response to Critics*. New York: S. Karger.

Kohn, A. (1997) 'How not to teach values: a critical look at character education', *Phi Delta Kappan*, 78, 6, 428–439.

Kulhavy, W., Woodard, K.A., Haygood, R.C. and Webb, J.M. (1993) 'Using maps to remember text: an instructional analysis', *British Journal of Educational Psychology*, 63, 161–169.

Kurfman, D.G. (ed.) (1977) *Developing Decision-making Skills*, 47th Yearbook. Virginia: National Council for the Social Studies, USA.

Kwan, E. (1994) 'Oaths and flags: an ambiguous heritage'. In D. Horne and P. Layland (eds) *Teaching Young Australians to be Citizens*. Monash University: National Centre for Australian Studies.

Labour Resource Centre (1990) *Pay Equity for Women in Australia*. Canberra: AGPS.

Lamerton, C. (1999) 'Toying with anarchy, discovering democracy', *EQ Australia*, Spring, 12.

Land, R. (ed.) (1994) *Invasion and After: A Case Study in Curriculum Politics*. Brisbane: Griffith University.

Larkin, J.M. (1995) 'Curriculum themes and issues in multicultural teacher education programs'. In J.M. Larkin and C.E. Sleeter (eds) *Developing Multicultural Teacher Education Curricula*. New York: SUNY Press.

Laughlin, M.A. and Haas, M.E. (1997) 'What do students learn about Australia by using United States published social studies/geography textbooks?', paper presented at the Education for Responsible Citizenship Conference, Sydney.

Laughlin, M.A., Hartoonian, H.M. and Sanders, N.M. (eds) (1989) *From Information to Decision-Making*. Washington: NCSS.

Lawton, D. (1981) 'Problems of the common curriculum', *Melbourne Studies in Education 1981*. Melbourne: University of Melbourne.

Learning Development Unit (1990) *Farm Development and Simulation*. Bristol: Learning Development Unit.

Lederman, L.C. (1984) 'Debriefing', *Simulation and Games*, 15, 4, 415–431.

Lederman, L.C. (1992) 'Debriefing: towards a systematic assessment of theory and practice', *Simulation and Gaming*, 22, 2, 145–160.

Lederman, L.C. and Kato, F. (1995) 'Debriefing the debriefing process: a new look'. In D. Crookall and K. Arai (eds) *Simulation and Gaming across Disciplines and Cultures*. London: Sage Publications.

Lederman, L.C. and Stewart, L.P. (1991) 'The rules of the game', *Simulation and Gaming*, 22, 4, 502–507.

Lee, V. and das Gupta, P. (1995) *Children's Cognitive*

and Language Development. Oxford: Oxford University Press.

Lee, A. and Taylor, E. (1996) 'The dilemma of obedience: a feminist perspective on the making of engineers', *Educational Philosophy and Theory*, 28, 1, 57–75.

Leeman, W. P. (1999) 'American history websites for use in secondary schools', *Social Education*, 63, 3, 144–151.

Leming, J.S. (1998) 'Some critical thoughts about the teaching of critical thinking', *The Social Studies*, 89, 2, 61–66.

Lepani, B. (1996) 'Education in the information society'. In K. Kennedy (ed.) *New Challenges for Citizenship Education*. Canberra: Australian Curriculum Studies Association.

Leppard, L. (1993a) 'Discovering a democratic tradition and educating for public politics', *Social Education*, 57, 1, 23–26.

Leppard, L.J. (1993b) 'Designing our futures by choice', *Social Education*, 57, 3, 127–130.

Levin, H.M. and Meister, G.R. (1985) *Educational Technology and Computers: Promises, Promises, Always Promises*. Stanford University, California: Institute for Research on Educational Finance and Governments.

Levitt, G.A., and Longstreet, W.S. (1993) 'Controversy and the teaching of authentic civic values', *The Social Studies*, 84, 4, 142–148.

Levitz, C.M. (1990) 'Nonadversarial conflict resolution: simulation in a school setting', *Social Education*, 54, 5, 263–266.

Levstik, L.S. and Smith, D.B. (1996) ' "I've never done this before". Building a community of historical inquiry, in a third-grade classroom', *Advances in Research on Teaching*, 6, 85–114.

Levy, T. (1999) 'Towards a humane world: making a difference with social studies', *Social Education*, 63, 1, 6–7.

Liesch, J.R. (1992) *The Education of Indians in North America: A Basis for Comparison*. Sydney: Aboriginal Education Unit, NSW Department of School Education.

Lingard, B. (1998) 'Contextualising and utilising the "what about the boys?" backlash for gender equity goals', *Change: Transformations in Education*, 1, 2, 16–30.

Long, C. (1906) *The Citizen Reader*. London: Cassell.

Lundeberg, M. (1997) 'You guys are overreacting: teaching prospective teachers about subtle gender bias', *Journal of Teacher Education*, 48, 1, 55–61.

McCrae, D. (1999) 'Lots of good pickings', *EQ Australia*, Spring, 16–18.

McElroy, B. (1984) 'Models and reality: integrating practical work and fieldwork in geography'. In J. Fien, R. Gerber and P. Wilson (eds) *The Geography Teacher's Guide to the Classroom*. Melbourne: Macmillan.

McGowan, T.M. (1987) 'Children's fiction as a source of social studies skill building', *ERIC Digest* (No. 37). Bloomington, Indiana: Clearinghouse for Social Studies/Social Science Education.

McGuire, M.E. (1996) 'Teacher education, some current challenges', *Social Education*, 60, 2, 89–94.

Macintyre, S. (Chair) (1994) *Whereas the people: Civics and Citizenship Education*. Canberra: AGPS.

Macintyre, S. (1995) 'Diversity, citizenship and the curriculum', Keynote Address, Biennial Conference of the Australian Curriculum Studies Association, University of Melbourne, 13 July.

Macintyre, S. (1996) 'Diversity, citizenship and the curriculum'. In K. Kennedy (ed.) *New Challenges for Citizenship Education*. Canberra: Australian Curriculum Studies Association.

Macintyre, S. (1999) *A Concise History of Australia*. Cambridge: Cambridge University Press.

McKay, S. and Pittam, J. (1993) 'Determinants of Anglo-Australian stereotypes of the Vietnamese in Australia', *Australian Journal of Psychology*, 45, 1, 17–23.

McKenna, R.J. (1991) 'Business computerized simulation: the Australian experience', *Simulation and Gaming*, 22, 1, 36–62.

McKeown, M.G. and Beck, I.L. (1999) 'Getting the discussion started', *Educational Leadership*, 57, 3, 25–28.

McLean, B. (1987) 'Multicultural studies'. In C. Marsh (ed.) *Teaching Social Studies*. Sydney: Prentice Hall.

McLean, K. and Wilson, B. (1995) 'The big picture', *Curriculum Perspectives*, 15, 3, 56–58.

McMillan, J.H., Workman, D. and Myran, S. (1999) 'Elementary teachers' classroom assessment and grading practices', paper presented at the Annual Conference of the American Educational Research Association Conference, Montreal.

McNeil, L.M. (1988) 'Contradictions of control, Part 2, Teachers, students and curriculum', *Phi Delta Kappan*, 69, 6, 432–438.

McRobbie, N. (1990) *Bip the Snapping Bungaroo*. Broome, WA: Magabala Books Corporation.

McTighe, J. (1997) 'What happens between assessments?', *Educational Leadership*, 54, 4, 6–13.

Mabry, L. and Stake, R. (1998) 'Schools and the children's museum: orthogonal space', paper presented at the Annual Conference of the American Educational Research Association, San Diego.

Mahoney, P. and Smedley, S. (1998) 'New times, old panics: the underachievement of boys', *Change: Transformations in Education*, 1, 2, 41–50.

Mahood, W., Bimer, L. and Lowe, W. (1991) *Teaching Social Studies in Middle and Senior High Schools*. New York: Macmillan.

Major, M.R. (1996) 'No Friends but the Mountains: a simulation on Kurdistan', *Social Education*, 60, 3, C1–C8.

Mann, L. (1989) 'Becoming a better decision maker', *Australian Psychologist*, 24, 2, 141–156.

Marsh, C.J. (1994) *Producing a National Curriculum: Plans and Paranoia*. Sydney: Allen & Unwin.

Marsh, C.J. (1995) *Assessment Support Materials for the Studies of Society and Environment*. Perth: Cross-Sectoral Consortium.

Martin, A. (1990) 'Social studies in kindergarten: a case study', *The Elementary School Journal*, 90, 3, 305–317.

Martin, K. (1995) *Teaching and Resource Unit*, Stradbroke Island, unpublished paper.

Martorella, P.H. (1976) *Social Studies Strategies: Theory into Practice*. New York: Harper and Row.

Massialas, B.G. (1992) 'The "new social studies"—retrospect and prospect', *Social Studies*, 83, 3, 120–124.

Massie, M. (1997) 'Intranets: spinning your own web'. In D. Ingvarson (ed.) *A Teacher's Guide to the Internet: The Australian Experience*. Melbourne: Heinemann.

Maxim, G.W. (1983) *Social Studies and the Elementary School Child*. Columbus, Ohio: Merrill.

May, S. (2000) 'Multiculturalism in the 21st century: challenges and possibilities', paper presented at the Annual Conference of the American Educational Research Association, New Orleans.

Mayer, E. (Chair) (1992) *Putting General Education to Work. The Key Competencies Report*. The Australian Education Council and Ministers for Vocational Education, Employment and Training.

Medley, R. and White, C. (1992) 'Assessing the national curriculum: lessons from assessing history', *The Curriculum Journal*, 3, 1, 63–74.

Mehlinger, H.D. and Davis, D.L. (1981) *The Social Studies*, 80th Yearbook of the National Society for the Study of Education. Chicago: University of Chicago Press.

Mehrens, W.A. (1998) 'Consequences of assessment: what is the evidence?', paper presented at the Annual Conference of the American Educational Research Association, San Diego.

Mellor, S. (1996) 'What can history contribute to the development of citizenship curriculum?', *Unicorn*, 22, 1, 72–81.

Midden, K.S. (1990) *Environmental Gaming Simulation*. Illinois: Carbondale.

Miller, M.L. (1991) 'School library media professionals: working for the Information Age', *NASSP Bulletin*, 75, 535, 43–48.

Milligan, S. (1994) *Women in the Teaching Profession*. Canberra: AGPS.

Ministerial Council on Education, Employment, Training and Youth Affairs (1999) *The Adelaide Declaration on National Goals for Schooling in the Twenty-First Century*. Canberra: DETYA.

Ministry of Education British Columbia (1994) *Performance Assessment*. Victoria, BC: Ministry of Education.

Ministry of Education Victoria (1987) *The Social Education Framework P–10, Effective Participation in Society*. Melbourne: Schools Division.

Mitchell, M. (1993) 'A teacher's view of the National Statement on Science', *Curriculum Perspectives*, 13, 1, 60–61.

Montague, E.J. (1987) *Fundamentals of Secondary Classroom Instruction*. Columbus, Ohio: Merrill.

Moore, S. (1988) 'The importance of a liberal education', Key Note Address, Annual Conference of the National Council for Independent Schools, Brisbane, 29 September–2 October.

Morgan, J.C. (1991) 'Using *Econ and Me* to teach economics to children in primary grades', *The Social Studies*, 82, 5, 195–197.

Morgan, J.R. (1984) 'An assessment of the suitability of chosen areas of the social studies K–10 syllabus being taught with the aid of computer-assisted learning techniques', unpublished paper, Murdoch University, Perth.

Morgan, S. and Bancroft, B. (1996) *Dan's Grandpa*. Fremantle: Sandcastle Books.

Morris, J. (1992) 'Back to the future': the impact of political ideology on the design and implementation of geography in the National Curriculum', *The Curriculum Journal*, 3, 1, 75–85.

Morris, P. (1994) *Introduction to Curriculum Development*. Hong Kong: University of Hong Kong Press.

Morrison, C. (1992) 'Open Letter', *The Society and Culture Association Journal*, 34, 45.

Moyles, J. (ed.) (1995) *Beginning Teaching: Beginning Learning in Primary Education*. Buckingham: Open University Press.

Mui, Y.H. (1993) 'From multiple media to multimedia—a convergence of vision', paper presented at the Australian Computers in Education Conference, Sydney.

Muir, S.P. (1996) 'Simulations for elementary and primary school social studies', *Simulation and Gaming* 27, 1, 41–73.

Murdoch, W. (1916) *The Australian Citizen*. Melbourne: Whitcomb and Tombs.

Murray, L. (1984) 'Learning geography through classroom and library research'. In J. Fien, R. Gerber and P. Wilson (eds) *The Geography Teacher's Guide to the Classroom*. Melbourne: Macmillan.

Musgrave, P. (1994) 'How should we make Australians?', *Curriculum Perspectives*, 14, 3, 11–18.

National Aboriginal Education Committee (1981) *Submission to the House of Representatives Standing Committee on Aboriginal Affairs*. Canberra: Commonwealth Department of Education.

National Aboriginal Education Committee (1985) *Philosophy, Aims and Policy Guidelines for Aboriginal and Torres Strait Islander Education*. Canberra: AGPS.

National Archives (1998) *Convict Fleet to Dragon Boat*. Canberra: Ripple Media/National Archives.

National Council for the Social Studies (1982) *Position Statement on Global Education*. Washington, DC: National Council for the Social Studies.

National Council for the Social Studies (1994) 'Ten thematic strands in social studies', *Social Education*, 58, 6, 365–368.

National Council for the Social Studies (1996) 'Handbook on teaching social issues', *Bulletin* No. 93.

National Council for the Social Studies (1997) 'Fostering civic virtue: character education in the social studies', *Social Education*, 61, 4, 225–227.

National Council for the Social Studies, Academic Freedom Committee (1991) 'Academic freedom and the social studies teacher', *Social Education*, 55, 1, 13–15.

National Council for the Social Studies Task Force (1984) 'In search of a scope and sequence for social studies', *Social Education*, 48, 4, April, 249–263.

Nean, P., Price, K., Tassell, D. and Tripcony, P. (1995) *Aboriginal Studies and Torres Strait Islander Studies: A Resource Guide for Schools*. Melbourne: Curriculum Corporation.

Neighbour, B. (1992) 'Enhancing geographical inquiry and learning', *International Research in Geographical and Environmental Education*, 1, 1, 14–23.

Neighbour, B.M. (1995) *A Committed Impartial Approach to Teaching Economic Controversies*. Unpublished PhD thesis, University of Queensland.

Neill, M. (1998) 'National tests are unnecessary and harmful', *Educational Leadership*, 55, 6, 45–46.

Nelson, M.R. (1992) *Children and Social Studies*, 2nd edition. New York: Harcourt Brace Jovanovich.

New South Wales Dairy Corporation (1988) *Food: Your Choice*. Sydney: New South Wales Dairy Corporation.

New South Wales Department of School Education (1992) *Anti-racism Policy Statement*. Sydney: Department of School Education.

New South Wales Department of School Education (1994) *Koori Images and Discussion Starters*. Sydney: Aboriginal Education Unit.

New South Wales Department of School Education (1995) *Aboriginal Visions*. Sydney: Aboriginal Education Unit.

New South Wales Department of School Education (1996a) *Aboriginal Education Policy*. Sydney: DSE.

New South Wales Department of School Education (1996b) *Is different, is interesting: Anti-racism Discussion Video for Secondary Schools*. Sydney: DSE.

New South Wales Department of School Education (1996c) *Principles for Assessment and Reporting in NSW Government Schools*. Sydney: NSW Department of School Education.

Newmann, F.M. (1990) 'Higher order thinking in teaching social studies: a rationale for the assessment of classroom thoughtfulness', *Journal of Curriculum Studies*, 22, 1, 41–56.

Newmann, F.M. and Wehlage, G.G. (1993) 'Five standards of authentic instruction', *Educational Leadership*, 50, 7, 8–12.

Nicholson, John (1997) *A Home Among the Gum Trees*. Sydney: Allen & Unwin.

Northup, T., Barth, J. and Kranze, H. (1991) 'Technology standards for social studies: a proposal', *Social Education*, 55, 4, 218–220.

Nuthall, G. (1995) *Understanding Student Thinking and Learning in the Classroom*, mimeograph, University of Canterbury, Christchurch.

O'Brien, Robert C. (1971) *Mrs Frisby and the Rats of NIMH*. London: Penguin Books.

O'Faircheallaigh, C. (1991) 'Uranium policy and the economy', *Current Affairs Bulletin*, 68, 3, 4–11.

OECD (1986) *Role of Women in the Economy: Australia*. Paris: OEDC.

Office of the Prime Minister (1995) *Government Response to the Report of the Civics Expert Group*. Canberra: Office of the Prime Minister.

Oliver, D.W., Newmann, F.M. and Singleton, L.R. (1992) 'Teaching public issues in the secondary school classroom', *Social Studies*, 83, 3, 100–103.

Olsen, D.G. (2000) 'Inquiry, problem solving and critical thinking: are these constructivist methods of teaching?', paper presented at the Annual Conference of the American Educational Research Association, New Orleans.

One Nation (1998) Web Page.

Orlich, D.C., Harder, R.J., Callahan, R.C. and Gibson, H.W. (1998) *Teaching Strategies*, 5th edition. Boston: Houghton Mifflin.

Oser, F.K. (1986) 'Moral education and values education: the discourse perspective'. In M.C. Wittrock (ed.) *Handbook of Research on Teaching*, 3rd edition. New York: Macmillan.

Ovington, D. (1986) *Kakadu*. Canberra: AGPS.

Owen, S. *et al.* (1978) *Educational Psychology: An Introduction*. Boston: Little, Brown.

Paley, V. G. (1979) *Oppression and Social Justice*. Needham Heights: Ginn Press.

Park, R. (1978) *Come Danger, Come Darkness*. Sydney: Hodder and Stoughton.

Parker, W. (1991) 'Social studies for the millennium', *Education Leadership*, 48, 4, 85.

Parker, W.C. (1996) 'Introduction: Schools as laboratories of democracy'. In W.C. Parker (ed.) *Educating the Democratic Mind*. Albany: SUNY Press.

Parker, W.C., McDaniel, J.E. and Valencia, S.W. (1991) 'Helping students think about public issues: instruction versus prompting', *Social Education*, 55, 1, 41–44.

Parkinson, A. (1913) *Civics Series for Schools*. Sydney: William Brooks.

Parks, S. (1999) 'Reducing the effects of racism in schools', *Educational Leadership*, 56, 7, 14–18.

Parry, L.J. (1998) 'Immigration and multiculturalism: issues in Australian society and schools', *Social Education*, 62, 7, 449–453.

Partington, G. and McCudden, V. (1992) *Ethnicity and Education*. Wentworth Falls: Social Science Press.

Pederson, P. (1995) 'Simulations: a safe place to take risks in discussing cultural differences', *Simulation and Gaming*, 26, 2, 34–41.

Peters, V., Vissers, G. and Heijne, G. (1998) 'The validity of games', *Simulation and Gaming*, 29, 1, 20–30.

Petranek, C.F., Corey, S. and Black, R. (1992) 'Three levels of learning in simulation: participating, debriefing, and journal writing', *Simulation and Gaming*, 23, 2, 174–185.

Phillips, A. and Taylor, B. (1980) 'Sex and skill', *Feminist Review*, 6, 55–66.

Pilkington-nugi Garimara, D. (1991) *Caprice— A Stockman's Daughter*. St Lucia: University of Queensland Press.

Piper, K. (1976) *Evaluation in the Social Sciences for Secondary Schools: Teachers' Handbook*. Canberra: AGPS.

Pixley, J. (1993) *Citizenship and Employment*. Melbourne: Cambridge University Press.

Poe, V.L., Ford, M.J. and Dobyns, S. (1998) 'Enhancing social studies instruction by exploring cultures through children's literature and technology', paper presented at the Annual Conference of the American Educational Research Association, San Diego.

Popkewitz, T. (1977) 'The latent values of the discipline-centred curriculum', *Theory and Research in Social Education*, 5, 1, 41–61.

Price, K. and Smith, S. (1997) 'I Spik Prapa'. In Curriculum Corporation, *Signposts ... to Country, Kin and Cultures*. Melbourne: Curriculum Corporation.

Pringle, R. (1973) 'Octavious Beale and the ideology of the birthrate: the Royal Commissions of 1904 and 1905', *Refractory Girl*, 3, 19–27.

Print, M., Kennedy, K. and Hughes, J. (1999) 'Reconstructing civics and citizenship education in Australia'. In J. Torney-Purta, J. Schwille and J. Amadeo (eds) *Civic Education Across Countries: Twenty-four National Case Studies from the IEA Civic Education Project*. Amsterdam: The International Association for the Evaluation of Educational Achievement.

Pugh, S.L., Garcia, J. and Margalef-Boada, S. (1994) 'Multicultural tradebooks in the social studies classroom', *The Social Studies*, 85, 2, 62–65.

Queensland Department of Education (1989) *For King and Country*. Brisbane: Government Printer.

Queensland Department of Education (1992) *Resources in Learning: A Focus on School Development*. Brisbane: Queensland Department of Education.

Queensland School Curriculum Council (1998) *Studies of Society and Environment Key Learning Area*. Brisbane: Queensland School Curriculum Council.

Queensland School Curriculum Council (1999) *Draft Studies of Society and Environment Years 1–10 Syllabus*. Brisbane: Queensland School Curriculum Council.

Radi, H. (ed.) (1989) *200 Australian Women: A Redress Anthology*. Sydney: Women's Redress.

Rainer, J., Guyton, E. and Bowen, C. (2000) 'Constructivist pedagogy in primary classrooms', paper presented at the Annual Conference of the American Educational Research Association, New Orleans.

Randel, J.M., Morris, B.A., Wetzel, C.D. and Whitehall, B.V. (1992) 'The effectiveness of games for educational purposes: a review of recent research', *Simulation and Games*, 23, 261–276.

Rank, H. (1994) 'Channel One: asking the wrong questions', *Educational Leadership*, 51, 4, 52–55.

Rawlins, Donna (1988) *Digging to China*. Melbourne: Penguin.

Reckase, M.D. (1997) 'Constructs assessed by portfolios: how do they differ from those assessed by other educational tests?', paper presented at the American Educational Research Association Conference, Chicago.

Regional Equity and Development School Support Centre (1995) *Torres Stait Islander Cultural Resource Kit*. Cairns: READ.

Reid, A. (1992) 'Social justice and the national curriculum', *Curriculum Perspectives*, 12, 4, 14–21.

Reid, A. (1995) 'Real problems or real gains—from

whose perspective?', *Curriculum Perspectives*, 15, 3, 76–80.

Renaud, L. and Stolovich, H. (1988) 'Simulation gaming: an effective strategy for creating appropriate traffic safety behaviours in five-year-old children', *Simulation and Games*, 19, 3, 325–345.

Resnick, L.B., Nolan, K.J. and Resnick, D.P. (1995) 'Benchmarking education standards', *Educational Evaluation and Policy Analysis*, 17, 4, 438–461.

Reynolds, H. (1995) *Fate of a Free People*. Melbourne: Penguin Books.

Reynolds, R. (1997) 'Changing conceptions of geography as exemplified in NSW. Syllabuses from 1965 to 1990', paper presented at the Biennial Conference, Australian Curriculum Studies Association, Sydney.

Reynolds, R.E. and Wade, S.E. (1986) 'Thinking about thinking about thinking: reflections on metacognition', *Harvard Educational Review*, 56, 307–317.

Rich, J.M. (1991) 'The conflict in moral education: teaching principles or virtues?', *The Clearing House*, 64, 5, 293–296.

Richardson, R. (1990) *Daring to be a Teacher*. Stoke-on-Trent: Trentham.

Richetti, C. and Sheerin, J. (1999) 'Helping students ask the right questions', *Educational Leadership*, 57, 3, 58–62.

Riddiford, B. (1992) 'Cultural studies', unpublished paper prepared for the second Aboriginal Studies Association Conference.

Risinger, C.F. (1996) 'The US Civil War on the World Wide Web', *Social Education*, 60, 3, 174–175.

Risinger, C.F. (1998) 'Separating wheat from chaff', *Social Education*, 62, 3, 148–150.

Roads and Traffic Authority of New South Wales (1988) *Are You in Control?* Sydney: Traffic Authority of New South Wales.

Roads and Traffic Authority of Victoria (1986) *Surveys*. Melbourne: RTA.

Rogers, P. (1990) 'Discovery, learning critical thinking and the nature of knowledge', *British Journal of Educational Studies*, 38, 1, 3–14.

Romanowski, M. (1996) 'Problems of bias in history textbooks', *Social Education*, 60, 3, 170–173.

Rosenshine, B. (1995) 'Advances in research on instruction', unpublished paper, University of Illinois at Urbana.

Rosenshine, B. and Meister, C. (1995) 'Direct instruction'. In L. Anderson (ed.) *International Encyclopaedia of Teaching and Teacher Education*, 2nd edition. Oxford: Elsevier Science Ltd.

Ross, E.W. (1996) 'The role of portfolio evaluation in social studies teacher education', *Social Education*, 60, 3, 162–166.

Rossi, J.A. (1995) 'In-depth study in an issues-oriented social studies classroom', *Theory and Research in Social Education*, 23, 88–120.

Rugen, L. and Hartl, S. (1994) 'The lessons of learning expeditions', *Educational Leadership*, 52, 3, 20–23.

Rushworth, M. *et al.* (1998–99) 'Resolving ethical dilemmas in the classroom', *Educational Leadership*, Dec–Jan., 38–41.

Russell, G. (1983) *The Changing Role of Fathers*. St Lucia: University of Queensland Press.

Rutter, M. (1972) *Maternal Deprivation Re-Assessed*. London: Penguin.

Ryan, B. (2000) 'Their future, not our past', *EQ Australia*, Winter, 2, 17–19.

Ryan, K. (1986) 'The new moral education', *Phi Delta Kappan*, November, 228–233.

Sage, S.M. (2000) 'The learning and teaching experiences in an online problem-based learning course', paper presented at the Annual Conference of the American Educational Research Association, New Orleans.

Salvia, J. and Ysseldyle, J.E. (1998) *Assessment*, 7th edition. Boston: Houghton Mifflin.

Sanchez, L.E. (1985) 'Controversial issues: practical considerations', *Educational Leadership*, December 1984/January 1985, 64–78.

Saunders, C. (1996) 'Challenges for citizenship', *Unicorn*, 22, 1, 30–34.

Savage, M.K. and Savage, T.V. (1993) 'Children's

literature in middle school social studies', *The Social Studies*, 84, 1, 32–36.

Savage, T.V. and Armstrong, D.G. (1987) *Effective Teaching in Elementary Social Studies*. New York: Macmillan.

Savoie, J.M. and Hughes, A.S. (1994) 'Problem-based learning as classroom solution, *Educational Leadership*, 52, 3, 54–57.

Saye, J. (1998) 'Creating time to develop student thinking', *Social Education*, 62, 6, 356–361.

Scheurman, G. (1998) 'From behaviourist to constructivist teaching', *Social Education*, 62, 1, 6–9.

Schneider, F. and Gullans, C. (1962) *Last Letters from Stalingrad*. New York: Morrow.

Schools Commission (1975) *Girls, School and Society*. Canberra: AGPS.

Schug, M.C. and Beery, R. (1987) *Teaching Social Studies in the Elementary School*. Glenview: Scott Foresman & Co.

Schug, M., Western, R.D. and Enochs, L.G. (1997) 'Why do social studies teachers use textbooks? The answer may be in economic theory', *Social Education*, 61, 2, 97–101.

Schunk, D.H. and Zimmerman, B.J. (eds) (1998) *Self-regulated Learning: From Teaching to Self-reflective Practice*. New York: Guilford Press.

Schwab, J. (1962) 'The concept of the structure of a discipline', *The Educational Record*, 43, 197–205.

Scieszka, J. (1989) *The True Story of the Three Little Pigs as Told by A. Wolf*. New York: Viking.

Segall, A. (1999) 'Critical history: implications for history/social studies education', *Theory and Research in Social Education*, 27, 3, 358–374.

Seidner, C.J. (1995) 'Simulation and the bottom line', *Simulation and Gaming*, 26, 4, 503–510.

Senate Employment, Education and Training References Committee (1998) *A Class Act: Inquiry into the Status of the Teaching Profession*. Canberra: Senate Printing Unit.

Shakeshaft, C. (1986) 'A gender at risk', *Phi Delta Kappan*, 67, 7, 500.

Shaw, Bruce (1995) *Our Heart is the Land*. Canberra: Aboriginal Studies Press.

She, Colleen (1995) *Teenage Refugees from China Speak Out*. New York: Rosen Publishing.

Shen, J. (1994) 'Ideological management in textbooks: a study of the changing image of the United States in China's geography textbooks', *Theory and Research in Social Education*, 22, 2, 194–214.

Shirts, R.G. (1976) *Rafa' Rafa'*. Lakeside: Interact Company.

Shirts, G. (1977) *BAFA–BAFA*. La Jolla, California: Simile II.

Shubik, M. (1989) 'Gaming: theory and practice, past and future', *Simulation and Games*, 20, 2.

Simon, S.B. (1972). *Values Clarification, A Handbook of Practical Strategies for Teachers and Students*. New York: Hart.

Simpson, M. (1996) Editor's notebook, 'Teaching controversial issues', *Social Education*, 60, 1, 5.

Singelis, T. and Pedersen, P. (1997) 'Conflict and mediation across cultures'. In K. Cushner and R. Brislin (eds) *Improving Intercultural Interactions: Modules for Cross-cultural Training Programs*, Vol. 2. Thousand Oaks, CA: Sage Publications.

Singer, A.J. (1997) *Social Studies for Secondary Schools: Teaching to Learn, Learning to Teach*. Mahwah, New Jersey: Lawrence Erlbaum.

Singer, A. (1999) 'Teaching multicultural social studies in an era of political eclipse', *Social Education*, 63, 1, 28–31.

Singh, M. (1993) 'Teaching social education from the standpoint of active citizens'. In K. Kennedy, O. Watts and G. McDonald (eds) *Citizenship Education for a New Age*. Toowoomba: University of Southern Queensland Press.

Singh, M.G. (1995) 'Translating studies of Asia: a curriculum statement for negotiation in Australian schools', unpublished paper, University of Central Queensland.

Sizer, T.R. (1999) 'No two are quite alike', *Educational Leadership*, 57, 1, 6–11.

Skilbeck, M. (1979) 'The nature of history and its place in the school curriculum', *Journal of the History Teachers' Association of Australia*, 6, 2–9.

Sklarz, D. (1993) 'Turning the promise of

multicultural education into practice', *The School Administrator*, 5, 50, 19–23.

Slavin, R.E. (1978) 'Student teams and achievement divisions', *Journal of Research and Development in Education*, 12, 39–49.

Sleeter, C. (1991) *Empowerment through Multicultural Education*. New York: SUNY Press.

Smith, D. (1991) 'Personal interest projects, a society and culture', paper presented at the biennial conference of the Australian Curriculum Studies Association, Adelaide.

Smith, D. and Halstead, B. (1990, 1992) *Lookin' for your Mob: A Guide to Tracing Aboriginal and Torres Strait Islander Family Trees*. Canberra: Aboriginal Studies Press.

Smith, R. (1986) 'Social studies education: the need for reappraisal', *Unicorn*, 12, 3, 147–153.

Smith, R. (1997) 'Make it plain, please', *Educational Quarterly*, 3, Spring, 22–23.

Smith, S. (1992) *Signposts*. Cairns: Education Office.

Smolicz, J.J. (1997) 'In search of a multicultural nation: the case of Australia from an international perspective'. In R.J. Watts and J.J. Smolicz (eds) *Cross Cultural Communication*. Frankfurt: Peter Lang.

Snelbecker, G.E. (1974) *Learning Theory, Instructional Theory and Psychoeducational Design*. New York: McGraw-Hill.

Soley, M. (1996) 'If it's controversial, why teach it?', *Social Education*, 60, 1, 9–14.

Southall, I. (1965) *Ash Road*. Sydney: Angus and Robertson.

Stafford, K. (1990) 'Media', unpublished paper, City Polytechnic of Hong Kong.

Stahl, R.J. and Van Sickle, R.L. (1992) *Cooperative Learning in the Social Studies Classroom*. Washington DC: NCSS.

Stanley, W.B. (1984) 'Approaches to teaching concepts and conceptualising: an analysis of social studies methods textbooks', *Theory and Research in Social Education*, XI, 4, 1–14.

Steinwachs, B. (1992a) 'How to facilitate a debriefing', *Simulation and Gaming*, 23, 2, 186–195.

Steinwachs, B. (1992b) *Some Resources on Simulation, Gaming and the Experiential Learning Methods*. New York: Organisational Planning and Participative Learning.

Stephens, M. (1997) 'Negotiating the curriculum: the discursive embodiment of gender', paper presented at Australian Curriculum Studies Association Conference, Sydney.

Stevens, Robert L. (1996) 'Teaching public values: three instructional approaches', *Social Education*, 60, 3, 155–158.

Stewart, N. (ed.) (1990) *Computers in the P–3 Classroom*. Lincolnville: Computer Education Centre.

'Stig of the Dump is in Maybury', Barry (1974) *Bandwagon*. Oxford University Press, Ely House, London W.1 pp 37–39, 'Stig of the Dump' was written by Clive King & reprinted in *Bandwagon* by permission of Hamish Hamilton Ltd. The acknowledgments page does not give a publication date for the original.

Stockhaus, S. (1979) *Selected Social Studies Skills*. Boulder, Colorado: Social Science Education Consortium.

Stonier, T. (1985) 'Computing the advantages', *Study of Society*, 26, 31–36.

Stradling, R., Noctor, M. and Baines, B. (1984) *Teaching Controversial Issues*. UK: Edward Arnold.

Strasser, B.B., Babcock, R.W., Cowan, R., Dalis, G.T., Gothold, S.T. and Rudolph, F. (1971) *Teaching Toward Inquiry*. Los Angeles: National Education Association of the United States.

Strike, K. (1996) 'The moral responsibilities of educations'. In J. Sikula (ed.) *Handbook of Research on Teacher Education*. New York: Macmillan.

Stroschein, T.M. (1991) 'Use a video camera to get to know your students', *The Social Studies*, 82, 1, 32–34.

Summers, A. (1975) *Damned Whores and God's Police*. Melbourne: Penguin.

Superka, D. *et al.* (1976) *Values Education Sourcebook, 176*. Boulder, Colorado: Social Science Education Consortium.

Swadling, M. (ed.) (1992) *Masterworks of Man and Nature: Preserving our World Heritage*. Melbourne: Harper-Macrae.

Swan Hill North Primary School Aboriginal Student Support and Parent Awareness Program Committee (1993) *Koori Photo Kit*. Swan Hill: ASSPA committee.

Szalay, A. (1995) 'Kakadu rock art', *Geo*, 17, 4, 41–52.

Taba, H. (1967) *Teachers Handbook for Elementary Social Studies*. Mento Park, California: Addison-Wesley.

Tamura, E. (1992) 'Should the minimum drinking age be changed? A simulation on the legislative process', *Social Studies*, 83, 5, 201–206.

Tapscott, D. (1999) 'Educating the Net Generation', *Educational Leadership*, 56, 5, 6–11.

Taylor, P. (1992) *Telling It Like It Is: A Guide to Making Aboriginal and Torres Strait Islander History*, Canberra: Australian Institute of Aboriginal and Torres Strait Islander Studies.

Teague, M. and Teague, G. (1995) 'Planning with computers: a social studies simulation', *Learning and Leading with Technology*, September, 20–22.

Teale, R. (ed.) (1978) *Colonial Eve: Sources on Women in Australia (1978–1914)*. Melbourne: Oxford University Press.

Tennyson, R. and Cocchiarella, M. (1986) 'An empirically based instructional design theory for teaching concepts', *Review of Educational Research*, 56, 1, 40–71.

Tetreault, M.K.T. (1987) 'Rethinking women, gender and the social studies', *Social Education*, 51, 3.

Thiagarajan, S. (1992) 'Using games for debriefing', *Simulation and Gaming*, 23, 2, 161–173.

Thiagarajan, S. and Steinwachs, B. (1990) *Barnga: A Simulation Game on Cultural Clashes*. Yarmouth: Intercultural Press.

Thiele, C. (1974) *Albatross Two*. Adelaide: Rigby, Opel Books.

Thomas, J. (1994) 'The history of civics education in Australia'. In Civics Expert Group *Whereas the people ... Civics and Citizenship Education*. Canberra: Australian Government Publishing Service.

Thompson, J.C. (1991) 'Resource-based learning can be the backbone of reform, improvement', *NASSP Bulletin*, 75, 535, 24–28.

Thompson, P. (1996) 'Citizenship and values', *Unicorn*, 22, 1, 44–53.

Thompson, P.J. (1996) 'Textbooks: sacred cow or sacred trust?', paper presented at the Annual Conference of the American Educational Research Association, New York.

Thorn, F. and Rigg, E. (1923) *Handbook of Civics*. Melbourne: Oxford University Press.

Thornton, S. (2000) 'Legitimacy in the social studies curriculum', paper presented at the Annual Conference of the American Educational Research Association, New Orleans.

Toffler, A. (1980) *The Third Wave*. New York: William Morrow and Company.

Tomlinson, C.A. and Kalbfleisch, M.L. (1998) 'Teach me, teach my brain', *Educational Leadership*, 56, 3, 52–55.

Tomlinson, P. and Quinton, M. (1986) *Values Across the Curriculum*. London: Falmer.

Torrance, H. and Pryor, J. (2000) 'Developing formative assessment in the classroom', paper presented at the Annual Conference of the American Educational Research Association, New Orleans.

Treadgold, C. (1999) 'The pedagogy of civics and citizenship education: a look into the Australian classroom', paper presented at the UNESCO/ACEID International Conference, Bangkok, 12–16 December.

Tripcony, P. (1990) 'The provision of access to education in remote areas (predominately Aboriginal)', unpublished paper.

Tripcony, P. (1998) 'Overview of indigenous issues impacting on students, families and communities', unpublished paper presented to the Anglican Schools Office Inaugural Indigenous Education Conference, 'Building partnerships for better learning'.

Trotman, J. (1994) 'Gender and teacher education', *Education Australia*, 28, 18–22.

Tunstall, P. and Gipps, C. (1996) 'How does your teacher help you to make your work better?: Children's understanding of formative assessment', *The Curriculum Journal*, 7, 2, 185–203.

Turner, T.N. (1994) *Essentials of Classroom Teaching*. Boston: Allyn & Bacon.

Upitis, R. (1990) 'Real and contrived uses of electronic mail in elementary schools', *Computers and Education*, 15, 1–3, 233–243.

Utemorrah, D. (1993) *Moonglue*. Broome, WA: Magabala Books.

Van Ausdall, B.W. (1994) 'Books offer entry into understanding cultures', *Educational Leadership*, 51, 8, 32–35.

Van Manen, M. (1977) 'Linking ways of knowing with ways of being practical', *Curriculum Inquiry*, 6, 3, 205–228.

Van Patten, J., Chun-I, C. and Reigeluth, C. (1986) 'A review of strategies for sequencing and synthesizing instruction', *Review of Educational Research*, 56, 4, 437–471.

Van Sickle, R.L. (1986) 'A quantitative review of research on instructional simulation gaming: a twenty year perspective', *Theory and Research in Social Education*, 14, 3.

Venezky, R.L. (1992) 'Textbooks in school and society'. In P. Jackson (ed.) *Handbook of Research on Curriculum*. New York: Macmillan.

Victorian Directorate of School Education (1993) *Voices on the Wind*. Melbourne: DSE.

WA Cross-Sectoral Consortium (1995) *Assessment Support Materials for the Studies of Society and Environment*. Perth: Education Department of WA.

Walford, R. (1995) 'A quarter-century of games and simulations in geography', *Simulation and Gaming*, 26, 2, 236–248.

Wapner, K. (1995) *Teenage Refugees from Vietnam Speak Out*. New York: Rosen Publishing.

Wasley, P. (1999) 'Teaching worth celebrating', *Educational Leadership*, 56, 8, 8–13.

Waters, T., Burger, D. and Burger, S. (1995) 'Moving up before moving on', *Educational Leadership*, 52, 6, 35–41.

Watt, M. (1998) 'National curriculum collaboration: the state of reform in the states and territories', *Curriculum Perspectives*, 18, 1, 21–34.

Watt, M. (2000) 'The National Education Agenda, 1996–1999: its impact on curriculum reform in the states and territories', *Curriculum Perspectives*, 20, 3.

Watts, R. (1995) 'Educating for citizenship and employment in Australia', *Melbourne Studies in Education*, 36, 2, 83–106.

Watts, R.J. and Smolicz, J.J. (1997) *Cross Cultural Communication*. Frankfurt: Peter Lang.

Wearing, B. (1984) *The Ideology of Motherhood: A Study of Sydney Suburban Mothers*. Sydney: Allen & Unwin.

Webb, J.M., Saltz, E.D. and Kealy, W.A. (1996a) 'Conjoint influences of maps and aided prose on children's retrieval of instruction', *Journal of Experimental Education*, 62, 3, 195–205.

Webb, J.M., Tiene, D., Verdi, M.P., Riltschof, K.A. and Saltz, E.D. (1996b) 'Learning from maps: multisensory instruction and visual literacy', paper presented at the Annual Conference of the American Educational Research Association, New York.

Webb, R.B. and Sherman, R.R. (1986) *Schooling and Society*, 2nd edition. New York: Macmillan.

Weepers, J. (1998) 'Jabiluka blockade', *Habitat*, 26, 2, 12.

Wellington, N. F. (1987) *Notes on Civics*. Moonee Ponds, Vic: Essendon City Council.

Welton, D.A. and Mallan, J.J. (1987) *Children and Their World*. Boston: Houghton Mifflin.

Western Australia Curriculum Council (1998) *Society and Environment Learning Area Statement*. Perth: Western Australia Curriculum Council.

Western Australian Aboriginal Education Resource Unit (1995a) *The Art Poster Kit*. Perth: EDWA.

Western Australian Aboriginal Education Resource Unit (1995b) *The Bush Food Poster Kit*. Perth: EDWA.

Western Behavioural Sciences Institute (1969) *Starpower*. La Jolla, California.

Wheatley, N. (1984) *Dancing in the Anzac Deli*. Melbourne: Oxford University Press.

Wheatley, N. and Rawlins, D. (1987) *My Place*. Melbourne: Collins Dove.

Wheatley, N. (1988) *Digging to China*, Melbourne: Penguin.

White, J.D. (1991) 'Review of the organisation', *Simulation and Gaming*, 22, 2, 254–258.

White, J.D. (1992) 'Review of *SimCity: The City Simulator*', *Simulation and Gaming*, 23, 1, 120–123.

Wildy, M. (1997) ' "Survival and Hope"—a refugee simulation game', *The Social Educator*, 15, 1, 21–24.

Wilen, W.W. and Phillips, J.A. (1995) 'Teaching critical thinking: a metacognitive approach', *Social Education*, 59, 3, 135–138.

Wilkinson, G.L., Bennett, L.T. and Oliver, K.M. (1997) 'Evaluation criteria and indicators of quality for internet resources', *Educational Technology*, 37, 3, 52–59.

Williams, A.E. and Eakins, C. (1970) *New Social Studies Through Activities Stage 6*. Perth: Carroll's.

Williams, C. (1989) *Gender Differences at Work: Women and Men in Nontraditional Occupations*. Berkeley: University of California Press.

Williams, C. (ed.) (1993) *Doing "Women's Work": Men in Nontraditional Occupations*. California: Sage Publications.

Williams, R.H. and Williams, S.A. (1987) 'Levels of identification as a predictor of attitude change', *Simulation and Games*, 18, 4.

Williamson, K. (1995) 'Independent learning and the use of resources: VCE Australian Studies', *Australian Journal of Education*, 39, 1, 77–94.

Willis, S. and Kissane, B. (1997) *Achieving Outcome-Based Education: Premises, Principals and Implications for Curriculum and Assessment*. Canberra: ACSA.

Willis, S. and Stephens, M. (1991) 'A national statement on mathematics for Australian schools', *Curriculum Perspectives*, 11, 1, 3–9.

Wilson, B. (1999) 'Packaging the curriculum', *EQ Australia* 4, Summer, 5–7.

Wilson, E.K. and Marsh, G.E. (1995) 'Social studies and the Internet revolution', *Social Education*, 59, 4, 198–202.

Wilson, J. (1990) *Single Fathers: Australian Men Take on a New Role*. Melbourne: Sun Books.

Wilson, V. and Litle, J. (1992) 'Social studies teaching: from eclecticism to cohesion'. *The Clearing House*, 65, 4, 198–199.

Wise, R. (1999) 'Open minds, defensible stances', *EQ Australia*, Winter, 12–14.

Withers, G. and McCurry, D. (1990) 'Student participation in assessment in a cooperative climate'. In B. Low and G. Withers (eds) *Developments in School and Public Assessment*. Melbourne: ACER.

Wolfe, D.P. and Reardon, S.F. (1996) 'Access to excellence through new forms of student assessment'. In J.B. Baron and D.P. Wolfe (eds) *Performance-based Student Assessment: Challenges and Possibilities*. Chicago: NSSE.

Wolfe, J. and Crookall, D. (1998) 'Developing a scientific knowledge of simulation/gaming', *Simulation and Gaming*, 29, 1, 7–19.

Woods, D. (1996) 'Aboriginality, citizenship and the curriculum—a response to Stuart Macintyre's Diversity, Citizenship and the Curriculum'. In K. Kennedy (ed.) *New Challenges for Citizenship Education*. Canberra: Australian Curriculum Studies Association.

Woolever, R. and Scott, K. (1988) *Active Learning in Social Studies: Promoting Cognitive and Social Growth*. Glenview: Scott Foresman & Co.

Worthen, B.R., White, K.R., Fan, X. and Sudwecks, R. (1999) *Measurement and Assessment in Schools*, 2nd edition. New York: Longman.

Wright, C. (1989) 'Black students—white teachers'. In B. Troyna (ed.) *Racial Inequality in Education*. London: Tavistock.

Wright, I. (1993) 'Civic education is values education', *The Social Studies*, 84, 4, 149–152.

Wright, W. (1989) *SimCity: The City Simulator*. Orinda, California: Maxis Software.

Wright, W. and Haslam, F. (1990) *Sim Earth: The Living Planet*. Orinda, California: Maxis Software.

Wyn, J. (1995) ' "Youth" and citizenship', *Melbourne Studies in Education*, 36, 2, 45–64.

Yates, L. (1993) *The Education of Girls: Policy, Research and the Question of Gender*. Melbourne: Australian Council for Educational Research.

Yates, L. (1996) 'Understanding the boys issues: what sort of challenge is it?', paper presented at American Educational Research Association Conference, New York.

Yoho, R. (1986) 'Effectiveness of four concept teaching strategies on social studies concept acquisition and retention', *Theory and Research in Social Education*, 14, 3, 211-233.

Yoho, R. (1988) 'Acquisition and retention of social studies concepts and principles', paper presented at American Educational Research Association Annual Meeting, New Orleans.

Young, C. (1993) 'Change and innovation in history curriculum: a perspective on the New South Wales experience'. In K. Kennedy, O. Watts and G. McDonald (eds) *Citizenship Education for a New Age*. Toowoomba: University of Southern Queensland Press.

Young, C. (1996) 'Civics and citizenship education and the teaching of history', *Unicorn*, 22, 1, 64-71.

Zehnder, S. and King, L. (2000) 'Student knowledge construction in cooperative small groups', paper presented at the Annual Conference of the American Educational Research Association, New Orleans.

Zinberg, D. (1998) 'Bad news from cyberspace?', *The Australian*, 11 November, 34.

Index

Page numbers in *italics* refer to figures. An "n" after a page number indicates a footnote.